Praise for
South to Freedom

"*South to Freedom* reorders the way we should think and teach about the slavery expansion crisis in the middle of the nineteenth century. Indeed, it reorders how to think about the huge question of the coming of the American Civil War. Not many books these days can make that claim. With astonishing research and graceful writing, this one can."

—DAVID W. BLIGHT, Pulitzer Prize–winning author
of *Frederick Douglass: Prophet of Freedom*

"Taken for granted, borders between two nations have the power to constrain curiosity and limit the self-understanding of both nations. But when the research of a gifted historian defies a border, as Alice L. Baumgartner's *South to Freedom* demonstrates, the result is the revelation of a story of great consequence. When Texas slaves seized the opportunities presented by Mexico's precedent-setting initiatives in emancipation, the actions of a comparatively small group of people shaped a historical event of enormous scale: the American Civil War."

—PATRICIA NELSON LIMERICK, author of *The Legacy of Conquest: The Unbroken Past of the American West*

"Enslaved freedom-seekers in the antebellum United States looked not only to the North Star, but also to the southern border with Mexico. In a fast-paced narrative that moves deftly between the histories of both countries, Alice L. Baumgartner demonstrates the far-reaching impact of Mexico's free-soil policies. She shows, with eloquence and insight, how enslaved people themselves ignited the fuse that led to a civil war—and the final abolition of slavery on the North American continent."

—W. CALEB McDANIEL, Pulitzer Prize–winning author of *Sweet Taste of Liberty: A True Story of Slavery and Restitution in America*

"In this deeply researched and pathbreaking study of southern slaves who escaped to Mexico and carved out new lives in the decades prior to the Civil War, Alice L. Baumgartner has succeeded in explaining a mystery that historians had been unable to unravel. How many slaves ran South to freedom, rather than North, and how did their assertiveness influence the coming of the Civil War? Baumgartner explores not only the familiar sectional controversy that led the southern states to secede from the union, but more importantly, *South to Freedom* examines the rich and complicated lives and the multifaceted roles that enslaved people played in Mexico. This book will contribute immensely to our understanding of sectional politics, as well as the manner in which Mexico asserted its 'moral power' to reject an inhumane institution and to assist fugitive slaves in recreating their lives as free men and women."

—ALBERT S. BROUSSARD, author of *Black San Francisco: The Struggle for Racial Equality in the West, 1900–54*

SOUTH
TO FREEDOM

SOUTH
TO FREEDOM

Runaway Slaves to Mexico
and the
Road to the Civil War

ALICE L. BAUMGARTNER

BASIC BOOKS
NEW YORK

Basic Books
Hachette Book Group
1290 Avenue of the Americas, New York, NY 10104
www.basicbooks.com

Printed in the United States of America
First Edition: December 2020

Published by Basic Books, an imprint of Perseus Books, LLC, a subsidiary
of Hachette Book Group, Inc. The Basic Books name and logo is a trademark
of the Hachette Book Group.

The Hachette Speakers Bureau provides a wide range of authors for speaking events.
To find out more, go to www.hachettespeakersbureau.com or call (866) 376-6591.

The publisher is not responsible for websites (or their content) that are not owned
by the publisher.

Print book interior design by Linda Mark

Library of Congress Cataloging-in-Publication Data
Names: Baumgartner, Alice, 1987– author.
Title: South to freedom : runaway slaves to Mexico and the road to the Civil War /
    Alice L. Baumgartner.
Description: New York : Basic Books, [2020] | Includes bibliographical references
    and index.
Identifiers: LCCN 2020011978 | ISBN 9781541617780 (hardcover) |
    ISBN 9781541617773 (ebook)
Subjects: LCSH: Fugitive slaves—Mexico—History—19th century. | Fugitive
    slaves—United States—History—19th century. | Slavery—Mexico—History—
    19th century. | Slavery—United States—History—19th century. | United
    States—History—Civil War, 1861–1865—Causes.
Classification: LCC HT1053 .B38 2020 | DDC 306.3/62—dc23
LC record available at https://lccn.loc.gov/2020011978

ISBNs: 978-1-5416-1778-0 (hardcover), 978-1-5416-1777-3 (ebook)

LSC-C

1 2020

TO MY TEACHERS

The road would always be open to Mexico.

—FREDERICK LAW OLMSTED

Contents

INTRODUCTION

N O ONE KNEW HOW THE TWO SAILORS ESCAPED—WHETHER they risked swimming from the *Metacomet*, anchored in the deep water off the port of Veracruz, Mexico, or whether someone had rowed them to shore under cover of darkness. It was the summer of 1857, and the *Metacomet* was due back in its home port of New Orleans, where another shipment of cotton awaited transport to Mexican markets. But the steamship could not leave Veracruz without the two missing sailors, and the shipmaster had reason to fear that the men were gone for good. Although it had become routine for Mexican authorities to arrest seamen who broke their contracts, George and James Frisby were no ordinary deserters: they were black slaves—brothers, in fact—hired out by their owner in Louisiana.[1]

If George and James Frisby had escaped in New York or Boston, they would have been returned, if captured, under the US Constitution and the Fugitive Slave Act, but Mexico's laws offered no such guarantees. Not only had Mexico abolished slavery, but its laws freed the slaves of "other countries" from the moment they set foot on its soil. To have any chance of returning the Frisby brothers, the shipmaster of the *Metacomet* avoided mentioning that the two men were black slaves. Assuming that the missing sailors were ordinary deserters, the local police "promptly" apprehended George. But his brother proved harder to find. As the police searched the streets and alleyways of Veracruz, James hid inside of a house. Nothing is known for certain about the house or its owners, though there is reason to believe that while in hiding, James learned about Mexico's antislavery laws. When the police finally found him, he did something that his brother did not: he claimed his freedom—ironically—by producing evidence of his enslavement.[2]

Since Mexican law abolished slavery and freed all slaves who set foot on its soil, the Commander of the Port of Veracruz refused to arrest James, even when the US ambassador to Mexico protested that the incident would undermine the "increasing and beneficent commerce" between Mexico and the US South. Much more was at stake than commercial relations. The freedom that Mexico promised would threaten slavery not just in the nearby states of Texas and Louisiana, but at the very heart of the Union.[3]

THERE WAS NO OFFICIAL UNDERGROUND RAILROAD TO MEXICO, only the occasional ally; no network, only a set of discrete, unconnected nodes. Some fugitive slaves received help while making their escape—from free blacks, ship captains, Mexicans, Germans, gamblers, preachers, mail riders, and other "lurking scoundrels." Most, though, escaped from the United States by their own ingenuity. They forged slave passes to give the impression that they were traveling with the permission of their masters. They disguised themselves as white men, fashioning wigs from horsehair and pitch. They stole horses, firearms, skiffs, dirk knives, fur hats, and, in one instance, twelve gold watches and a diamond breast pin. And then, while either gathering oysters or collecting firewood or walking to a camp meeting, they disappeared.[4]

Two options awaited most runaways in Mexico. The first was to join the military colonies, a series of outposts that the Mexican government established to defend its northeastern frontier against foreign invaders and "barbarous" Indians. The second was to fill Mexico's labor shortage by seeking employment as servants and day laborers. Both alternatives came at a cost. The demands of military service along the northeastern frontier constrained the autonomy of former slaves. Runaways who worked as servants endured other forms of coercion. In parts of southern Mexico, such as Yucatán and Chiapas, indentured servitude sometimes amounted to slavery in all but name. Even in regions where the labor system differed from human bondage, coercion continued in other forms. In northern Mexico, hacienda owners enjoyed the right to physically punish their employees. Farther to the south, in San Luis Potosí, Querétaro, and Zacatecas, indentured servants often had no choice but to work on haciendas because their alternatives were far worse. These labor systems were coercive, even though the mechanism of coercion was economic necessity rather than physical violence.[5]

The differences between the southern route to freedom and its more renowned northern counterpart are not as pronounced as they might appear. Although popular understandings of the Underground Railroad describe hundreds of white antislavery activists ferrying largely anonymous runaways to freedom, recent scholarship has shown that the "conductors" on the northbound route, like the southbound one, were individuals and small groups who were largely oblivious to one another's existence. Runaways who escaped to the North also found that their "freedom" was abridged, just as it was in Mexico. In the "free" states, runaways enjoyed only a "doubtful liberty," as Frederick Douglass later put it. The Constitution, reinforced by the Fugitive Slave Acts of 1793 and 1850, provided for the return of runaways who managed to get across the Mason-Dixon Line. Even "free" blacks were denied the same rights as their white neighbors. Although they paid taxes, they were not always allowed to vote, and their children were often denied access to public schools. Nor could "free" blacks travel freely or settle where they wished. In Ohio, black residents had to post a five-hundred-dollar bond "to guarantee their good behavior." The state of Illinois excluded African Americans altogether in 1853.[6]

For all of their similarities, the northern and southern routes differed in one important respect: numbers. Determining how many enslaved people actually reached Mexico is difficult. My estimate, based on scattered and incomplete Mexican sources, puts the number somewhere between three and five thousand people—considerably fewer than the thirty thousand to one hundred thousand runaways who crossed the Mason-Dixon Line. The number of slaves who reached Mexico was undeniably small. Still, each escape was important in its own right. And their collective story had strategic and political significance out of all proportion to the numbers involved. Their experiences reorient our understanding of the Civil War, showing that one of the most distinctively "American" events in US history was in part ignited by the enslaved people who escaped to the south and the laws by which they claimed their freedom in Mexico.

BLACK SLAVERY TOOK ROOT IN THE VICEROYALTY OF NEW SPAIN (as Mexico was then known) at the end of the sixteenth century, when a series of epidemics decimated the indigenous population that had provided the bulk of the viceroyalty's labor force. Between 1580 and 1640, New Spain imported more slaves than any other European colony in the Western Hemisphere except Brazil. But after 1640, a decline in sugar prices and an increase in the indigenous population slowly shifted New Spain's labor system away from black slavery. As former slaves became free laborers, they formed black militias; they joined lay religious organizations known as *cofradías*; they worked as butchers and barbers, domestic servants and ranch hands; and they married people of European and indigenous descent.[7]

By the time Mexicans took up arms against Spain in 1810, Mexico's population of eight million included only around nine to ten thousand black slaves. Though the enslaved population was comparatively small, Mexican leaders could not abolish slavery outright. Like the United States, Mexico was founded on two competing principles: liberty and property. In both countries, masters insisted that enslaved people be counted as chattel—that is, movable property. Slaveholders in the United States capitalized on this logic to argue that any interference with slavery amounted to a violation of "property" rights. In 1787, when the Continental Congress prohibited slavery north of the Ohio River, disgruntled slaveholders convinced the territorial governor that the measure did not apply to enslaved people already in the region. Eleven years later, the US Congress rejected a bill to abolish slavery in the Mississippi Territory, after slaveholders around Natchez made clear that they would sooner revolt than submit to such a measure. In 1804, Congress succeeded in prohibiting the importation of slaves to the Louisiana Territory, but reversed course the following year in the face of resistance from slaveholders. Pressured not to interfere with the "peculiar institution," Congress hesitated to abolish slavery or even to enact gradual emancipation policies.[8]

In Mexico, slaveholders also opposed any interference with their "property," but local and national authorities did not comply with these demands as often as politicians in the United States. The threat of a revolt convinced Mexico's leaders that the only way to ensure political stability was to bring slavery to a gradual end. Between 1824 and 1827, more than half of Mexico's states promised that the children born to enslaved people would be free—a free womb law that would end slavery within a generation. Meanwhile, Mexico's Congress prohibited the introduction of enslaved people to the republic, promising freedom to illegally imported slaves from the moment they set foot on the national territory. In 1829, Mexico's president tried to end slavery by executive decree, but Mexico's Congress overturned the decree less than two years later, in the face of resistance from cotton growers, mine operators, hacienda owners, and sugar refiners. Although Mexico's leaders would not abolish slavery outright, they remained committed to putting the "peculiar institution" on the path to ultimate extinction.[9]

As Mexican politicians tried to enforce their gradual emancipation policies, Anglo-American slaveholders who had moved to the province of Téjas in the 1820s and 1830s realized that the future of slavery was not as assured in their adopted country as it was in the United States. In the fall of 1835, the Anglo colonists revolted, and a year later, declared their independence. The Texas Revolution confirmed the danger that slaveholders posed to Mexico. In 1837, Mexico's Congress prohibited slavery across the nation. This abolition policy boosted morale among Mexicans, galvanized international support for Mexico, and encouraged slaves in Texas to revolt or escape. But Mexico's attempts to undermine slavery in Texas gave credence to rumors that another foreign power—Great Britain—was scheming to promote abolition in Texas, in violation of the Monroe Doctrine. To prevent such interference, the US Congress voted in favor of annexing Texas in 1845. Within a year, war broke out between Mexico and the United States.[10]

Southern planters predicted that the war with Mexico would extend slavery to the Pacific. Instead, the conquest of Mexican territories threatened the very existence of slavery in the United States. Although US congressmen believed they had an obligation to respect the existing "property" rights of slaveholders, Northern representatives refused to reestablish slavery where it had been abolished, including in the territories that the United States seized from Mexico. Southern politicians' attempts to extend slavery into the former Mexican territories ignited a sectional controversy—that is, a controversy between North and South—that would lead to the overturning of the Missouri Compromise, the outbreak of violence in Kansas, and the birth of a new political coalition, the Republican Party, whose success in the election of 1860 led to the US Civil War.

THIS BOOK TELLS THE STORY OF ENSLAVED PEOPLE LIKE GEORGE and James Frisby, the law by which they claimed their freedom in Mexico, and the crisis that they provoked in the antebellum United States. It begins in the early nineteenth century, with the United States Congress caught up in debates over slavery and the rebels in Mexico fighting for their independence from Spain. It ends in 1867, when civil wars in Mexico and the United States had concluded and both countries began to take up the question of what freedom meant in the wake of emancipation. The pages in between take us from the floor of the US Senate in Washington, DC, to the stage of the National Theatre in Mexico City, from the barricaded doors of the Alamo to the military outposts of northern Mexico. In the process, this book makes the case that enslaved people who escaped to Mexico and the antislavery laws that entitled them to freedom contributed to the outbreak of a major sectional controversy over the future of human bondage in the United States.

To make this argument, this book weaves together three narrative threads. The first examines why the United States permitted human bondage to expand without check across the Southern territories. The second explores why Mexican leaders restricted and eventually abolished slavery, and the profound consequences that these policies had for the United States. The third takes up the lives of some of the thousands of slaves who escaped to Mexico in defiance of their masters, bringing forceful but forgotten figures into the light: Jean Antoine, who hid in the hold of a ship bound for Campeche; Honorine, who escaped with the help of a Louisiana merchant; François Dupuis, who joined an artillery unit of the Mexican Army; and Burrill Daniel, who demanded compensation before a claims court for being held as a slave in Mexico.

The histories of Mexico and the United States are not often told together. During most of the nineteenth century, people in the United States described themselves as irreconcilably different from Mexicans. "Among the nations of the earth, we are the one above all others," noted

Nicholas Trist, the diplomat who negotiated the treaty that ended the US-Mexican War. "Mexico occupies the very lowest point of the same scale, a point beneath even the one proper to the Indian tribes without our borders." Trist was expressing a common view. People in the United States considered themselves enlightened, educated, democratic, hard-working, generous, and just; while, to them, Mexicans seemed bigoted, tyrannical, obstructionist, lazy, fanatical, and treacherous.[11]

Although such comparisons now sound outdated, the histories of Mexico and the United States continue to seem distinctly unrelated. Mexico was so unstable that forty-nine presidents took office between 1824 and 1857, while the United States enjoyed political stability and economic prosperity. In the first half of the nineteenth century, the population of the United States doubled and then doubled again; its territory expanded by the same proportion, as its leaders purchased, conquered, and expropriated lands to the west and south. By almost every metric, the United States was stronger than Mexico, and according to most accounts, the US government could impose its will on its Latin American neighbors without consequence.[12]

But Mexico's relative lack of power did not mean that it was pow-er*less*. Power can take on other, subtler forms than economic success or brute force. In the nineteenth century, newly independent Mexico gained moral power through the rejection of slavery. These policies would alter the lives of enslaved people in Texas and Louisiana, and ultimately obstruct the expansion of slavery across the southwestern United States. By showing that we cannot understand the coming of the Civil War without taking into account Mexico and the slaves who reached its soil, this book ultimately contends that "American" histories of slavery and sectional controversy are, in fact, Mexican histories, too.

A NOTE ON TERMINOLOGY

During my first research trip to Mexico City, a man on the subway asked where I was from. I told him that I was an American. The man responded that so was he. He gestured to everyone on the subway. "We are all Americans," he said. And he was right. Derived from the name of the sixteenth-century explorer Amerigo Vespucci, the word "America" originally referred to the entire hemisphere. From the sixteenth century to the present, Mexicans have called themselves Americans or *americanos*. To most of the inhabitants in the Americas, this label did not—and does not—only refer to people living in the United States. Instead my sources referred to US residents as *norteamericanos*. I have adopted this term, because I believe that it is inaccurate to use the word "American" to describe residents of the United States when the rest of the hemisphere refers to themselves as Americans, too.[13]

I take similar care when referring to Southerners. Although this term embraces the population of the Southern states as a whole, historians often use it when discussing *white* Southerners. I am careful to specify when I am talking about Southern whites, in order to remind readers that a substantial proportion of Southerners were free and enslaved blacks, with very different experiences and views than their white neighbors and owners.

I have also adopted an unusual lexicon to discuss Texas. During the fourteen years that Texas belonged to Mexico, the province was known as Téjas. I refer to it as such, in order to help mark the complicated shifts from Mexican Téjas to the Republic of Texas to the State of Texas. I have also adopted this terminology in order to call into question the deeply rooted assumption that even when Téjas belonged to Mexico, the province was an extension of the United States, destined to join the Union.

I refer to the nonslaveholding states as "free" states, as a reminder that the freedom people of African descent enjoyed in these states was not the same as the freedom available to whites. I also put the "property" rights of slaveholders in quotations to draw attention to the casuistry of any argument to define human beings as property.

All of the translations from original sources are my own unless otherwise noted.

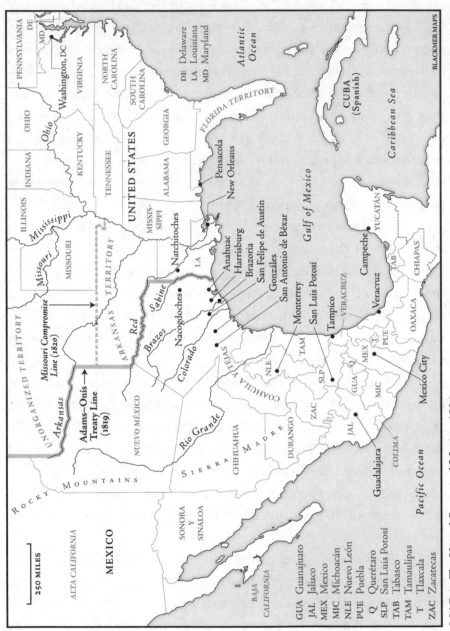

MAP 1: The United States and Mexico, 1824

ONE

DEFENDING SLAVERY

F ROM THE DENSE MAGNOLIA FORESTS AROUND PORT HUDSON, Louisiana, rose the strains of "The Star Spangled Banner" on July 7, 1863. As Confederates gathered to listen at the parapets and behind piles of sandbags, they began to make out something else: the Union soldiers were shouting through cupped hands that Vicksburg, a major Confederate stronghold in Mississippi a hundred and fifty miles to the north, had surrendered three days earlier. Suddenly the Confederate soldiers understood why the Union forces were singing. If Vicksburg had fallen, Port Hudson was next.[1]

Among the soldiers who heard the news was John H. Kirkham of Lamar County, Texas. For three generations, Kirkham's family lived in the Mississippi Valley. Like other slaveholders in the region, the Kirkhams defended their right to hold human beings as property, without interference from the United States government or from foreign powers. And for the most part, they succeeded. The threat of a revolt dissuaded congressmen in Washington, DC, from passing legislation to restrict slavery in the Southern territories. The remonstrations of slaveholders convinced the executive branch to wield the power of the federal government repeatedly against neighboring empires that granted asylum to fugitive slaves from the United States. But over the previous two decades, a political faction had risen to prominence on a platform that promised to halt the expansion of slavery. Their candidate, Abraham Lincoln, won the presidency in 1860, and in response, John Kirkham and thousands of other Southern white men enlisted in the Confederate Army to fight for their right to hold people as property.

After enlisting in the First Battalion Texas Sharpshooters in 1862, Kirkham spent more time in hospitals than in battle. In February 1863, he was laid up at an infirmary in Mandeville, Louisiana, while the rest of his regiment captured a federal ironclad named the *Indianola* on the Red River. Two months later, he fell ill again in Clinton, Louisiana, where the local hospital did not have enough medicine, despite the best efforts of its matron, who slipped in and out of Union-occupied New Orleans with vials of morphine and quinine sewn into her skirts. By the time that Kirkham recovered, the Sharpshooters were marching toward Jackson, Mississippi. Kirkham was ordered to join a detachment of his company that had been assigned to serve with the Louisiana Legion at Port Hudson, halfway between Vicksburg and New Orleans. His detachment arrived just before the Union Army put Port Hudson under siege on May 22, 1863. In the weeks that followed, neither food nor munitions entered the town. The soldiers began skinning rats, knowing that in another month the rats would be gone, and their only sustenance would likely be shoe leather.[2]

Six weeks into the siege, the men gathered on the parapets understood that they would not starve after all. The rebels could not hold Port Hudson now that Vicksburg had fallen. After the Confederates gave their word not to bear arms against the United States, they would return home, parole in hand. John Kirkham must have felt relief but also fear. After Port Hudson surrendered, the Union Army would take control of the Mississippi, dividing Texas, Arkansas, and Louisiana from the other Southern states. The Confederate States of America seemed unlikely to survive. Nor did the system of slavery that the Kirkham family had defended for generations. "This [is] the darkest day of the war," wrote a Confederate War Department clerk when he heard the news. The future that awaited Confederate soldiers looked bleak. "Your negroes will be taken from you, the men put into the army to fight against you, the able-bodied women and men not too old to labor will be put on *your farms* to work under Yankee overseers," Brigadier General Henry Eustace McCulloch predicted. When Kirkham laid down his arms on July 9, 1863, he knew he stood to lose much more than his country—and much else.[3]

THE FIRST OF THE KIRKHAMS TO CROSS THE MISSISSIPPI RIVER was James, the brother of John H. Kirkham's grandfather. Born in Hillsborough, North Carolina, in 1775, James Kirkham came of age during the American Revolution. A year after he was born, Thomas Jefferson drafted the Declaration of Independence. When James turned six, the British surrendered at Yorktown, Virginia, three hundred miles away from his home. The War of Independence in the United States transformed the political system under which Kirkham lived, but the revolution that would have the greatest impact on his life was not the one that began at Lexington and Concord. This revolution was an economic transformation, which was taking place at almost the exact same time in northwestern England, and it would lead *norteamericanos* like James Kirkham to turn away from the Declaration of Independence's revolutionary claim that "all men are created equal."[4]

At the end of the eighteenth century, small factories in northwestern England began to turn cotton into thread using water-powered machines. To spin one hundred pounds of cotton by hand took upward of fifty thousand hours. In 1790, the mechanized hundred-spindle mule decreased the time to one thousand hours. Five years later, the water mule took only three hundred hours to spin the same amount. Productivity had increased, in less than a decade, by a factor of three.

These innovations transformed what was once a luxury good—cotton cloth—into an everyday fabric. To meet the growing demand, bales of cotton arrived from Jamaica, Saint-Domingue, the Ottoman Empire, and the Gold Coast of Africa, but not even the thirty-one million pounds imported to England in 1790 was enough to keep the water mules humming. Paying two to three times more for the fiber than a decade earlier, English manufacturers were "quite convinced that unless some new source of supply could be found, the progress of the rising industry would be checked, if not altogether arrested."[5]

The high price of cotton did not go unnoticed in the United States. But the short staple cotton that thrived along the Eastern Seaboard had a significant disadvantage compared to the long staple varieties cultivated elsewhere. The seeds of the short staple variety were so difficult to remove that it took an entire day to clean one pound of cotton by hand. In 1793, a recent graduate of Yale College named Eli Whitney solved this problem by inventing a machine that could clean fifty pounds of short staple cotton in a day. With the turn of a crank, a studded roller picked up the cotton fibers, forcing them through a metal grate through which seeds could not pass. Following the invention of the cotton engine—or cotton gin, for short—planters who had grown tobacco, rice, or indigo began to cultivate cotton. The price of prime cotton lands tripled. Cotton production skyrocketed from 1.5 million pounds in 1790 to 36.5 million pounds ten years later.[6]

The invention of the cotton gin positioned the United States to become the world's leading producer of cotton. The United States had land in abundance. Since cotton depleted the soil within two to three years, access to land was crucial. Cotton production also depended on a large labor force, and in the United States, planters could rely on enslaved people to plant, tend, and harvest the crop. Although the Founding Fathers declared that all men were created equal, the Constitution they drafted extended several important protections to slaveholders in the United States: fugitive slaves would be "delivered up" to their owners;

the international slave trade would be sanctioned under federal law until at least 1808; and three-fifths of "all other persons"—that is, slaves—would be counted when determining the number of seats that a state would have in the House of Representatives.[7]

The United States had millions of acres of land on which to grow cotton, and a system of slavery that could meet the crop's enormous labor demands, but the ideas that inspired the American Revolution endangered the future of cotton production. In Washington, DC, a growing number of congressmen argued that human bondage violated the founding principles of the young republic. If they succeeded in prohibiting slavery in the newly opened territories to the west, the United States would never become the world's largest exporter of cotton, as Southern planters hoped.

AFTER THE AMERICAN REVOLUTION, EVERY STATE EXCEPT GEORgia and South Carolina banned the international slave trade. New Hampshire, Vermont, and Massachusetts abolished slavery outright. Pennsylvania, Connecticut, and Rhode Island adopted gradual emancipation policies that would end human bondage within a generation or two. Every Southern state except North Carolina made it easier for owners to manumit—or free—their slaves. Between 1782 and 1790, slaveholders manumitted over ten thousand people in Virginia alone. But as cotton prices continued to rise during the late eighteenth century, planters defended their right to hold slaves, particularly in the newly opened territories to the west.[8]

The US Constitution granted Congress the power to make "all needful rules and regulations" for the territories—the lands west of the Appalachian Mountains that seven of the thirteen states had ceded to the federal government in the late eighteenth century. The First Congress acted on the assumption that this authority included the power to restrict slavery. Early in its first session, on July 21, 1789, Congress ratified the Northwest Ordinance of 1787, which prohibited slavery and involuntary servitude in the territory north of the Ohio River.[9]

The antislavery provision of the Northwest Ordinance posed a threat to slaveholders, not because they expected the Northwest to become a plantation society, but because the legislation established a precedent for the federal government to interfere with their "property" rights. Since slavery already existed north of the Ohio River, slave-holders in the region insisted that their "property" was protected under the Fifth Amendment, passed in 1789 and ratified two years later. The territorial governor, Arthur St. Clair, agreed with their interpretation. In 1790, he wrote that the Northwest Ordinance did not "extend to the liberation of those [slaves] the People were already possessed of." As a result, enslaved people in the territory remained in bondage. The famous provision that "there shall be neither slavery nor indentured servitude" north of the Ohio River became, in practice, a prohibition on the importation of new slaves.[10]

Slaveholders also invoked "property" rights to defend slavery in the territories south of the Ohio River. North Carolina ceded its western territories (what would become the state of Tennessee) to the United States on the express condition that "no regulations made or to be made by Congress shall tend to emancipate slaves." The United States gov-ernment could have rejected the condition, but with more than three thousand slaves already living in the Southwest Territory, congressmen feared they could only do so at the risk of a revolt. An uprising in the distant Southwest Territory threatened to become part of the much larger conflict: across the Mississippi River from the Southwest Ter-ritory was Louisiana, which Spain owned, France hoped to regain, and Britain was scheming to seize. To avoid provoking a revolt that would be difficult to contain or suppress, Congress organized the territory in 1790 without any prohibition of slavery. With protections for human bond-age in place, the population exploded, from 35,691 in 1790, to 105,602 in 1800, and to 261,727 in 1810.[11]

Concerns about the loyalty of distant citizens also derailed efforts to abolish slavery in the Mississippi Territory (what would become the states of Mississippi and Alabama). On March 23, 1798, Representative George Thatcher of the District of Maine moved to prohibit unfree labor in the territory on the grounds that Congress ought not to "legalize the existence of slavery any farther than it at present exists" out of "respect for the rights of humanity." Southern politicians were quick to point out that slavery did, in fact, exist already in the Mississippi Territory. Enslaved people in the Natchez District produced over 1.2 million pounds of cotton for the New Orleans market in 1798—nearly four times the amount they had produced a mere three years earlier. "Are not these men property?" asked John Rutledge Jr. of South Carolina. "Do not the people in this territory hold them as such?" Prohibiting slavery "would be a serious attack upon the property of that country"—an attack that risked the revolt of a region whose loyalty to the Union was far from assured. When a vote was called on March 23, the prohibition on slavery did not pass. The only restriction Congress approved was a ban on the importation of slaves into the territory from abroad. By invoking the Constitution, slaveholders secured the right to extend human bondage across the prime agricultural lands to the south and west.[12]

As the territories formed new states, and the original states passed additional laws with respect to slavery, a pattern began to emerge. Slavery became more entrenched in the Southern states than in the Northern ones. Tennessee joined the Union as a slave state in 1796. During the 1790s, South Carolina, Georgia, and Alabama made it impossible for slaveholders to manumit their slaves without approval from the legislature. Meanwhile, the economy of the Northern states moved in a different direction, toward wage labor. In 1799, New York enacted a gradual emancipation law. Four years later, Ohio, the first state to be organized from the Northwest Territory, joined the union without slavery. In 1804, New Jersey became the last state north of the Mason-Dixon Line to pass legislation to end slavery. A geographical boundary began to form between slaveholding and nonslaveholding states.[13]

These developments held a particular interest for James Kirkham. In Hillsborough, North Carolina, the local economy revolved around tobacco, whose leaves, when stripped and dried, were among the most profitable exports from mainland North America. But by the early nineteenth century, tobacco prices were declining and yields from the overworked soil were plummeting. Producing cotton with enslaved labor in the western territories presented a lucrative alternative. Less than a year after the United States purchased the Louisiana Territory from France for $15 million in 1803, James Kirkham loaded his belongings onto a wagon and set out west, determined to make a life for himself across the Mississippi River.[14]

ALONG THE RED RIVER, IN WESTERN LOUISIANA, THE LAND WAS almost constantly waterlogged. When it rained, the river rose so high that it left debris on the tops of trees. For good reason, few whites settled in western Louisiana in the early nineteenth century. The roads were narrow and often impassable. The land was "unhealthy," "unfit for cultivation," and "not of much value." The largest town was Natchitoches ("pronounced Nacatosh," one visitor helpfully explained). Located on the banks of the Red River, the town boasted a population of six hundred, excluding several companies of the Second Infantry of the United States Army, stationed at nearby Fort Claiborne.[15]

Forty miles west of Natchitoches, James Kirkham staked out two thousand acres, "bounded North, East, and South, by vacant land." Eventually he intended to claim his property by preemption, a policy under which settlers could gain title to the acres that they had improved "by virtue of occupation, habitation, and cultivation." Kirkham, however, had no intention of cultivating the land himself. Instead he purchased a man named Martin for $800 and a woman named Fivi (perhaps Phoebe) for $1,000. He exchanged a donkey for an older man named Richard Moran.[16]

The US Congress made no attempt to abolish slavery in the Louisiana Territory. Enslaved people numbered thirty thousand in 1803—nearly half the total population, excluding indigenous peoples. Not only did the Constitution seem to guarantee the "property" rights of Louisiana slaveholders, but the treaty that ceded the territory provided that "the inhabitants . . . shall be incorporated in the Union of the United States," where they would enjoy "all these rights, advantages and immunities of citizens of the United States." Congress could not abolish slavery in Louisiana, but many of its members were committed to stopping human bondage from expanding. In 1804, Congress prohibited the introduction of new slaves to the territory for anything other than personal use. Citizens of the United States could only bring enslaved people with them if moving to Louisiana "for actual settlement."[17]

Prohibiting importation was the kind of policy that could have restricted slavery while respecting existing rights to "property." But slaveholders still threatened to revolt. Louisiana Governor William Claiborne warned that even the rumor of a policy "prohibiting the foreign importation of Slaves into this Province . . . occasioned great agitation in this City and in the adjacent Settlements." A petition from the white residents of the territory confirmed Claiborne's warning. "The necessity of employing African laborers," the petitioners explained, was "all important to the very existence of our country" for without slavery, "cultivation must cease, the improvements of a century be destroyed."[18]

Discontented masters, living a thousand miles from Washington, DC, were an ongoing threat to the young republic. The army was not strong or large enough to put down every rebellion, and in the Mississippi Valley, an uprising would likely become a larger geopolitical conflict. A New Orleans attorney cautioned in 1804 that "there are men who speak seriously of appealing to France & requesting the first Consul [Napoleon Bonaparte] to give them aid." Another businessman in New Orleans warned that "if even the slightest advantage were held out" to white Louisianans by European powers, the "majority of them" would take up arms against the United States. These warnings were enough to dissuade Congress in 1805 from renewing the prohibition on the importation of slaves to Louisiana.[19]

Louisiana slaveholders like James Kirkham successfully protected their property from any interference by the United States Congress. But slavery in the Mississippi Valley faced other threats besides unfavorable legislation from Washington. In 1805, a year after James Kirkham staked out his claim in western Louisiana, several enslaved people were tied down outside of Natchitoches, their wrists and ankles bound, their limbs splayed. Then they were whipped with a rawhide lash. Their crime had been to try to escape to the neighboring viceroyalty of New Spain, where, according to one *norteamericano* in Natchitoches, they expected to "obtain freedom, which everybody said was a sweet thing."[20]

EXTENDING FROM THE ISTHMUS OF PANAMA TO THE NORTHERN coast of California, New Spain was the richest viceroyalty of the Spanish Empire. From the southern provinces of New Spain came sugar and cotton, from the north, cowhides and tallow, but the main source of the viceroyalty's wealth was the silver ore extracted by pickax from mines in the central highlands of Zacatecas, Guanajuato, and San Luis Potosí. Between 1800 and 1809, total exports from New Spain averaged $14 million in US dollars a year. Total production—$240 million in US dollars in 1800—outpaced that of every other Spanish colony. Few *norteamericanos* would see the viceroyalty with their own eyes, but the power of the Spanish Empire was never far from view. At the time that James Kirkham settled in Louisiana, the monetary standard in the United States was the Spanish dollar, made from silver mined in the Mexican highlands, and minted in Mexico City.[21]

The geography that gave rise to an abundance of natural resources also made New Spain remarkably difficult to govern. The dominant feature of the viceroyalty was a central plateau. Flanked by two mountain ranges—the Sierra Madre Oriental to the east and the Sierra Madre Occidental to the west—the central plateau extended to the south for a thousand miles, until it intersected a rift in the earth's crust. Along this tectonic seam rose a line of volcanoes, whose snow-capped peaks could be seen on clear days from the Gulf of Mexico. In the valley formed by the Sierra Madre and the volcanic belt was the capital of the viceroyalty, Mexico City. By 1800 it was one of the largest cities in the Americas, with over a hundred churches, twelve hospitals, a botanical garden, and the oldest university in the hemisphere, founded in 1551. With a population of 138,000 in 1800, Mexico City was more than twice the size of New York City. To the Prussian explorer Alexander von Humboldt, who visited in 1803, the metropolis was among "the finest cities ever built."[22]

Most of the population of New Spain lived on the central plateau. A harsh and rugged landscape divided the rest of the viceroyalty into distinct regions. Along the eastern coastal plain, where moisture from the Gulf of Mexico delivered up to five feet of rain per year, outbreaks of yellow fever were so common that even the major port cities of Tampico and Veracruz emptied during the disease-ridden summer months. Farther to the south, the coastline curved upward, forming the Yucatán peninsula. The unforgiving terrain made land transportation from Yucatán to Mexico City impractical, giving the peninsula a reputation for independence rivaled only by the *gran septentrión*—the far north. Native peoples dominated the lands north of the Rio Grande. The only presence that Spain had in the region was a line of missions and forts. The presidios, as the forts were known, were so isolated from the rest of the viceroyalty that the few thousand soldiers who occupied them used pelts as a medium of exchange instead of silver.[23]

Race divided New Spain as sharply as geography. The viceroyalty was astonishingly diverse, with over fifty distinct language groups. To classify the population, Spaniards developed a system of sixteen racial categories: the child of an Indian and a Spaniard was a *mestizo*; that of a person of African descent and a Spaniard, a *mulato*; and so forth. As in the United States, the racial hierarchy in New Spain privileged white-ness. Indians and blacks, *mestizos* and *mulatos*, worked almost exclusively in menial occupations, as artisans and muleteers, domestic servants and market vendors. Less than 1 percent of the population knew how to read or write. The only university that admitted people of mixed race was the second-rate Colegio de San Juan de Beltrán, whose limited in-struction included lessons in begging. Travelers to Mexico City often commented on the number of men and women living on the streets, their arms outstretched for alms. "Mexico is the country of inequality," Alexander von Humboldt commented in 1803. "Nowhere does there exist such a fearful difference in the distribution of fortune, civilization, cultivation of the soil and population."[24]

Only two forces seemed capable of uniting the people of New Spain. The first was religion. The viceroyalty developed its own distinc-tive brand of Catholicism that integrated the religious practices of local native peoples with the traditional celebrations of the liturgical calendar. It also drew upon an appearance of the Virgin Mary to a poor Indian man outside of Mexico City in 1531—a miracle that convinced the sub-jects of the viceroyalty, no matter their race or status, that they were a chosen people. Catholicism was a powerful driving force in a country where communication from heaven was sometimes required to approve treaties, where men and women processed on their knees to pay homage to saints, and where royal salutes were fired in the Virgin's honor.[25]

Divided by race, class, customs, and even language, the subjects of New Spain also forged a common identity through the experience of living under Spanish rule. New Spain was divided into adminis-trative units known as audiencias, each with a commandant general who reported directly to Madrid. The audiencias were, in turn, divided into provinces, ruled over by Spanish governors. The laws these gov-ernors enforced regulated almost every aspect of life in New Spain. A decree from 1538 prohibited the introduction of dice or cards to the Americas. Another from 1716, entitled "Against the Abuse of Cloth-ing and Other Superfluous Expenses," prohibited people of African descent from wearing pearls, and people of mixed race from dressing as Indians.[26]

Human bondage drove the economy of New Spain from as early as the sixteenth century. Enslaved people were a common sight in the shops and households of the capital, which, by 1570, boasted the largest African population of any city in the Americas. In Guadalajara, a city in northwestern New Spain, the population of one thousand included more than five hundred black or mulatto slaves in 1606. Enslaved people also labored on the sugar plantations in central and southeastern Mexico. At the San Cosme y San Damián plantation, 130 miles south of Mexico City, a census in 1691 counted 156 slaves. Even the ranches and haciendas on the northern frontier sometimes relied on enslaved labor. At San Antonio de Béxar, one of the three Spanish garrisons in the province of Téjas, twenty of the 1,248 residents in 1783 were black slaves.[27]

The lives of enslaved people were by no means easy in New Spain. Black slaves worked long hours in silver mines and textile workshops, cotton fields and sugar mills. They did not always have enough to eat. They could be whipped, branded, or put in chains for even minor infractions. But they did have a number of legal protections, because Spanish law recognized people of African descent as human beings, not simply as property. Enslaved people were subjects of the Spanish Crown. As such, they enjoyed protections against cruel and excessive punishments that enslaved people in the United States did not. In New Spain, slaves were also members of the Catholic Church, which entitled them to receive the sacraments, including the rite of marriage. By law, their owners could neither forbid enslaved people from marrying nor separate husbands from their wives, both common occurrences in the slaveholding United States.[28]

Perhaps no legal protection was as significant as the right for enslaved people to seek their freedom. Beginning with the thirteenth-century legal code known as the Siete Partidas, which condemned slavery as the "most evil and the most despicable thing which could be found among men," Spain's legal tradition established that "all of the laws of the world should lead towards freedom." No onerous or costly restrictions discouraged owners from manumitting their slaves. Enslaved people also enjoyed the right to purchase their freedom under a process known as *coartación*, and they could file claims against their masters in cases of abuse.[29]

As news of Spanish legal protections spread across the Americas, enslaved people fled the Dutch islands of Aruba, Bonaire, and Curaçao for Venezuela; they left the rice plantations of South Carolina for Spanish Florida. When their owners tried to secure their return, enslaved people took up arms in defense of their freedom. Their actions convinced royal officials that formerly enslaved people could help to populate and protect the borders of Spain's far-flung empire. In 1693, King Charles II issued a decree promising freedom to enslaved people who escaped to Spanish Florida. In 1733, the Spanish Crown added an additional caveat: fugitive slaves would be free if they converted to Catholicism and swore allegiance to the Spanish Crown. The policy proved so useful that, in 1750, the Spanish king extended this promise to New Spain.[30]

The promise of freedom in New Spain was a mounting concern to slaveholders in the Mississippi Valley. On May 23, 1806, seven slaves arrived at the Spanish garrison of Nacogdoches, Téjas, with a forged passport from a judge in Kentucky. Two years later, between thirty and forty slaves went missing from a plantation outside of Natchitoches, Louisiana. Their owners petitioned for their return, but Spanish officials refused to turn over the runaways. "Things cannot long remain in this state," complained one *norteamericano* in Natchitoches, Louisiana. Indeed, they would not. The geography of freedom in the Mississippi Valley would soon be redrawn by larger geopolitical developments taking place far from the border between the United States and New Spain.[31]

On September 16, 1810, a priest named Miguel Hidalgo shouted "Death to bad government!" from the open window of a parishioner's house in the small town of Dolores in central New Spain. Two years earlier, the French army had crossed the Pyrenees and deposed the Spanish king, Fernando VII. Across the Spanish Empire, loyal subjects revolted against French rule. With Hidalgo's call to arms, New Spain joined the growing movement to demand the restoration of the rightful king. In 1815, Spanish forces finally drove the French army from the Iberian Peninsula. But upon being restored to power, Fernando VII established an absolutist government. The revolutionaries who had originally taken up arms against the French now revolted against their own king. As the stakes of the war increased, the fighting became more desperate. Entire towns were massacred. A royalist commander replaced his epaulets with the severed ears of an insurgent.[32]

With the Spanish Crown distracted by the wars of independence, the United States, under the direction of President James Monroe, invaded Florida. The commander of the Florida expedition was Major General Andrew Jackson. At six feet tall, with bright blue eyes and a pronounced jaw, Jackson was a commanding presence who had become a national hero when his men decisively defeated the British at the Battle of New Orleans, the final battle of the War of 1812. Jackson recognized the strategic importance of seizing Florida: whoever ruled over this mosquito-infested peninsula would control the Gulf of Mexico. As the owner of more than thirty slaves, Jackson also understood that Spanish rule in Florida posed a threat to slavery in the United States. Enslaved people who escaped from Georgia and the Carolinas could claim their freedom on Spanish soil, and they did so in droves. Some runaways headed toward a Spanish establishment on the Apalachicola River called the Negro Fort. Others joined the Seminoles, a tribe of Creek extraction that fled Georgia and the Carolinas during the eighteenth century.[33]

On March 15, 1818, Jackson crossed into Florida at the head of five thousand men. Three weeks later he took St. Marks, on Apalachee Bay. He then led his men a hundred miles to the east, where they set fire to a town along the Suwannee River, which was established by fugitive slaves. All that was left when they turned back toward the west were the charred foundations of three hundred houses. From the Suwannee River, Jackson's forces marched three hundred miles to the west to Pensacola, the center of Spanish rule in the Florida panhandle. On May 24, 1818, the town surrendered.[34]

When news from Florida reached Washington, DC, the Spanish minister, Luis de Onís, was irate. Onís demanded that the United States government apologize, end the occupation of Pensacola and St. Marks, and censure General Jackson. But Secretary of State John Quincy Adams flatly refused, and Spain was in no position to remove Jackson's army by force.[35]

Across the Americas, the revolutionaries were gaining ground. In 1817, José de San Martín, the son of a Spanish military officer stationed in Argentina, led more than five thousand men (half of them former slaves) over the high passes of the Andes to attack the loyalist stronghold of Lima, Peru. Two years later, Simón Bolívar, a wealthy planter who styled himself the Liberator of Spanish America, led an army that drove the Spanish forces across the plains of Venezuela. Bolívar's forces would soon take control of New Granada, what is now Colombia. Revolutionaries, dispersed across the Spanish viceroyalties, were about to achieve what once seemed impossible. The Spanish Empire, one of the first truly global empires in human history, the empire that had defeated the Aztecs, the Incas, the Berbers of Algeria, and the Sultanate of Brunei, was on the verge of collapse.[36]

Faced with the prospect of losing its empire, the Spanish government ceded its claim to Florida on February 22, 1819. In exchange, the United States paid Spain $5 million. US and Spanish diplomats also resolved a long-standing dispute over the border between the United States and New Spain. After Thomas Jefferson purchased Louisiana from France in 1803, the United States maintained that the territory extended as far south as the Rio Grande, because the French explorer Robert de La Salle had established a short-lived settlement on the coast of Téjas in 1685. Spanish officials countered that La Salle had abandoned his settlement in a matter of months, while Spanish subjects had occupied and defended Téjas since 1716. Now both powers recognized the Sabine River as the border between Louisiana and New Spain.[37]

The invasion of Florida underscored the danger of protecting fugitive slaves. The United States government was committed to protecting the rights of slaveholders against domestic and foreign threats. And federal officials were not the only ones who defended slavery. State legislatures also enacted policies designed to keep enslaved people in bondage. In Louisiana, where James Kirkham settled, slaves could not carry arms, ride on horseback, or leave their plantation without a pass. They could not drink alcohol or dance at night. They were forbidden from buying, selling, negotiating, or trading, because they possessed nothing, not even their bodies, in their own right. Slaveholders familiarized themselves with the code by paging through the thick legal digests that the legislature circulated across the territory. Enslaved people learned of the laws through the punishments inflicted on runaways tied to the public whipping post, and on the faces of slaves branded with the letter "R"—for "runaway." And yet enslaved people continued to escape.[38]

TWO

THE MEANING OF LIBERTY

MARTIN WAS PICKING COTTON ON JAMES KIRKHAM'S PLANTA-
tion in the summer of 1819 when he mentioned his plan of
escaping to New Spain to another field hand. Later he discussed the
details with some of the other slaves while they were chopping wood.
Another slave—a woman named Fivi—stopped her washing to listen.
Richard Moran, an older man with a peg leg, agreed to accompany Martin. At night they told Samuel, a slave from a neighboring plantation,
who decided to join them.[1]

Martin had tried to run away once before. In the winter of 1814,
near the close of the War of 1812, a British fleet appeared off the coast
of Louisiana. Throughout the war, enslaved people who escaped to British lines had proven useful, digging trenches, piloting ships, and pow-
dering officers' wigs. To encourage enslaved people to escape, British
commanders promised to free "all interested Americans" who reached
their lines. Martin, then twenty-two, slipped away from Kirkham's
plantation to try to join the invaders. Before he had gotten far, he was
caught. As punishment, he was branded on each cheek with the letter

"R"—for "runaway." The marks on his face were meant as a warning
to him and others, though his branding only seemed to strengthen his
determination to escape.[2]

In the winter of 1819, Martin, Samuel, Fivi, and Richard stole two
horses and a mule and rode west for more than a hundred miles. The
journey presented a variety of dangers: the sheer distance; the huge
alligators, which could maim a horse and do worse to its rider; the
Karankawa Indians, who were rumored to have a taste for human flesh,
and who adorned themselves, according to one traveler, with "astronom-
ical instruments" salvaged from shipwrecks. The dangers did not end
when the four runaways arrived at Nacogdoches, in eastern Téjas. The
town consisted of several log cabins, a church, and a two-story stone
fort, which stood on a low hill, surrounded by immense forests of holm
oaks, sugar maples, and, at higher elevations, pines, which, according to
one visitor, gave "a dark, somber aspect to the land."[3]

In Nacogdoches, the four slaves claimed their freedom before the
military commander of the garrison, General Ignacio Pérez. Spanish
law provided a number of protections to the runaways, ranging from
the thirteenth-century legal code, the Siete Partidas, which shielded
enslaved people against excessive punishments, to the royal decrees
that promised freedom to slaves escaping from neighboring jurisdictions. But General Pérez was wary of freeing the runaways. Ever since
General Andrew Jackson seized Florida, Spanish officials feared that
protecting fugitive slaves would provoke another invasion. Rather than
emancipate Richard, Martin, Fivi, and Samuel, Pérez sent them to
Monterrey, nearly six hundred miles to the south, where they would
have to petition for their freedom before a judge. The four runaways
escaped the plantation society of Louisiana, only to face the consequences of a foreign policy that actively defended the interests of
slaveholders abroad.[4]

Diplomats from the United States were not the only ones trying to
check emancipatory legislation in New Spain. As Martin, Fivi, Samuel, and Richard were making their way to Monterrey, *norteamericanos*

were moving to the province of Téjas in hopes of opening up new lands to cotton cultivation. These immigrants intended to defend slavery in their adopted country as they had in the United States: by protesting unfavorable laws and, if necessary, breaking them.

FOR THE FIRST FEW WEEKS AFTER THEIR DISAPPEARANCE, JAMES Kirkham likely assumed that his slaves were hiding in the swamps west of the Red River and that they would return as soon as they ran out of food. But when spring arrived, Martin and Richard were not there to plow the fields, with Fivi trailing behind, a bag of cottonseed around her neck. The summer of 1820 passed, without the familiar sight of their rounded shoulders, as they bent to hoe weeds from the rows of cotton. By the harvest, Kirkham must have understood that his slaves had escaped to New Spain. In November, after the valuable cotton was tied into bales and loaded onto flatboats, he packed his saddlebags for the journey west.[5]

Near the Sabine River, Kirkham met another traveler, also making his way to New Spain. Moses Austin had dark, close-set eyes and side-whiskers that reached almost to his jaw, but his most striking feature was a high forehead, made even more pronounced by a receding hairline. He rode a gray horse, a shotgun tied to his saddle, a pistol at his side. An enslaved man named Richmond rode beside him on a mule. The fine figure that he cut overstated his means. The horse did not belong to him; nor did the slave who accompanied him. Moses Austin was bankrupt.[6]

Austin was not accustomed to penury. In 1797, he opened a lead mine forty miles southwest of St. Louis. His fortunes rose as Missouri, part of the Louisiana Territory, was transferred from Spain to France to the United States. By 1810, his assets totaled $190,000—approximately $4 million in today's dollars. But as lead prices started to drop, Austin took on debt to keep his mine in operation. He borrowed thousands of dollars from the Bank of Saint Louis. He leased sixty slaves from Colonel Anthony Butler, a wealthy slaveholder from Kentucky who would later become the US minister to Mexico. In 1819, a financial panic swept the United States, and Austin could no longer hold off his creditors. His mine was seized, but the proceeds from the sale had not been enough to repay all of his debts.[7]

At the age of fifty-three, Austin needed to remake himself, and he saw an opportunity in New Spain. In the fall of 1820, he set out for San Antonio de Béxar to petition Spanish authorities for permission to settle three hundred families from the United States in the province of Téjas. The petition, if granted, would open thousands of acres along the Gulf Coast to cotton production, and the demand for such lands was mounting. As aspiring cotton planters moved west, the population of Alabama, Mississippi, and Louisiana exploded from 93,202 in 1810 to 356,756 in 1820. Land prices soared as high as forty dollars an acre— far too much for a man of modest means. A recent controversy over the admission of Missouri made clear that although the US Congress remained committed to protecting slavery where it existed, the prime cotton lands in the United States were running out.[8]

AT THE END OF 1818, MISSOURI PETITIONED TO JOIN THE UNION as a slave state. Although the territory occupied the same latitude as the "free" states of Illinois, Indiana, and Ohio, Missouri's petition did not come as a surprise. Slavery had existed in Missouri since the eighteenth century, and as the region was transferred from Spain to France to the United States, masters adamantly defended their right to hold slaves. In 1804, a year after the Louisiana Purchase, a *norteamericano* in Kaskaskia, Illinois, reported that the people of Missouri were "very much interested in obtaining an unlimited slavery." The same year, a judge in Vincennes, Indiana, warned that Missourians were "wonderfully alarmed lest their Slaves should be liberated." Faced with such threats, the United States

Congress decided against imposing any restriction on slavery. By the time the population of Missouri reached sixty thousand—the minimum to apply for statehood—the number of slaves in the territory had jumped from 3,011 in 1810 to 10,222 in 1820.[9]

Missouri's admission as a slave state alarmed Northern representatives. As they saw it, slavery contradicted the founding principles of the United States. According to Representative Arthur Livermore of New Hampshire, human bondage was "the foulest reproach of nations." Another representative from New York condemned slavery as the "bane of man" and the "abomination of heaven." The political consequences of Missouri's admission could not have been far from their minds, either. In 1818, there were eleven slave states and eleven "free" states, giving each section equal representation in the Senate. If Missouri joined the Union as a slave state, the balance of power would shift in favor of the South.[10]

On February 13, 1819, Representative James Tallmadge Jr. of New York proposed that Congress authorize Missouri to form a state government on the condition that its constitution ban the further introduction of new slaves, and free at age twenty-five the children of slaves already in the state. To Tallmadge and his supporters, Congress's authority to impose such a condition was indisputable. The Constitution gave the legislative branch the power to make "all needful rules and regulations" for the territories and authorized it only to admit those states that had adopted republican forms of government. Just as Louisiana had to provide for free elections for state officials, Missouri would have to limit slavery in order to be admitted to the Union.[11]

Southern politicians vehemently disagreed. Although the Constitution gave the legislative branch the authority to make "all needful rules and regulations" for the territories, Representative Philip Barbour of Virginia pointed out that Congress only imposed those regulations when the territories were being organized, not after they met the requirements for statehood. No other territory had been ordered to restrict slavery as a condition of admission. To impose such a condition on Missouri would deny it the rights that belonged to every other state in the Union. Henry Baldwin, a states' rights advocate from Pennsylvania, captured what he saw as the injustice of the Tallmadge Amendment when he asked whether Missouri would make her own laws "like the other states, new and old," or whether Congress would make laws for her and "keep her out of the Union and in a state of colonial vassalage until she will give up the power and right of deciding as to her own internal policy."[12]

On February 16, 1819, the House of Representatives passed the bill to admit Missouri, with the Tallmadge Amendment attached. But the Senate rejected the amendment. On March 2, when the bill to admit Missouri returned to the House, without the provisions to prohibit the introduction of new slaves and to free enslaved children at age twenty-five, the Northern majority rejected the Senate's revisions, 78 to 76. "We have kindled a fire which all the waters of the ocean cannot put out, which seas of blood can only extinguish," Representative Thomas Cobb of Georgia thundered, as he glared at Tallmadge. The representative from New York was unmoved. "My hold on life is probably as frail as that of any man who now hears me, but while that hold lasts, it shall be devoted to the service of my country—to the freedom of man," Tallmadge explained defiantly. "If blood is necessary to extinguish any fire which I have assisted to kindle . . . I shall not forebear to contribute my mite."[13]

The two houses had reached an impasse, and the nation was beginning to take notice. Southern whites protested that Northerners' supposed humanitarianism was nothing more than a bid for increased regional power. There was no better proof, they argued, than the hypocrisy of Northern congressmen. These politicians invoked the "rights of humanity" for enslaved people in the territories, but not for the poor whites, who labored for long hours in the North. This accusation would often be repeated by Southern debaters in the decades ahead. "Power, power—the preponderance of political power is the great desideratum," exclaimed the proslavery *Louisville Public Advertiser*.[14]

Northerners took an entirely different view. The editorial board of the *New-York Daily Advertiser*, which routinely condemned the mistreatment of soldiers, blacks, Indians, mental patients, and even lobsters, now turned its attention to the Tallmadge Amendment. "This question involves not only the future character of our nation but the future weight and influence of the 'free' states. If now lost—it is lost forever." The legislatures of nine states passed resolutions supporting Congress's decision not to admit Missouri as a slave state. The citizens of Boston, Providence, Hartford, New Haven, Albany, and Cincinnati urged their representatives to stop the expansion of slavery in the territories. Every "dog-hole town and blacksmith's village" had organized a mass meeting, the proslavery *Saint Louis Enquirer* complained.[15]

CONGRESS HAD NOT REACHED A DECISION ON MISSOURI WHEN, ON January 3, 1820, the House of Representatives authorized Maine, formerly a part of Massachusetts, to petition for statehood. When the House bill went to the Senate, Southern politicians recognized that it gave them leverage to end the impasse over Missouri. They moved to add a provision to the bill that would allow both Maine *and* Missouri to petition for statehood without restriction. The message was clear. The Senate would not admit Maine until the House admitted Missouri.[16]

The debates up until this point had turned on whether the legislative branch could impose conditions on the territories at any point, or only during the earliest stages of territorial organization. Now senators began to make a different argument. If the Constitution protected the right to "property," then, they reasoned, Congress could *never* interfere with slavery where it already existed. Thomas Cobb challenged his colleagues "to point out, and lay their finger upon, that clause of the Constitution of the United States which gives to this body the right to legislate upon the subject." The Constitution had clearly set out the powers of the legislative branch: to tax, to spend, to borrow, to regulate commerce, to declare war, to raise armies, to build post offices. Nowhere, Cobb explained, did the Constitution authorize Congress to abolish or even restrict slavery.[17]

The theory that the national government could not interfere with slavery became known as the principle of nonintervention, or the principle of noninterference. Southern politicians embraced this principle. To abolish slavery in territories where it existed, Representative Hugh Nelson of Virginia argued, was "to prepare the way for an attack by Congress on the property of masters . . . in the several states." Noninterference also appealed to Northern politicians who favored interpreting the Constitution as it was written. After reading "every paper, pamphlet and essay written upon the subject," Representative Jonathan Mason of Massachusetts concluded that "the power to impose this restriction was not to be found either in the letter or spirit of the national compact." For congressmen like Mason, the principle of noninterference was part of a larger vision of limited government—a government with no authority to impose tariffs, fund internal improvements, or meddle in the domestic concerns of the individual states. On February 16, the Senate voted to admit Maine and Missouri without condition.[18]

Not everyone accepted the principle of noninterference, however. On February 23, the House defeated the bill to admit Missouri and Maine, 93 to 72. Two weeks later, the House again voted to make gradual emancipation policies a condition for Missouri's admission. The Senate rejected this condition. In a last-ditch effort to break the deadlock, the two houses convened a conference, which proposed to admit Missouri as a slave state and Maine as a "free" state, while prohibiting slavery in the Louisiana Purchase north of 36°30'—the approximate latitude at which the Ohio River meets the Mississippi. Though Congress had neglected to restrict slavery while organizing the Missouri Territory, the compromise measure would avoid this mistake in the unorganized territories of the Louisiana Purchase that lay north of 36°30'. On March 2, the Senate passed the compromise measure. The same day, the House followed suit.[19]

The controversy over Missouri was settled and the Union remained intact. But the Democratic-Republican Party, the main political coalition in the United States, was beginning to splinter into two camps, with opposing views of federal power. One camp—the Whigs—envisioned an activist government that had the power to exclude slavery from the territories. The other camp, known as Democrats, favored a more limited government that could neither abolish slavery where it existed nor establish it where it had been abolished. Both parties took the Missouri Compromise as confirmation of their political convictions. To Northern Whigs, the compromise line proved that the legislative branch could, in fact, restrict forced labor in the territories, while Northern and Southern Democrats countered that slavery did not exist north of 36°30' in the Louisiana Purchase and that the compromise simply maintained the status quo.[20]

The Missouri controversy exposed a serious disagreement over matters of constitutional interpretation, and at the same time it created a major problem for slaveholders. Only a narrow swathe of the unorganized territories of the Louisiana Purchase remained open to forced labor. To keep growing cotton—a crop that depleted the soil in which it was grown after only three years—planters needed land. Moses Austin understood this problem more clearly than most, and he staked his future on the possibility that Spanish officials would open up the province of Téjas to cotton planters from the United States.

Both Moses Austin and James Kirkham were headed to the provincial capital of San Antonio de Béxar. To better find their way, and to protect themselves from bandits and Indians, the two men agreed to travel together. Following an old Indian road, Austin and Kirkham traveled west, passing fertile, blackland prairies intersected by rivers: the Trinity, the Brazos, the Colorado, and the Nueces. As they moved farther inland, the land gradually rose, until they reached a sheer limestone escarpment—the Balcones Fault—beyond which lay the high plains of western Téjas. With an average annual rainfall of less than twenty inches, the existence of every living thing in western Téjas was tenuous. The vegetation was sparse—bunchgrass, yuccas, a few mesquite trees. Even the ground seemed impermanent. During the long, hot summers, travelers sometimes woke to find their tents covered with earth deposited overnight by the wind.[21]

Austin and Kirkham were not the only *norteamericanos* to arrive in Téjas around this time. In the summer of 1819, a plantation owner from Natchez, Mississippi, named James Long organized a company of volunteers to cross the Sabine River and liberate Téjas from "Spanish rapacity." Spanish soldiers promptly turned back the invasion, but rumors soon began to circulate of a second expedition from Louisiana. In the weeks before James Kirkham and Moses Austin arrived in San Antonio de Béxar, dozens of *norteamericanos* crossed the Sabine River—ostensibly, to hunt, wrangle horses, recover debts, search for mules, or peddle silk handkerchiefs to the Spanish troops. Governor Antonio Martínez did not believe these pretexts. By the time that Kirkham and Austin reached San Antonio de Béxar, Governor Martínez was convinced, not without reason, that *norteamericanos* were involved in some new scheme to occupy Téjas. Rather than receive Kirkham and Austin at the Palacio de Gobierno, Governor Martínez ordered them to return immediately to the United States.[22]

As the two men walked across the plaza in the waning afternoon light, dejected at the thought that their journey had been in vain, Austin spotted Philip Nering Bögel, whom he had met several decades earlier in a tavern in New Orleans. Bögel was born in the Dutch colony of Guiana but raised in Holland, where he worked as a tax collector until the government issued a reward of one thousand gold ducats for his arrest on charges of fraud. Bögel fled to New Orleans, where he took advantage of his anonymity to pass himself off as minor royalty, calling himself the Baron de Bastrop, and using his purported status to secure a land grant in Spanish Téjas.[23]

When Austin explained why he had come to San Antonio de Béxar, the Baron de Bastrop promised to intercede on his behalf. The day after Christmas, Austin and Kirkham found themselves in the Palacio de Gobierno, presenting their petitions to the Spanish governor. With Bastrop interpreting, James Kirkham presented a letter from the governor of Louisiana, requesting the return of his slaves, which Governor Martínez promised to forward to the proper authorities. Next, Austin proposed settling three hundred Catholic families from the United States along the Colorado River in Téjas. Although Spanish officials were wary of admitting *norteamericanos*, Austin promised that his colonists would "bind themselves by oath to take up their arms in defense of the Spanish government against either the Indians, filibusters or any other enemy that may plan hostilities." With three-quarters of the military budget of the Provincias Internas devoted to the defense of Téjas, Governor Martínez was beginning to believe that colonization might "provide for the increase and prosperity of this province." He promised to consider Austin's proposal.[24]

SEVERAL DAYS AFTER MEETING WITH GOVERNOR MARTÍNEZ, Moses Austin and James Kirkham set out for Louisiana. Austin felt uneasy about their return journey. Kirkham was driving a herd of mules that he had stolen from outside of San Antonio de Béxar, and Austin feared that the Spanish authorities would never issue his land grant if they discovered that he had knowingly accompanied a criminal. Kirkham, for his part, chafed at Austin's apprehension. Not far into their journey, Kirkham stole Austin's mule and provisions, and slipped away under cover of darkness. For eight days, Austin and his slave, Richmond, lived off roots and berries, as they made their way eastward. They stumbled into Natchitoches barely alive in January 1821.[25]

After convalescing for three weeks in Natchitoches, Austin began his return journey to Missouri, traveling by boat down the Red River to the Mississippi, and then north on the Mississippi to Missouri. Less than a week after reaching his home state, a messenger arrived from Téjas to inform him that his petition had been approved. Moses Austin was overjoyed. "Times are changing," he wrote to his son, Stephen, who was working as an apprentice lawyer in New Orleans. "A new chance presents itself. Nothing is wanting but concert and firmness." Although he was thirty thousand dollars in debt, and still sick with pneumonia—or as he called it, "flux"—Moses prepared to leave Missouri for good. As he hurried to settle his affairs, barely eating or sleeping, Moses experienced a "Violent attack of Inflamation on the brest and lungs." His wife called a doctor to blister and bleed him, but his fever only worsened. As he lay dying, Moses motioned for his wife to come toward him. "Tell dear Stephen that it is his dying father's last request to prosecute the enterprise that he had commenced."[26]

Moses died, as the Spanish Empire continued to disintegrate. In 1820, fourteen thousand Spanish soldiers in Cádiz, Spain, revolted against Fernando VII's absolutist reign, forcing the king to establish a constitutional government. This development alarmed a royalist brigadier in New Spain named Agustín de Iturbide. After the war of independence broke out in 1810, six hundred thousand people in the viceroyalty lost their lives—a tenth of the total population. The economy ground to a halt. The viceroyalty's mines produced less than half of what they did before the revolution began, and agricultural production fell by a similar margin. Government revenues plummeted from 24.7 million pesos in 1809 to 7.6 million in 1821. To Iturbide, the scale of destruction confirmed the dangers of republicanism. Now that Fernando VII had agreed to establish a constitutional government, the republican principles that had wreaked such havoc in New Spain seemed likely to spread across the empire. As Iturbide saw it, the only way to stop the rabble from taking hold of political power was to establish a monarchy in the name of the king.[27]

But Vicente Guerrero, the leader of the rebels in New Spain, rejected Iturbide's plan. Born in Tixtla, sixty miles inland from Acapulco, Guerrero was the descendant of African slaves. He was working as a muleteer when the war of independence broke out. Guerrero joined the rebels, rising through the ranks until he took control of the insurgency in the south. Guerrero was fighting in defense of republicanism, and he refused to give up the fight unless Iturbide promised to establish the independence of New Spain and to extend citizenship to all men, regardless of their race. Unable to defeat Guerrero's army in battle, and desperate to end the fighting, Iturbide agreed.[28]

On February 24, 1821, Iturbide issued a manifesto to the people of New Spain, which called for the independence of Mexico, the ascendance of the Catholic Church, and the equality of all *americanos*. These three guarantees brought together liberals and conservatives, rebels and royalists. Across the viceroyalty, Spanish commanders came out in favor of the plan. So few garrisons remained loyal that the Spanish viceroy, Juan O'Donojú, signed a treaty on August 24, 1821, recognizing Mexican independence. A month later, on September 27, Iturbide's army processed through Mexico City in triumph.[29]

Mexico was no longer a viceroyalty of the Spanish Empire, but what would independence actually bring? For some, the promise of equality signaled a fundamental transformation in Mexican society, particularly with respect to slavery. José Trinidad Martínes, a black slave born in Havana, Cuba, who had come to Mexico with his owner, took this promise to mean that he could no longer be held in bondage. "All the inhabitants of this vast continent are free," he reasoned, "and only I am a slave, for no other crime than having descended from Africans." Enslaved people from the United States acted on the same reasoning. In the months after Agustín de Iturbide issued his manifesto, fourteen slaves fled from the town of Grande Prairie, located about a hundred miles west of New Orleans. Seventy-five were unaccounted for in neighboring Vermilion Parish. Four more were caught outside of St. Martinville. All of them seemed to be heading west toward the Sabine River, on the other side of which, according to the *Courrier de la Louisiane*, they would enjoy "an unrestrained equality of human rights, without regard to birth, or condition, title, name, descent, or color."[30]

Others, however, took a different interpretation. Although Iturbide's new government proclaimed all *americanos* equal, it also swore to defend property rights. These two high principles had been central to the American Revolution a generation earlier, and as bickering members of Congress could attest, the two ideals sometimes clashed, because slaves counted as both people and property. *Norteamericanos* who hoped to open up the rich lands of eastern Téjas rejected the idea that equality took precedence over property. Decades of making these arguments in the United States gave them hope of success in Mexico. But while the US Congress organized territory after territory without any restriction on the "peculiar institution," the leaders of New Spain often adopted a different course, as James Kirkham learned.[31]

In the spring of 1820, Martin, Fivi, Richard, and Samuel arrived in Monterrey. Samuel, who had fallen sick during the journey, was taken to a hospital, while the others were ushered, one by one, into the former mission that served as the Palacio de Gobierno. A judge, speaking through an interpreter, asked them to swear to tell the truth. Kirkham's slaves must have known about the royal decrees that promised liberty to fugitive slaves from neighboring jurisdictions, because Richard Moran testified that he could no longer be held in bondage now that he had "cross[ed] the line" into New Spain. When the judge asked why they crossed the Sabine River, they invoked the Siete Partidas, which protected enslaved people against mistreatment. Martin pointed to his "bad treatment" in Louisiana, of which the scars on his face bore physical proof. Richard Moran testified that "his owner did not treat him well." The woman, Fivi, believed that the Spanish would treat her better. These laws gave the runaways a claim to freedom that they never would have enjoyed in the United States, where the Constitution's fugitive slave clause guaranteed their capture and return. Even more important was the distance that the journey to Monterrey placed between themselves and their owners. For James Kirkham, this distance would ultimately prove insurmountable. As far as the records indicate, the four runaways never returned to Louisiana.[32]

THREE

THE RIGHT TO PROPERTY

O N July 16, 1821, Stephen F. Austin crossed the Sabine
River, accompanied by an escort of fifteen Spaniards. As he rode
south and west, he began to see what drew his father, Moses, to the
province. Across the Brazos River, the red clay soil gave way to rich,
black earth. The pine forests opened into large prairies, flush with long,
native grasses. Each river valley was "more luxuriant" than the last,
Austin recorded in his journal. The deer were fat and the grass was
"abundant." This country, he wrote, was "the most beautiful" he had
ever seen.[1]

By the time he reached San Antonio de Béxar, Austin had a plan
for how to distribute land to the three hundred families that he planned
to bring to Téjas. At the Palacio de Gobierno, he reviewed the details
with Governor Antonio Martínez. Each head of household would receive 320 acres of agricultural land and 650 acres of grazing land. This
standard grant would increase with the size of the household. Austin
proposed to offer an additional 200 acres to men who brought their
wives and another 100 acres for each child. For every slave, colonists

would receive another 50 acres. While prime agricultural lands in the United States sold for as much as $50 an acre, Austin proposed charging no more than the costs of surveying: 12.5 cents per acre.[2]

After securing approval for his plan, Austin turned to the task of deciding where to establish his colony. On August 21, he and his party left for La Bahía, a fort on the banks of the San Antonio River. When they arrived, they found the town in "a state of ruin." The houses had "but little furniture or rather none at all." Lacking knives, the inhabitants ate with "forks & spoons" and occasionally "their fingers." The surrounding region had no more promise than the town itself. The soil was "mirey" and timber was scarce. "The whole country round this Bay is a dead level Prairie, not a bush growing," Austin recorded. In wet weather, the "deep black" soil "will mire a horse almost any where" and "in dry weather cracks open so that a horses foot would go into them." Here was no place for a colony.[3]

From the coast, Austin continued north. "Land is better," he noted, as he reached the Colorado River. His outlook brightened as his party approached the Brazos River. "Prairies of the richest kind of black sandy land," he gushed, "intersected by branches and Creeks of excellent water—heavyly timbered, beautifully rolling." Austin had seen enough; he knew where he wanted to settle. The area between the Colorado and Brazos Rivers was as rich as any tract in Mississippi and Alabama, and there seemed to be more free land than anywhere else in North America.[4]

Other *norteamericanos* shared Austin's enthusiasm for Téjas. By the time Austin returned to Louisiana in October 1821, nearly a hundred letters had arrived from *norteamericanos* in Missouri and Kentucky who were interested in moving to Téjas. The roads to western Louisiana were soon choked with immigrants. "I am convinced that I could take on fifteen hundred families as easily as three hundred if permitted to do so," Austin boasted.[5]

Anglo colonists were already clearing land on the banks of the Colorado River when Austin received troubling news from Governor Martínez that the newly installed government in Mexico City under

Agustín de Iturbide would have to confirm Austin's grant before any more lands could be distributed. Worse still, Mexico's Congress was debating whether to abolish slavery. To protect his colony and the system of forced labor upon which it depended, Austin would have to go to Mexico City. In the United States, Southern planters had prevented the US Congress from prohibiting or even restricting slavery by invoking their "property" rights and threatening to revolt, and Austin planned to make the same arguments in his adopted country. Over the years, he would have to make this case again and again. The early decades of Mexico's independence were turbulent, and each administration adopted its own policies with respect to slavery. But no administration fully accepted Austin's arguments. Mexico's policies, however numerous and varied, were consistent in one respect: they would not permit slavery to expand unchecked.[6]

IN THE SPRING OF 1822, AUSTIN SET OUT FOR MEXICO CITY, OVER a thousand miles to the south. The journey was a catalog of disappointments. "No one after reading Humboldt and other writers can pass through this country without being sorely disappointed at every step," Austin wrote, recalling the Prussian explorer. Alexander von Humboldt had marveled at the natural resources of the country, when he visited in 1803, but as Austin made his way southwest from San Antonio de Béxar, he saw "nothing but Sand, entirely void of Timber, covered with scrubby thorn bushes and Prickly Pear." Near the Nueces River, fifty Comanches surrounded him, taking four blankets, a bridle, his Spanish grammar book, and all of his provisions. On March 21, he crossed the Rio Grande, gaining elevation as he headed south along the central plateau, the limestone peaks of the Sierra Madre Oriental looming to the east. At the end of April, he reached Mexico City. Humboldt, he discovered, had been wrong about everything except for the capital. "This city is truly a magnificent one," he marveled.[7]

Austin expected the new government to confirm his land grant within a matter of days. "The Congress here do business in good order and with great deliberation," he wrote. But he was less certain that the legislative branch would arrive at a satisfactory decision with respect to slavery. The thirty-eight members of the recently convened Mexican Congress had a number of reasons to end human bondage. To many Mexicans, colonialism was a kind of slavery. As a popular political catechism explained: "Q: What is liberty? A: To not be a slave, nor subject to any foreign power." From this perspective, masters had no more right to own slaves than European monarchs had to rule over distant colonies. National independence, in other words, had to be accompanied by personal emancipation. Championing antislavery would also help to distinguish Mexico from Spain—an important task for any fledgling government, but particularly for the Latin American republics. Unlike Great Britain, which grudgingly recognized the independence of the United States after the American Revolution, Spain continued to launch expeditions from Cuba to recover her former colonies, and did so until 1830. By abolishing or at least restricting slavery, the Mexican authorities could cast themselves in a different, more enlightened mold than the Spanish government, which continued to permit human bondage across its empire.[8]

In addition, antislavery would allow Mexicans to differentiate their independence movement from its more renowned forebear, the American Revolution. Although the Latin American republics took inspiration from the independence movement in the United States, Mexican politicians predicted that the *norteamericanos'* "glorious uprising" would be forgotten because of the contradiction between its professed ideals and the millions of slaves who cultivated "the lands of the South with their sweat." Mexico, by contrast, had heard the "scream of nature" against slavery. While *norteamericanos* commemorated their independence by wearing cockades and raising liberty poles, antislavery Mexicans wanted to celebrate their own emancipation from the "yoke of slavery" by emancipating African slaves.[9]

For all of its advantages, abolition was risky. Although slavery was declining at the national level, it remained significant in certain regions, though it is impossible to say exactly how significant. Estimates of Mexico's slave population after independence are speculative, because the independent Mexican government abolished distinctions of caste and census takers stopped recording racial categories. Anecdotal evidence, however, suggests that the remaining enslaved population was concentrated in the sugar-producing south and the cotton-growing north. Abolition would undermine the "property" rights of owners in those regions. "We cannot in any way attack the right to property," said one of Mexico's congressmen, Francisco Manuel Sanchez, in 1821.[10]

In Mexico City, the representatives had not reached a decision on slavery when they found themselves confronted with an even more pressing issue. Agustín de Iturbide, the former royalist brigadier who helped to win Mexico's independence, hoped to install Fernando VII, or some other member of the Bourbon line, on the throne. But the Spanish king and his relatives refused this offer. After a year without a monarch, conservatives in Mexico were growing impatient. On May 18, Austin heard the "firing of Musketry and cannon" and "loud Shouts from the Soldiers and Citizens proclaiming Iturbide Emperor under the title of Agustin 1st." The next day, Congress elected Iturbide emperor, as the people demanded.[11]

AFTER AGUSTÍN DE ITURBIDE WAS CROWNED EMPEROR OF MEXico at the main altar of the Cathedral of the Assumption late in the summer of 1822, he exited the cathedral, throwing medals to the crowd gathered outside. These tokens were a paltry sop to revolutionaries like Vicente Guerrero who had risked their lives to transform Mexico from a Spanish viceroyalty into an independent nation. But to Stephen F. Austin, the new government was not conservative enough.[12]

Norteamericanos would do almost anything for the opportunity to grow cotton along the rich soil of the Gulf Coast. They agreed—in theory, at least—to convert to Catholicism. They pledged their loyalty first to the Spanish Empire and then to Iturbide's constitutional monarchy. But they would not subject themselves to a government that prohibited or even restricted slavery, as Iturbide's government was now threatening to do. After Iturbide's coronation, the Mexican Congress drafted three separate bills, each of which imposed significant restrictions on forced labor. One permitted the introduction of slaves to Mexico on the condition that slaves receive wages so that they could buy their freedom after a few years. Another prohibited the introduction of slaves and emancipated at age fourteen children born to enslaved mothers. A third bill abolished slavery altogether, freeing enslaved people already in Mexico, and forbidding colonists from bringing any more into the country.[13]

As news of these proposed laws reached the United States, interest in moving to Téjas waned. Most of Austin's prospective colonists hailed from the nearby states of Louisiana, Mississippi, Alabama, and Arkansas, and they either owned slaves or aspired to. "A great many is very anxious to know the system of government which now exists and whether slavery is abolished or not," a *norteamericano* informed Austin in 1822.[14]

Austin was starting to despair for the future of his colony when, on October 31, 1822, Emperor Iturbide dissolved Mexico's Congress, establishing a governing council in its place. Seeing his chance, Austin set to work to convince the forty-five members of the new council of "the necessity that there was in Téjas . . . and all of the other depopulated provinces, that the new Colonists could bring their slaves with them." Francisco Argandar, a deputy who hailed from the state of Michoacán, located to the west of Mexico City, was not convinced. He argued that slavery was "inhuman and against all right," and the *norteamericanos* who planned to settle in the province of Téjas would be better off without it. "If they wish to come, they will do it under the condition that they will not have slaves," he exclaimed. "This will be the highest honor of the Mexican nation." But others recognized, as Deputy Salvador Porras of the Mexican state of Durango put it, that abolition would pose "powerful and invincible obstacles" to the settlement and development of Mexico's frontiers. A disregard for "property" would discourage immigration (what one booster later called the "bone, nerve, and marrow" of Mexico's prosperity).[15]

On January 3, 1823, eight months after Stephen F. Austin reached Mexico City, Emperor Iturbide signed a colonization bill. The terms were generally favorable. The Mexican government would issue contracts to agents known as empresarios to recruit foreign immigrants. Each family would receive 4,438 acres for grazing livestock and 177 acres for farming—twice as much land as Stephen F. Austin had originally requested. Better yet, they would be exempt from paying taxes for the first six years that they lived in Mexico. But the colonization law had a major shortcoming: it prohibited the slave trade and freed the children of enslaved people at age fourteen. "The article is very different from what I hoped," Austin wrote.[16]

Although the colonization law did not abolish slavery outright, it did guarantee that human bondage would end within a generation or two. Austin understood that planters would no sooner move to a country that had adopted gradual emancipation policies than to the Northern states. During the late eighteenth and early nineteenth centuries, Pennsylvania, Connecticut, Rhode Island, New York, and New Jersey had adopted laws to emancipate the children of slaves once they reached a specified age. The process was excruciatingly slow, since slavery would come to an end only after existing slaves died and their children reached the age that the laws specified. The last slave in Pennsylvania gained freedom in 1847. Slavery only ended in Connecticut the following year. Despite these delays, gradual emancipation policies did eventually bring slavery to an end in these states. Mexico's colonization law would have the same result, if Iturbide's government remained in power.[17]

But in December 1822, while the governing junta was finalizing the colonization law, a young military officer named Antonio López de

Santa Anna, who commanded the garrison at the port city of Veracruz, revolted against the emperor. A man of "very extraordinary powers" and few scruples, Santa Anna would go on to preside over some of the most important events in Mexican history. He forfeited Mexico's military advantage during the Texas Revolution and lost a leg during a French invasion of Veracruz; he led the country to defeat in the Mexican War and five years later, declared himself dictator. But before his defeat during the Texas Revolution, before pilgrimages were made to the cemetery where his amputated leg had been ceremoniously interred, before he christened himself "His Most Serene Highness," he organized an insurrection against Agustín de Iturbide.[18]

In February 1823, the soldiers that Iturbide sent to Veracruz to crush Santa Anna's uprising joined it instead. To shore up his flagging legitimacy, Iturbide convened a new congress on March 5, but this compromise measure came too late. By the end of March, Iturbide sailed to exile in Italy. Mexico's Congress, which ruled over the country after Iturbide's ouster, proved much more receptive to Austin's wishes than the emperor's governing junta. On April 14, 1823, Mexico's Congress approved Austin's contract to settle three hundred families along the banks of the Colorado River. In addition, it annulled all of the laws that the governing council had passed, including the gradual emancipation policies included in the colonization law. But Mexico's Congress stopped short of adopting laws to recognize and protect black slavery— the laws upon which the success of Austin's Colony seemed to depend. "If the colonists are permitted to bring slaves, we will have workers to cultivate the land," Austin wrote. But "without this, we will have nothing but poverty for a long time, perhaps the rest of our lives."[19]

AFTER ITURBIDE'S DEPARTURE, HIS NASCENT EMPIRE BEGAN TO fracture, as one province after another asserted its independence. Chiapas, Oaxaca, Yucatán, Querétaro, San Luis Potosí, Michoacán,

Guanajuato, Zacatecas, Coahuila, and Jalisco, as well as the five provinces of Central America, declared themselves sovereign. Nothing, it seemed, could bind these diverse regions together. The difficulties of transportation and communication, along with the tremendous variation in climate and natural resources, made Mexico, as one historian put it, "an archipelago of local societies."[20]

Convinced that only a federal republic could bind together a divided country, the members of Mexico's Congress set to work on a new system of government. The Constitution of 1824, as it became known, created a "popular, representative, and federal republic," composed of nineteen states, which governed their own affairs, and four territories, which would be governed from Mexico City. The constitution declared Mexico "forever free and independent of the Spanish government and of every other power," and it established Catholicism as the official religion of the nation. By erasing distinctions of race and class, and adopting universal male suffrage, the constitution took important steps toward fulfilling the egalitarian principles of Mexico's independence movement.[21]

The constitution established three branches of government: the legislative, the executive, and the judicial. The legislative branch was bicameral. Representatives were elected to the chamber of deputies by popular vote on the basis of population, while each state legislature would appoint two delegates to the senate. The state legislatures also voted for the president. In 1824, they elected General Guadalupe Victoria, a hero of the independence movement whose political views were so moderate that when he rode in his carriage, Mexicans joked that he always sat in the exact middle. Antonio López de Santa Anna, who organized the uprising against Iturbide in 1822, had to settle for a posting as the commandant-general of Yucatán.[22]

Although federalism gave local interests greater control over their own affairs, the future of Austin's Colony was far from secure. The province of Téjas was too sparsely populated to become its own state. Either the province could merge with the neighboring sovereign state of Coahuila, or it could become a separate territory of Mexico. A union with Coahuila would mean that most legislative decisions would be made hundreds of miles away in the state capital, Saltillo, but the alternative was worse. If Téjas became a territory, Mexico City would govern the province, and it would do so in the same way that the US Congress drafted all "needful rules and regulations" for Arkansas and Missouri before they became states. Faced with such an alternative, the representatives from Téjas agreed to become a part of Coahuila. The new state became known as Coahuila y Téjas.[23]

On the whole, though, the news from Mexico City was a relief to Austin. The system of government that Mexico adopted was reassuringly similar to that of the United States. "The Federal Republican System, that last and glorious hope of persecuted freedom, first established by the great fathers of North American Independence on the ruins of British Colonial oppression, and which soon raised a new born nation to a degree of prosperity and happiness unequaled in the history of the world—Now Spreads its fostering arms over the vast dominions of Mexico," Austin exclaimed in 1824. "The hitherto enslaved Spanish Provinces are now free and independent States." Slaveholders in the United States had used the federal system to their advantage in the United States. By invoking the constitution and threatening to revolt, they persuaded the US Congress not to impose any restriction on slavery in the territories where the institution already existed, but these arguments would not carry the same weight in Mexico.[24]

ON JULY 13, 1824, MEXICO'S CONGRESS PASSED A LAW TO BAN THE importation of new slaves from abroad. Although many countries had imposed such prohibitions, Mexico's law departed in subtle ways from similar policies in the United States and elsewhere. No other government promised freedom to illegally imported slaves "from the moment they set foot on the national territory," as Mexico did. Africans sold in violation of the United States' 1808 Act Prohibiting the Importation of Slaves were turned over to the state authorities, who often auctioned them off to the highest bidder, lest they become public charges or, worse, "vagabonds." In the British Empire, the law abolishing the slave trade made no mention of "freedom" or "emancipation," either; instead, it authorized British officers to enlist "liberated" Africans as "Soldiers, Seamen, or Marines" or to hire them out as indentured servants for as many as fourteen years. The timing of Mexico's prohibition posed as great a threat to human bondage as any of the law's specific provisions. One million slaves lived in the US when the 1808 ban went into effect. By contrast, less than 1 percent of that number lived in Mexico. While the United States' enslaved population could sustain itself by natural reproduction, Mexico's could not. If Mexico's laws prohibited *norteamericanos* from bringing enslaved people across the Sabine River, slave-based plantation agriculture seemed unlikely to take root in Téjas.[25]

Mexico's congressmen understood the risk they were taking by prohibiting the "commerce and traffic in slaves." While debating the law, Congressman Miguel Ramos Arizpe of Coahuila pointed out that forbidding the importation of new slaves to Mexico would discourage immigration to the province of Téjas. To promote the development of Mexico's northern frontier, Ramos Arizpe proposed permitting continued slave imports for ten years. But his colleagues balked at his suggestion. "Let us not populate our country by oppressing humanity," exclaimed Congressman Rafael Mangino of Puebla. "Excitement was very high whenever the subject of slavery came up," observed Congressman Erasmo Seguin of San Antonio de Béxar, who served on the committee that drafted the ban. Seguin doubted that there was any way to defeat the bill. In a letter back to San Antonio, he reported that the other representatives were "determined that trade should be forever abolished" and "introduction into our territory should not be permitted under any pretext."[26]

The Anglo colonists and their supporters responded to the new law in the same way that slaveholders had reacted to unfavorable legislation from the US government for decades: they tried to circumvent it. On October 11, 1824, Juan Antonio Padilla, the *jefe politico* of Téjas, wrote to the Department of Justice in Mexico City to ask whether the law applied to Austin's Colony. The land grant that the Spanish government had issued to Stephen Austin's father, Moses, in 1821 ostensibly permitted colonists to immigrate with their slaves, and Padilla warned that the *norteamericanos* who had decided to settle in Austin's Colony under those terms were now "wary of settling down because they all have slaves that they have introduced for cultivation, industry, and arts." One of the bureaucrats at the Department of Justice who read the letter wrote beneath Padilla's signature that the law "left no doubt that the new colonists cannot introduce slaves." But on October 18, 1824, the Department of Justice informed Padilla that the "North American colonists and others who wish to establish themselves in Téjas can introduce those slaves which they have for their personal use (whose status should be accredited with legal documents) on the condition that they treat them with leniency." According to this interpretation, the law did not apply to slaves imported to Mexico for personal use. The floodgates were opened for immigration of slave owners from the Southern states. Austin's strategy appeared to be working.[27]

On March 24, 1825, the legislature of Coahuila y Téjas passed a new colonization law under which the governor would enter into contracts with empresarios. According to the law, the contracts would parcel out lands in Téjas, on which empresarios would settle a certain number of families. Like the bill drafted by Iturbide's governing junta, this law imposed no taxes, charged only a nominal fee for land, and granted citizenship to colonists who converted to Catholicism and swore allegiance to Mexico. But unlike the earlier measure, which included gradual emancipation policies, the new bill only required "the new settlers [to] subject themselves to the laws that are now, and shall be hereafter, established on the subject," and the only law in force at the time was the ban on the introduction of slaves.[28]

At the capital of Saltillo, in the foothills of the Sierra Madre Oriental, dozens of empresarios petitioned for contracts. In 1825, Haden Edwards, a land speculator from Mississippi, received a concession to settle eight hundred families near Nacogdoches. A year later, the legislature issued a grant on the Colorado River to Benjamin Milam, despite the fact that the Kentuckian had joined the expedition that James Long and other filibusters organized against Téjas in 1819. The legislature of Coahuila y Téjas issued nearly forty contracts, but no colony was more successful than Austin's. Ninety percent of the *norteamericanos* who joined the colony between 1825 and 1831 hailed from slaveholding states, with more than half coming from Louisiana, Arkansas, and Alabama. Many of the colonists brought slaves with them. William Rabb left the Arkansas Territory with one slave. James Ross, also of Arkansas, owned six. Jared Groce, originally from Georgia, crossed the Sabine River with ninety slaves. By 1825, 1,790 people, including 443 slaves, had settled along the banks of the Colorado River.[29]

Anglo immigration transformed Téjas. Not only did the colonies provide a measure of defense against the Comanches and Lipan Apaches, whose raids had devastated the frontier for decades, but they also jump-started the local economy. By 1827, the province was exporting somewhere around 400,000 pounds of cotton each year. Two of every three bales found their way to the textile mills of northwestern England. The rest supplied the growing manufacturing industry of the northeastern United States. This economic growth benefitted Mexicans living in Téjas. Nearly every prominent family in San Antonio made a living by importing goods from the United States and selling them at double or even triple the price in Téjas. Their business picked up as the population expanded.[30]

But the legislature of Coahuila y Téjas was taking a risk by permitting immigration from a nation whose leaders had set their sights on Mexican lands north of the Rio Grande. As early as 1822, the Mexican minister to the United States, José Zozaya, warned his government of "the haughtiness of these Republicans who see us not as equals but inferiors, and who think that Washington will become the capital of all the Americas." As if to prove Zozaya's fears, President John Quincy Adams instructed the chargé d'affaires in Mexico City to offer one million dollars for the province of Téjas in 1825. Around the same time, the Secretary of the Mexican legation in Washington, DC, reported overhearing General Andrew Jackson explain that the best way to annex Téjas was to seize the province and then negotiate for it, as he had done with Florida. In the event of an invasion by the United States, the *norteamericanos* who moved to Téjas seemed unlikely to take up arms in defense of their adopted country. Although Stephen Austin converted to Catholicism and mastered Spanish to the point where he could write to Mexican officials without the assistance of a translator, his assimilation proved the exception, not the rule.[31]

Did the benefits of Anglo colonization outweigh the costs? No consensus had been reached when the legislature of Coahuila y Téjas set to work drafting a state constitution. On November 30, 1826, a representative from Saltillo named Manuel Carrillo proposed an article that, if passed, threatened to destroy everything that Austin and the other empresarios had built. "The state prohibits absolutely and for all time slavery in all its territory," the proposed Article 13 read, "and slaves that already reside in the state will be free from the day of the publication of the constitution in this capital."[32]

THE ARTICLE PROHIBITING SLAVERY WAS EXACTLY WHAT STEPHEN F. Austin feared from the union with Coahuila. "More than one half of these people are awaiting the decision of Congress in regard to their slaves, as they intend to leave the Country if their emancipation is decreed," the empresario wrote from San Felipe de Austin. "The remainder of the settlers are so disheartened that they have no energy to make an effort."[33]

Austin had invested too much for his colony to fail so soon. On August 11, 1826, he wrote a strongly worded letter to the Constituent Congress in Saltillo. His original empresario contract permitted colonists to enter the province with their slaves. "What would the world say," Stephen F. Austin demanded, "if in direct violation of that law and that guarantee, the Government were to take away that property from those colonists against their will?" José María Viesca, who served as the president of the Constituent Congress, recognized "the impossibility of freeing all of the slaves in the state in an instant," because "the funds of the state are very short to be able to compensate the masters for their slaves' value."[34]

Abolishing slavery with only a vague promise of compensation would not only dissuade foreigners from immigrating to Mexico in the future, it would also provoke the colonists who had already settled in Téjas. The mayor of Nacogdoches reported that the *norteamericanos* along the Sabine River would never submit to abolition, accustomed as they were "to living with total liberty in those deserts without respect for the laws or subjection to any authority." According to another report from San Antonio de Béxar, the Anglo colonists were "conspiring against the authorities" over the proposed constitution. In the United States, these kinds of threats derailed legislation to restrict slavery. But in Mexico, they convinced state and national officials of the urgent need for gradual emancipation policies.[35]

Governor Victor Blanco of Coahuila y Téjas was convinced that as long as slavery existed, slaveholders would pose a risk to the stability of the republic. On October 16, 1826, Blanco forwarded a letter to the Constituent Congress, urging its members to amend Article 13, the proposed article to abolish slavery. To uphold both "liberty and property, which are the greatest interests in regularly organized societies," Blanco recommended a gradual emancipation policy: acknowledging the "property" rights of slaveholders already in the province, while banning the slave trade and freeing the children of enslaved people.[36]

The final draft of the Constitution, published on March 11, 1827, acted on Blanco's recommendation. "In the state no one is born a slave," the revised Article 13 read, "and six months after the publication of this constitution . . . neither will the introduction of slaves be permitted under any pretext." The constitution did not abolish slavery, but it did promise to end the institution within a generation by prohibiting the importation of slaves and freeing children born to enslaved people. "The binds of slavery that the legislator cannot cut in one stroke, time can loosen bit by bit," Dionisio Elizondo, a representative from northern Coahuila, explained. "The march of liberty is no less secure for being slow." To the consternation of slaveholders in Téjas, the state legislatures of their adopted country enacted the same policies as the Northern "free" states in the three decades after the American Revolution.[37]

COAHUILA Y TÉJAS JOINED A GROWING NUMBER OF STATES MAKING inroads against slavery. Between 1824 and 1827, nine of Mexico's nineteen states, including Coahuila y Téjas, prohibited the slave trade or decreed that "no one is born a slave"—what was known as a free womb law. Seven states abolished slavery altogether, promising to compensate slaveholders for their losses.[38]

Slaveholders across Mexico circumvented these laws by exploiting the blurred distinction between slavery and other forms of coerced labor. On September 29, 1826, the legislature of Veracruz debated a bill to promote European immigration by legalizing indentured servitude. Although the law limited terms of indenture to twenty years, some legislators denounced such contracts as a kind of slavery. Every colonist, they insisted, should enjoy the "liberty and protection of our laws." Those who supported the bill countered that servants did, in fact, have recourse before the law. So long as laborers had the right to appeal to the courts, their contracts bore none of the hallmarks of slavery. There was "no injustice" in requiring servants to repay the cost of their passage from Europe, remarked one legislator. At the end of the debate, the bill passed.[39]

In the spring of 1828, the legislature of Coahuila y Téjas debated a similar measure. Two representatives, José Antonio Navarro and José Antonio Tijerina, proposed a bill guaranteeing enforcement of all labor contracts signed in other countries. The Mexican government, they argued, had an obligation to respect those contracts on the principle of comity—the idea that governments should respect one another's laws. Moreover, they claimed that the law would fill the northern reaches of the state with white laborers from Ohio and Illinois, who would sign a contract "as is the custom in that country" to work in Mexico for "two or three or more" years. As in Veracruz, the bill was "debated at length" and, finally, approved on May 5, 1828. Although the final version of the bill reiterated that the state constitution prohibited the introduction of enslaved people, Stephen F. Austin sent sample contracts to prospective colonists in the United States anyway.[40]

An unconditional respect for contracts provided an opening that slaveholders exploited, and no one stopped them. The Mexican government was not strong enough to guarantee compliance with every law. (Nor, for that matter, was the United States.) For most of the nineteenth century, legislation was implemented at the "convenience" of local officials, as the US consul to Tampico put it. In the Anglo colonies, the local authorities were often *norteamericanos* themselves. Most saw no reason to stop the colonists from forcing enslaved people to sign contracts with terms as long as ninety years.[41]

Still, the future of slavery in the province was far from secure. The gradual emancipation policies that state and national authorities enacted over the objections of slaveholders spoke to Mexico's commitment to ending slavery. In 1823, Iturbide's junta prohibited the introduction of slaves and emancipated the children of enslaved people at age fourteen, in spite of the lobbying of Stephen F. Austin. A year later, Mexico's congressmen again prohibited the introduction of slaves to the country, despite recognizing that such a measure would discourage *norteameri- canos* from immigrating to the province of Téjas. In 1827, the Consti- tution of Coahuila y Téjas banned the introduction of slaves and freed enslaved children at birth, again over the protests of slaveholders.

As news arrived that the Anglo colonists were ignoring the prohi- bition on the introduction of slaves, Mexico's leaders decided to investi- gate. In 1827, Congress appointed an engineer named Manuel de Mier y Terán, who served as a brigadier general during the wars of indepen- dence and as the minister of war afterward, to head a commission that would survey Mexico's boundary with the United States. At the same time, the commissioners were instructed to report on the state of affairs in the province of Téjas. What they found was even more alarming than Mexico's congressmen had expected.[42]

FOUR

AN ANTISLAVERY REPUBLIC

I N THE SPRING OF 1828, THE COMMISSIONERS TASKED WITH
surveying the border between the United States and Mexico arrived
in San Antonio de Béxar. Manuel de Mier y Terán, the head commis-
sioner, was taken aback by the derelict condition of the provincial capital.
The mission on the east bank of the San Antonio River had been converted into a military storehouse. At the presidio on the opposite bank,
the cannons were only fit for firing the occasional celebratory salvo, and
the soldiers survived on meager rations of corn mush and dried salted
beef. The condition of San Antonio de Béxar concerned Terán, but not
as much as what he saw when he continued his journey north and east.
The farther that Terán traveled from San Antonio de Béxar, the more
"Mexican influence" diminished. From the window of his large coach,
whose wood exterior was carved and inlaid with silver, Terán saw a province that hardly seemed to be a part of Mexico at all.[1]

Thousands of *norteamericanos* had settled in Téjas since 1821—many
more than were allowed under the terms of the nearly forty land grants
issued by the state legislature. These squatters crossed into Mexico

without the permission of the state or national government and settled on lands "without anyone's knowledge." To Terán, their arrival amounted to an invasion. "Instead of armies, battles, or invasions—which make a great noise and for the most part are unsuccessful—these men lay hand on means that, if considered one by one, would be rejected as slow, ineffective, and at times palpably absurd," he wrote. "They begin by assuming rights, as in Téjas, which it is impossible to sustain in a serious discussion, making ridiculous pretensions based on historical incidents which no one admits." But from those extravagant claims, "adventurers and empresarios . . . take up their residence in the country."[2]

The colonization law was not the only statute that went unenforced in Téjas. Terán observed that the Anglo colonists were doing everything in their power to undermine "the favorable intent of Mexican law" with respect to slavery. *Norteamericanos* brought their slaves into the province "with forged letters of freedom and with the name of free laborers who must forfeit the salaries that they have received." To keep their slaves in bondage, the colonists "commit[ed] the barbarities on their slaves that are so common where men live in a relationship so contradictory to their nature: they pull their teeth, they set dogs upon them to tear them apart, and the mildest of them will whip the slaves until they are flayed." Without slavery, Terán reported, "they say that their settlement cannot prosper, nor can much of the land be cultivated, because there are forests so thick that only with negro labor can they be cleared."[3]

Mexico's hold over Téjas was precarious. *Norteamericanos* outnumbered Mexicans ten to one, and the undermanned garrisons at Nacogdoches and Béxar would be unable to stop an insurrection in the colonies or an invasion from the United States. "If timely measures are not taken," Terán warned, "Téjas will put down the entire federation." Exactly what measures would prevent such an outcome was far from obvious. Slaveholders had forced hundreds of enslaved people to cross the Sabine River, in violation of state and national laws against the importation of slaves. These statutes gave enslaved people a claim to freedom, but Terán did not dare acknowledge that these laws were "definitive not provisional measures" for fear that the colonists would revolt.[4]

Instead, Terán recommended protecting slavery in the Anglo colonies. Protecting slavery, he argued, would "indirectly contribute" to the security of the northern frontier. So long as their "property" rights were secure, Terán doubted that slaveholders would run the risk of starting a revolution in which enslaved people would take up arms against them. "Experience has taught, and the colonists cannot ignore, how dangerous uprisings are in countries where there are many slaves," Terán observed. "Spain owes her possession of Cuba to them, and the residents of Téjas, tied up with these shackles, would never expose themselves to the consequences of a revolution. The slaves would be the best guarantee of their submission and the most powerful weapon of the government." This was the very argument that the United States Congress accepted. But most of Mexico's leaders, no matter their political affiliation, took the opposite view—that only by limiting slavery would they be able to defend Mexico against a domestic insurrection or a foreign invasion.[5]

WHILE THE BOUNDARY COMMISSION WAS TRAVELING ACROSS TÉJAS, the rest of Mexico was preparing to elect a new president. In 1828, the minister of war, a moderate federalist named Manuel Gómez Pedraza, was running against the rebel war leader, Vicente Guerrero, whom the US chargé d'affaires in Mexico City described as "a man of vigorous intellect and of determined character, but uneducated."[6]

Vicente Guerrero bore striking similarities to Andrew Jackson, who was running for president in the United States at the same time. Both men were military heroes: Guerrero for his exploits against the Spanish during the war of independence, and Jackson for his role in defeating the British during the War of 1812. Both candidates claimed to speak

for the common man, though they had both risen from humble begin-
nings to achieve an uncommon measure of wealth and success. And
yet for all of their similarities, the two candidates differed in significant
ways. Jackson owned upward of fifty slaves. Guerrero could trace his
bloodline to the African slaves shipped to New Spain during the sixteenth and seventeenth centuries. While Jackson campaigned for the
equality of all white men, regardless of wealth, Guerrero fought for the
equality of all men, regardless of race.[7]

The outcome of the two men's presidential bids also diverged. In the
United States, Jackson won the election, with 56 percent of the popular
vote; while in Mexico, the state legislatures voted to install Guerrero's
opponent, Gómez Pedraza. Rather than admit defeat, Guerrero refused
to recognize the election results. Lorenzo de Zavala, a liberal journalist
and former senator for Yucatán, organized a coup on Guerrero's behalf
in Mexico City. On December 4, 1828, the lower classes took to the
streets. They broke into the upscale shops near the central plaza and
ransacked the storerooms of the National Palace, destroying twenty-
five million pesos' worth of property within twenty-four hours. For the
next ten days, fires burned across the city. In January 1829, Manuel
Gómez Pedraza resigned and Guerrero was "elected."[8]

When Guerrero took office in April, he had almost no support
from within the Mexican government. The unconstitutional means by
which he took power concerned federalists, who opposed any kind
of executive overreach, while the policies he advocated alarmed conservatives, who otherwise tended to support a strong central government. Shortly after taking office, Guerrero expelled all Spaniards
from the country except for those who were physically incapacitated.
He revised the tax code, hiking rates on the wealthy, foreigners, and
medium-to-large businesses. Guerrero also imposed heavy tariffs on
the cheap cotton cloth from England and the United States that had
nearly destroyed the domestic textile industry, earning him the support of cotton farmers and urban artisans, but the enmity of importers
and consumers.[9]

While Mexico City descended into political controversy, Manuel de Mier y Terán drafted a set of recommendations to forestall a revolution in the Anglo colonies. He recommended strengthening the military presence in Téjas, encouraging the immigration of Mexican and European families, and appointing a Mexican consul in New Orleans to keep tabs on the *norteamericanos*. But the political controversy in Mexico City distracted from the immediate threat on the northern frontier. Terán was beginning to despair that the national authorities would take any action in Téjas when he learned of an even more pressing threat to Mexican sovereignty than the Anglo colonists. In the late summer of 1829, Terán received word that the Spanish Army was invading Mexico.[10]

ON A LATE JULY MORNING IN 1829, JOSEPH CRAWFORD SCRAMBLED onto a rocky outcropping, and a broad expanse of water and sky, barely visible from the low, flat shelf of land below, opened suddenly before him. Crawford was the British consul to Tampico, a small city on the northeastern coast of Mexico, and he knew that Spain hoped to reconquer its former colonies in the Americas. He was aware of the rumors that Spain had secured a loan in London, mustered an army of ten thousand men at Cádiz, and dispatched a fifty-gun frigate (fittingly called the *Restoration*) to Havana. But on that late July morning, neither Crawford nor anyone else knew where the Spanish forces would attack. The press gave varying accounts of the army's destination. First the Spanish fleet had landed at Campeche. Then it was sailing toward Yucatán. All the while, Tampico seemed safe from invasion. But when Crawford reached the top of the outcropping, he spotted fourteen ships just beyond the sandbar at the mouth of the harbor. Tampico was under attack.[11]

Guerrero's shaky new government managed to organize three armies, according to the British minister to Mexico, Richard Pakenham, with "a degree of activity which does not usually attend operations in

this country." Manuel de Mier y Terán left Téjas to assume command of
the two thousand soldiers stationed in Tampico; another general, Antonio López de Santa Anna, recruited men in Veracruz; a third army, led
by Vicente Guerrero's vice president, Anastasio Bustamante, was held
in reserve at Xalapa, sixty miles northwest of Veracruz. Although Guerrero's legitimacy was tenuous, Mexican citizens supported his efforts to
turn back the Spanish invasion. Mexico State raised a civic militia. The
ladies of Monclova, Coahuila, did what was "compatible with their sex"
and raised 128 pesos for the nation's defense. The colonists in Anahuac,
Téjas, volunteered their services against "the odious misrule and tirani-
cal [sic] sway" of Spain.[12]

The Spanish invasion touched a patriotic nerve in Mexico. The only
question was whether these efforts would be enough to defeat the invading army. In Tampico, residents vowed to burn their houses to the
ground rather than watch them fall into Spanish hands. But as the
invading Spanish soldiers patrolled the adjacent beaches and lagoons,
no patriots razed their homes in defiance. Instead, local militias qui-
etly disbanded. Tampico's merchants loaded chests of books and papers
onto ships waiting in the harbor, leaving behind only their heaviest
furniture and "some Brandy." On July 31, 1829, Spanish forces attacked
the city, and Terán's outnumbered men were forced to retreat, leaving
behind a nine-pounder cannon, some ammunition, and the scattered
instruments of the military band.[13]

Mexico's army was not strong enough to turn back a Spanish invasion.
And so Guerrero began to entertain a bold countermeasure that might
help to defend Mexico's independence. Spain had launched its expedition
from its colony of Cuba, the largest and most westerly of the Caribbean
islands. To permanently remove the threat of an invasion, the Guerrero
administration resolved to deprive Spain of its base of operations. "If they
invade us, they will also be invaded," Mexico's minister to London sum-
marized, "if they come to Mexico to put an end to anarchy, as they say, we
will go to Cuba to put an end to the enslavement of the blacks."[14]

AFTER TAKING TAMPICO, THE SPANISH ARMY PLANNED TO AT-
tack the more strategically important city of Veracruz, two hundred forty
miles to the south. In anticipation of this attack, the Mexican Congress
granted emergency war powers to Vicente Guerrero, allowing the president to rule by decree. Finding the treasury almost empty, he authorized
the seizure and sale of church property to fund the war effort. He also
decided to use his emergency powers to issue another decree, an "act of
justice and charity" that he planned to announce during the celebrations
of Mexican Independence Day.[15]

On September 16, 1829, Guerrero abolished slavery across the country. Now, he said, Mexico's "disgraced inhabitants" would at last enjoy
"their sacred, natural rights." Aware that his decree marked a departure
from the precedent of respecting "property" even at the expense of freedom, Guerrero promised to compensate owners "when the state of the
revenue permits." But compensation would likely be deferred for a long
time. "As this indemnification obviously cannot take effect for years to
come," the British consul general, Charles O'Gorman, observed the next
day, "great injustice will no doubt be suffered by some proprietors."[16]

Slave owners unsurprisingly protested the new abolition decree. On
October 18, 1829, three slaveholders from Chiapas demanded the immediate payment of 11,660 pesos in compensation. "At the time of lib-
erating those who were unfortunately plunged into the degradation and
misery of slavery," they explained, "we should not forget those who are
entitled as owners, having purchased their slaves when your institutions
permitted it, and who now find themselves without the help of their
servants and with budgets to balance."[17]

Two months later, the town council of Córdoba, Veracruz, made its
own complaint to the Department of Justice. Abolition "would cause
the ruin of this population that labors exclusively in the cane fields;
the owners of the twenty-two sugar refineries in which the slaves work
will be without recourse," leading to "the ruin of the property owner."
And in states where slavery remained a substantial institution, wealthy

officials were prepared to go further. Within months, Yucatán seceded from the Mexican confederation. The legislature of Yucatán lambasted the national government for assuming powers that rightly belonged to the states, as Guerrero had done in issuing his decree. They argued that the abolition of slavery was a "cruel attack on property" that disadvantaged Yucatán more than any other state.[18]

Anglo colonists in Téjas also objected to Guerrero's decree. "Slavery, if an evil, is one that will correct itself," wrote the proslavery *Constitutional Advocate and Texas Public Advertiser*. "Legislative interference in this will be found to be impolitic." But when judges in the Anglo colonies of Austin, Brazoria, and Gonzáles refused to enforce the emancipation decree, enslaved people escaped and appealed to the authorities of other jurisdictions. In October 1829, a black man named José Francisco Laviña petitioned the mayor of Allende, Coahuila, to free his wife, an enslaved woman in San Antonio de Béxar. Several months later, two men and a woman from De León's Colony of Téjas arrived in Guerrero, Coahuila, just south of the Rio Grande, and asked "to know if they were free." The mayor of Guerrero considered it his duty to "the cause of humanity" to grant them their liberty.[19]

Why would Guerrero adopt such a controversial policy in the midst of a Spanish invasion? The president, who could neither read nor write, left few clues. His minister of finance, Lorenzo de Zavala, suggested one explanation for the decree: the president and his supporters had always wanted to establish "absolute equality" among Mexicans. Since Congress had not abolished slavery, Guerrero might have seen his wartime powers as an opportunity to make good on the republic's founding principles. Another possible explanation came from Congressman José María Tornel of Veracruz, who claimed, in 1852, to have written the emancipation decree and convinced Guerrero to sign it. "In the abolition of slavery was involved a highly political consideration," Tornel recalled more than two decades later, "that of establishing a barrier between Mexico and the United States, where slavery is maintained in open contradiction with the principles solemnly proclaimed in its act of independence of 1776."[20]

The expansion of the United States did concern the Mexican government, but this concern was a reason against—not for—issuing the decree. On December 8, 1829, Colonel José de las Piedras reported from Nacogdoches that the US Army was moving troops to the frontier and that hundreds of *norteamericanos* were entering Téjas. Local authorities feared that "the Department of Téjas and much more [would be] irremediably lost" if the US Army attacked Mexico in the midst of the Spanish invasion. Convinced that the decree abolishing slavery would undermine further colonization and economic development, President Guerrero agreed on December 2, 1829, to exempt the province, ordering that no change "be made as respects the slaves that exist legally in that part of your State." The expansion of the United States did not convince Guerrero to abolish slavery; instead, he exempted Téjas from his decree in order to discourage *norteamericanos* from seizing Téjas.[21]

Vicente Guerrero may have had another aim in mind when he abolished Mexican slavery. Unbeknownst to the public and even to many in his administration, Guerrero had already sent a secret agent, Ignacio Basadre, to Port-au-Prince to negotiate a Treaty of Alliance with President Jean-Pierre Boyer of Haiti. It was no coincidence that Mexico sought an alliance with a nation that had abolished slavery in 1804 and promised freedom to all enslaved people who set foot on its soil in 1816. Only a government that had enacted the most radical antislavery policies in the western hemisphere would have entertained the plan that Guerrero had in mind. The purpose of the proposed treaty between Mexico and Haiti was to invade Cuba and free its slaves.[22]

ON SEPTEMBER 20, 1829, FOUR DAYS AFTER ABOLISHING SLAVERY, Vicente Guerrero was watching a play at the Teatro Principal in Mexico City when a messenger, still covered with dust from the unpaved roads, stepped into the president's box, apologized for the disturbance, and delivered the latest news from Tampico. Several weeks earlier, yellow fever had broken out in the Spanish camp. Reinforcements did not seem to be forthcoming, and so the Mexican commanders ordered an attack that forced Spanish General Ignacio Barradas to surrender unconditionally on September 11, 1829.[23]

At the Teatro Principal, President Vicente Guerrero rose in his box, interrupting the performance to announce the news. The audience broke into cheers. Outside, in the streets, strangers clapped each other on the back, and hastily assembled brass bands struck up the national anthem. Storekeepers uncorked bottles from their shelves, and newspaper vendors shouted, "Barradas has surrendered!" But the celebrations only lasted as long as that night's fireworks. In Spain, word of the battlefield defeat turned the subjugation of Mexico into a royal fixation. Within months, the Spanish Army was planning a second expedition on an even larger scale than the first. Mexico was not prepared to resist another invasion. The treasury was nearly empty, and the small navy had rotted in the harbor of Veracruz while waiting for the Spanish to attack.[24]

To defend against another Spanish invasion, Guerrero kept three thousand soldiers in reserve in Xalapa. Their commander was Vice President Anastasio Bustamante. On December 4, 1829, Bustamante and his troops in Xalapa rebelled against Guerrero. Although their only demand was that Guerrero renounce his extraordinary powers, their rallying cries—"Long live centralism" and "Death to *el negro* Guerrero"—left no doubt as to their long-term aims. The sudden revolt succeeded shortly after it began: on December 25, Guerrero resigned the presidency, calling on Mexico's Congress to decide who should replace him. As the ousted president made his way back to his hacienda in Tixtla, Congress declared that Guerrero was "mentally and morally unfit" and that Vice President Anastasio Bustamante would rule in his stead.[25]

The new administration purged the government of any official who supported Guerrero, engineering the dismissal of federalist governors and legislators across Mexico. Bustamante also ordered the arrest of two hundred of Guerrero's allies on charges of conspiracy. Executions occurred almost daily. An official explained to the US minister Anthony Butler in Mexico City that leniency would only embolden the opposition.[26]

Upon taking power, the Bustamante administration met with pressure from abroad to rescind Guerrero's orders to Ignacio Basadre to negotiate an alliance with Haiti. The minister of relations, Lucas Alamán, claimed to be appalled by "the mere idea of the disasters and horrors that would result from this project, the varied accusations of the civilized world against Mexico for this attack against the law of nations." But Alamán did not immediately revoke the orders that Guerrero had issued.[27]

Guerrero's secret agent, Ignacio Basadre, was making progress in forging an alliance. Independent Haiti had recently annexed the Spanish colony of Santo Domingo and would soon face a Spanish invasion of its own. The Haitian government appeared eager to make common cause with Mexico. A Spanish agent in Nassau, Bermuda, reported that Haiti was raising three thousand troops to sail for Cuba. In Cuba, the Grand Legion of the Black Eagle, the secret society founded by Mexican freemasons, started to prepare for a revolution. In June 1830, slaves revolted on a coffee plantation fifty miles outside of Havana. A few days later, two more revolts erupted nearby. Rumor had it that the slaves were expecting troops from Mexico and Haiti. "On the landing of these troops, the standard of independence was to be raised, and liberty proclaimed to the slaves, who were to be invited to assist in putting down the government of Old Spain," reported the proslavery *Louisiana Advertiser* in 1830. "The terrific and universal bloodshed which must have resulted from carrying this plan into execution, makes us hesitate in yielding entire belief to this account."[28]

Forestalling a slave rebellion in Cuba prevented the Spanish Army from carrying out its plans to reconquer Mexico. In January 1830, Spanish commanders diverted frigates bound for Veracruz to patrol the coast of Haiti. An entire fleet remained in Cuba, and its warships detained every vessel that had managed to set sail from the black republic and elude patrolling royal vessels along the Haitian coast. A second invasion of Mexico would have to wait.[29]

THE IDEA OF TURNING SLAVES INTO A FIFTH COLUMN WAS NOT unprecedented. During the American Revolution, British commanders promised freedom to enslaved people who flocked to their banners. Spanish generals adopted the same policy during the wars of independence in Latin America, as did their opponents. European powers justified their actions by invoking what became known as the "just war" tradition, which argued that any measures were warranted that contributed to victory. In defense of justice, soldiers could raze fields and sack cities; they could free slaves and execute peasants. As the sixteenth-century Spanish theorist Francisco de Vitoria wrote from Salamanca in western Spain, "A prince may do everything in a just war which is necessary to secure peace and security from attack." From this perspective, generals had every right to emancipate enemy slaves who reached their lines.[30]

But the just war tradition had been under attack ever since 1758, when a Swiss-born diplomat named Emmerich de Vattel published *Le Droit des Gens*, or *The Law of Nations*. The book set out rules that sought to limit the devastation wrought by war. According to Vattel, the only justifiable violence in war was between uniformed soldiers on the field of battle. The Law of Nations itself protected entire categories of people during wartime: women, children, the elderly, the infirm, scholars, churchmen, and "other persons whose mode of life is very remote from military affairs." And Vattel argued that the Law of Nations also protected civilian property, which slaveholders took to include their slaves.[31]

The proposed alliance between Haiti and Mexico plainly violated this interpretation of the Law of Nations. "A democratic general was about to march through Cuba, with the torch of revolution in his hand, announcing instant freedom to the slaves," as the British Foreign Secretary, George Hamilton Gordon, Fourth Earl of Aberdeen, saw it. More was at stake than a single uprising in Cuba. Lord Aberdeen feared that the "contagion of anarchy" would spread across the West Indies. Although abolitionism was on the rise in England, three-quarters of a million people remained enslaved in British colonies. A generation after the French Revolution had inspired hopes of liberation, slavery still flourished in the French colonies of Guadeloupe and Martinique. To Lord Aberdeen, an alliance between Mexico and Haiti portended "the final destruction of the world." To stop the plan from going forward, he hastily scheduled a meeting with a member of the Mexican legation.[32]

On February 13, 1830, Lord Aberdeen found himself sitting across from the Mexican diplomat Manuel Eduardo de Gorostiza. When the Foreign Secretary expressed his concerns about Mexico's plan to free the slaves in Cuba, Gorostiza did nothing to dispel his fears. In the event of an invasion, the Mexican diplomat acknowledged that Cuban slaves would probably throw down their plows and flock to the banner "pronouncing the magic name of Liberty." Cuba's slaves, once armed, would no doubt think of their brothers in chains; the Haitian government would "stoke the flames"; and the contagion would spread to Jamaica, Trinidad, and Martinique. This response infuriated Lord Aberdeen. Fomenting a slave revolt was an unacceptable tool of statecraft, he sputtered, and the British government would not stand for its use. Gorostiza responded that the Mexican government was willing to acquiesce to Lord Aberdeen's demands—on the condition that the British government throw its diplomatic weight against a renewed Spanish invasion.[33]

British subjects, especially prosperous commercial leaders who had adapted quickly to the prospect of independent governments in Latin America, were also putting pressure on their government to intercede on behalf of Mexico. To protect their "general interests," English businessmen formed a Mexican and Colombian Association, a South American and Mexican Association, and a North and South American Coffee House to advocate for the Latin American republics. The "menacing and injurious attitude" of Spain, they argued, threatened to disrupt British trade with Mexico.[34]

Faced with the prospect of a slave insurrection in Cuba and urged by their own subjects to change course, British officials pressured the Spanish Crown to renounce its plans to invade Mexico. "From this day forth, Spain would be made to keep the peace," the Mexican minister reported from London. The United States government followed the British lead. Secretary of State Martin Van Buren told the Mexican minister to the United States that he would encourage the Spanish Crown to recognize the independence of its former colonies, in exchange for a guarantee that, in the case of another invasion, "the government of Mexico will never try to foment rebellion among the people of color in the Spanish Antilles, to which the US could never be indifferent, seeing as they have so many of that class in the Southern states." The fear that consumed the British and US governments—the fear that motivated the change in policy—was that enslaved people would rebel at the encouragement of Mexico and Haiti.[35]

This was not necessarily the result that President Guerrero had intended when he ordered his secret agent Ignacio Basadre to negotiate an alliance with the Republic of Haiti. No slaves revolted. Cuba did not win its independence. But his plan did remove the threat of a Spanish invasion. The widespread fear that "the Cubans would replicate the bloody scenes of Santo Domingo" convinced the British and US governments to abandon their policy of neutrality and intercede on Mexico's behalf in Madrid. Antislavery was a powerful weapon in the hands of a weak government. And the tactic that turned back a Spanish invasion seemed like it could protect the republic against any number of threats, including the one that most concerned Manuel de Mier y Terán: the Anglo colonists in Téjas.[36]

On January 6, 1830, Lieutenant Colonel Constantino Tarnava, one of the soldiers who accompanied the boundary commission, delivered a report from Terán to the minister of war in Mexico City. The report communicated "the urgency of taking prompt steps to prevent the shameful loss of the department of Téjas—a loss whose consequences would vitally affect the safety of the entire nation, because of the condition which would then exist on the frontier, Chihuahua, Nuevo México, and part of Sonora being exposed to and half surrounded by our dangerous neighbors, who would thus be at the doors of our richest states."[37]

The minister of war immediately forwarded Terán's report to the minister of relations, Lucas Alamán. Born in 1792 in Guanajuato, the center of silver production in New Spain, Alamán came from a distinguished Spanish family. His father was a wealthy mining magnate, and his mother was the fifth marchioness of San Clemente, who could trace her lineage back to the reign of Queen Isabella. Alamán was eighteen when the war of independence broke out and revolutionary forces under Father Miguel Hidalgo attacked his native city, storming the municipal granary and executing the Spanish officials and militiamen who had barricaded themselves there. The violence that Alamán witnessed that day convinced him that the people could never rule themselves. As minister of relations, Alamán aimed to impose a modern rationalized system of government in Mexico in which a powerful executive would oversee the church and the army, the courts and the legislatures. Punishing even the most minor of infractions with severity would, he hoped, help to restore order, while shutting down brothels and gambling houses would take an important step toward cultivating a moral and civilized society.[38]

Alamán's conservative worldview aligned with a number of Terán's recommendations. In a report that he wrote on January 14, 1830, the minister of relations agreed that the Mexican Army needed to increase its military presence in Téjas, that Mexican families should be encouraged to move to the province, and that appointing a Mexican consul in New Orleans would help "to keep an eye on the preparations of our neighbors, now almost our enemies." But Alamán pointedly rejected Terán's recommendation to permit *norteamericanos* to bring enslaved people to Téjas. To strengthen Mexico's hold over its northern frontier,

Alamán wanted to stop further immigration from the United States, and he saw the prohibition on the introduction of new slaves as the most straightforward means to this end.[39]

Over the next several weeks, Mexico's Congress met in a secret session to draft a law based on Alamán's report. The Law of April 6, 1830, as it became known, strengthened the military posts along the northern frontier and promised cash advances to Mexican families who moved to Téjas. Convicts would no longer languish in prison. Instead they would serve out their sentences building fortifications, public works, and roads on the northern frontier. To encourage trade between Mexico's northern states and the Gulf Coast ports of Matamoros, Tampico, and Veracruz, no customs duties would be levied on coastal trade for four years. The law also included a number of provisions designed to force the *norteamericanos* in Téjas to submit to Mexican rule. "No change shall be made with respect to the slaves now in the states," Article 10 of the Law of April 6, 1830 stated, "but the federal government and the government of each state shall most strictly enforce the colonization laws and prevent the further introduction of slaves." The article that followed banned "migrants from nations bordering on this Republic from settling in the states or territory adjacent to their own nation." Any empresario who had not yet recruited the agreed upon number of colonists would have his contract canceled.[40]

The Law of April 6, 1830 provoked immediate protests in Coahuila y Téjas. The legislature in Saltillo criticized the law as an attack "against the sovereignty and rights of the state." The town council of Béxar pointed out that by prohibiting any *norteamericanos* from settling in Téjas, the law prevented "the emigration of some capitalists or other industrious and honored men" and instead "left open the door to the adventurers and other dregs of society, who have nothing to lose and who have entered in large numbers furtively and may cause incalculable evils." The state governor, Ramón Múzquiz, argued that a ban on immigration from the United States simply could not be enforced. As Múzquiz predicted, the increased military presence on the northern frontier did not stop *norteamericanos* from crossing the Sabine River. Neither did the ban on the importation of slaves, which *norteamericano* planters avoided by forcing their slaves to sign lifelong indenture contracts. Between 1830 and 1834, the number of *norteamericanos* in Téjas doubled. Although immigration from the United States continued, the Law of April 6 underscored the reluctance of the Mexican government to protect slavery. "No one will be willing to risk a large capital in negroes under contracts with them," Stephen F. Austin despaired, "for they are free on their arrival here."[41]

WHILE THE BUSTAMANTE ADMINISTRATION DEFLECTED A SPANish invasion and drafted a plan to avoid an uprising in the province of Téjas, revolts against Bustamante's centralism broke out in Puebla, San Luis Potosí, and Morelia. In March 1830, Guerrero left his hacienda for the mountains, where he started to organize an uprising of his own. Guerrero called for new elections, a return to federalism, and a restoration of state sovereignty. But his rebellion came to a sudden end when an Italian ship captain named Francisco Picaluga invited Guerrero aboard his vessel, the *Colombo*, anchored at the port of Acapulco. Guerrero accepted his friend's invitation, unaware that the captain had struck a deal with the Bustamante administration to betray him. After finishing his lunch on board the *Colombo*, Guerrero found himself under arrest. Picaluga delivered the former president to federal troops in the port of Huatulco and then claimed his reward: fifty thousand pesos. Transported to Oaxaca and tried before a court martial, Guerrero was sentenced to death. On February 14, 1831, he stood before the firing squad and was killed.[42]

The next day, Mexico's Congress formally abrogated "all the laws, decrees, regulations, ordinances and orders" issued by Guerrero under his wartime powers, including the decree abolishing slavery. After a sixteen-month hiatus, human bondage was again permitted in Mexico.

But slavery was not destined to become a permanent feature of Mexican society. At both the state and national levels, gradual emancipation policies promised to end slavery within a generation. In 1824, Mexico's Congress had prohibited the slave trade, promising freedom to illegally imported slaves from the moment they set foot on Mexican soil. Three years later, the constitution of Coahuila y Téjas had imposed the same restriction over the objections of Anglo colonists. And in the Law of April 6, 1830, the national government had renewed its commitment to enforcing the ban. Taken together, these policies presented an opportunity to enslaved people—and a challenge to their owners.[43]

FIVE

"IN ACCORDANCE WITH THE LAWS, THEY ARE FREE"

O N MARCH 1, 1831, AN ENSLAVED WOMAN NAMED HONORINE disappeared from a plantation in Ascension Parish, Louisiana, just south of Baton Rouge. The plantation owner, Louis Elic Laroque Tourgeau, assumed that the "dark mulatto" woman had "fallen into the river and drowned herself." At any time of year, the Mississippi was dangerous from its bends and sandbars, and the trees buried in the riverbed. The river was particularly treacherous in the early spring of 1831. That winter was unusually cold. The citrus trees in New Orleans died after the first frost. Bayou St. John froze over. By early March, snow throughout the huge watershed started to melt, and as the river rose, it overflowed its banks, inundating the broad bottomlands of the river valley.[1]

Honorine would have had reasons to drown herself in the swollen river. The chances that she would win her freedom in Louisiana were vanishing. After planters protested legislative efforts to abolish slavery in the Mississippi Territory in 1798 and to prohibit the importation of slaves into the Louisiana Territory in 1804, the US Congress permitted slavery to expand across the south-central United States. By the time that Honorine turned twenty-five, the Democratic Party, the largest and most powerful political coalition in the United States, took it as a matter of historical precedent and constitutional principle that the federal government had no authority to interfere with slavery. Honorine witnessed the consequences of these policies firsthand. During her lifetime, the number of enslaved people in Ascension Parish doubled, from 1,031 in 1810 to 2,129 in 1820. By 1830, slaves made up 65 percent of the population of the parish.[2]

As the pressure on enslaved people mounted, some resisted in small, almost unnoticeable ways, by breaking tools, working slowly, or feigning illness. But others acted out in more open and destructive ways. In 1830, three slaves on Tourgeau's plantation murdered a fourth—a crime for which all three were hanged. They were not the only ones to have reached a breaking point. Honorine had also had enough of the endless days of planting sugarcane. But rather than ending her own life, as Tourgeau suspected, she tried to start a new one.[3]

In the spring of 1831, while the other slaves on the plantation were perhaps searching the banks of the Mississippi for a body, Honorine was making her way to Mexico with the help of a local merchant named John Franz. At some point on their journey, Franz drew up a term of indenture, as the laws of Coahuila y Téjas ostensibly permitted, and asked Honorine to sign it under a new name, Susan. It is possible that John forced Honorine to make her mark or forged the cross that supposedly indicated her consent, but it is just as likely that he convinced her to sign the contract as the only way to travel across Téjas without raising the suspicions of Anglo slaveholders or Mexican officials. When John and Honorine at last arrived in San Felipe de Austin, their joint journey came to an abrupt end. John made use of the indenture papers that Honorine had signed, not to dispel suspicions, but to turn a profit for himself: John sold Honorine to Samuel May Williams, a wealthy businessman and land speculator from the United States, who had made a fortune issuing stamps for legal documents in the early Mexican Republic.[4]

What to do with fugitive slaves like Honorine was a pressing question. Mexican leaders did not want to give the United States any pretext to invade their country, and a policy that protected fugitive slaves risked provoking the same recriminations that led to the seizure of Florida in 1818. At the same time, Mexican officials had to enforce the nation's laws against the introduction of slaves. *Norteamericanos* forced hundreds if not thousands of enslaved people to sign indenture contracts before crossing the Sabine River into Téjas. Although slaveholders insisted that these lifelong indentures were valid under an 1828 law recognizing labor contracts signed abroad, Mexican authorities countered that the practice violated state and national laws and that illegally imported slaves were entitled to their freedom. As Mexican leaders redoubled their efforts to enforce these laws, the Anglo colonists in Téjas made good on their threats to defend their enslaved property at all costs.

SIX MONTHS AFTER HONORINE DISAPPEARED, HER OWNER received "positive information" that she was not, in fact, dead. As far as Louis Elie Laroque Tourgeau knew, the news came "at the express request" of Honorine herself, who purportedly begged the man who discovered her whereabouts to urge Laroque "to come . . . and recover her possession." Whether or not Honorine wanted to return to the plantation, Laroque was determined to bring her back.[5]

Five days after learning that Honorine was alive, Laroque arrived in New Orleans to petition the Mexican consul for her return. Even in September, the heat was stifling. From the "damp alluvial soil" came the smell of "vegetable composition." On Gravier Street, an even "more offensive" odor arose from the piles of rodent carcasses—the bounty of the local rat-killing clubs. As Laroque made his way through the wide streets, laid out in the gridiron pattern favored by eighteenth-century French engineers, he might have noticed the boats dredging up "property long submerged and supposed to be lost" from the tidewaters of the

Mississippi. Perhaps he saw their task as a metaphor for his. He, too, was trying to recover what he had once taken for lost.[6]

At an office on the outskirts of the French Quarter, Laroque presented his case to Francisco Pizarro Martínez, the Mexican consul. Pizarro had slipped into New Orleans five years earlier with a commission from the Mexican government to act as a secret agent. But he was an unlikely spy. Fretful and rule abiding, he constantly worried that his mission had been discovered. After a year, he asked to act in a more public capacity as consul. Manuel de Mier y Terán, who organized the boundary commission to Mexico's northeastern frontier, had recommended appointing a consul in New Orleans, and so Mexico's minister of relations, Lucas Alamán, agreed to Pizarro's request. Pizarro threw himself into his work. He commissioned a steam engine from a Philadelphia manufactory and contracted a *norteamericano* engineer to build a paper mill in Veracruz; he shipped boxes of Osage orange tree saplings from the Territory of Arkansas, and he recommended the purchase of a herd of merino sheep from France.[7]

That September afternoon, when Laroque explained what had happened to Honorine, Pizarro listened with concern. This was the second case of "negro stealing" to reach his desk since May. Lawbreaking was not unusual in Louisiana. Even murders often went unreported or unprosecuted, and bodies regularly washed up on the banks of the Mississippi River. But no crime concerned Louisiana's slaveholders as much as "negro stealing." "A theft of this nature has not ceased to alarm the inhabitants of this country," Pizarro wrote in 1831.[8]

The lengths to which slaveholders would go to keep their property in bondage struck Pizarro as "scandalous," but he believed that the Mexican government had an obligation to return fugitives. Andrew Jackson, the general who had commanded the expedition against Florida, was now the president of the United States. Jackson made no secret of his desire to acquire the province of Téjas. Shortly after taking office on March 4, 1829, Jackson instructed the US minister to Mexico to renew negotiations for the region. "Early attention to be paid to the bound-ery [sic] between the U. States and Mexico—" the president noted in his Memorandum Book. "The line must be altered." At the same time, newspapers in the United States were urging Jackson to seize Téjas so that it would not become "a place of refuge for debtors, malefactors, and fugitive slaves." If the Mexican government protected runaways, Jackson would have an excuse to march on Téjas, as he had invaded Spanish Florida in 1818.[9]

Pizarro believed that he had to return Honorine, and he had every reason to believe that he could. At that very moment, Mexico's Congress was debating a Treaty of Amity and Commerce with the United States, which would, among other things, provide for the extradition of fugitive slaves and criminals. But to Pizarro's dismay, Mexico's Congress would not ratify the treaty as quickly as he hoped.[10]

At the beginning of every month, Anthony Butler, the United States minister to Mexico, wrote a report to his superiors in Washington. He folded the thick sheets of dispatch paper, placed them in an envelope, and deposited the package in the mail that would be transported by mule to Veracruz. From that port, the mail bags traveled by steamship to New York or Philadelphia, and then overland to Washington, DC.[11]

The monthly reports from Mexico City were encouraging and, in general, highly colored. Butler was an inexperienced diplomat. A political appointee of the Jackson administration, he did not speak Spanish. He irked his subordinates in the US Legation by never repaying the money that he borrowed from them. In 1833, the US consul in Mexico City, James Wilcocks, resigned in protest of Butler's having "converted the dignified and honorable office of the Legation of the United States of America, into a usurious, mean, money lenders' shop."[12]

Although Butler's colleagues at the embassy doubted his ability to acquire Téjas and negotiate a commercial treaty—the principal aims of the Jackson administration—the US minister boasted shortly after assuming his post in 1830 that he would settle every question committed to his charge in six months. Butler assumed that the $5 million Jackson authorized him to offer would be more than enough to convince Mexican leaders to sell Téjas. "As the influence of money is well understood and as readily conceded by these people as any under Heaven," Butler informed the president, "I have no doubt of its doing its office."[13]

Butler failed to appreciate the determination of the Mexican government to keep Téjas. Only a few days after he arrived, the Mexico City newspaper *El Sol* published the details of his mission, including the specific amount that Jackson had authorized him to offer for Téjas. When Butler tried to open negotiations for the province, Mexican diplomats refused to sell, leaving Butler no choice but to accept the Sabine River as the western boundary of the United States in the Treaty of Limits that he eventually forwarded to Washington, DC.[14]

Butler hoped to redeem himself by negotiating a commercial treaty between Mexico and the United States. The treaty would "establish on a firm basis the relations of friendship" by enshrining the principles of free trade, enumerating the protections given to the citizens of one country living in the other, and providing guidance for dealing with events like shipwrecks and pirate attacks. To the wide-ranging treaty, Butler included a final article "that criminals and slaves taking refuge in the territories of either party shall be given up on the formal demand of the other." Although Mexico's Congress had overturned Guerrero's decree of abolishing slavery, Southern planters in the US could not be certain how long the more conservative administration under Anastasio Bustamante would remain in place. An extradition treaty would insulate the burgeoning cotton frontier in the United States from any future antislavery legislation that the Mexican government might adopt.[15]

But Butler was wrong to anticipate "no serious difficulty in [the treaty's] adoption" by Mexico's Congress. During the administration of John Quincy Adams, the US chargé d'affaires to Mexico, Joel R. Poinsett, insisted in "very strong language" that any commercial treaty between the

United States and Mexico include an article for the return of fugitive slaves. As a result, Mexico's Congress rejected the treaty that Poinsett negotiated. "It would be most extraordinary," Mexico's senators argued, "that in a treaty between two free republics slavery should be encouraged by obliging ours to deliver up fugitive slaves to their merciless and barbarous masters."[16]

MONTHS PASSED WITHOUT A RATIFIED TREATY. ANTHONY BUTLER blamed the delay on "the movements of these people always [being] slow." Only after the months turned to a year did the US minister admit that "either through ignorance or perverseness, great opposition [was] manifested to the Treaty."[17]

Mexico's Chamber of Deputies was in an uproar over one article in particular: the clause providing for the return of fugitive slaves from Mexico. The Mexican government had been wary of Butler's intentions ever since his diplomatic instructions appeared in *El Sol*, and the representatives suspected that his proposed article was a backhanded method of acquiring Téjas. To arrest, detain, and deliver fugitive slaves to their owners, some representatives argued, the Mexican government would have "to maintain a large army on the frontiers that would hunt for blacks who had sought refuge there." Delivering up every runaway would prove difficult, if not impossible, and this failure would give the United States government an excuse to invade the province of Téjas. The Chamber narrowly rejected the article, 28 to 27, on October 21, 1831.[18]

Next, the treaty went to the Mexican Senate. Over a six-week period, the Senate Committee on Foreign Relations presented a case for the extradition of fugitive slaves. As a practical matter, the committee members argued that a formal extradition policy would discourage enslaved people from seeking freedom in Mexico in the first place. "Slaves will not come to a country where they would be apprehended or at least in which they would not be able to live in safety or liberty," they explained. By discouraging enslaved people from fleeing across the Sabine River, they argued, the treaty would remove one of the major pretexts for an invasion from the United States.[19]

The Committee also made a legal argument for extradition. The laws of both nations recognized slaves as property. All that the treaty asked was that the Mexican government uphold a basic guarantee of its political system: the right to "property." Promising to extradite fugitive slaves, without being able to fulfill this promise, might lead to the loss of Téjas, as the Chamber of Deputies feared. But the Senate Committee on Foreign Relations argued that *not* making such a promise might lead to the same result. On December 2, 1831, the Senate voted to accept the treaty, with the article on fugitive slaves.[20]

The revised treaty returned to the Chamber of Deputies. To reject the article a second time required a two-thirds majority—a difficult task given the narrow margins by which the provision had been defeated in the first place. But this time the article permitting the extradition of fugitive slaves generated even more opposition in the Chamber of Deputies. As the impasse threatened to derail ratification of the entire treaty, Anthony Butler despaired. It was December 1831, and with the legislative session drawing to a close, it looked as though Mexico's Congress would adjourn without ratifying the commercial treaty.[21]

Desperate, Anthony Butler wrote to Lucas Alamán, the minister of relations, on December 14, 1831. The two men met three days later. After a "very free interchange of opinions," they agreed to withdraw the article relating to fugitive slaves. The next day, Mexico's Congress ratified the treaty. The extradition of slaves who escaped to Mexico would be "a matter for discussion in the future."[22]

Mexico's Congress rejected any formal obligation to return fugitive slaves. But neither did it adopt an official policy to free them. Without specific instructions from Mexico City, local officials had to make their own decisions, which, more often than not, were to return runaways to their owners. In 1831, Colonel Peter Ellis Bean, a military commander in eastern Téjas, ordered the local Indians to turn over any person of color who they came across west of the Sabine River. The following year, when a slaveholder from Louisiana tried to reclaim three black slaves from Nacogdoches, the governor of Coahuila y Téjas told the local authorities that "there is no inconvenience in returning them" if they "can prove their ownership." The danger of not returning runaways would become clear within a matter of months.[23]

IN THE SPRING OF 1832, THREE SLAVES ESCAPED TO THE TOWN OF Anahuac, where the Trinity River emptied into Galveston Bay, along the Gulf Coast of Téjas. Anahuac was a small settlement, with fifteen to twenty log cabins and a handful of shops. The largest building was the barracks that housed approximately one hundred soldiers, whose task it was to collect customs duties, stop the immigration of *norteamericanos*, and generally remind the Anglo colonists that Téjas did not, in fact, belong to the United States.[24]

The commander of the garrison at Anahuac was John "Juan" Davis Bradburn. Born in Virginia in 1787, Bradburn moved with his family to Kentucky in 1810, where he learned that the viceroyalty of New Spain had taken up arms against the Spanish Crown. Keen for adventure, Bradburn traveled down the Mississippi to fight on behalf of the republicans. In 1812, he joined an expedition that captured Nacogdoches, La Bahía, and San Antonio. Five years later, he started a powder factory in the Sierra Madre Oriental and then joined Vicente Guerrero's forces in Acapulco. After Mexico won its independence, Bradburn did not return to the United States. By that point, he went by the name of Juan, instead of John. He saw himself as a Mexican, not a *norteamericano*, and his loyalty to his adopted country only increased as he joined the Mexican Army, married into a titled Mexican family, and purchased a ranch on the north side of the Rio Grande, where he tried, without much success, to establish a steamboat line. In 1830, he abandoned his steamboat venture to take command of the new garrison on Galveston Bay, Anahuac.[25]

The Anglo colonists did not expect a countryman like Bradburn to enforce what struck them as arbitrary and sometimes contradictory laws from Mexico City. But Bradburn was determined to force "the colonists and the other inhabitants of the State to obey the Mexican laws, since up until now they have only observed Anglo-American laws." He turned away colonists with the Galveston Bay and Texas Land Company, whose uncompleted contracts had been suspended under the Law of April 6, 1830. He made every effort to collect the customs duties that the Anglo colonists were unaccustomed to paying. He arrested a surveyor who tried to lay out a town within ten leagues of the coast, also in violation of Mexican laws.[26]

Bradburn was determined to enforce the law, but when the three runaways from Louisiana petitioned for "protection under the Mexican flag," Bradburn was not sure exactly what the law required. The Treaty of Amity and Commerce that Anthony Butler had negotiated did not provide for the extradition of fugitive slaves, and Bradburn was not aware of any other law that established a clear policy on the subject. "Since my instructions did not foresee this case," Bradburn wrote, "I sent them [the runaways] immediately to the fort to work while I consulted with the commandant general of these states." Several weeks later, when a planter named William H. Logan claimed the runaways as his property, Bradburn refused to return them until he received further guidance from Mexico City. "Military commanders," he explained, "are not posted to the frontier to determine national questions."[27]

Discouraged but not deterred, William H. Logan enlisted the services of a lawyer in Anahuac named William Barret Travis. Born in South Carolina, and raised on a farm in southwestern Alabama, Travis worked as a teacher, lawyer, newspaper publisher, and adjutant of the Twenty-Sixth Regiment of the Alabama Militia, but succeeded at none of these pursuits. The newspaper that he edited was losing money. The irregular fees that his law practice brought in were hardly enough to make up the difference. The only thing that Travis had succeeded in doing was impregnating the daughter of a wealthy planter, who had been one of his students while he was a schoolteacher. They married when she was sixteen and he nineteen. But neither fatherhood nor matrimony made Travis into a family man. In March 1831, he abandoned his wife, their young son, and his mounting debts. Determined to make "a splendid fortune" in the Mexican province of Téjas, Travis headed west to San Felipe, where he paid ten dollars as a down payment on a quarter league of land in Austin's Colony. He originally intended to set up a law practice in San Felipe, but the town was already overstocked with attorneys, so Travis moved to Anahuac.[28]

William H. Logan was one of Travis's first clients. Exactly what course of action Travis recommended to the Louisiana planter was not recorded, but whatever it was, it did not seem to involve the law. On a cold, rainy night, several days after their meeting, a tall, cloaked figure delivered a message to a soldier posted outside of the garrison at Anahuac. It warned that a hundred men were gathering on the banks of the Sabine River to kidnap the runways. Bradburn kept the garrison under arms for several days, only to discover that the message had been a ruse. No forces were gathering on the Sabine River. William Barret Travis had only wanted Bradburn to *think* that an invasion was imminent so that the commander would return the runaways to his latest client.[29]

Incensed, Bradburn arrested Travis and another man he suspected of being an accomplice. Concerned that his prisoners would escape from the guardhouse, Bradburn moved them to an empty brick kiln, where they survived on a meager diet of beans and stale bread. Meanwhile, anger against the supposed despotism of Juan Davis Bradburn mounted among the *norteamericanos* in neighboring communities. In early June, thirty armed colonists from Brazoria rode toward Anahuac. By the time they reached the garrison, a hundred miles to the north, the force had more than tripled in number. The armed colonists quickly overwhelmed Bradburn's nineteen cavalrymen, but they did not have the artillery that they needed to capture the fort.[30]

While the armed colonists waited for a cannon to arrive from Brazoria, Colonel José de las Piedras, the Mexican commander at Nacogdoches, rode into Anahuac. Piedras wanted to avoid an uprising. When he asked to negotiate, the rebels demanded that the Mexican commander release the prisoners and relieve Juan Davis Bradburn of his duties. Piedras agreed. To resolve the issue that had started the revolt in the first place, he signed an agreement on June 29, 1832, which provided "that the private property appropriated by Colonel Bradburn for the use of the Garrison at Anahuac shall be restored upon legal proof." William H. Logan's slaves would return to Louisiana.[31]

The disturbance at Anahuac was over, but the debates over the authority of the Mexican government over its citizens were not. On October 1, 1832, fifty-eight delegates met at San Felipe de Austin to enumerate their complaints. They called on Mexico's Congress to modify the Law of April 6, 1830, which prohibited the introduction of enslaved people and the immigration of *norteamericanos* to Téjas. They came up with a plan to organize militias that could defend their settlements in case of an emergency. They also decided to petition Mexico's Congress for Téjas to become a separate state, independent from Coahuila. The delegates made the case that the differences between the regions were so great that the same laws could not govern them both. The petition did not mention the greatest difference between Coahuila and Téjas: their views on slavery.[32]

IN THE FALL OF 1831, FRANCISCO PIZARRO MARTÍNEZ, MEXICO'S consul in New Orleans, reported that *norteamericanos* were contracting "individuals of color" to serve "them, their heirs, or their representatives" for periods of "sixty, seventy, eighty, and up to ninety years—and this in exchange for an insignificant sum." For the next five months, Pizarro counted over two hundred "disguised slaves" bound for Téjas. This was not what the legislature of Coahuila y Téjas intended when it voted in favor of recognizing labor contracts signed in foreign countries. On April 28, 1832, the state legislature issued a new colonization law that closed the loophole the Anglo colonists had been exploiting to introduce enslaved people as indentured servants. According to Article 36 of the new law, "Servants and day laborers, hereafter introduced by foreign colonists, cannot be obligated by any contract to continue in the service of the latter longer than ten years." The indentures for seventy, eighty, and up to ninety years were now annulled.[33]

Within months, enslaved people started to claim their freedom under the new law. In the late spring of 1832, Peter and his son John, two slaves who had escaped from a plantation in Austin's Colony, arrived in San Antonio de Béxar. After gaining an audience with the mayor, they petitioned for their freedom on the grounds that they had been imported to Mexico in violation of the prohibition against the slave trade. The mayor granted their request. As more slaves filed suit, the Mexican consul, Francisco Pizarro Martínez, predicted that *norteamericanos* would find themselves "in a tumult" for having "secretly introduced a large number of slaves, among whom word has already spread that, in accordance with the laws, they are free." As Mexican officials redoubled their efforts to enforce the ban on the importation of slaves, the Anglo colonists in Téjas grew increasingly concerned about the future of slavery under Mexican rule.[34]

Other states in the federation were growing restive as well. Since taking office in 1830, Anastasio Bustamante had limited civil rights, authorized the execution of Vicente Guerrero, and curbed the power of the state legislatures. On January 2, 1832, a garrison in Veracruz took up arms against Bustamante. By late summer, the states of Tamaulipas, Jalisco, Zacatecas, Durango, and San Luis Potosí joined Veracruz in open rebellion.[35]

By the end of 1833, the rebels had ousted Bustamante from power and called for a new election. Antonio López de Santa Anna, one of the leaders of the uprising, handily won. But Santa Anna neither attended his own inauguration nor made any attempt to govern. Claiming illness, he left his administration in the hands of his liberal vice president, Valentín Gómez Farías. Santa Anna wanted to let Gómez Farías enact his liberal reforms, while he watched from his hacienda in Veracruz. If the reforms were popular, Santa Anna could claim credit, but if they were unpopular, he could blame his vice president.[36]

While Santa Anna supposedly convalesced, Gómez Farías set to work. One of the most pressing issues that faced the new administration was preventing an uprising in the province of Téjas. At the urging of the vice president, the legislature of Coahuila y Téjas made a number of concessions to the colonists: no one could be harassed for his religious views. Legal documents could be printed in English as well as Spanish. The province could elect two additional representatives to the state legislature. At the end of 1833, Mexico's Congress also repealed the provision of the Law of April 6, 1830, that prohibited the immigration of *norteamericanos*. But the administration remained committed to enforcing the ban on the importation of slaves. In 1834, Valentín Gómez Farías dispatched a secret agent to Téjas with instructions to "seek by every possible and prudent means to make it known to the slaves who have been brought into the Republic in circumvention of the law, that [the law] gives them freedom by the mere act of stepping on the territory of the Republic." Mexico's leaders were willing to compromise on a number of issues, but they would not permit slavery to expand unchecked.[37]

Gómez Farías also wanted to reform the church and the army, which, he believed, wielded too much power in the republic. His administration secularized the educational system, prohibited priests from sermonizing about politics, taxed the church to finance the government, decreased the size of the army, and eliminated the *fuero militar*—the immunity from civil prosecution—that military officers traditionally enjoyed. Revolts soon broke out across the country, giving Santa Anna the answer he needed. Returning to Mexico City on June 12, 1834, the president denounced the liberal reforms, removed Gómez Farías, and dissolved Congress and most of the state legislatures.[38]

"The political character of this country seems to partake of its geological features—all is volcanic," Stephen F. Austin wrote in 1835. Since arriving in the province of Téjas in 1821, the empresario had watched Agustín de Iturbide crown himself emperor and then sail to exile in Italy; Guadalupe Victoria establish a federal system of government, in which the church and the army retained undue power; Vicente Guerrero declare himself president and then die before a firing squad. The upheaval continued in the 1830s, as Antonio López de Santa Anna ousted Anastasio Bustamante and fourteen months later, overturned the federal system he had once taken up arms to defend. The Anglo colonists in Téjas tried to keep abreast of political developments in Mexico City, for one reason in particular. "It matters not to me what form of government Mexico adopts," wrote William Barret Travis, "so that we are guaranteed in the security of persons & property."[39]

On the morning of October 20, 1835, the Mexican consul, Francisco Pizarro Martínez, made his way to the New Orleans waterfront. Hundreds of boats lined the wharf, creating the impression that the city extended beyond the riverbank—and, in certain respects, it did. Boats of all sorts brought a steady supply of goods down the Mississippi and across the Gulf to New Orleans. Over twenty-three hundred steamboats arrived in the city in 1835—more than ten times the number of vessels that entered the port when the Jefferson administration purchased Louisiana in 1803. Baton Rouge would eventually become Louisiana's political capital, but New Orleans was its mercantile center.[40]

Due to arrive that October morning was a fifty-six-ton schooner from Campeche called the *Iris*. As consul, Francisco Pizarro Martínez was required to record the arrival of every Mexican ship at New Orleans, but his work that morning would go beyond jotting down the port the *Iris* had come from and the number of days its crew had spent at sea. The schooner carried a more unusual cargo than the ten thousand dollars in Mexican silver reported on its customs declaration. Chained below deck was an enslaved mulatto man named Jean Antoine.[41]

Three months earlier, while a brig called the *General Santa Anna* lay alongside a New Orleans dock, Jean Antoine slipped on board and bolted down the single ladder from the main deck to the hold. If the summer air was damp and hot outside, the conditions below deck were stifling. The "animal and vegetable substances that commonly accumulate after a ship has been some time in commission"—the brine that sloshed from a barrel of salt pork, the flour that leaked from a torn burlap sack—decomposed slowly in the windowless hold. Despite the heat and the putrid smell of rot, Jean Antoine managed to keep himself out of sight until the unsuspecting crew set sail for Campeche in early August.[42]

The *General Santa Anna* was "a long distance from New Orleans" by the time the captain began to suspect that someone was hiding in the hold. The crew searched but found no one. The odds were against them. The waves turned the hull into a drum, whose cadence drowned out the sound of a cough or a step that might otherwise have betrayed a man in hiding. In the windowless hold, it was impossible to see without lighting a match, and if a spark touched the loose oakum on the floor, a fire would consume the wooden ship. So the crew had to navigate using other senses: the touch of wire cables or the knowledge of each crate's position. For the eleven-day journey to Campeche, Jean Antoine remained hidden.[43]

Toward the south, the Yucatán Peninsula curves like a beckoning finger. On the western coast was Campeche, with a population of around thirty thousand in 1835. Not long after the brig dropped anchor, the captain, a naturalized Mexican citizen named Ignatius William Cantarell, asked the local authorities to help him arrest the runaway in his hold. Alejandro Duque de Estrada, the mayor of Campeche, did what his predecessors had done for decades. He dispatched a small police force to the *General Santa Anna*. Now that the hatches were under constant watch by a crew no longer distracted by their duties at sea, Jean Antoine was trapped. As a result of their "very thorough diligences," the police caught "said mulatto" and hauled him to the municipal prison.⁴⁴

In Campeche, Mayor Alejandro Duque de Estrada decided to return the runaway on the next ship bound for New Orleans: the *Iris*. The captain of the *Iris* was Domingo Hernández, a Mexican citizen who had been arrested the previous year in New Orleans for carrying a "black slave" to freedom in Matamoros. Hernández must have been chastened by his arrest, because he did not help Jean Antoine escape on the journey between Campeche and New Orleans. Instead, the *Iris* was towed upriver on October 20, 1835, docking at the waterfront without incident. After the customs agent boarded the schooner, examined the ship's manifest, and cleared the *Iris* for entry, the work of unloading began: cranks turned, ropes coiled, sails folded. From below deck, the fugitive slave emerged. As he was being led toward a justice of the peace, Jean Antoine suddenly made use of a knife that "no one had seen." Before anyone could take back the blade, Jean Antoine gave himself "various wounds," or so official reports would state. An uncharacteristically terse Francisco Pizarro Martínez noted only that the "unhappy slave" died the next day.⁴⁵

From 1821 to 1835, Mexico's system of government shifted from a constitutional monarchy to a federal republic to a centralist regime. All the while, Mexican officials returned fugitive slaves to their *norteamericano* owners in order to deny the United States government an excuse to invade Mexico, as it had Spanish Florida. At the same time, Mexico's domestic policies sought to restrict slavery in order to eliminate the threat of an internal revolt that could dismember the republic. At the state and national level, Mexican authorities seemed to doubt that slaveholders would have any cause for protest against gradual emancipation laws, since these policies did not interfere with "property" rights. But discontent was growing among the Anglo colonists.

Although slavery remained legal in Téjas, *norteamericanos* recognized the threat that Mexico's gradual emancipation policies posed to the future of human bondage in the region.

Perhaps no one in the province was more dissatisfied with Mexico's policies on slavery and more vocal about his dissatisfaction than William Barret Travis, the lawyer at Anahuac who helped to return fugitive slaves to their owner in Louisiana. In 1832, the legislature of Coahuila y Téjas limited labor contracts to ten years, preventing *norteamericanos* from importing their slaves as indentured servants. Although Mexico's Congress had overturned the prohibition on immigration from the United States, the national authorities continued to enforce the other provisions of the Law of April 6, 1830, including the prohibition on the slave trade. As Mexican officials renewed their efforts to enforce the ban, the Anglo colonists concluded what they had long suspected—that their rights would never be safe under Mexican rule. The government in Mexico City was "a plundering, robbing, autocratical, aristocratical, jumbled up govt which is in fact no govt at all," as William Barret Travis put it on May 6, 1835. "There is no security for life, liberty, or property."[46]

Travis wanted to take action. In the late spring of 1835, he learned that customs officials, appointed by Mexico City, were imposing tariffs on trade in Anahuac. The development "aroused the indignation & resentment of the whole people," as he put it. On June 30, 1835, Travis and fifty men mounted a six-pounder cannon onto a cart, wheeled it onto a small vessel, and sailed across Galveston Bay. The garrison at Anahuac surrendered without a fight. Travis hoped that his raid would be the opening salvo of a war for independence. But most of the other colonists prioritized keeping the government—and the army—out of the province. On July 4, the town council of Mina, on the upper Colorado River, criticized the "misconduct of designing men" like Travis. A week later, the people of Columbia, sixty miles south of Galveston, declared themselves to be "true, faithful, loyal, and unoffending Mexican citizens," who disapproved of the "incautious and unreflecting" rebels who had disturbed the "peace quiet harmony and concord" at Anahuac.[47]

In September, Mexico's president, Antonio López de Santa Anna, ordered his brother-in-law, General Martín Perfecto de Cos, to investigate the disturbances at Anahuac. The news that Mexican forces were marching northward set the Anglo colonists on edge. Slaveholders could not shake the suspicion that the invading forces would try to "excite the negroes." Rumors circulated that the commander of a Mexican schooner in Galveston Bay had announced his intention to "take all the negro slaves in the country that he could get in his possession and offer them their liberty after one year's service." In October, the Matagorda Committee of Safety and Correspondence condemned Mexico's "merciless soldiery" for marching on Texas "to give liberty to our slaves and to make slaves of ourselves." When over a hundred slaves in Brazoria, fifty miles south of Galveston Bay, were hanged or "whipd [sic] nearly to death" for allegedly planning a revolt, fear turned to hysteria, and the Anglo colonists began to prepare for the worst.[48]

SIX

THE TEXAS REVOLUTION

O N SEPTEMBER 29, 1835, LIEUTENANT FRANCISCO DE Castañeda arrived on the banks of the Guadalupe River in Téjas with orders to retrieve a cannon from the town of Gonzáles on the opposite bank. Located about seventy-five miles east of San Antonio de Béxar, Gonzáles was a small town that suffered from frequent Comanche and Karankawa raids. In 1831, the people of Gonzáles asked the Mexican government to send troops to protect the town, but the garrisons at Nacogdoches, La Bahía, and San Antonio de Béxar had no men to spare. The best that the commandant general of Coahuila y Téjas could do was to send a cannon to the town so the people of Gonzáles could defend themselves. But now the Mexican Army needed the cannon back to confront an even more pressing danger than Indian raids. A year earlier, President Antonio López de Santa Anna overturned the Mexican constitution on the grounds that the people were unsuited to representative government. The already "feeble" bonds between the states snapped. Zacatecas seceded, and the Mexican authorities were desperately trying to stop other states from following suit.

The Mexican Army needed every weapon it could find, including the cannon in Gonzáles.[1]

Lieutenant Castañeda reached the Guadalupe River to find the banks swollen from the recent rains. Where the shore ought to have been, there was nothing more than partly submerged willows, bending beneath the current. After scouting for a natural crossing on September 29, 1835, Castañeda concluded that neither he nor his men would be able to reach the town on the opposite side without a boat. He had no choice but to shout until someone—anyone—came out to listen.[2]

Soon the people of Gonzáles began to gather on the banks. When Castañeda shouted across the river that he had a message for the mayor, the townspeople shouted back that the mayor was away on business. Castañeda decided to wait. While his men whiled away the hours in their tents, the eighteen white men who lived in Gonzáles met to discuss their options. They did not, strictly speaking, need the cannon. They had never even used it until several days before the arrival of Mexican forces, when they fired it at a sycamore tree on the banks of the Guadalupe River. Still, they objected on principle to returning the weapon. "This cannon was as I have always been informed given in perpetuity to this Town for its defense against the Indians," the mayor wrote. "The dangers which existed at the time we received this cannon still exist and for the same purposes it is still needed here."[3]

Refusing to return the cannon was only the town's most recent act of disobedience. In Gonzáles, as in the rest of Téjas, the ban on the introduction of slaves was a dead letter. The provision of the state constitution that freed the children of enslaved people also went unenforced. Town councils were supposed to send a report to the state authorities four times a year, listing the names of the children born to enslaved people who would become free under the terms of the state constitution. But the authorities in Gonzáles never complied with the requirement, even when the governor of Coahuila y Téjas threatened to levy a fifty-peso fine. This lawbreaking would not continue, at least not to the same degree, under the centralized system of government that Santa Anna envisioned. Enforcing the ban on the introduction of new slaves would have predictable and devastating results. Not only would hundreds of illegally imported slaves win their freedom, but the entire system of forced labor in Téjas would be endangered. To defend against Antonio López de Santa Anna's centralizing tendencies, the cannon would have to remain in Gonzáles.[4]

Over the next several days, the citizens of Gonzáles stockpiled weapons, moved their families into the woods, and sent messengers to the surrounding settlements, asking for reinforcements. By October 1, they were ready. After nightfall, a small force crossed the Guadalupe River by ferry, the brass cannon in tow. The next morning, with a heavy fog over the river, they pointed the cannon toward Castañeda's camp, unfurled a flag that read "come and get it," and opened fire.[5]

ON NOVEMBER 3, 1835, FIFTY-EIGHT DELEGATES CONVENED AT AN unfinished hotel in San Felipe de Austin to "set forth to the world the causes which have impelled [them] to take up arms." Some of the delegates wanted to declare independence from Mexico. But others feared such a bold move, preferring, in the words of James Kerr of Gonzáles, to "keep the pease" until "our rights and privileges are invaded."[6]

Samuel Houston, a delegate from Nacogdoches, was expected to brashly champion independence. Born in 1793 in Virginia, Houston fought under Andrew Jackson during the War of 1812, acted as an Indian subagent to the Cherokees, and served two terms in Congress. After being tried by the US House of Representatives for beating one of its members with a hickory cane in 1832, Houston left Washington, DC, for Nacogdoches, Téjas. The Mexican authorities suspected that his arrival had less to do with his alleged misdeeds than a secret commission from Andrew Jackson to "revolutionize" Téjas. Houston was, according to one British diplomat, "well calculated" to stir up the "lawless bands" in the Anglo colonies. Anthony Butler, the US minister to

Mexico, called him a "drunkard," a "blackguard," a "Rogue," a "liar," and a "most unqualified braggadocio representing himself on all occasions as the ne plus ultra of sagacity, foresight, tact & talent." Even David Burnet, who would go on to serve as interim president of the Republic of Texas, attributed to Houston "all the vices, without one of the virtues of Alcibiades."[7]

At the convention, Houston surprised the other delegates by urging them to proceed cautiously. Beneath an open sky—the roof of the half-built hotel had not yet been finished—he argued in favor of fighting for federalism, rather than independence. The committees of safety that the Anglo colonists organized after Santa Anna's coup had not yet reached a consensus about what was to be done—some demanded a return to federalism, while others urged conciliation. Houston understood that this lack of consensus would only exacerbate the practical challenge of organizing an uprising in a province that spanned thirty-five thousand square miles. Across this vast area were thirty thousand *norteamericanos*, five thousand slaves, and four thousand Mexicans. The only newspaper in the entire province was the *Texas Republican*, published weekly in Brazoria, just outside Galveston. Communication would be slow and coordination difficult. The Anglo colonies seemed more likely to unite behind the cause of federalism—at least for now.[8]

Declaring themselves in favor of federalism would also win the support of other Mexicans who had taken up arms against the centralist government in Mexico City, which only seemed to grow more authoritarian by the day. The latest grievance was the constituent congress that Antonio López de Santa Anna convened to draft an entirely new charter for Mexico in the fall of 1835. The Constitución de las Siete Leyes, as the new constitution became known, restricted the franchise to citizens with annual incomes of more than one hundred pesos; it established a fourth branch of government—the Supreme Conservative Power— with the power to veto laws, remove judges, and shut down Congress; and it reduced the states to the status of departments, with no financial autonomy or political sovereignty.[9]

To Houston, a more conservative defense of federalism would win over liberal Mexicans, encourage the donation of war matériel from the United States, and give the revolutionaries time to organize an army. The delegates followed his advice. On November 7, they voted to express their support for the principles of the recently overturned Constitution of 1824, promising "their support and assistance to such of the members of the Mexican Confederacy, as will take up arms against military despotism."[10]

Although the delegates stopped short of declaring independence, they quickly set about forming a government to organize the war effort. They appointed a Kentuckian named Henry Smith as governor and directed him to oversee military affairs in concert with a legislative body—the Governing Council—to which each district would elect one representative. On November 12, the delegates elected Sam Houston as major general of the Texas Army, authorizing him to appoint an adjutant general, an inspector general, a quartermaster general, a paymaster general, and a surgeon general. To recruit, equip, and train as many men as possible, they also created a powerful incentive for men to join the army. After serving out a two-year enlistment, each volunteer would receive 640 acres of land.[11]

These measures came none too soon. The Anglo colonists faced an immediate military threat. In the fall of 1835, General Martín Perfecto de Cos transported five hundred men from Veracruz to Brazoria. From the Gulf Coast, he and his men marched west to San Antonio de Béxar. In response, three hundred Texas volunteers placed the town under siege. Dressed in buckskin breeches, and armed with single-barreled flintlock rifles, the Texians (as they now called themselves) lacked almost everything except "great purpose," and for most of the fall, their purpose did not seem to extend beyond getting drunk off corn liquor shipped by the barrel from San Felipe. "In the name of Almighty God," their commander, the empresario Stephen F. Austin, wrote to the Governing Council in November, "send no more ardent spirits to this camp."[12]

The odds were against the Texas volunteers. Cos's forces occupied a strong position in the presidio at San Antonio de Béxar. Reinforcements were on the way. From intercepted letters, Major General Sam Houston learned that Antonio López de Santa Anna was recruiting ten thousand men at San Luis Potosí to march on Téjas. Houston needed to impose discipline—fast.[13]

IN EARLY DECEMBER 1835, WITH WINTER UPON THEM, THE VOL-unteers led by Stephen F. Austin decided to attack San Antonio de Béxar. Their objective was to take the presidio. To create a diversion, they feigned an attack on the Alamo, the former mission that stood on the east bank of the San Antonio River. Before dawn on December 5, an artillery company fired a few salvos at the Alamo. Then the men made as much noise as they could, shouting and stomping their feet, until they saw a rocket flare above the presidio, calling the Mexican forces to come to the defense of the Alamo. The Texians' plan had worked. General Martín Perfecto de Cos, mistaking their raid on the Alamo for a much larger attack, rushed across the San Antonio River, leaving the presidio undefended.[14]

As Mexican soldiers marched toward the Alamo, two columns of volunteers crept along the San Antonio River, trampling the gardens that the locals tended along the banks. The volunteers entered the town without resistance, firing into the narrow streets, as the residents ducked into their doorways and backed away from their windows. By the time that General Cos realized his mistake and ordered his men back across the river to Béxar, the volunteers had taken up positions inside the presidio. From every loophole in the walls extended the barrel of a gun.[15]

The Mexican forces desperately tried to retake Béxar. Some engaged in brutal hand-to-hand combat through the streets of the town. Others took up a position behind a line of mesquite trees along the San Antonio River, until the Texians' artillery set the trees on fire. On

December 7, five hundred reinforcements arrived, but they were so exhausted from their forced march from the Rio Grande that they could hardly stand. The next day, General Martín Perfecto de Cos surrendered, giving his word that his men would "retire with their arms and private property into the interior of the republic under parole of honor" and not in any way "oppose the reestablishment of the federal constitution of 1824."[16]

As Cos's army retreated toward the Rio Grande, the Texas volunteers surveyed what they had won. The Alamo was in shambles. Flies circled over mule carcasses. Strewn across the ground were "cannon balls & shot of every description." The walls, which enclosed a central courtyard of three acres, were extensive and crumbling. "Everything looked miserable," one soldier remembered, as he studied the charred breastworks.[17]

Sam Houston did not want to defend San Antonio de Béxar. Even if he could have spared the four hundred men needed to occupy the Alamo, he saw no point to staking out a position so far removed from the Anglo colonies in central and eastern Téjas. He reasoned that the surest way for his men to defeat a superior Mexican force was to lure them deeper into the province, where the terrain was unfamiliar and the people hostile.[18]

Nonetheless, General Sam Houston ordered thirty or so of his volunteers to go to San Antonio de Béxar. They were under the command of a tall, heavyset man with sandy blond hair and deep-set gray eyes named James Bowie. Born in Kentucky, and raised in southeastern Louisiana, Bowie made a name for himself in 1826, when he thrust a long hunting knife into a man's chest and twisted it, as he later boasted, "to cut the heart strings." Four years later, by the time that any long hunting blade was known as a Bowie knife, James Bowie moved to the province of Téjas, where he speculated in lands, traded in slaves, and married into one of the most distinguished Tejano families in San Antonio de Béxar.[19]

Bowie's instructions were to remove the artillery and then destroy the fort and the former mission. But when he reached San Antonio de Béxar, the Louisianan decided against carrying out his orders. After capturing Béxar, the seventy or so men who remained in the town had reinforced the walls of the Alamo. The cannons that they mounted on the batteries gave the former mission a formidable appearance. As James Bowie inspected the Alamo, he became increasingly convinced that he could defend it. And by defending the Alamo, Bowie and his men could keep the Mexican Army far from the plantations of eastern Texas—and the enslaved people who worked on them. "The salvation of Texas depends in great measure in keeping Béjar out of the hands of the enemy," he wrote to Governor Henry Smith on February 2, 1836. "It serves as the frontier piquet guard."[20]

Governor Henry Smith agreed with Bowie's assessment, and so he ordered Lieutenant William Barret Travis to reinforce the Alamo. Travis was eager to take part in the war he helped to start six months earlier when he and fifty men seized the garrison at Anahuac. But when Travis asked for one hundred soldiers, Governor Smith told him that the only men he would be taking with him were the ones he recruited himself. Travis only managed to enlist twenty-six cavalrymen. "The people are cold and indifferent," Travis complained. "I have strained every nerve; I have used my personal credit, and have neither slept day nor night since I received orders to march, and, with all this, I have barely been able to get horses and equipments for the few men I have."[21]

Travis had reservations about "going off into the enemy's country with such little means, so few men, and with them so badly equipped," but in the end, he complied, setting out for the Alamo in January with his twenty-one-year-old slave Joe and twenty-six white men. He believed the position was worth defending. Travis owned several slaves in addition to Joe: Jared, age six; Eliza, age twelve; Simon, age twenty-six; Jack, age fifty-one. Like James Bowie, Travis wanted to stop Antonio López de Santa Anna from reaching the plantations of eastern Texas, where the presence of the Mexican Army might encourage enslaved people to escape—or worse, revolt. "This neighborhood will be the great and decisive ground," he later wrote. "The power of Santa Anna is to be met here or in the colonies; we had better meet them here than to suffer a war of devastation to rage in our settlements."[22]

AT THE REAR OF THE MEXICAN ARMY WERE TWO THOUSAND mules hauling beans, cornmeal, dried meat, and Brown Bess muskets purchased from the British after the Battle of Waterloo. The marching army spanned several miles, and the din of braying animals and ungreased axles faded only at night, when the foot soldiers folded their dark blue coats into pillows and the cavalrymen pulled off their boots, careful to avoid the tin-plated iron spurs screwed to the wooden heels.[23]

Their commander was Antonio López de Santa Anna. "Plain and unostentatious in manner," "notable in conversation," and "read somewhat," according to one US diplomat, Santa Anna styled himself the "Napoleon of the West." He collected Napoleonic memorabilia, devoured biographies of the French general, and insisted on always riding at the head of his army because he had once seen a portrait of Napoleon leading a charge, his sabre raised. Santa Anna had grandiose ambitions for his invasion of Téjas. The previous month, before leaving Mexico City, he told the French and British ambassadors that if the US government backed the Texians, "he would continue the march of his army to Washington and place upon its Capitol the Mexican Flag."[24]

Antonio López de Santa Anna believed that he had justice on his side. Although the rebels claimed to have taken up arms in defense of federalism, their own words seemed to reveal their true intentions. The rebels compared themselves not to other Mexican Federalists but to the "illustrious patriots" of the American Revolution. They adopted the same battle cry as the Virginian Patrick Henry: "Liberty or Death!" They wrote poems about how their uprising would teach "chain'd nations that they can be free." The Texians believed that they were sustaining the "principles of 1776" so devoutly that they later considered naming their new nation the Republic of Washington. "We are the descendants of that immortal man," boasted one Anglo colonist. It seemed only a matter of time before the rebels declared independence. Santa Anna was determined to crush the uprising before they did.[25]

In the fall of 1835, Santa Anna raised an army of six thousand men. From San Luis Potosí, two hundred and fifty miles north of Mexico City, they marched toward Téjas during the coldest months of the year. The soldiers survived on half rations. Forage was so scarce that the mules began to gnaw on the wagon boxes. To keep up with the general on horseback at the front of the column, the soldiers resorted to throwing boxes of munitions from their overloaded carts. By the time the Mexican forces could make out the white walls of the Alamo on February 23, 1836, four hundred men had died. Those who survived were exhausted. But they did enjoy a critical advantage—the element of surprise.[26]

THE DEFENDERS OF THE ALAMO DID NOT EXPECT THE ENEMY TO arrive so quickly. They spent the previous weeks exploring the acreage they hoped to claim after the war was over. The night before the Mexican forces appeared on the horizon, they celebrated George Washington's birthday in San Antonio with ample amounts of corn liquor. Distracted by scouting expeditions and patriotic celebrations, they had not reinforced the walls of the former mission. Neither had they stockpiled supplies in preparation for a long siege. The Texians were unprepared to defend the Alamo when a sentry in the bell tower of the San Fernando Cathedral in San Antonio shouted on February 23, "The enemy are in view!"[27]

Antonio López de Santa Anna was determined to score a major victory at the site of General Cos's defeat. "I shall convert Téjas into a desert," he declared. His determination only increased when on March 1, 1836, a convention met at Washington (later Washington-on-the-Brazos). The delegates, over half of whom had arrived in Téjas within the last two years, assembled in a shed. After working through the night, they declared the independence of Texas by unanimous vote. Their justification was that the Mexican government had "ceased to protect the lives, liberty and property of the people." Houston was ebullient. Another delegate, George C. Childress, expressed the common view that the defense of federalism had been "but a mere *pretence* from the beginning."[28]

IN THE EARLY MORNING HOURS OF MARCH 6, 1836, INSIDE THE Alamo William Barret Travis and his slave Joe woke in darkness to cannon fire and the acrid smell of smoke. The explosion of cannon fire was an almost common feature of their lives. By Travis's estimate, over two hundred shells had hit the Alamo since the siege began. But the commotion outside was louder and more frenzied than ever before. Travis grabbed two rifles, one in each hand, and headed toward the north wall, yelling for the men to take their positions. Joe followed close behind.[29]

By the time they sprinted up the earthen ramp that led to the north wall, Joe could see what the garrison was up against. The previous night, six thousand Mexican soldiers had surrounded the former mission. The first column had filed toward the west wall, closest to San Antonio de Béxar. The second had staked out a position beneath the heavy artillery of the north wall. The third had circled around to the east. The fourth had prepared to assault the main gate, on the south side of the former mission. In the early morning darkness, Joe heard the sound of the bugle—the signal to attack. All at once, the men stormed the walls, shouting, "*Viva Santa Anna*" and "*Viva México*."[30]

As Mexican soldiers scaled the wood outer work that reinforced the crumbling north wall, Joe could see that the odds were against the Texians. The Mexican forces numbered in the thousands. The rebels had somewhere around two hundred men. Flying from the bell tower of the San Fernando Cathedral in San Antonio de Béxar was a bloodred banner, emblazoned with a skull and crossbones. What this meant for the rebels was clear—they would receive no quarter—but what it meant for Joe and the other enslaved people forced to fight alongside their masters at the Alamo was uncertain.[31]

Outnumbered thirty-to-one, the Texians fought for their lives. Their immediate priority was to keep the Mexican forces from gaining the walls. Travis urged them to keep firing, while he loaded the cannons with nails, chain links, horseshoes, and whatever else he could find that would withstand the blast of powder. Joe was firing and reloading, like all of the other men on the north wall, when a bullet struck William Barret Travis through the forehead. Travis froze and then slumped over the gun carriage, dead.[32]

Mexican soldiers continued to pour over the wall, armed with axes, crowbars, picks, planks, and ladders. "The first to climb were thrown down by bayonets already waiting for them behind the parapet, or by pistol fire," a Mexican colonel recalled. But the Mexican forces had a numerical advantage and soon the defenders fell back, fighting and firing as they ducked into the barracks along the east wall. Some of the defenders fashioned white flags out of handkerchiefs and socks, but the Mexican soldiers, who had orders to give no quarter, smashed down the doors of the barracks and shot whomever they found inside.[33]

Joe hid, desperately hoping that no one would find him. From where he had concealed himself in the barracks, he could not see the battle going on around him, but he must have been able to hear the screams and the gunfire, the dull thud of rifle butts against bone and the labored breaths of men bayonetted through the chest. After what seemed like hours, the noise died down. As Joe emerged from where he had been hiding, a Mexican soldier shot at him, buckshot grazing his side. Another lunged at him with his bayonet. But their captain interceded, ordering them to spare Joe. No slave would have taken up arms against the Mexican Army, the captain explained, except by "force."[34]

Cautiously, Joe made his way toward the central courtyard of the former mission. Somewhere around two hundred rebels were dead. As Mexican soldiers piled up the bodies, they probably would not have known that William Barret Travis, slumped near the north wall with a bullet in his head, owned five slaves, or that James Bowie, the man who insisted on defending the Alamo, made a fortune smuggling slaves into Texas and Louisiana. But Joe must have known that even the ordinary soldiers whose bodies lay strewn across the Alamo were slaveholders. William and Mial Scurlock came to Texas from Tennessee with three slaves: a man, a woman, and a young child. Anthony Wolfe joined a slave-smuggling business when he moved from London to Nacogdoches in 1835. The Texians claimed to have taken up arms in defense of freedom and democracy, but they had, in fact, been fighting for something other than liberty. When the soldiers finished piling the bodies, their commanders gave the order to douse them in oil and set them to burn.[35]

THE TEXAS REVOLUTION INAUGURATED A NEW ERA OF ANTISLAVERY activism in Mexico. Mexican political theorists argued that the revolt was unjustified, because the Anglo colonists had violated the social contract by importing slaves in "contradiction of the laws of this country." If the Texians had flouted the law, they were no longer entitled to its protections. "The lack of compliance," President Santa Anna explained, "destroyed the pact." This argument placed the blame for the war on the Anglo colonists, at the same time that it emboldened the Mexican government to take stronger measures against slavery. On March 8, 1836, Santa Anna directed his generals to "give protection to all those unhappy slaves who groan beneath the whip."[36]

This reversal of Mexico's long-standing respect for "property" rights was not a principled defense of liberty. As a Mexico City newspaper put it, Santa Anna's supporters were people "who preach a liberator in order to enthrone a sultan." The president was no more committed to antislavery than his hero, Napoleon Bonaparte. Rather, Santa Anna's decree to free all slaves who reached Mexican lines was a calculated attempt to undermine the rebellion in Texas, and the plan seemed to have its intended effect. As Santa Anna marched northward, slaveholders in Texas reported that their "negroes, G—d—'em, were on the tip-toe of expectation, and rejoicing that the Mexicans were coming to make them free!" On March 17, 1836, eleven days after the fall of the Alamo, a group of citizens from Brazoria railed against the "horrid purpose of our treacherous and bloody enemy, to unite in his ranks, and as instruments of his unholy and savage work, the negroes." A week later, the commander at Galveston Island warned that "the Negroes . . . have manifested a disposition to become troublesome and in some instances, *daring*." The daring led to action. On April 3, 1836, fourteen slaves and their families reached the Mexican Army on the Navidad River and petitioned for their freedom. The Mexican commander sent them "in liberty" to Tamaulipas.[37]

To prevent their slaves from escaping to Mexican lines, Anglo colonists fled eastward, loading their belongings onto whatever conveyances they could find. Oxen hauled carts loaded with housewares. Mules carried burlap bags stuffed with provisions. Slaves pushed wheelbarrows piled with their owners' possessions. Women walked alongside their children who were too tired or frightened to complain, even though there was much to complain about: the driving rain, the strong winds, the distance that lay before them. "I have never witnessed such scenes of distress and human suffering," remembered a Texian named Creed Taylor, who was sixteen at the time.[38]

As families fled eastward, General Sam Houston continued to order his men to retreat. He was prepared to fall back to the Sabine River, where reinforcements from the United States waited. Major General Edmund Gaines, who destroyed the Negro Fort in Florida on Jackson's orders in 1818, and who now commanded the Western District of the United States Army, had moved his headquarters to Natchitoches, Louisiana, fifty miles east of the Sabine River. "Should I find any disposition on the part of the Mexicans or their red allies to menace our frontier," Gaines informed the United States Secretary of War Lewis

Cass, "I cannot but deem it to be my duty not only to hold the troops of my command in readiness or action in defense of our frontier, but to anticipate their lawless movements, by crossing our supposed or imaginary national boundary." Edmund Gaines only needed an excuse to invade Texas, as Andrew Jackson had invaded Florida, and the emancipatory policies of the Mexican forces gave him one. "Santa Anna has proclaimed the emancipation of the slaves in Texas and called the Indians to his aid," read the *New York Herald*, a newspaper that supported the Democratic Party. "Santa Anna not only wars against the colonists of Texas, but he has unfurled the flag against the domestic institutions of the South and West."[39]

As General Houston's forces fled eastward, the Mexican Army scored triumph after triumph. It presided over the Texians' defeat at Nuestra Señora del Refugio Mission, and their surrender at Coleto Creek. The Mexican forces seemed on the cusp of victory when President Antonio López de Santa Anna made a fateful mistake. On April 20, 1836, he ordered his men onto a peninsula near Harrisburg, Texas. The only retreat was over a single bridge that spanned the San Jacinto River. Sensing an opportunity, Houston's forces quickly followed. After building a breastwork using trunks, baggage, packsaddles, and brush, they launched an attack that within eighteen minutes claimed the lives of six hundred Mexicans. After the Battle of San Jacinto, President Santa Anna fled into the marshes, dressed as a common soldier. The next day, the Texians found him, took him prisoner, and forced him to sign a treaty that ended the war.[40]

For years, the authorities in Mexico City feared losing Téjas to an invasion from the United States or an uprising among the Anglo colonists. Now that the province had won its independence, Mexican diplomats predicted that it would not take long for the United States to annex the Republic of Texas, with the ultimate aim of fortifying "the institutions peculiar to the Southern States" and opening "a new field for the execrable system of the slavery of the negroes." The Mexican minister in Washington expected that Texas would soon join the United

States as "four to five slave states" and that the secession of the Southern states would follow soon thereafter.[41]

THE SHINE OF INDEPENDENCE QUICKLY DIMMED IN THE REPUBLIC of Texas. Maintaining a separate government, with its judicial, executive, and legislative branches, its soldiers and diplomatic agents, was costly. To avoid such heavy expenses, the people of Texas voted to annex their fledgling republic to the United States in September 1836—a mere five months after the defeat of Santa Anna's army.[42]

Texians welcomed the possibility of joining a stable and prosperous democracy. Political participation was on the rise in the United States, as state legislatures abolished property requirements for voting. Between 1824 and 1836, the proportion of adult white males who voted nearly doubled from 25 percent to 58 percent. The states and territories were more connected than ever before. New technologies revolutionized travel, as steamships plied the major rivers of the United States, and railroad cars hurtled at speeds up to thirty miles an hour on an expanding network of tracks. Improvements in communication also made distant places seem closer and more familiar. Rotary presses churned out ten thousand pages an hour, transforming the grueling manual labor of typesetting into an industrial process. As the cost of printing decreased, readership exploded. By 1832, newspapers accounted for 95 percent of the weight of the mail transported by the US Post Office.[43]

The United States also experienced unprecedented economic growth, driven by the system of forced labor that in Mexico politicians tried to restrict. As cotton production expanded, the total value of goods produced in the United States increased by 38 percent from 1820 to 1829 and 36 percent from 1830 to 1836. Federal land sales skyrocketed from 1,930,000 acres in 1830 to 12,565,000 in 1835. By 1836, cotton grown by enslaved people in the Southern states accounted for more than half of the United States' total exports. To finance the economic expansion, the number of banks tripled from 307 in 1820 to 901 in 1840, while banking capital over that period surged from $102,000,000 to $358,000,000. The most important of these financial institutions was the Second Bank of the United States. Chartered in 1816, the Second Bank of the United States regulated the supply of money and credit by exchanging or holding banknotes issued by the hundreds of state banks across the nation.[44]

The United States also stood to benefit from annexing the Republic of Texas. With this acquisition, the United States would take control of the Gulf of Mexico. The US Army would be better able to stop Indian raids from the Great Plains. The markets for beef, pork, horses, mules, corn, hemp, and other agricultural products would expand. But annexation also threatened to undermine the political stability of the United States. Abolitionism was on the rise. On January 1, 1831, an abolitionist named William Lloyd Garrison published the first issue of the antislavery *Liberator* in Boston. In 1833, the same year that the British Empire freed the slaves in its colonies, Garrison founded the American Anti-Slavery Society, which would have 1,350 chapters and 25,000 members by 1836. Although most *norteamericanos* saw the Texas Revolution as an uprising against despotism, abolitionists condemned it as a war to preserve slavery. Late in 1835, David Lee Child, the husband of the abolitionist Lydia Maria Child, offered to recruit a corps made up "either wholly or principly [sic] of *colored* persons" to fight for the nation that had "done so much to establish real liberty and the imprescriptible, inalienable, and impartial rights of man." Benjamin Lundy, who tried to establish a free black colony in Mexico several years earlier, expressed the views of most abolitionists in the title of a pamphlet that he wrote in 1836: *The War in Texas: A Review of Facts and Circumstances, Showing That This Contest Is a Crusade Against Mexico, Set on Foot and Supported by Slaveholders, Land Speculators, &c., in Order to Re-establish, Extend, and Perpetuate the System of Slavery and the Slave Trade.*[45]

Northern congressmen also suspected that the Anglo colonists had rebelled against Mexico in defense of slavery. "One of the complaints made by the Texans is, that the Mexican government will not permit the introduction of slaves," observed state legislator William B. Reed of Pennsylvania on June 11, 1836, "and one of the first fruits of independence and secure liberty (natural as is the paradox) will be the extension of slavery . . . over the limits of a territory large enough to form five states as large as Pennsylvania." John Quincy Adams, the former president who went on to serve in the House of Representatives, described the Texas Revolution as "a war between slavery and emancipation." Adams opposed annexation as a matter of principle, as well as a matter of interest. The Mexican Army already promised freedom to slaves who reached its lines in Texas. No amount of diplomatic pressure would stop a weakened Mexican government from seeking the assistance of the recently removed Cherokees and the three million slaves in the Southern states. "And how far will it spread, sir, should a Mexican invader, with the torch of liberty in his hand, and the standard of freedom floating over his head, proclaiming emancipation to the slave and revenge to the native Indian, as he goes, invade your soil?"[46]

The constitution that the Republic of Texas drafted in the fall of 1836 only seemed to confirm that the Anglo colonists had taken up arms in defense of slavery. "All persons of color who were slaves for life previous to their emigration to Texas, and who are now held in bondage, shall remain in the like state of servitude," read the ninth section of the Constitution. "Congress shall pass no laws to prohibit emigrants from bringing their slaves into the republic with them, and holding them by the same tenure by which such slaves were held in the United States." The Whig *Pawtucket Chronicle* editorialized in 1837 that "the Americans then fought for their own liberty" and by extension, "the "liberty of the world," while the Texians fought for slavery and "the perpetuity of slavery throughout the world."[47]

The connection between slavery and the Texas Revolution made annexation a divisive issue. Any suggestion that the Jackson administration had annexed Texas in order to expand the power of the slaveholding south threatened to jeopardize the Democratic Party's northern support. Jackson could not hazard such a risk, particularly during an election year, when his handpicked successor, Martin Van Buren, was running for president. Although Jackson would not entertain proposals of annexation, he did take another unusual step. Ten months after Santa Anna's defeat, the Jackson administration recognized Texas's independence, claiming that this decision acknowledged by law what Texas had established in fact. Mexican officials, who insisted that the Texas Revolution was unjustified and the newly founded republic illegitimate, were taken aback. Who could think that the upstart colonists had already proved themselves capable of independence? Texas's Congress still convened in a tavern. The documents that it printed contained a disproportionate number of typographical errors. As Britain's Secretary of War observed, the Texians were, literally and figuratively, "a *nation of herdsmen.*"[48]

Recognizing Texas's independence seemed to tip the United States' hand. By extending diplomatic recognition, Mexicans reasoned, the *norteamericanos* clearly hoped that other nations would follow suit. The greater the number that recognized Texas, the easier it would be for the United States to justify its annexation at a later date. Against such a threat, Mexican leaders felt they had little recourse. The recently defeated army was in no position to mount another invasion, and Mexico's diplomatic corps lacked leverage to pressure foreign governments. Worse still, the treasury was empty, and the citizenry demoralized. But, despite its weak hand, the Mexican government still had one card to play.

ON APRIL 5, 1837, A LINE OF BLACK CARRIAGES MADE ITS WAY through the streets of Mexico City, past the priest in his cowl, the leper in his serape, the *gallinera* with her crate of hens, a letter-writer-for-hire with a board on his knees, charging 6.5 cents for a scolding letter and twice as much for a declaration of love. At the National Palace, the carriages converged. Mexico's Congress was in session.[49]

None of the bills under consideration that day was particularly contentious, and the velvet seats in the legislative hall were unevenly occupied. During that day's session, the deputies discussed the military honors to be awarded to the navy for its defense of Tampico during the Spanish invasion in 1829, the duties to be charged on the 275 crates of paper imported to print Manuel de la Peña y Peña's *Lecciones de práctica forense*, and, finally, a proposed decree to abolish slavery "without exception" that they had been discussing since November of the previous year. For nearly two decades, Mexico's national government had resisted abolition for fear of disregarding the "property" rights of slaveholders in Téjas and, in the process, igniting a revolt. Now, however, there was little sense of hesitation or division. The congressmen voted unanimously in favor of abolition.[50]

That Mexico's Congress abolished slavery in the wake of the Texas Revolution was no coincidence. The loss of Texas eliminated one of the largest slaveholding regions in Mexico. Because the Anglo colonists had revolted, the national authorities were under no obligation to compensate them for any loss. Only the slaveholders in Texas who remained loyal would be compensated for their slaves under the new abolition law.[51]

If the costs of abolition were less, the benefits appeared greater. The Mexican government was in no position to press its claims to Texas by force. Mexico had defaulted on its international loans ten years earlier. The annual deficit exceeded eighteen million pesos in 1837. Sonora, Puebla, and Oaxaca were in revolt. Yucatán was on the verge of declaring independence. In 1843, Mexico's minister of war estimated that it would cost twenty-two million pesos to put down these insurrections— nearly double the *total* annual revenues.[52]

Ending slavery allowed Mexicans to assume the mantle of righteousness. José María Tornel, who served as minister of war during the Texas Revolution, denied that the Texians had taken up arms for liberty. Instead they had broken Mexico's laws and turned the province into "a mart of human flesh, where the slaves of the south might be sold and others from Africa might be introduced." Mexico's abolition legislation only seemed to confirm that the Texas Revolution was a conflict between slavery and freedom.[53]

In addition, the new legislation allowed Mexicans to find victory in defeat. Mexican diplomats did not hesitate to point out that Texians, for all their talk of "liberty" and "rights of man," were destroying the "true liberty" of slaves. This sentiment was a powerful antidote to the demoralization that accompanied military defeat. If Christianity promised justice only in the next life, the antislavery law could still deliver a striking moral triumph in the here and now. The Anglo-Americans might boast of their military successes, but only Mexico could stand "upright" before the world. As Mexico's Secretary of State would later boast: "Let the world now say which of the two has reason and justice on its side."[54]

Abolishing slavery also transformed a question of national honor into a matter of common humanity, galvanizing support for Mexico's government around the world. European governments expressed dismay at the developments in the Gulf of Mexico. In Paris, members of the Chamber of Deputies argued against recognizing Texas's independence by pointing out how glaringly the colonists had flouted Mexico's antislavery laws. British diplomats decried the "restless and roving propensity" of *norteamericanos*. "I see more reason to hope for the improvement and safe keeping of the principles of true freedom and real liberality certainly in Prussia, or even in Austria, or Russia, than in the United States of America," the British minister Charles Elliot wrote from Mexico. To maintain a balance of power in the Americas, British diplomats advised keeping Mexico's weight on the scales. "We should use every fair means to prevent an ally from being ruined, that can serve us in time of need," cautioned one consul, "and this Mexico can evidently do in the event of a war with the United States of America."[55]

Although European support for Mexico would wane in the next several years, abolition did secure another, more lasting alliance. Free blacks in the United States signed petitions and organized meetings in protest of the annexation of Texas. Enslaved people escaped in droves to the south, undercutting the fledgling republic at the moment it most needed to gain the respect of the international community. "The African race is beginning to wake up," Mexico's minister to the United States wrote to the Department of Relations. "In the case of a war between Mexico and this country, we should count on them."[56]

JOE, THE SLAVE OF THE LATE WILLIAM BARRET TRAVIS, PAID CLOSE attention to these developments. On the evening of April 27, 1837, he drove a carriage into Houston. Eight months earlier, the town consisted of a single log cabin, barely visible behind the brush that lined the banks of Buffalo Bayou. By the time Joe arrived at the capital, Houston was transformed, with over a hundred houses in various states of construction.[57]

Joe stopped the carriage in front of a two-story frame building, where a ball was being held to commemorate the Battle of San Jacinto. Although Joe fought at the Alamo, the invitation printed on white satin was not for him. Instead it was addressed to John Rice Jones, the first postmaster of the Republic of Texas and the executor of William Barret Travis's estate. From the box seat of the carriage, Joe watched as Jones and his wife stepped onto the street and strode toward the brightly lit house. Then Joe flicked the reins and kept moving.[58]

At a safe distance from the ball, Joe unhitched the horses from the carriage. Still dressed in his white cotton pantaloons and dark satinet vest, he coaxed a bit into the mouth of the small bay horse that, like Joe himself, belonged to the estate of William Barret Travis. A Mexican servant named Domingo, who also accompanied Jones to Houston, swung a Spanish-style, Texas-made saddle, covered in blue cloth, onto another horse, a chestnut sorrel. To Joe and Domingo, the anniversary of the

Battle of San Jacinto was not an occasion to celebrate an independence movement waged in defense of slavery; instead it was an opportunity to seize the freedom that Mexico promised in the wake of the Texas Revolution. As John Rice Jones and his wife toasted General Sam Houston for defeating the Mexican Army, Joe and Domingo mounted the horses and spurred them south and west.[59]

SEVEN

ANNEXATION

W HEN THE TEXAS MINISTER TO THE UNITED STATES, MEMU-
can Hunt Jr., presented a formal proposal of annexation on
August 4, 1837, President Martin Van Buren hesitated. The economy
of the United States was beginning to falter, and Van Buren's predeces-
sor in the White House, Andrew Jackson, was at least partly responsible. Distrustful of banks in general and the Second Bank of the United
States in particular, Jackson directed his Secretary of the Treasury to
withdraw federal deposits from the national bank. In 1834, a former
slaveholder from Maryland named Roger Taney, who would go on to
serve on the Supreme Court, carried out the president's orders. After
withdrawing federal funds from the Second Bank of the United States,
Taney deposited them in state-chartered banks. British creditors, who
had invested heavily in the United States, panicked.[1]

In March 1837, just after Martin Van Buren took the oath of office, an economic recession swept across the United States. Prices rose.
Major banks closed. Nearly a third of the population of New York

City became unemployed as businesses declared bankruptcy. The older brother of the writer Herman Melville, Gansevoort, shuttered his hat and fur shop in Albany, New York, forcing Herman to take a series of jobs on whalers and merchant ships to help support their fatherless family. Another writer, Ralph Waldo Emerson, captured the sense of desperation that had fallen over the United States. "Cold April; men breaking who ought not to break; banks bullied into the bolstering of desperate speculators; all of the newspapers a chorus of owls," he wrote in his journal.[2]

The Panic of 1837 united the Whig Party, so called because they opposed Andrew Jackson and his successor, Martin Van Buren, as the revolutionary Whigs in England had opposed George III. The Whigs included strong nationalists, like Senator Henry Clay of Kentucky, who defended the national banking system that Democrats opposed. But the coalition also included states' rights advocates who opposed what they considered to be Jackson's excessive use of presidential power, particularly during the Nullification Crisis of 1833, when the South Carolina legislature refused to enforce a tariff that it deemed unconstitutional. The Whigs agreed on so little that some contemporaries insisted that they did not constitute a formal political party at all. But by the time that Martin Van Buren took office, the Whigs had an issue upon which their diverse coalition could agree: the Democratic Party was to blame for the Panic of 1837.[3]

With the economy in a tailspin, and his presidency in crisis, Van Buren was wary to accept the proposal from the Texas minister. Annexing Texas was likely to provoke a war with Mexico. Moreover, the Republic of Texas had racked up $1.25 million in debts since declaring its independence, and the United States was in no position to assume responsibility for those debts. What concerned Martin Van Buren most, though, was that annexation would divide the United States—not between Whigs and Democrats, but between North and South.[4]

ACROSS THE NATION, *NORTEAMERICANOS* VOICED THEIR CONCERNS about the annexation of Texas. Some argued that the Union was already large enough, and that any further expansion would, in the words of one state legislator in Ohio, "certainly and naturally tend to weaken and destroy those bonds of union" of "our already Colossal Confederacy." Others pointed out that annexation would almost certainly lead to armed conflict. "We could not incorporate Texas into the Union without involving the United States in a war with Mexico," Senator Henry Clay of Kentucky explained, "and, I suppose, nobody would think it wise or proper to engage in war with Mexico for the acquisition of Texas." Still others argued that annexation was unconstitutional. "If we have the power to annex Texas, we have the power to annex Cuba, Great Britain & even all of Europe," a constituent wrote to Representative Daniel Barringer of North Carolina. "No such power [is] to be found in this constitution."[5]

No argument against annexation was stronger—at least for Northern voters—than the one that William Ellery Channing made in a public letter to Senator Henry Clay on August 1, 1837. Channing, a Unitarian minister at the Federal Street Church in Boston, argued against annexation on the grounds that the Texians had taken up arms in defense of slavery. Channing explained that the Mexican government had prohibited the importation of enslaved people. "It is a matter of deep grief and humiliation," the minister wrote, "that the emigrants from this country, whilst boasting of superior civilization, refused to second this honorable policy, intended to set limits to one of the greatest social evils." Channing recounted how *norteamericanos* introduced slaves "under formal indentures for long periods, in some cases it is said for ninety-nine years," only to have the legislature of Coahuila y Téjas block their subterfuge by canceling any contract whose term exceeded ten years. "This settled, invincible purpose of Mexico to exclude slavery from her limits created as strong a purpose to annihilate her authority in Texas." The cause of Texas, Channing concluded, was the cause of slavery. "Are we

prepared to couple with the name of our country the infamy of deliberately *spreading* slavery? And especially of spreading it through regions
from which the wise and humane legislation of a neighboring republic
had excluded it?" he demanded. "We call Mexico a semi-barbarous people; and yet we talk of planting slavery where Mexico would not suffer
it to live."[6]

Southern voters were irate that Northerners would oppose annexation on the grounds that slavery existed in Texas. "To refuse to extend
to the Southern and Western States any advantage which would tend to
strengthen or render them more secure, or increase their limits, or population, by the annexation of new territory or States, on the assumption
or under the pretext that the institution of slavery, as it exists among
them, is immoral, or sinful, or otherwise obnoxious would be contrary
to that equality of rights and advantages which the constitution was
intended to secure alike to all members of the Union," argued John C.
Calhoun in 1837. "It is vain to arrest the course of things," the proslavery Washington, DC, *Telegraph* wrote the same year. "Slavery will exist
until men, of their own accord change their opinions."[7]

Annexation threatened to divide the United States between the
slaveholding South and the nonslaveholding North. On January 4,
1838, Senator William Preston of South Carolina drafted a resolution
calling on Congress to annex Texas as soon as it could be accomplished
"consistently with the faith and treaty stipulations of the United States."
When the resolution came to a vote six months later, it exposed the
depth of the division between North and South over Texas. Six of the
seven state delegations that voted unanimously against annexation were
"free" states. The five that voted unanimously for it were slave states.
When Representative Waddy Thompson proposed a similar measure in
the House of Representatives, John Quincy Adams railed against it for
the last three weeks that Congress was in session. Eight states issued
resolutions in protest. Petitions, memorials, and resolutions flooded
Congress. The House Committee on Foreign Affairs measured the cor-

respondence that it received on the subject "by cubic feet." One of the petitions against annexation included six hundred thousand signatures.[8]

President Martin Van Buren, who spent most of his career trying to forge the Democratic Party into a national political coalition, wanted to avoid sectional controversy. Annexing Texas as a slave state would only add to the turmoil unleashed by the financial panic. Unwilling to hazard a political firestorm over the issue, the Van Buren administration notified the Texas minister that it would not pursue annexation in the next session. On October 12, 1838, Texas diplomats formally withdrew the annexation proposal.[9]

AFTER THE REPUBLIC OF TEXAS REVOKED ITS OFFER OF ANNEX-ation, Martin Van Buren turned his attention back to the Panic of 1837. In 1840, the president issued an executive order that limited the workday of federal workers on public works projects to ten hours, without any reduction in pay. That same year, on the president's recommendation, Congress established an independent treasury. Van Buren hoped that an independent treasury would help to avoid another financial panic, but this measure was not enough to shake off his nickname, Martin Van Ruin. Nor did it reverse his flagging prospects for reelection.[10]

In the Election of 1840, Van Buren ran against the elderly war hero William Henry Harrison, who had famously defeated the Shawnee leader Tecumseh at the Battle of Tippecanoe in 1811. The Whigs described their candidate as a man of the people, who was born in a log cabin and who displayed a down-home fondness for hard cider. (Harrison had, in fact, grown up in a brick mansion on the banks of the James River in Virginia.) In the months before the election, *norteamericanos* could purchase everything from Tippecanoe Tobacco to Tippecanoe Shaving Soap or Log-Cabin Emollient. At the Whig convention in Baltimore, Harrison supporters rolled a stuffed leather ball, eight or nine feet in diameter, inscribed with the comic verse: "Farewell, dear Van / You're not our man; / To guide the ship / We'll try Old Tip."[11]

Frustrated by the Panic of 1837 and energized by the log cabin campaign, two and a half million voters went to the polls in the fall of 1840. With 80 percent of adult white men voting, the Whigs won majorities in the House and the Senate. And their candidate, William Henry Harrison, took the White House, winning 234 electoral votes to Van Buren's 60. At sixty-eight, Harrison was the oldest president yet elected. His age proved to be an enormous liability. A month after taking office, he died of pneumonia.[12]

Harrison's vice president was John Tyler. A Virginian by birth, Tyler won election to the state House of Delegates at age twenty-one. He went on to serve in the governor's house, in the US Senate, and in the House of Representatives. The nominating convention added John Tyler to the ticket in order to secure the votes of the Whigs who advocated for Southern rights and state sovereignty. Tyler objected to nearly every plank of his party's platform. He favored a limited government, while the Whig platform envisioned an activist one. He dismissed tariffs as unconstitutional, while the platform saw them as essential to promoting domestic industries. He thought that the individual states should build roads and dig canals, while the platform asserted that the federal government should fund such internal improvements. After Harrison's death, party leaders realized their mistake. The man who would now occupy the White House was, in the words of George W. Julian of Indiana, "not a Whig in any sense."[13]

John Tyler arrived in Washington, DC, on April 6, 1841, to find the houses draped in black crepe and the flags at half-mast. The political elite in the capital lamented his arrival as much as they mourned Harrison's death. Andrew Jackson called the vice president "an imbecile." John Quincy Adams railed against the White House being occupied by "a man never thought for it by anybody." Tyler, on the other hand, thought of himself as an "instrument of Providence" and an heir to another president from Virginia, Thomas Jefferson. In the same way that Jefferson negotiated the Louisiana Purchase, Tyler hoped to annex the Republic of Texas. "Could anything throw so bright a luster around us?" he asked Secretary of State Daniel Webster in October 1841. "I really believe [that] it could be done." First, though, Tyler had to win over the Northern public. His greatest asset in this endeavor was neither a member of his own administration nor even a diplomat from the Republic of Texas, but a Kentucky-born newspaper editor named Duff Green.[14]

DUFF GREEN ARRIVED IN LONDON IN THE SPRING OF 1843. IT WAS his second trip in as many years. The first time he acted as an unofficial agent of the United States government, with instructions to pressure the British authorities to reverse their restrictive trade policies and to monitor their diplomacy in Texas. Now he came as a private citizen, though with much the same aim in mind. He wrote to British statesmen. He attended debates at the House of Commons. He made a case for free trade to Prime Minister Robert Peel. Even as a private citizen, Green wielded influence. "I am one of the American people who in the United States direct and control the government itself," he explained to the prime minister.[15]

Duff Green's claims to power were only a slight exaggeration. Born near Versailles, Kentucky, in 1791, Green speculated in lands, invested in railroads, and purchased lead and copper mines. But his greatest ambition was to harness the new, inexpensive printing technologies of his era to champion the cause of state sovereignty and Southern rights. In 1823, Green purchased the *St. Louis Inquirer* in order to promote the presidential campaign of General Andrew Jackson. Although Jackson lost the election the following year, Green was determined to help his candidate take the White House in the next election. In 1828, Green moved to Washington, DC, and took over the *United States Telegraph*. He used the pages of his new newspaper to defend Andrew Jackson against charges of adultery, dueling, bigamy, and murder, among other transgressions. He also used the *Telegraph* to attack Jackson's enemies, and he did not limit those assaults to the printed word. In 1828, he walked into the rooms of the Senate Committee on Claims and bludgeoned a reporter for the *National Intelligencer* who had, apparently, misquoted a report from the *Telegraph*. Two years later, at the entrance to the US Capitol, Green drew a pistol on an editor who had proposed that Martin Van Buren, a Northerner, succeed Andrew Jackson as president.[16]

As an unabashed defender of slavery, Duff Green was in favor of annexing Texas. During his second trip to England, he gleaned something "from a source entitled to the fullest confidence" that he believed would unite the Northern public behind annexation. According to Green, British leaders had come to the conclusion that enslaved labor was both cheaper and more efficient than free labor and that Parliament's decision to abolish slavery in 1833 had put British planters at a disadvantage on the global market. The only way for Britain to remove this handicap was to convince its competitors, especially Cuba, Brazil, Texas, and the United States, to abolish slavery as well. To that end, the British authorities allegedly offered to guarantee a loan to the Texas government on the condition that it abolish slavery. A Texas lawyer named Stephen Pearl Andrews was already on his way to London to try to organize a company "who shall advance a sum sufficient to pay for the slaves now in Texas, and receive in payment Texas lands." The obvious intention of "purchasing and emancipating the slaves of Texas," Green wrote to the US Secretary of State, was not only to end human bondage in Texas, but to incite "rebellion and servile war in the South."[17]

Duff Green's letter from London arrived in Washington, DC, four months after Daniel Webster resigned as Secretary of State. President Tyler nominated his Secretary of the Navy, Abel P. Upshur, to replace Webster. Upshur had distinguished himself as Secretary of the Navy, overseeing, among other things, the construction of the *Princeton*, a state-of-the-art warship, mounted with two 228-pounder cannons and propelled by a six-bladed screw instead of the usual paddle wheel. Now, as Secretary of State, Upshur was determined to negotiate the annexation of Texas. "I do not care to control any measure of policy except this," he wrote to a friend.[18]

Abel Upshur had reason to be skeptical of Duff Green's report. Only the British cabinet or parliament itself could have approved a loan to the Republic of Texas, and there was no evidence to suggest that either had done so. Any campaign to abolish slavery stood at odds with the primary aim of British diplomacy, which was to prevent the US government from annexing Texas. "*There* lies the danger to the Maritime and Commercial supremacy of Great Britain," wrote the British consul in Galveston in 1845. For the "security and tranquility" of North America, British leaders encouraged the Mexican government to recognize the independence of Texas—with or without slavery. In their own negotiations with the Republic of Texas, Britain's Secretary of State for Foreign Relations cautioned against making "the question of the Slave Trade a *champ de bataille* in any discussion" for fear that it would drive the leaders of the new republic to seek annexation.[19]

Though British leaders were not conspiring to abolish slavery in Texas, another government was. Mexico's Congress refused to ratify any treaty with Texas "except on the basis of reannexation and the abolition of slavery." In 1841, Mexico's minister of war ordered the decree abolishing the slave trade to be printed in Spanish, English, and French, and posted in the "most public places" in Texas. That same year, fourteen hundred Mexican troops seized the city of San Antonio and the nearby towns of Goliad and Refugio.[20]

Texians complained that their slaves displayed "a very refractory disposition" and blamed the Mexican government for sending emissaries "to excite an insurrection." In 1842, a Mexican man had both of his ears cut off for "lurking upon a plantation near San Felipe" and "enticing several of [the] slaves to run away with him to Mexico." That same summer, a Mexican man stole "two fine horses" and rode toward the Rio Grande with an enslaved woman "with whom he had been living as a wife." The Texians who pursued and eventually overtook them promptly hanged the Mexican from the nearest tree.[21]

The threat of the Mexican Army marching across Texas also struck fear in the hearts of *norteamericanos*. The *New-Orleans Commercial Bulletin* reminded "the slaveholders of the United States" that the Mexican soldiers who would march on Texas were "avowed abolitionists." Representative Henry A. Wise of Virginia warned that "the tyrant of Mexico" would invade Texas and "never stop till he had driven slavery beyond the Sabine" and forced back "the slaves of Texas . . . upon Louisiana and Arkansas." If Mexico reconquered Texas and abolished slavery, Secretary of State Upshur predicted that the territory would "afford a ready refuge for the fugitive slaves of Louisiana and Arkansas, and would hold to them an encouragement to run away, which no municipal regulations of those states could possible counteract."[22]

In his official capacity as Secretary of State, Abel P. Upshur disclaimed any concern about abolition in Mexico, insisting that the federal government did "not possess" and would "never attempt to exercise, any authority" over slavery "as a domestic question." So long as the Mexican government claimed jurisdiction over Texas, it could send as many decrees as it pleased. Yet to Upshur, Duff Green's letter gave this question "a different aspect." For a European country to interfere with the domestic institutions of any nation in the Americas violated an obscure principle that President James Monroe had included in his annual message to Congress in December 1823. The Monroe Doctrine, as pro-annexationists termed it, forbade European interference in the Americas. If Britain's "policy were confined to her own dominions, we should have no right to complain," wrote Upshur in 1843. "But if it be her purpose to extend her policy to other countries, and to use her influence to bring about a state of things calculated seriously to affect the institutions of nearly half the states of our Union, the duty which we owe, not only to our interests, but to our independence and dignity, demands a prompt and decided counteraction on our part."[23]

Crediting Mexico's antislavery policies to Great Britain made annexation into an issue of national security, not sectional partisanship. To drum up support for annexation, US newspapers made "strenuous endeavors" to "create and fix the impression that Mexico was secretly prompted by England in her persevering hostility to Texas." The *Pennsylvanian*, which supported the Democratic Party, wrote that "foreign European powers, and England especially, are striving by every art . . . to obtain influences and privileges there which must be adverse to the United States, and deeply injurious to their interests and commerce." The *Philadelphia Ledger* agreed. "Let us suppose that Britain seeks a colonization, or offensive and defensive alliance with Texas, and then ask what, in such a contingency, is our duty? Our reply is annexation." It did not seem to matter that British diplomats were making no effort to abolish slavery in Texas. "No falsehood is too rampant to serve the purpose of the hour," wrote the British consul in Galveston.[24]

On February 27, 1844, Abel P. Upshur and the Texas negotiator Isaac Van Zandt finished drafting a treaty of annexation. Texas agreed to cede all of its territory to the United States. In return, the US government would assume Texas's debts. To guarantee "the liberty and property" of the citizens of Texas, the existing laws would "remain in force" until "further provision shall be made." All that remained to be done was to sign the treaty and send it to both governments for ratification.[25]

THE DAY AFTER UPSHUR FINISHED THE TEXAS NEGOTIATIONS, HE took a carriage to the waterfront outside of Washington, DC. The *Princeton*, the steam-powered warship that he commissioned as Secretary of the Navy, had been completed the previous year and was now anchored in the Potomac River. Captain Robert F. Stockton, who commanded the vessel, organized a cruise to show off the warship to members of the government and their families. Upshur received an invitation. So did President John Tyler, Secretary of the Navy Thomas Gilmer, the

Mexican ambassador Juan Almonte, the Texas negotiator Isaac Van Zandt, and seventy-five-year-old former First Lady Dolley Madison. On February 28, 1844, four hundred men and women gathered at the waterfront to board the launches that would ferry them to the *Princeton*, anchored in the channel of the Potomac, half a mile away.[26]

Even from shore, the ship looked impressive, with three masts and flags flying from the rigging. Beneath the waterline was the innovative six-bladed screw that powered the *Princeton* forward. But what most impressed the guests as they stepped on board the ship were the two enormous guns mounted on the deck. John Ericsson, the Swedish-born inventor who designed the *Princeton*, built one of the cannons. Nicknamed the Oregon, the cannon was fifteen feet long with a twelve-inch bore. The breech where the shot was loaded was reinforced with wrought iron that was heated and then shrunk—a process that strengthened the material so that the breech would not burst when the gun was fired. Captain Stockton built the second gun, but rather than go through the cumbersome process of heating and shrinking the wrought iron, he decided simply to reinforce the breech with more wrought iron. Stockton named his thirteen-and-a-half-ton gun the Peacemaker. He tested the gun a half dozen times, certified it as sound, and dismissed Ericsson's concerns about the design as jealous nitpicking.[27]

After the four hundred passengers boarded the ship on February 28, 1844, the six-bladed screw began to turn and the *Princeton* gained speed. Near Alexandria, a crowd gathered at the wharf gave three cheers. The ship band struck up "Hail Columbia," while the crew fired a twenty-six-gun salute, one for every state in the Union. Soon, Abel P. Upshur knew, US naval officers would have to fire an extra shot for Texas.[28]

On reaching the lower Potomac, where the river widened, Stockton ordered a demonstration of the Peacemaker. The passengers gathered on the deck plugged their ears as the gun was fired, watching in amazement as the 228-pound shot hurtled across the estuary. The passengers tried to keep track of how many times the ball struck the water before sinking. Some counted seven, others fifteen or sixteen. Stockton ordered one more shot fired and then announced that it was time for lunch. The tables below deck were piled high with "every delicacy of the season"— fruit, ham, and roast fowl. President Tyler proposed a toast. "To the three big guns—the Peacemaker, the Oregon, and Captain Stockton!"[29]

Near the end of the luncheon, Thomas Gilmer, who took over from Upshur as Secretary of the Navy, asked for another demonstration, and Stockton obliged. A hundred or so people were milling about the deck as the sailors swung the thirteen-and-a-half-ton gun into position. Stockton placed his foot nonchalantly on the carriage, but when the firing hammer released, flames suddenly burst from the breech. A cloud of white powder smoke filled the air. Two tons of wrought iron—a piece of the breech—flew backward, pinning three men against the deck. As the smoke cleared, the people on deck began to make out the bodies. Abel Upshur and Thomas Gilmer were dead; as were Captain Beverley Kennon, chief of the Bureau of Construction of the US Navy; Virgil Maxcy, who had just returned from a diplomatic posting in The Hague; and David Gardiner, a former New York state senator. Two sailors and President Tyler's enslaved butler, Henry, were also killed. No one spoke. Captain Stockton stood, his hair singed, his face blackened with powder, unable to form words. On the water floated ten or twelve hats, blown off by the explosion.[30]

PRESIDENT TYLER WAS DETERMINED NOT TO LET UPSHUR'S DEATH derail the annexation of Texas. Within a matter of weeks, he nominated a new Secretary of State: the outspoken proslavery politician from South Carolina, John C. Calhoun. Even more than Upshur, Calhoun was convinced that slavery was essential to "free and stable political institutions." "There is and always has been, in an advanced stage of wealth and civilization, a conflict between labor and capital," as he saw it. "The condition of society in the South exempts us from the disorders and dangers resulting from this condition; and this explains why it is that the political condition of the slaveholding States has been so much more stable and quiet than the North"—to say nothing of Mexico. Abolish slavery, Calhoun warned, and "the next step would be to raise the negroes to a social and political equality with the whites." Democracy, as *norteamericanos* knew it, would be over.[31]

To defend the entwined institutions of slavery and democracy, Calhoun wasted no time in wrapping up the details of annexation. Arriving in Washington, DC, at the end of March, he signed the treaty of annexation two weeks later, on April 12, 1844. But before he forwarded the treaty to the Senate, Calhoun decided to respond to a letter from Lord Aberdeen that the British minister, Richard Pakenham, had forwarded to the State Department on February 26. Calhoun intended to send his response to the Senate, along with the treaty of annexation.[32]

In his letter, Lord Aberdeen denied the rumors that the British government was conspiring to abolish slavery across North America. "The British Government, as the United States well know, have never sought in any way to stir up disaffection or excitement of any kind in the slaveholding States of the American Union." According to Lord Aberdeen, the Foreign Office had done everything in its power to stop slave uprisings in North America, including preventing an alliance between Mexico and Haiti in 1829. "We shall never interfere unduly or with an improper assumption of authority," Lord Aberdeen continued, though he acknowledged that "it must be and is well known, both to the United States and to the whole world; that Great Britain desires, and is constantly exerting herself to procure, the general abolition of slavery throughout the world."[33]

Calhoun took no comfort in knowing that the British government had done nothing "secretly or underhand." To him, *any* interference with slavery was unacceptable. Calhoun spent a week furiously drafting a response explaining his position. In dense, legalistic prose, Calhoun acknowledged that "no other country had a right to complain" when the British government abolished "slavery in her own possessions and colonies." But, he continued, "when she goes beyond and avows it as her settled policy and the object of her constant exertions, to abolish it throughout the world, she makes it the duty of all other countries, whose safety or prosperity may be endangered by her policy, to adopt such measures as they may deem necessary for their protection." Slavery was "essential to the peace, safety, and prosperity of those States of the Union in which it exists." To preserve US slavery in the face of British opposition, Calhoun argued, the US government had no choice but to annex the Republic of Texas.[34]

Calhoun included his response to the British minister in the packet of documents he sent to the Senate along with the treaty. By justifying annexation in terms of slavery rather than the Monroe Doctrine, the letter made annexation, in the words of one Northern senator, "odious in the north & peculiarly a southern question." On June 8, the Senate rejected the treaty, 35 to 16.[35]

THE SENATE VOTE WAS A RELIEF TO MARTIN VAN BUREN, THE former president who refused to annex Texas in 1837, and who was now the frontrunner for the Democratic presidential nomination. A few weeks before the treaty came up for a vote, Van Buren wrote a letter arguing against annexation on the grounds that it would destroy the union and provoke an unjust war with Mexico. When the Washington *Globe* ran Van Buren's letter, Southern members of his party were outraged. But Van Buren doubted that their protests would prevent him from winning the Democratic nomination in 1844. The Whig candidate, Henry Clay of Kentucky, also opposed annexation, which meant that the issue would not be disputed in the presidential race.[36]

But Van Buren miscalculated. Enthusiasm for annexation was growing, and at the Democratic Convention, held in Baltimore in late May 1844, he failed to secure enough votes to become the nominee. Instead the party selected a little-known politician from Tennessee named James K. Polk. Polk's political career was undistinguished. The previous

year, he ran for governor of Tennessee and lost. But Polk had one char-
acteristic that the other candidates did not. He was unabashedly in favor
of annexation. "It is impossible to arrest the current of the popular opinion," Polk wrote to another politician from Tennessee, "and any man
who attempts it will be crushed by it."[37]

Now that the Democrats had their candidate, the delegates at the
convention set to work drafting a platform. To make expansion appealing to Northern and Southern Democrats, they called not only for the
annexation of Texas but also the occupation of the entire Oregon Territory. The exact borders of the Oregon Territory had been under dispute since the early nineteenth century, and every attempt to resolve the
conflict had failed. In 1818, United States diplomats proposed drawing
the border at the forty-ninth parallel, but British negotiators insisted on
retaining control of the Columbia River. The two sides remained at an
impasse, until the expansionists in the United States began to demand
a boundary even farther north. Their rallying cry—"Fifty-four forty or
fight!"—became Polk's campaign slogan.[38]

The Whig nominee, Henry Clay, opposed annexation on the
grounds that it would provoke an unjust war with Mexico. But now that
he was running against an avowed annexationist, he hedged his position,
explaining that he could "have no objection to the annexation of Texas"
if the Mexican government consented. By bringing his position closer
to Polk's, Clay hoped to neutralize the annexation issue. But Clay's waf-
fling did little to convince white Southerners that he would champion
annexation. At the same time, it led at least some Northerners to cast
their ballots for the Liberty Party, a coalition of Whigs and Democrats
whose presidential candidate, James Birney, promised to take more ac-
tive measures against slavery.[39]

The November election was close. Polk won, with 38,000 more votes
than Clay, out of 2.7 million cast. If Clay had attracted just 5,107 more
votes in New York State, he would have won the Electoral College. Despite these thin margins, Democrats took Polk's victory as a mandate
to annex Texas. "The decision of the people and the States on this great

and interesting subject has been decisively manifested," the outgoing president John Tyler explained in his annual message to Congress on December 3, 1844. "A controlling majority of the people and a large majority of the States have declared in favor of immediate annexation." Tyler urged Congress to act quickly. Negotiating another treaty would take months, and the resulting agreement might again fail to secure the required two-thirds majority in the Senate. In his annual message, Tyler recommended that Congress issue a joint resolution in favor of annexation, which would avoid lengthy discussions with Texas, and could be enacted with a simple majority in both houses.[40]

Drafting a joint resolution meant that the two houses of Congress would have to agree upon the terms of annexation—not an insignificant feat. Texas's debts had skyrocketed from $1.25 million in 1836 to $9.9 million in 1845, raising the question of whether the United States government should agree to repay those loans. The borders of the Republic of Texas were also under dispute. According to the Texians, the boundary was the Rio Grande, from its mouth to its source. But the Mexican government placed the border at the Nueces River, a hundred miles north. "Would we take 2,000 miles of the Canadas in the same way?" Senator Thomas Hart Benton of Missouri asked. "I presume not. And why not? Because Great Britain is powerful and Mexico weak."[41]

Another source of controversy was the issue of slavery. Some congressmen opposed annexation under any circumstances, because it would, in the words of Representative Freeman H. Morse of Maine, lead to the "perpetuation of slavery." Other congressmen advocated extending the Missouri Compromise line to Texas. On January 13, 1845, Representative Milton Brown of Tennessee proposed a resolution to admit Texas as a state, from which four additional states could be formed. "Such states as may be formed out of that portion of said territory lying south of 36 degrees and thirty minutes north latitude, commonly known as the Missouri compromise line, shall be admitted into the Union, with or without slavery as the people of such State asking admission may desire." (The Republic of Texas claimed, rather dubiously, to extend as far north as the forty-second parallel, the same latitude as Boston.[42])

No politician, however, proposed to restrict or abolish slavery where it existed in Texas, as James Tallmadge had during the debates over the admission of Missouri. The fact that no congressman even raised this possibility spoke to the growing consensus, particularly among Democrats, that the legislative branch could neither abolish slavery where it existed nor establish it where it did not. Unlike the Mexican government, which sought to restrict slavery at both the state and national levels, the United States Congress followed the principle of noninterference. This point of agreement helped to prevent a major sectional controversy over the status of slavery in Texas. On January 25, 1845, the House of Representatives voted on a resolution to admit Texas as a state, from which up to four additional states could be formed "with or without slavery, as the people of each State asking admission may desire." The measure also required that the United States government assume responsibility for Texas's debts and adjust "all questions of boundary that may arise with other Governments." The resolution passed, 120 to 98. But when the House resolution went to the Senate, the Committee on Foreign Relations rejected it. The only measure that the Senate managed to pass was an appropriation of one hundred thousand dollars to fund annexation negotiations with the Republic of Texas.[43]

To avoid a showdown between the two houses, Senator Robert Walker proposed combining both bills and letting the president decide which to sign. After President-elect James K. Polk intimated that he would sign the Senate bill to open negotiations with Texas, rather than the House bill to annex the Republic, the Senate narrowly approved the joint resolution, 27 to 25. A day later, on February 28, the House followed suit. When the joint resolution arrived at the White House, the outgoing President John Tyler did not know whether he should decide between the two bills, or if he should leave the choice to his successor. On March 3, with only one day remaining in his term, he signed the bill from the House of Representatives to admit Texas as the twenty-eighth state.[44]

"COULD PROCEEDINGS MORE HOSTILE ON THE PART OF THE UNITED States have taken place?" asked Secretary of State José María Bocanegra of Mexico. Annexing a territory claimed by a friendly power violated the Law of Nations. To do so in defense of slavery, the Mexican Congress resolved, was a "monstrous novelty dangerous to the peace of the world and the sovereignty of nations." Many Mexicans hoped that Britain would declare war on the United States. But, distracted by the continued disintegration of the Ottoman Empire and other affairs in Europe, the British did little more than look on "with amazement."[45]

The Mexican government had long threatened that it would take war to the slave states in the event that the United States annexed Texas. As early as 1830, Lucas Alamán, the conservative minister of relations, explained that if the *norteamericanos* crossed the Sabine, Mexican leaders would have every right to provoke a slave rebellion in the Southern states. "Louisiana is an open country and its extension along our frontier makes it an easy matter to penetrate it with a force even smaller than that of the enemy and by burning their own homes perhaps diminish the number of those advocating the conquest of Téjas." Now Mexican leaders made good on Alamán's promise.[46]

Given the United States' action on Texas, the Mexican government saw no reason to continue to respect the "property" rights of United States citizens, as it had in the past. In 1844, the minister of relations ordered no more runaways to be returned to the United States, "or else we will not be able to count on the slaves of the Southern states in case of a war with that country. We risk losing their sympathies at the moment that we most need them to conquer Texas." That same year, Mexico's Congress passed a law that fugitive slaves be given passports "wheresoever they may land" to permit them to remain in the country. "*Libre sois!*," Mexican newspapers announced to the people of color in Louisiana, Texas, and Florida. "What would happen if a Mexican army of twenty thousand crossed the Sabine with their Trigarantine flag?" asked *El Amigo de Pueblo*. "Four million slaves with many grievances to avenge would hear this magic voice of liberty and revolt against the

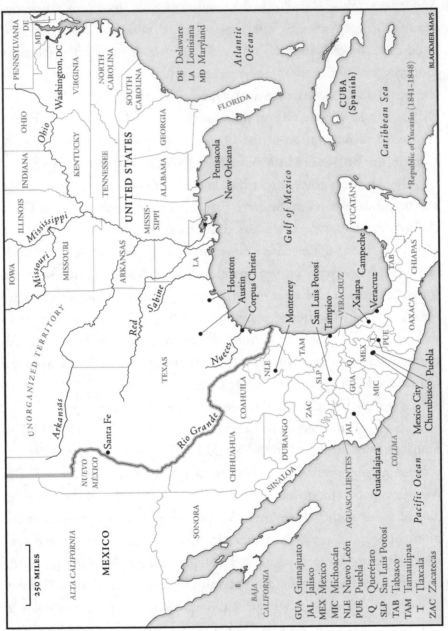

MAP 2: The United States and Mexico, 1846

South." The message to the United States was that a war with Mexico would also be a "war with the blacks and with the Indians."[47]

As Mexican newspapers cheered the plan to pursue "the rebels of Texas" into "the very center of the Union," the Mexican government broke diplomatic relations with the United States. The heavy double doors of the US Legation in Mexico City were locked shut. Both keys were wrapped in thick paper and sealed with wax. Then the package was placed into a box, and after being nailed shut, deposited within a strong iron chest that would not be opened again until the war between the two nations was over.[48]

EIGHT

COMPROMISE LOST

S ECOND LIEUTENANT JOHN J. PECK DID NOT ENJOY LIVING IN A
tent. Damp clothes hung from the guylines. The only light came
from a candle jammed into the mouth of an empty bottle. The lieutenant
from New York was among the thirty-five hundred soldiers stationed at
Corpus Christi, Texas, just south of the Nueces River. Although the US
Army was occupying disputed territory—the United States claimed the
Rio Grande as its southern boundary, while the Mexican government
claimed that the boundary was the Nueces River—the men made no
effort to disguise their presence. For two miles, their white, Army-issue
tents formed orderly rows. At night, as the soldiers paged through books
or wrote to their families from inside their tents, the canvas walls lit up
like "so many transparencies."[1]

The United States Army was trying to provoke a war. Like many
soldiers at Corpus Christi, Peck hoped to be "thundering over the plains
of Mexico" in no time. "We are in Mexico, have invaded their soil, and
it is their business to drive us off," Peck wrote to his sister. But the Mexican Army did not drive them off. Mexico's President José de Herrera

wished to avoid a war in which his country stood to lose all of its northern territories. Decades of Indian raids laid waste to northern towns and haciendas, leaving the frontier vulnerable to attack. The Mexican Army was in disarray, and military enlistments were dismal. Only thirty-seven men registered for the civic militia in Morelia, twenty-seven in Zacatecas, ten in Querétaro, three in Guadalajara, two in Aguascalientes, and one in Puebla. Mexico's chances worsened in December 1845, when General Mariano Paredes y Arrillaga, the army commander at San Luis Potosí, refused to follow Herrera's orders to join Mariano Arista's regiment in the north, instead calling for Herrera's resignation and marching on the capital. In January 1846, Paredes assumed the presidency.[2]

At Corpus Christi, the US soldiers were growing restless. "I am heartily tired of this dull & uncertain camp life," Peck wrote to his father in February 1846. "We need some excitement." The Polk administration was growing impatient, too. On January 13, 1846, anxious either for the completion of negotiations or the commencement of war, the president ordered General Taylor to move his forces from Corpus Christi to the mouth of the Rio Grande, near where Mexican forces were stationed. On April 25, 1846, a seventy-man unit was on patrol near the Rio Grande when a Mexican cavalry detachment attacked, killing eleven US soldiers. The US-Mexican War had begun.[3]

Peck was overjoyed. From what he read, Mexicans were uneducated, lazy, and disinclined to fight except "at long distances." As the United States Army scored decisive victories at Palo Alto and Resaca de Palma, and occupied Matamoros without a fight, he predicted that the war would be over within months. Notwithstanding the acrimonious debates over the annexation of Texas, the war seemed to have united the nation. Legislatures from Louisiana to Michigan appropriated funds to raise volunteer companies. Even the Whig *Cleveland Herald* swallowed its opposition to annexation and urged "every American citizen" to "stand by his country and hold himself ready to fight its battles." Second Lieutenant Peck felt certain that a war with Mexico would put an end to the "trivial difficulties about the tariff, slaves &c."[4]

To the Southern volunteers, who made up the majority of the United States forces in Mexico, the future of slavery depended on the outcome of the war. The Southern economy depended on the availability of land, and slaveholders expected that at least some of the territories conquered from Mexico would be suitable for cotton production. The Aztec Empire produced 116 million pounds of cotton per year—more than the United States had grown before 1816. The Prussian explorer Alexander von Humboldt, who traveled through New Spain in 1803, noted that the central plateau of Mexico produced cotton in abundance. But the conquest of Mexican territory was more than an economic opportunity for Southern planters; it was a political necessity. The remaining territories of the Louisiana Purchase, as well as the recently acquired Oregon Territory, were expected to join the Union as "free" states. To maintain a balance between North and South in Congress, the United States needed land from Mexico.[5]

But it soon became clear that the war would neither unite the country nor ensure the expansion of slavery. The cause for disagreement in Washington was not the justice of the war, but the status of slavery in the territories that the United States stood to acquire from Mexico. This was the first time that the United States had ever incorporated territories where slavery was explicitly abolished, and Northern politicians argued that Congress had no authority to reestablish the practice. This argument forged a dangerous alliance between Northern Democrats and Northern Whigs that Southern politicians feared would bring an end to slavery—and the Union. No one knew how, or if, their representatives in Washington, DC, would be able to resolve this crisis. With Congress in gridlock, some volunteers began to fear that "we shall have a Mexican war of some years."[6]

ON AUGUST 8, 1846, WHEN THE CONGRESSMEN REASSEMBLED AT the US Capitol after dinner, David Wilmot, a first-term Democrat from Pennsylvania, raised his hand. Under discussion was a $2 million appropriation bill that the Polk administration had requested to fund the US-Mexican War. On taking the floor, the freshman congressman kept his remarks brief. Congress had been in session for eight grueling months. With two days before the recess, the House had limited speeches to ten minutes and debates to two hours. The freshman representative had only enough time to propose an amendment to the appropriation bill, guaranteeing that "neither slavery nor involuntary servitude shall ever exist" in any territory that the United States might acquire from Mexico. This would not have been a surprising position for a Northern Whig. But this stance seemed unusual for a Democrat, and particularly a Democrat like David Wilmot, who never gave any sign of antislavery convictions and who supported the annexation of Texas as a slave state a year earlier. Wilmot seemed so unlikely an author that historians have speculated that someone else wrote the amendment.[7]

But David Wilmot had a principled reason to oppose the expansion of slavery into the territories seized from Mexico. The Democratic Party envisioned a limited government in which the legislative branch only did what the Constitution explicitly authorized it to do. According to this interpretation, the national government could not interfere with slavery where it existed—a theory that was known as the principle of noninterference. It was according to this principle that David Wilmot voted to annex Texas as a slave state. As he saw it, the Constitution did not authorize Congress to interfere with slavery where it "already existed." But the territories that the United States stood to acquire from Mexico were unlike Texas. In Mexico, slavery was abolished, and the Constitution did not authorize Congress to reestablish slavery where it did not exist, any more than it authorized Congress to interfere with slavery where it did. "God forbid," Wilmot exclaimed, that he or any other Democrat should "be the means of planting this institution" upon a free territory.[8]

Representative James C. Dobbin of North Carolina immediately recognized the threat that the Wilmot Proviso posed to the balance of power in the United States. Under the Missouri Compromise, slavery could not exist north of 36°30' in the Louisiana Purchase. Nor was it likely to extend to the recently acquired Oregon Territory. If Congress could not reestablish slavery in the territories that the United States stood to seize from Mexico, then all of the remaining western territories would be closed to the peculiar institution. As those nonslaveholding territories became "free" states, the balance of power in Washington would shift decisively in favor of the North. To prevent this future from coming to pass, Representative Dobbin rose from his seat, exclaiming that the Wilmot Proviso was out of order, because slavery had no connection to the appropriation bill. But the speaker overruled him.[9]

Soon nearly every representative was on his feet. Above the floor, men and women crowded into the gallery, fanning themselves with newspapers to stave off the heat of the August evening. The fact that slavery was abolished in Mexico set the constitutional principle of not interfering with slavery against the political necessity of maintaining a sectional balance between North and South, and it was unclear whether principle or pragmatism would triumph. At the end of the allotted two hours, the House voted 83 to 64 for the Wilmot Proviso and 86 to 64 for the $2 million appropriation bill to which it was attached. All but two Southern representatives opposed the appropriation bill. Eighty-three out of ninety-five Northerners voted in favor. The House of Representatives was divided along sectional lines.[10]

On August 10, the last day Congress was in session, the Senate took up the appropriation bill with its attached proviso. The debate started promptly, with final adjournment set for noon, but the proceedings stalled when Whig John Davis of Massachusetts took the floor. Davis demanded to know why the Polk administration needed such a large sum to negotiate a peace treaty with Mexico.[11] The United States did not owe money to Mexico, so the sum of $2 million was not meant to cancel any financial obligations. "What, then, is its purpose?" Davis asked. The unavoidable conclusion, he continued, was that it was "an appropriation for the purpose of acquiring territory" and not just any territory—a territory where slavery was abolished. "The House of Representatives has seen fit to insert in the bill that, if there be an acquisition of territory, involuntary servitude shall not exist within that territory," Davis continued. "Now, I should like to hear some reasons, if there be any, why it should exist. I should like to hear some good and sufficient reason, such as would satisfy the country."[12]

Dixon Lewis of Alabama interjected that only twenty minutes remained in the session. If Davis wanted to make a speech, Lewis suggested that he propose a resolution to extend the session beyond twelve o'clock.

"I shall occupy but a few minutes," Davis replied.

"Will you allow me to introduce the resolution?" Lewis asked, hoping to extend the session.

"After I have finished."

"But it will then be too late."

Davis continued for another twelve minutes. As a matter that would "agitate the country from one end of it to the other," the Wilmot Proviso deserved a full debate. Davis also hoped that by refusing to yield the floor until the very last moment, he could force his colleagues to take the appropriations bill as the House offered it—with the proviso.

With the clock showing eight minutes to noon, Lewis interrupted Davis again.

"Does the Senator from Massachusetts yield the floor?" Vice President George Dallas asked.

"For a question of order," Davis answered. "Otherwise not."

At this point, it did not matter. Lewis announced that the House, whose clock was faster, had already adjourned.[13]

The bill was dead. Yet *norteamericanos* did not fool themselves into thinking that the debate was over. The Wilmot Proviso was not merely a gratuitous slap at the South or a defensive movement by Northern Democrats to protect themselves in the face of growing antislavery sentiment among their constituents. Prohibiting slavery in the former Mexican territories was also a matter of principle. Slavery was abolished in Mexico and, Northern Democrats argued, Congress did not have the power to reestablish it. Congress remained divided, as the fighting continued in Mexico.[14]

MEXICO WAS A COUNTRY OF "DECEPTIVE DISTANCES." AS THE US Army marched deeper into the country, the mountains seemed as distant at the end of a day's march as at the beginning. Volunteers who expected the war to end in a matter of months began to lose track of the days. "Is this Sunday?" they asked one another. Between drilling and marching, cleaning guns and polishing swords, a private remarked that "we have no Sunday here."[15]

Four months into a war that was supposed to have been over in weeks, the volunteers in northern Mexico were tiring of the "soldier's life." They had had enough of the spiders that scuttled across their arms and the brackish water to which they had no choice but to add a "*little spirit.*" They complained of sore teeth. ("Hard bread . . . *is* rather hard.") Now they understood why the army classified a hatchet and a Bowie knife as "utensils."[16]

Second Lieutenant John Peck's enthusiasm for the war was also dwindling. In September, he arrived in Monterrey, the largest city in northeastern Mexico, which had been transformed since the start of the war. Locals barricaded the streets and drilled loopholes for musketry in their garden walls. Mexican soldiers erected a battery on Federation Hill, which guarded the entrance to the city. As General William Jenkins Worth surveyed the enemy defenses, he came up with a plan to take the city. "Men," he ordered, "you are to take that hill." Once in possession of Federation Hill, the United States Army would be able to march into Monterrey.[17]

On September 20, 1846, two detachments crossed the Arroyo San Juan toward Federation Hill. The fire from above was so heavy that the water in the streambed steamed with shot. As the *norteamericanos* advanced up the hill, clinging to whatever vegetation they could to keep from sliding on the loose dirt, the enemy plunged down the slopes to meet them. Mexican officers waited behind the batteries, urging their troops on with an occasional "Bravo!" Facing heavy fire from above, the *norteamericanos* drove the Mexicans from their position. At the top of Federation Hill, Peck commandeered a cannon and turned it upon the enemy.[18]

The war defied John Peck's predictions. He continued to regard the Mexican officers as "generally ignorant," but after fighting at Federation Hill, he acknowledged that the soldiers against whom he had fought were "as brave as our own." Mexicans were determined to defend their local communities—the *patria chica*, or the little homeland. They also fought to forestall what they feared awaited under United States rule. The Protestant invaders, according to *El Mosquito Mexicano*, threatened "the safety of the Catholic religion." Another newspaper warned that Mexicans would be "sold as beasts" since "their color was not as white as that of their conquerors." The "triumph of the Anglo-Saxon race," *El Estandarte Nacional* predicted, heralded "the enslavement of the Mexican people" and "the destruction of their language and customs."[19]

For some of the soldiers in the Mexican Army, the prospect of enslavement was not at all hypothetical. During the war, fugitive slaves from the United States fled to Mexican lines. Six runaways joined the Mexican Army in Matamoros in 1845. Twenty more received instruction in the "handling of firearms" as members of the National Guard. General Mariano Arista boasted that the African Americans who joined his army defended "with determination" the country "in which they found liberty." As "natural enemies" of the United States, the commanding general of the State of Tamaulipas reported that African Americans "had always been quick to lend their services to the Mexican Republic."[20]

Even after the United States Army took control of Alta California, Nuevo México, and much of northeastern Mexico, Mexicans would not surrender. Parishes across the country melted down their church bells to cast into cannonballs. At weekend markets, vendors sold US soldiers candied fruit, gleaming with syrup, that, according to army intelligence, was "purposefully prepared to cause sickness & untimely death." Only a decisive victory by the US would force the Mexican government to surrender.[21]

The United States Army would have to seize Mexico City. Since it would take months for General Taylor's Army of Occupation to march south to the capital, President Polk instructed General Winfield Scott to occupy the port city of Veracruz and then march inland, taking the same route as the Spanish conquistador Hernán Cortés three centuries earlier. To defray the mounting expenses of the war, Polk planned to make "an adequate appropriation" of Mexican territories—Alta California and Nuevo México, which the army had already seized, and perhaps even Sonora, Chihuahua, Coahuila, Nuevo León and Tamaulipas. What "splendid schemes of conquest," Senator Jacob W. Miller of New Jersey scoffed. "Mexico is to be conquered, and her people made to pay for their own subjugation" by ceding their national territory. But the United States would also pay, in ways that its leaders were only just beginning to understand. Unless Congress reached some consensus about the status of slavery in the ceded territories, Polk's "appropriation" would unleash a major sectional controversy that threatened to destroy the Union.[22]

HENRY WASHINGTON HILLIARD SPENT HIS LIFE IN PURSUIT OF some great accomplishment. He worked as the chair of the English Department at the University of Alabama, honed his oratorical skills in the state legislature, and served as chargé d'affaires to Belgium. But it was only when he won election to the House of Representatives that his moment seemed finally to have arrived. Hilliard believed that he had a solution to the sectional controversy over the US-Mexican War.[23]

On January 5, 1847, Hilliard proposed that Congress extend the Missouri Compromise line to the Pacific. Dividing the western territories had maintained the balance of power between North and South for decades, as Congress admitted one "free" state for every slave state: Missouri for Maine, Arkansas for Michigan. Extending the line would permit the admission of the remaining western territories in the same plodding fashion. "If it is provided that the states on this side the Mississippi shall be equally balanced in respect to slavery," Hilliard asked, "why should not the same balance be permitted to exist on the other side?"[24]

Northern Democrats, however, refused to reestablish slavery where it had previously been abolished. The principle of noninterference embodied the ideal of limited government that Democrats championed. A government that could interfere with slavery might also have the power to enact tariffs, establish a national bank, and fund internal improvements—policies that most Democrats opposed. Southern slaveholders proved willing to advocate for a strong federal government when it served their purposes, but Northern Democrats would not change their interpretation of the Constitution to defend an institution about which they felt ambivalent at best. Those who faced growing antislavery sentiment among their constituents or who resented the outsized influence of Southern politicians within party leadership had even less reason to vote in favor of Hilliard's proposal.[25]

Northern Whigs found themselves in agreement with Northern Democrats. Although the two parties had a very different view of federal power, with Democrats favoring a limited government and Whigs an activist one, Northern Whigs denied Congress the power to "fasten" slavery upon territories where it did not exist. The United States was "the great republic of the world—the model government—the home of freedom—the asylum of the oppressed," as Representative James Dixon of Connecticut put it. Like their Democratic colleagues, Northern Whigs could never sacrifice the "blood of their countrymen" to "turn a free into slave soil."[26] When Northern Democrats and Northern Whigs combined forces, they wielded a majority in the House. They intended to use it.[27]

On February 8, 1847, David Wilmot reintroduced his famous proviso. "All we ask in the North is, that the character of its territory be preserved," Wilmot said. "There is no question of abolition here, sir. It is a question whether the South shall be permitted, by aggression, by invasion of right, by subduing free territory, and planting slavery upon it, to wrest this territory to the accomplishment of its own sectional purposes and schemes." A week later, the measure passed, 115 to 106, and the bill was sent to the Senate.[28]

The Wilmot Proviso alarmed Senator John C. Calhoun of South Carolina. Nicknamed the cast-iron man for his unwavering commitment to the proslavery cause, Calhoun had grown so wan—a symptom of advanced tuberculosis—that his face looked as if it were literally wrought in iron. On February 19, 1847, Calhoun asked for the floor. He explained that the Wilmot Proviso was not a "mere question of policy" to Southern whites; it was "a question of safety, of self-preservation." Prohibiting slavery in the former Mexican territories virtually guaranteed that "free" states would eventually outnumber slave states. "We shall be at the entire mercy of the non-slaveholding States," Calhoun concluded, and he placed no confidence in "their justice and regard for our interests." By destroying the "balance between the two sections," the proviso would bring "political revolution, anarchy, civil war, and widespread disaster."[29]

Calhoun went on to make a constitutional argument against the Wilmot Proviso. He explained that the territories were the "common property" of the states. Therefore, preventing "the citizens of any of the states" from taking their personal property to the territories was a "violation of the Constitution." From this perspective, the Missouri Compromise line was unconstitutional. Previously, Calhoun had been "willing to acquiesce in a continuance of the Missouri Compromise, in order to preserve, under the present trying circumstances, the peace of the Union." But now that "an overwhelming majority" had voted against extending the line to the Pacific, Calhoun argued against federal interference with slavery under any circumstances. "Let us be done with compromises," Calhoun urged. "Let us go back and stand upon the Constitution!" Now that the principle of noninterference threatened to undermine the extension of slavery into the former Mexican territories, Southern moderates started to come around to Calhoun's more radical view. At the end of February, the Senate approved a separate appropriation bill, without the proviso.[30]

When the House of Representatives considered the appropriation bill, the Polk administration pressured Democrats to vote for the bill without the Wilmot Proviso attached. But this was an era when political debate turned on constitutional exegesis, when politicians consulted manuals of elocution to find appropriate hand gestures, when speeches were so long that a president died from exposure after attending lengthy ceremonies on the National Mall. With Wilmot Proviso Leagues being founded in the North, Northern Democrats could not vote against the measure without some sort of explanation.[31]

TO RETURN TO THE PARTY FOLD, WITHOUT ABANDONING THEIR principles, Northern Democrats explained that though they supported the Wilmot Proviso, they considered it unnecessary. If slavery was abolished in Mexico, and Congress had no power to reestablish it, then slavery could not exist in the former Mexican territories, regardless of whether Northern Democrats voted for an explicit prohibition.[32]

The Law of Nations seemed to bolster the Democrats' argument. After a territory was conquered or ceded, *public* law, which defined the relationship between citizens and their sovereign, would be extinguished. But *private* law, which governed dealings among individuals, enforced contracts, guaranteed property rights, and protected against negligence, nuisance, and defamation, remained in force "for the preservation of society."[33] To maintain order, property—including property in persons—would be respected and contracts would continue to be valid. As David Wilmot himself argued, the territories were "free; and it is part of the established law of nations, and all public law, that when [they] shall come into this Union, all laws there existing not inconsistent with its new allegiance will remain in force. This fundamental law, which prohibits slavery in California, will be in force; this fundamental law, which prohibits slavery in New Mexico, will be in force."[34]

The courts of the United States supported this interpretation of the Law of Nations. Judges in California already ruled that Mexico's laws on slavery remained in force. In 1846, when an enslaved woman named Mary petitioned for her freedom in San Jose, California, the justice of the peace, appointed by the United States forces occupying California, ruled in her favor, on the grounds that Mexico's laws had abolished slavery. In another case three years later, a judge in Sacramento reached the same conclusion, that "Mexican law prohibited slavery in California."[35]

The Law of Nations, as well as judicial decisions from California, suggested that slavery would not—indeed, could not—extend to the ceded territories, proviso or no proviso. "If the territory will be free when it is annexed, and Congress has no power to make it slave, where is the necessity for the adoption of the amendment?" wondered Richard Brodhead of Pennsylvania. Isaac Parrish of Ohio credited the "advocates of this proviso" with showing that "slavery cannot exist in any territory that may be acquired of Mexico." According to these Northern Democrats, Mexico's laws prohibited the expansion of slavery. The Wilmot Proviso served no purpose except to antagonize the Southern states.[36]

The press agreed with Democrats' assessment that the Wilmot Proviso was unnecessary. "Is it not strange that the legislatures of every free State in this Union should resolve in favor of the prohibition of slavery in territories from whence it is *already* excluded?" the *Semi-Weekly Union* of Washington, DC, asked. The Democratic *Coldwater Sentinel* of Coldwater, Michigan, concluded that the "present uproar" was over "the abstract right of doing what cannot be done!"[37]

On March 3, twenty-two Northern Democrats voted along with Southern congressmen for the appropriation bill without the proviso attached. Southern politicians expected slavery to extend to the conquered Mexican territories, while Northern Democrats assured themselves that

Mexico's laws prohibiting slavery would remain in force. Looking back a year later at all that had transpired during the previous summer, one Massachusetts Democrat boasted, "The inflated bladder of free soil has been pricked and has collapsed." But the man spoke too soon. The war was not over yet.[38]

On March 9, 1847, John Peck disembarked from the *Massachusetts* onto a windswept beach two miles south of Veracruz. For two weeks, he and his fellow soldiers went about preparing to attack the port city. Then, on March 22, General Winfield Scott gave the order to open fire. Over the next three days, three thousand shells rained down on Veracruz. By daybreak on the fourth day, the Mexican forces raised a flag of truce. When Scott's army occupied the city, they found the walls and batteries pockmarked by gunfire, the buildings so raked with grapeshot that it looked as though "iron harrows had been dragged over them." The extent of the destruction astounded Peck. "War is a terrible calamity," he wrote.[39]

With Veracruz under occupation, the United States Army marched westward. The first major engagement on the march took place on April 18, 1847. At the Battle of Cerro Gordo outside of Xalapa, Veracruz, General Winfield Scott's army took three thousand prisoners, forty-three artillery pieces, and the presidential carriage, complete with Antonio López de Santa Anna's cork leg, papers, toilette case, wardrobe, and luncheon. ("I was voraciously hungry and enjoyed the latter immensely," one soldier boasted, with pen and ink pilfered from Santa Anna's stores.) John Peck, for his part, claimed "an elegant camp bed" from Santa Anna's headquarters.[40]

On May 15, Scott's forces placed Puebla under siege. The sprawling haciendas and fragrant orange groves that surrounded the city impressed Peck, even as he was taking quinine to stave off the chills and fevers associated with malaria. "You forget you are in Mexico," he remarked of his surroundings. When reinforcements arrived in July, General Scott prepared to march toward Mexico City, eighty miles to the west. On August 8, 1847, his men, John Peck included, set out from Puebla. They faced almost no resistance until eleven days later, when the enemy attacked the *norteamericanos* as they picked their way across a lava field south of Mexico City known as the Pedregal. Three hundred *norteamericanos* were killed or wounded. Mexican casualties were over four times as high. The night after the battle, it rained so hard that the soldiers could not even pitch their tents. They slept in the mud, their arms clutched in their hands. "It poured down in torrents, and was extremely dark, save when the flash of the Mexican artillery told that the enemy was still there," Peck wrote. He remembered it later as the worst night of his life.[41]

The next morning, the *norteamericanos* arrived at the town of Churubusco, three miles outside of Mexico City. Thousands of Mexican infantrymen guarded the town, backed by heavy artillery. Scott's forces surged forward, advancing over ditches and cornfields. "Round shot, grape, canister, and musket balls swept over the ground like hail," Peck remembered. "Regiments were in confusion, wagons strewn in pieces, and roads locked with dead horses, and mules. It seemed as if annihilation awaited us." The wheels of the guns could not turn against the "blockade of dead." To pass from caisson to gun, the volunteers had to climb over "windrows" of bodies. Every blade of grass seemed weighted with blood. The United States Army won the battle, but at tremendous cost. One hundred thirty-three *norteamericanos* were killed, and another 865 wounded. Mexican casualties numbered 723. "My heart sickens at the thought of the field of Battle," Peck wrote. "I did not expect to live from moment to moment, so fierce was the contest."[42]

After the Battle of Churubusco, Scott's forces marched to Mexico City, taking the capital on September 14, 1847. The volunteers fashioned themselves after the Spanish conquistadors who conquered Mexico City three centuries earlier. They used the crosses on church steeples as flagpoles. They donned the armor of Cortés and his men from the National Museum. Meanwhile, their commanders imposed martial law. The US Army appointed military governors to maintain order, and the laws that they observed were those of the United States. Eager to exploit the shift in jurisdiction, Southerners began efforts to recover slaves who had escaped to Mexico. One Louisiana woman traveled to Veracruz in 1847 on the steamship *Palmetto* to oversee personally the return of a fugitive. "Her pursuit is represented as successful," the proslavery *Richmond Enquirer* noted approvingly. The following year, a widow from New Orleans sent an agent to Veracruz, armed with a letter from the governor of Louisiana. The letter demanded that the military governor of Veracruz return the runaway, Abraham, under the terms of the Fugitive Slave Act of 1793.[43]

At the town of Hidalgo, just north of Mexico City, diplomats discussed the terms of the treaty that would end the US-Mexican War. During the negotiations, Mexico's foreign minister Luis de la Rosa asked that the treaty formally exclude slavery from the ceded Mexican territories. Human bondage, he explained, was already abolished. But the US delegation, led by envoy Nicholas Trist, dismissed his suggestion out of hand. Prohibiting slavery was "an absolute impossibility." With Mexico City under occupation, and military governments ruling over northern Mexico, Nicholas Trist felt no obligation to acknowledge Mexico's laws against forced labor. The Treaty of Guadalupe Hidalgo, which ceded the northern half of Mexico's territory to the United States for $15 million, made no mention of slavery.[44]

But congressmen in Washington, DC, and their constituents refused to dismiss Mexican abolition so easily. Six months after the treaty was signed, Secretary of State James Buchanan circulated "correct translations of the decree of President Guerrero of the 15th September 1829 and of the act of the Mexican Congress of 5th April, 1837" to the editors of the *Washington Union*. Across the United States, newspapers reprinted the decrees. "There is no slavery, at this time, either in Mexico or California, in law or in fact," proclaimed the *Coldwater Sentinel*.[45]

Many *norteamericanos* balked at the prospect of reestablishing slavery in the territories seized from Mexico. Greene Bronson, the conservative chief justice of the New York Supreme Court, declared that he was "utterly opposed to the extension of slavery into any territory of the United States where it does not now exist." On July 28, 1848, a public meeting in New York City resolved that "the laws of Oregon, California and New Mexico, by which slavery has been abolished in those territories, will remain in force until altered by or under the authority of Congress, or by the proper authority of these territories after they shall be formed into states yet." The war with Mexico was over, but debate over slavery in the ceded territories had hardly begun.[46]

JOHN PECK SPENT HIS FINAL DAYS IN MEXICO CITY "TAKING A cigar with this one and some refreshment with that one." On December 9, 1847, he set off by mule toward Veracruz. The "long and tedious" journey retraced the steps that he had taken over the previous months with General Scott's army. Two weeks later, he arrived in Veracruz. "The sight of the sea is most joyful, after our long and dry and dusty marches," he wrote. "We breathe fuller and freer at its side!"[47]

As Peck traveled to New Orleans and from there, to New York, a chance discovery brought the crisis over slavery in the ceded territories to a head. In the Sierra Madre of California, a crew of Mormons and forty Miwok Indians was constructing a sawmill, when, on January 24, 1848, something caught the light at the bottom of a millrace. The foreman at the sawmill rolled up his sleeves and, from about a foot of water, extracted a small, warped-looking pebble. Gold. As news spread, almost the entire male population of San Francisco decamped for the American River. US soldiers posted at Monterey, California, deserted, leaving nothing but the flag. With no one to write or print the local *American*, newspapers became as scarce as pickaxes and tin pans. Thirty-five thousand gold seekers set out for California in 1849. Some of these '49ers sailed around Cape Horn. Others disembarked at Panama and trekked across the isthmus. Thousands more drove covered wagons overland,

loaded down with sluices, pickaxes, collapsible houses, and other ne-
cessities. John Peck joined the western migration, though for a different
reason than the '49ers. Several months after returning to his hometown
of Manlius, New York, he set out for Jefferson Barracks, Missouri, and
from there, to his next military posting in New Mexico.[48]

With tens of thousands of *norteamericanos* charging west, a major
sectional controversy over the status of slavery in the former Mexican
territories seemed imminent. Zachary Taylor, the US-Mexican War hero
who had recently been elected president of the United States, owned
over a hundred slaves and a Louisiana plantation, but he privately opposed any plan to extend the "peculiar institution" into the territories
that he had helped to win from Mexico. As he had observed to General
Jefferson Davis during the Mexican campaign, slavery had "been abolished by the people of Mexico" and could "never be revived by ours." No
man of "ordinary capacity" would believe "for a moment" that Congress
would open the ceded territories to slavery.[49]

The problem was that Southern whites refused to accept that the
former Mexican territories would be closed to slavery. To spare the nation a major controversy over slavery, Taylor schemed for New Mexico
and California to avoid the territorial stage altogether. The admission
of Missouri in 1820 had established the precedent that the people of a
territory could decide whether to permit or prohibit slavery when they
petitioned for statehood, and Taylor hoped that the people in the ceded
territories would decide for themselves before Congress took up the
divisive question again. Admitting California and New Mexico as states
became "the *great object* of the administration."[50]

On September 1, 1849, a convention met at Monterey, California, to
draft a constitution, as Taylor hoped. Most of the delegates were in their
twenties or early thirties. Among their ranks were lawyers, farmers, merchants, and a Texan whose occupation was listed as "elegant leisure." The
exuberant delegates discussed forming as many as six new states. They
debated the merits of annexing the Sandwich Islands and perhaps even
China. Ultimately, they decided to establish a single state. The delegates

also voted unanimously to prohibit slavery. Delegates with Southern roots conceded that California was "utterly unfitted for slave labor." Northerners like Kimball Dimmick hoped that "the first great republican state on the borders of the Pacific" would further "the progress of human freedom." By abolishing slavery, the convention "acted in accordance with the dictates of the whole civilized world," according to New York–born Edward Gilbert. "The people of Mexico have said by their action that they do not want slavery," explained Winfield Sherwood, also from New York. "We have said by our action that we do not." After the convention adjourned on October 13, 1849, the people of California voted on the constitution. More than ninety-four thousand eligible men did not go to the trouble of casting ballots. The small minority who did vote overwhelmingly supported the convention's work. The constitution passed, 12,061 to 811.[51]

The people of New Mexico were also eager to apply for statehood. Since the end of the US-Mexican War, New Mexicans had "suffered under the paralyzing effects of a government undefined and doubtful in its character, inefficient to protect the rights of the people, or to discharge the high and absolute duty of every government, the enforcement and regular administration of its own laws." Commerce slowed. Indian attacks went unpunished. "Ruin appears inevitably before us, unless speedy and effectual protection be extended to us by the Congress of the United States." Since the United States Congress failed to establish a territorial government, the people of New Mexico resolved to apply for statehood. As in California, the constitution that the New Mexico delegates drafted in the spring of 1850 did not equivocate on the issue of slavery. Article 1, Section 1 declared: "No male person shall be held by law to serve any person as a servant, slave or apprentice, after he arrives at an age of twenty-one years; nor female in like manner, after she arrives at the age of eighteen years."

The delegates submitted the constitution to the people of New Mexico, with a statement that elaborated on the antislavery position. "Slavery in New Mexico is naturally impracticable, and can never, in reality, exist here;—wherever it has existed it has proved a curse and a blight to the State upon which it has been inflicted,—a moral, social, and political evil." On June 20, 1850, the people of New Mexico went to the polls. The constitution passed, 6,771 to 39.[52]

The political power of the slaveholding states was in jeopardy. Building on the precedent established by the Missouri Compromise, President Zachary Taylor was working to admit California and New Mexico as states, and both territories drafted constitutions that prohibited slavery. To the consternation of Southern slaveholders, Mexican abolition prevented the expansion of slavery to the Southwest. At the same time, the promise of freedom in Mexico would also undermine the labor system where it was expanding most rapidly: the Mississippi Valley and eastern Texas.

NINE

LIBERTY FOUND

O N THE INSIDE FOLD OF ALMOST EVERY NEWSPAPER IN TEXAS
was the headline "TAKEN UP." The text that followed listed
the name, age, height, color, and "perceivable marks" of fugitive slaves
who had been captured while trying to escape. The listings also noted
where the runaways had been caught and where their owners lived.
From this information, slaveholders could approximate the general
direction that fugitive slaves took. The notices could sometimes be
misleading. Some runaways got lost and were caught far from their
intended destination. Others purposefully misidentified their owners
to delay and possibly even avoid being returned to slavery. Still, diligent readers would have noticed a troubling pattern. According to
these notices, over three-quarters of the fugitive slaves caught in Texas
between 1837 and 1861 were headed toward Mexico.[1]

In the summer of 1850, Secretary of State John M. Clayton of the
United States proposed a solution: an extradition treaty with Mexico
that included an article "relative to fugitives held to service or labor
in the territory whence they may have escaped." The article applied to

fugitive slaves who escaped from the United States, as well as the indentured servants—or peons—who fled from Mexico. The demand for such a provision was growing in Mexico. In 1850, the towns of Nuevo Laredo, Reynosa, Mier, Matamoros, and Camargo demanded the extradition of escaped peons. The legislature of Tamaulipas pleaded for a treaty to correct this "lamentable situation." Even the Mexican consul in Brownsville, Texas, asked that any treaty with the United States include an article "relative to the debts that servants or dependents contracted to the owners of agricultural and industrial establishments."[2]

Mexico's minister to the United States, Luis de la Rosa, acknowledged that "this additional provision might be useful to Mexico." But his instructions forbade him from agreeing to any treaty that provided for the return of fugitive slaves. Under Mexico's laws, enslaved people were "free" and "their liberty guaranteed." As a result, the proposed article would involve Mexico in "very odious" questions. "There are laws in Mexico which it would be necessary to abolish in order that this additional provision might be admitted," de la Rosa explained, "and it seems very certain that the National Congress can never be persuaded to abolish such laws."[3]

De la Rosa was referring to one law in particular. On March 22, 1849, Mexico's Congress decreed that "the slaves of other countries" would be "free by the act of stepping on the national territory." This promise, known as the freedom principle, made territory into a mechanism of emancipation. By promising freedom not just to the slaves within a particular jurisdiction, but to *all* slaves who set foot on its soil, Mexico's policy transformed the landscape of freedom across North America.[4]

Few countries enshrined the freedom principle in law. Although fugitive slaves generally found safety in Canada, no law explicitly promised to free all enslaved people. As a result, a small number of fugitive slaves who committed crimes before reaching Canada were denied asylum. One freedom seeker was returned to the United States in 1842 for having stolen a beaver overcoat, a racing mare, and a gold watch while escaping from Arkansas. Eight years later, a Canadian court ruled in favor of extraditing a fugitive slave accused of murder.[5]

Only one other nation in the Americas passed laws as radical as Mexico's. In 1804, Haiti abolished African slavery; and twelve years later, promised to free all slaves who set foot on its soil. These laws destabilized black slavery in the neighboring islands of Cuba and Jamaica. In the United States, they struck fear in the hearts of Southern slaveholders. But Haiti lay five hundred miles by sea off the southernmost tip of Florida. Mexico, by contrast, directly bordered the US South—and not just any part of the US South: the Deep South, where slave-based agriculture was booming.[6]

In 1850, Mexico's minister to the United States followed his instructions to protect fugitive slaves. Negotiations for an extradition treaty failed. Mexico's commitment to the freedom principle gave runaways a chance to forge new lives for themselves across the Rio Grande. Some joined the military colonies that protected the northeastern frontier against "barbarous" Indians, gravitating in particular to an outpost in northern Coahuila that Seminoles and their black allies established in 1849. Others helped fill Mexico's labor shortage by seeking employment as servants and day laborers. Their freedom was far from complete. Exposed to the risk of military service or the coercion of labor in a cash-poor economy, former slaves did not enjoy unabridged freedom. But these choices—indeed, the very opportunity to make a choice—were to many a victory.[7]

NORTHERN MEXICO WAS POOR AND SPARSELY POPULATED. DURING the winter months, Comanches and Lipan Apaches crossed the Rio Grande to rustle livestock from Mexico, and the garrisons posted to the frontier lacked even the most basic supplies to stop them. Local militiamen had no saddles. Military commanders asked for "the cooperation of the female population" to provide their men with uniforms.

TABLE 1: THE DIRECTION OF FLIGHT

	Total
To Non-Mexican Destinations	193
To Mexico	584
% to Mexico	75.2%

Destinations	Total	Percentage
Dallas	9	2%
Houston	48	10%
Indian Territory	39	8%
Louisiana	6	1%
Mexico	359	75%
Northern states	2	0.4%
Union lines	14	3%
Total	477	

This table is based on a database of 777 runaway notices from newspapers in Texas and Louisiana. Where runaways were caught and where their owners were reported to live gives a sense of where they seemed to be heading. These data are only a loose proxy of intention. A runaway who seemed to be heading toward Indian Territory might have been aiming to continue to the Northern states; similarly, a runaway who was caught near Houston might have intended to continue to Mexico. Regardless, these data give a sense of what slaveholders would have seen as they read these notices, namely that a large proportion of runaways seemed to be escaping toward Mexico.

Town councils pleaded for more gunpowder. Desperate to restore order, Mexico's Congress passed a law on December 4, 1846, that established a line of forts on the south bank of the Rio Grande. According to the law, foreigners who joined the military colonies would receive land and become "citizens of the Republic upon their arrival."[8]

This new policy caught the attention of Wild Cat, also known as Coacoochee, the leader of the Seminole Indians. After General Andrew Jackson invaded Florida in 1818, and Spanish diplomats agreed to cede the peninsula to the United States, the US Army drove the Seminoles and their black allies (known as Black Seminoles) onto a reservation south of the Apalachicola River. In 1833, another treaty removed them to the Creek reservation west of the Mississippi. There, the Creeks denied the newcomers land and sold the Black Seminoles into slavery in Arkansas and Louisiana. Eventually, the Seminoles and their black allies had had enough. Sometime around November 10, 1849, Wild Cat convinced over three hundred men, women, and children to leave Indian Territory—what is now Oklahoma—and head south.[9]

After six months of slow, grueling travel, the weary emigrants stopped on the Llano River, just west of Austin, Texas, while a delegation continued on to Mexico. As the Seminole delegation made its way south, the hills, once barely visible, now loomed, shimmering in the heat. Beyond those hills lay the poor and sparsely settled state of Coahuila, where the delegation met with Antonio María Jaúregui, inspector general of the eastern military colonies. With the Black Seminole leader, John Horse, interpreting, the Seminole leader Wild Cat explained that the US government had "without conscience" driven the Seminoles and their black allies "far to the north" of their Florida home. Wild Cat expressed his "very true wishes" to escape the "insecurity" of Indian Territory by settling in Mexico. In return, the Seminoles pledged to take up arms against the "wild" Indians. To add weight to his word, Wild Cat produced a sheet of paper. More than three decades after being driven from Florida, the Seminoles still carried a "message from the Spanish government," attesting to their good conduct. Seeking to return to the warm Gulf latitudes that resembled their Florida homeland, they were ready to be of service.[10]

Inspector General Antonio María Jaúregui did not need much convincing. To defend against Comanches and Lipan Apaches, Mexico's government had long turned to "civilized" Indians. In 1826, the legislature of Coahuila y Téjas approved a colonization law that promised lands to any native peoples who declared their allegiance to Mexico. These *indios de paz* were "peaceful" and "hardworking," occupying "another state of culture" than those who "harassed" the northern frontier. The hope was that Mexico's native allies would form a "barrier" against the "incursions of the barbarous nations" as well as *norteamericano* filibusters. And it seemed that they had succeeded. In 1826, General Antonio Gaona boasted that the Cherokees, Caddos, and other native peoples who moved to Mexico from the United States evinced such hatred for "foreigners" that they promised to "wipe our territory clean of intrusive adventurers." During the Texas Revolution, the Caddos proposed raising a force of three thousand men, and the Cherokees promised the same number. General José de Urrea reported that the Indians hated the *norteamericanos* who had revolted against Mexico as much as the ones "who removed them from the lands they occupied."[11]

The Seminoles and their black allies struck Inspector General Antonio María Jaúregui as suitable colonists. In exchange for their taking up arms against the "barbarous" Indians, the inspector general promised them seventy thousand acres near Guerrero and Monclova Viejo in northern Coahuila, along with financial subsidies, agricultural tools, and work animals. The terms seemed generous, but the Seminole delegation asked a final question. They needed assurances that Mexico was, in fact, "a free country." Eighty-four of the 351 people who had accompanied Wild Cat to Mexico in 1849 were black.[12]

SEVERAL MONTHS AFTER ARRIVING IN NORTHERN COAHUILA, Wild Cat returned to Indian Territory to recruit more emigrants. The task proved easier than expected. During his absence in the spring and summer of 1850, the discontents of his followers in Indian Territory multiplied, as Creek and Cherokee slave hunters repeatedly seized blacks from Seminole country. Thirty to forty Seminole families and most of the remaining Black Seminoles began to prepare for the journey south. In early October, Wild Cat and the emigrants left Indian Territory for the last time.[13]

Their lives in Mexico would not be easy. Few spoke Spanish. ("Couldn't even ask for a chaw of terbacker!" one remembered.) Most had so little taste for Mexican food that they scraped the red beans from the tortillas their neighbors handed them. But the Mexican government did what it could to help them settle and assimilate at the military colony, thirty miles from Piedras Negras. A priest arrived from nearby Santa Rosa to baptize the Black Seminoles. A schoolteacher followed. Crates of tools arrived from Eagle Pass, the town across the Rio Grande from Piedras Negras. With the help of the 370 pesos a month that the government funneled to the colony, the Seminoles and their black allies set to work clearing fields, raising stock, and building their wood-frame houses around a square where they kept their animals at night.[14]

Fugitive slaves were already starting to arrive at the military colony and the surrounding towns. In 1849, David Thomas "save[d] his family from slavery" by escaping with his daughter and three grandchildren to Coahuila. A year later, seventeen African Americans appeared in Monclova Viejo, asking to join the Black Seminoles. Meanwhile, two men, José and Sambo, arrived "straight from Africa." By 1851, 356 blacks lived at the military colony—more than four times the number of blacks who had arrived with the Seminoles the previous year.[15]

Concentrated around a single community, the Black Seminoles managed to maintain their own faith and cultural traditions while also respecting the efforts of the priest in Santa Rosa. They fasted every Friday and they baptized the faithful in the Sabinas River. But when they kept vigil over the dead, there was traditional stamping, swaying, hooting, and singing around the bier. And when they took sick, the Black Seminole leader, John Horse, ministered to them, using old folk methods. Despite his efforts, two died from smallpox in the 1850s, while others suffered from more unusual ailments. A father gave his daughter a Comanche necklace he had stolen on a patrol, its white beads whittled from bones. Almost as soon as she put it on, she grew weak. Taking one look at the ailing child, John Horse snatched the beads away. He placed a buffalo horn with the tip cut out on her chest, sucking on it until he had "drawn the poison out."[16]

Although the Black Seminoles retained much of their cultural heritage, the demands of military service constrained their autonomy. To ensure "good order," police were posted to the military colonies. They levied fines on Black Seminoles for infractions like neglecting to clean their irrigation ditches. Deputies noted and commented upon how much alcohol John Horse consumed. Meanwhile, the Seminoles proved unreliable allies. In a fit of drunkenness in 1850, Wild Cat was said to have sold the daughter of a runaway from Louisiana to a barkeep in Fredericksburg, Texas, only to have John Horse steal her back as she sat on the bar, sucking on a piece of candy. In 1853, the Seminole leader purportedly sold another runaway for eighty pesos to a *norteamericano* in Eagle Pass.[17]

Fugitive slaves who joined the military colony frequently risked their lives in campaigns against the Comanches and Lipan Apaches. Fathers, husbands, and sons had to take up arms at a moment's notice. When the Black Seminole leader John Horse put his hand to his mouth to announce an expedition, bright-kerchiefed heads appeared in the low doorways of the houses; women unhobbled the horses, slipping bits into their mouths. Then the men emerged, a powder horn and a bullet pouch slung across a shoulder, a machete or a horse pistol in hand. The weapons that the Mexican government supplied did not afford much of an advantage over the Comanches and Lipan Apaches. The muskets were so old that the men had to pour the powder into the barrels, tamp it down with some paper, put in a bullet, and tamp it down again with more paper—a cumbersome process made the guns more useful as clubs than firearms.[18]

Fugitive slaves who joined the military colony also risked being kidnapped. On September 20, 1851, John Crawford crossed the Rio Grande at Eagle Pass and requested a pass—called a *salvoconducto*—in Piedras Negras, Mexico. Then Crawford turned his horse south and east.

As he neared Guerrero, a small ranching town on the banks of the Rio Grande, the president of the town council stopped him. Crawford produced the *salvoconducto*. The municipal president waved Crawford on, but then warned the other members of the town council of the stranger from Texas. The president of the town council was right to be suspicious. The military colony where the Seminoles and their black allies had settled was several miles from Guerrero, and Crawford was no ordinary citizen. He was the sheriff of Bexar County, and he had ridden nearly two hundred miles from San Antonio to fulfill his sworn duty to enforce the laws of Texas. Upon arriving at the military colony, he kidnapped two men he suspected of being runaways. One of the prisoners was John Horse, the leader of the Black Seminoles. The other was a black man named Hongo de Agosto. Then Crawford carried them back across the Rio Grande and imprisoned them at Fort Duncan near Eagle Pass.[19]

Mexican military authorities immediately condemned the kidnapping as an "outrage to our laws and the cause of liberty that they protect." Promoting freedom was one way that Mexicans distinguished their republic from the United States. In 1850, *El Demócrata*, a liberal newspaper in Mexico City, published a poem from the perspective of a Southern slave: "Blessed be the nations / of the noble Spanish race. . . . There we are called brothers / and the laws shield us." *La Religión y La Sociedad*, a religious newspaper in Guadalajara boasted that their republic's "respect for the dignity of man without any distinction of blood" could not be "exceeded by any other nation." What Mexico lacked in wealth it made up for in righteousness. Steam engines could not be heard in Mexico, but, as *El Universal* put it, neither could "the clink of chains" or "the crack of the whip." Defending runaways underscored the contrast between Mexico's "philanthropy" and the United States' "barbarity."[20]

Mexican officials had another, more practical reason to defend the Seminoles and their black allies. Not only did these "hardworking men" contribute to the economic development of the northern states, but their "warriors" helped to defend against the "very bellicose" Indians.

In 1851, the commander of Mexico's military colonies reported that the "faithful" Black Seminoles never abandoned the "desire to succeed in punishing the enemy." Another general concluded that same year that their service provided a "great benefit" to the country. The victories that they scored against the Comanches and Lipan Apaches proved to Mexican military commanders that the Seminoles and their black allies were "worthy of every confidence"—and deserving of protection against kidnappers from the United States.[21]

On September 21, the day after John Crawford crossed the Rio Grande, the subinspector of Mexico's eastern military colonies demanded that the commander of Fort Duncan release John Horse and Hongo de Agosto. The subinspector insisted that both were "under the protection of our laws & government and considered as Mexican citizens." When the commander of Fort Duncan refused to release the two men, explaining that a court in San Antonio had ordered their arrest, Mexico's military authorities and their Seminole allies decided to secure the release of John Horse and Hongo de Agosto by other means. On the evening of September 22, a force of blacks and Indians from Mexico crossed the river, charged the fort, and freed the prisoners.[22]

The demands of military service both undermined and underscored the freedom of former slaves in northern Mexico. Blacks who joined the military colonies risked their lives in campaigns against the Comanches and Lipan Apaches. Expected to take up arms at a moment's notice, blacks found their mobility circumscribed and their habits scrutinized. At the same time, their military service convinced Mexican authorities to defend them against their former owners, and the experience that they gained fighting hostile Indians prepared them to take up arms against the kidnappers who sought to return them to the United States.

NOT EVERY RUNAWAY JOINED THE MILITARY COLONIES. IN MEXICO, fugitive slaves could trade the risks of military service for the demands of a labor contract. Some settled in cities like Matamoros, with a growing black population of merchants and carpenters, bricklayers and manual laborers, who hailed from Haiti, the British Caribbean, and the United States. Others hired themselves out to local hacendados, who were in constant need of extra hands. Evaristo Madero, a businessman who carted goods from Saltillo, Mexico, to San Antonio, Texas, hired two black servants. Espiridion Gomez employed several others on his ranch near San Fernando in Coahuila.[23]

Seeking employment came at a risk. Former slaves who worked on haciendas and in households were often the only people of African descent on the payroll, leaving them no choice but to assimilate into their new communities. Most learned Spanish. To avoid being found by their masters, many changed their names. A former slave named Dan called himself "Dionisio de Echavaria." The mayor of Guerrero, Coahuila, christened another runaway Maria Guadalupe Guerrero—Guadalupe for the Virgin who guided her to Mexico, and Guerrero for the town where she won her freedom.[24]

Fugitive slaves entered an economy defined by a shortage of labor. In the Yucatán and the southeastern lowlands, where the production of cash crops depended upon an enormous labor force, and where the local Indians generally refused to give up their largely independent existence for the regimented routine of a hacienda, planters often turned to coercive labor practices. Overseers meted out corporal punishments as harsh as any on plantations in the United States. And debt tied laborers to plantations as effectively as violence. At the *tienda de raya*—the hacienda store where workers purchased goods on credit—prices were several times higher than market value. Debts mounted to the point where laborers could not pay them off within their lifetimes. A Veracruz newspaper reported in 1849 that indentured servants occupied a state of dependence worse than slavery. *El Monitor Republicano* in Mexico City complained in 1857 that laborers had earned their "liberty in name only."[25]

But in other parts of Mexico, hacendados persuaded peons to work by means of voluntary incentives rather than outright violence. The dispossession of Indian lands in central Mexico had given rise to a large, landless labor force that worked on haciendas because the alternatives were far worse. By some estimates, fewer than half of these workers in the late eighteenth and early nineteenth centuries were in debt, and the amounts that they owed generally came to three weeks of wages or less. In northern Mexico, where livestock ranged far beyond the hacienda, and where the ranch hands responsible for herding them could easily escape to the United States, voluntary incentives also produced a more reliable labor force than violence. At one hacienda in Zacatecas, the state to the south of Coahuila, only one-fifth of the peons were indebted to their employer in any given year between 1820 and 1880. On average, indebted peons owed no more than a month's wages. The hacienda employed a schoolmaster to teach the children of peons, and the *tienda de raya* did not charge higher prices than other purveyors nearby. Similar conditions prevailed in San Luis Potosí, to the east of Zacatecas, where haciendas sometimes owed money to laborers, rather than the reverse.[26]

Enslaved people who escaped to Mexico would have encountered labor conditions that resembled slavery in the United States in certain respects. But in contrast to the southern United States, where enslaved people knew no other law besides "the caprice of the masters," laborers in Mexico enjoyed a number of legal protections. Laborers could file suits when their employers lowered their wages or added unreasonable charges to their accounts. They could also sue in cases of mistreatment, as Juan Castillo of Galeana, Nuevo León, did in 1860, after his employer hit him, whipped him, and attempted to run him over with his horse. (His employer admitted to a certain "excess of anger.") Even if the courts dismissed their suits, laborers had the right to seek new employment for any reason. All they had to do was ask their employer how much they owed and find someone who would assume their debts.[27]

Of course, employers did not always obey the laws that protected workers. In 1856, when Encarnación Baldenama asked how much he owed, Manuel Gutiérrez, his employer in Cañas, Nuevo León, claimed not to have his account. Several weeks later, Encarnación asked again.

This time, Gutiérrez showed him his account, but when Encarnación examined it closely, he discovered that Gutiérrez had lowered his daily wages from five pesos to four. Encarnación stormed off, and when he returned to the hacienda, Gutiérrez tied him up "like a goat" until he agreed to work for another three months. Gutiérrez's tactics were coercive—and illegal. Before Encarnación served out his three months, he fled. His mother filed suit on his behalf, and the courts of Nuevo León ruled in his favor.[28]

Seeking employment in Mexico carried a number of risks. In households and haciendas, former slaves did not often find a large community of people of African descent, forcing them to assimilate in ways that those who joined the Black Seminoles did not. Fugitive slaves were also vulnerable to coercion, as employers desperately tried to secure an adequate labor force on their haciendas. Mexican law provided some protection against violence and unfair dealings, but the greatest concern for former slaves was not their new employers: it was their former masters.

On August 20, 1850, Manuel Luis del Fierro stepped outside his house in Reynosa, Tamaulipas. The night was hot, and a band was playing in the plaza. As he stood, listening, two foreigners approached, asking if he wanted to join them at the concert. Del Fierro politely refused their invitation. He did not give the incident much thought until later that night, when he woke to the sound of a woman screaming. Throwing off the sheets, del Fierro took his rifle and hurried toward the commotion. In the living room, he came upon the two foreigners waving a pistol at his wife's maid, Mathilde Hennes, who "had been held as a slave in the United States."[29]

Born in Cheneyville, Louisiana, a town about hundred and fifty miles northwest of New Orleans, Mathilde belonged to a planter named William Cheney. From her years working on Cheney's plantation, Mathilde must have known that Mexico's laws gave her a claim to freedom. In

1837, not far from Cheneyville, nine slaves were hanged for planning a "crusade to Mexico" where "they would be free." The knowledge of Mexico's laws did not die with the executed slaves. Solomon Northrup, a free black man who was kidnapped and sold into slavery, heard of the plan several years later, when he arrived at a plantation in a neighboring parish. Even then, he remembered, the aim of the plot was "a subject of general and unfailing interest in every slave hut on the bayou." At some point—when or how is unclear—Mathilde acted on that knowledge, escaping from Cheneyville, making her way to Reynosa, and finding work in Manuel Luis del Fierro's household.[30]

To del Fierro, Mathilde Hennes was not just a runaway. As his wife's servant, she was a member of his household, and in the patriarchal culture of northern Mexico, he must have felt that it was his duty to protect her. In the living room of his house, del Fierro shouldered his rifle, ordering the kidnappers to stop. The two men froze. Mathilde stopped screaming. Del Fierro could faintly hear his wife calling for help from the balcony. One of the kidnappers managed to escape, but the police arrived in time to arrest the other, Mathilde Hennes's owner, William Cheney. In Mexico, Cheney found that he could not treat people of African descent with impunity, as slaveholders often did in the United States. While Cheney sat in prison, Judge Justo Treviño of the district of Northern Tamaulipas began an investigation into the attempted kidnapping.[31]

Del Fierro's actions were not unusual. In the fall of 1851, the townspeople of a small village in northern Coahuila took up arms "in the service of humanity" to stop a slave catcher named Warren Adams from kidnapping "an entire family of negroes." Several months later, the Mexican Army posted a "respectable" force and two field pieces on the Rio Grande to stop a group of two hundred *norteamericanos* from crossing the river to seize fugitive slaves. In 1852, four town councilmen from Guerrero, Coahuila, chased after a slaveholder from the United States who had kidnapped a black man from their town. Cornered in a clearing, the slaveholder pulled a six-shooter from his holster, but one of the town councilmen drew faster, killing the man. Unable to bring the kidnapper to court, the town councilmen brought his corpse to the judge of Guerrero, who certified that he was, in fact, dead, "for not having responded when spoken to, and other cadaverous signs."[32]

Why did ordinary Mexicans protect runaways? For one thing, labor was scarce. Runaways who worked as indentured servants and day laborers reduced the shortage. Fugitive slaves who intermarried with their Mexican and Indian neighbors also formed part of the local community. José, one of the men who supposedly came "straight from Africa," married a Mexican woman named Jesusa Montalvo. Two free blacks from South Carolina who arrived in Múzquiz married Black Seminole women. Mexicans protected fugitive slaves, just as they defended any other member of their community.[33]

Mexicans also might have acted out of genuine opposition to slavery. In the United States, some white Northerners took up the cause of antislavery after witnessing an enslaved person being whipped or sold, and this kind of firsthand experience also seems to have galvanized Mexicans. Particularly in northern Mexico, human bondage was more than a theoretical injustice. Northern Mexicans likened the captives traded by the Comanches and Lipan Apaches to a "mass of slaves of both sexes, children and adults." They feared that these "wild" tribes would impose on Mexico the "ominous yoke" of slavery. *Norteamericanos* posed a similar threat. During the US-Mexican War, Mexican generals rallied their recruits with the rumor that the US Army hoped to enslave them. Politicians cautioned that the chains of this conquest would not be forged of the same metal as those of the Spanish Empire, for theirs would not merely be a figurative enslavement to a colonial power, but an oppression "more insupportable than that of the African negroes."[34]

However exaggerated, this call to arms contained a kernel of truth. Mexico boasted a sizable mixed-race population. After the US-Mexican War, the United States government balked at the prospect of such an addition to the US body politic. A Massachusetts representative exclaimed that he would rather admit the Choctaws or Cherokees than the "mongrel races of Mexico." A congressman from Pennsylvania said he would prefer a "den of exasperated rattlesnakes." Even those of the "highest social and political class" in Mexico have "negro blood in their veins," wrote the *New-York Daily Tribune* in 1859. To *norteamericanos*, Mexico's *mulatos* and *morenos* were, simply, blacks.[35]

The fear of enslavement was made real by news of Mexicans being kidnapped and sold into slavery in the United States. In 1848, a Mexican boy named Severo Lugo was living in the suburbs of Monterrey, Nuevo León, when Captain Fleming Ames persuaded the boy to return with him to Mississippi. In the United States, Lugo worked for several years as a hired hand on the steamer *Telegraph No. 3*, as a shoemaker in New Albany, Indiana, and as a barber in Winchester, Kentucky. After a few years, Lugo decided to head to Louisiana. On the turnpike to New Orleans, a fellow traveler asked him who his master was. When Severo replied that "he was a Mexican and free," the man tied him with a silk handkerchief and locked him in the stateroom of a steamer bound for New Orleans. From a depot on Gravier Street, Severo was sold and re-sold until a judge learned of his predicament in 1857 and issued a writ of habeas corpus.[36]

Severo Lugo was not the only Mexican citizen who claimed to have been sold into slavery in the United States. In the spring of 1854, a "very intelligent little fellow" stumbled into a town in Indiana, telling a "romantic" story to the family who took him in. Seven years earlier, he was living with his family in Campeche, Mexico, when French pirates kidnapped him and five other boys while they were swimming one morning in the sea. For four years, the boys worked on board the ship. Then they were sold to a US merchant vessel and, two years later, to a Louisiana planter, at which point the boy escaped. On his arrival in Indiana, the boy told his story "with so much simplicity and with such apparent correctness" that the man who took him in raised a "great deal" of money to return him to Mexico.[37]

Ordinary Mexicans took up arms against kidnappers because fugitive slaves defended the frontier, added to the labor force, and formed part of the local community. The protection that Mexican citizens provided to escaped slaves was significant, because the national authorities in Mexico City did not have the resources to enforce many of their policies. Due process guarantees did not stop men from being jailed on the "most frivolous pretexts." Commercial regulations did not keep the country from becoming a "Republic of Smugglers." Mexico's freedom principle might also have been a dead letter if not for the ordinary citizens, both black and white, who risked their lives to protect fugitive slaves. These men and women were neither political hopefuls jockeying for power, nor elected officials hoping to defend their country against the United States. They were ranchers and merchants, soldiers and bricklayers, servants and barbers, and the cause of antislavery had become their own.[38]

As Mexico became known as "a sort of *REFUGIUM PECCATORUM*," the landscape of slavery in the south-central regions of the United States began to shift. No man "in his senses" risked "a large gang of negroes south of the Colorado." Prospective immigrants chose not to settle in South Texas for the "*unsafety of bringing slaves.*" The area from the township of Point Isabel to the mouth of the Rio Grande was deemed "non-slaveholding" due to its "proximity to Mexico." Slaveholders in Texas and Louisiana were concerned by the number of enslaved people escaping to the south. Diplomats from the United States pressured their Mexican counterparts to sign an extradition treaty that would return fugitive slaves to their owners. But negotiations failed in 1850—and 1851, 1853, and 1857. Mexico's extradition of fugitive slaves would not be entertained "for a moment," lamented the US Secretary of State in 1853.[39]

The flight of enslaved people to Mexico posed a threat to slavery, but Mexico's freedom principle was hardly the most significant threat that Southern politicians faced. The seizure of Alta California and Nuevo

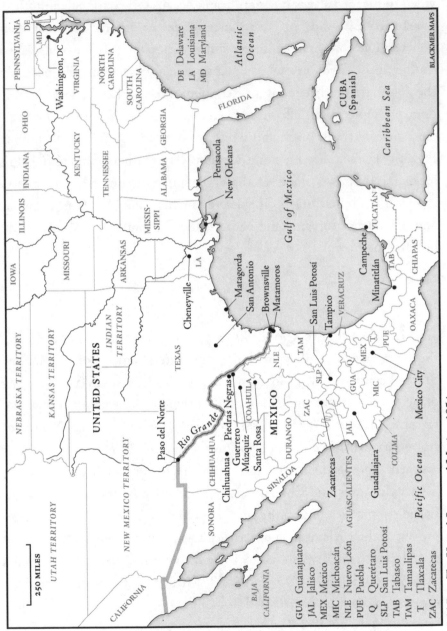

MAP 3: The United States and Mexico, 1854

México during the US-Mexican War ignited a major sectional controversy over whether the legislative branch could reestablish slavery where
it had been abolished. Efforts to prohibit slavery in the former Mexican
territories failed, but so too had measures to permit slavery. Congress
had not arrived at a solution when California petitioned to join the
Union as a "free" state in 1849. Given that the Union consisted of fifteen "free" states and fifteen slave states, the admission of California
threatened to shift the balance of power in favor of the North, and the
organization of the remaining Mexican territories would only make the
problem worse.

TEN

THE BALANCE OF POWER

O N JANUARY 29, 1850, SENATOR HENRY CLAY OF KENTUCKY rested several times as he climbed the Capitol's steps. At seventy-two, Clay was one of the oldest and most experienced politicians in Washington. He represented his state with distinction in both houses of Congress and served for four years as John Quincy Adams's Secretary of State, but he had also lost three elections for the presidency. To console or perhaps to spite him, the state of New Hampshire named a peak in the Presidential Range of the White Mountains after him in 1848— right between Mt. Washington and Mt. Jefferson.[1]

That January morning, Clay introduced a set of compromise measures that he hoped would save the Union. Each component of the compromise stoked controversy. Clay's proposal to admit California as a "free" state would shift the balance of power in favor of the North. His recommended solution to a boundary dispute in New Mexico angered neighboring Texas. Slaveholders opposed his plan to prohibit the slave trade in the District of Columbia, while abolitionists condemned his suggestion to draft a more effective fugitive slave law. But no measure was more contentious than his proposal to organize "appropriate Territorial Governments" for New Mexico and Utah without any provision on slavery. Although the measure would not prohibit slavery in the territories, Clay made clear that Mexico's laws abolishing slavery would remain in effect, until the "people" voted to alter or to uphold those laws. "Slavery does not exist by law" in the former Mexican territories, Clay explained, and if Congress reestablished slavery where it was abolished, then the "posterity of the present inhabitants" would blame the representatives "for doing just what we reproach Great Britain for doing to us."[2]

Forbidding slavery from the former Mexican territories was, of course, unacceptable to Southern politicians. "The necessary consequence" of the compromise measures, Senator John C. Calhoun objected, "is to exclude the South from that territory just as effectually as would the Wilmot Proviso." Southern politicians repeatedly proposed extending the Missouri Compromise line west to the Pacific, which would maintain the balance of power, at the expense of the principle of noninterference. To justify reestablishing human bondage in New Mexico and California, Southern congressmen argued that the Mexican government had not *really* abolished slavery. "I understand the Mexican Confederation to have been formed upon the model of our own," Senator John Berrien of Georgia stated on February 12, 1850. "The power over this subject of slavery belonged to the separate States of the Mexican Republic."[3]

The premise that Mexico had not actually abolished slavery strained Northerners' credulity. "The people of Mexico will be highly edified when they learn that their old acquaintances, the 'Norte Americanos,'" had discovered that "slavery was in full force and operation in that country, without the people themselves being aware of the fact," quipped Senator James Shields of Illinois. "I think when they hear this they will come to the conclusion that we are as invincible in logic as we are in battle." To prove that Mexico's Congress had, in fact, abolished slavery, Senator Thomas Hart Benton, a Democrat from Missouri, quoted Mexico's laws in the original Spanish. "*Ninguno es esclavo en el territorio de la nación*," Benton read. ("The Senate cannot understand a word of what he reads," complained another congressman.) Mexico's laws meant that Congress could not reestablish slavery in California and New Mexico, even if that meant destroying the balance of power between North and South. "I repeat what I have said before," Henry Clay explained. "I cannot vote to convert a territory already free into a slave territory."[4]

Despite these disagreements, Clay hoped that his fellow senators would vote for the compromise "in a spirit of mutual concession." But when he combined his compromise measures into a single bill, his colleagues rejected it on July 31, 1850. Exhausted, depressed, and ill, the senator left Washington, DC, to recuperate in Newport, Rhode Island. The task of compromise fell to an Illinois Democrat named Stephen A. Douglas. At five feet three inches, Douglas was short and barrel-chested with a square forehead and unruly brown hair that, when combed, curled outward just above his ears. Douglas had enjoyed an early and meteoric rise. At age twenty, he left his native Vermont for the Illinois prairies, where he served as a state legislator, a register of the General Land Office, the Secretary of State, and a justice on the Illinois Supreme Court. By age twenty-nine, he won election to the United States House of Representatives. Four years later, he became one of the youngest men to join the Senate. Illinois voters admired his tireless energy and his down-home manner. Not all of his colleagues shared their view. "His legs are too short," Thomas Hart Benton of Missouri noted. "That part of his body, sir, which men wish to kick, is too near the ground."[5]

Over the next six weeks during the summer of 1850, Douglas brought the original Clay resolutions to a vote as five separate measures. The admission of California passed, 150 to 58. The bill to organize the New Mexico and Utah territories left the status of slavery to the will of the people, without determining whether Mexico's laws abolishing slavery remained in force. The slave trade was abolished in the District of Columbia. The boundary dispute between New Mexico and Texas was resolved.

The most significant concession to the South was the Fugitive Slave Act of 1850, which was passed by Congress on September 18. It denied jury trials to fugitive slaves, forbade them from disputing their detention in court—the basic right of habeas corpus—and authorized federal commissioners to call upon ordinary citizens to assist in their capture.[6]

But for all that it achieved, the Compromise of 1850 did not maintain the balance of power between the North and the South. With the admission of California, the "free" states enjoyed a majority in the Senate—a majority that would prevent Southern senators from blocking legislation that ran counter to their sectional interests. The future admission of the Utah and New Mexico territories would further increase the majority that the "free" states wielded in Congress. Rather than promote and protect slavery, the annexation of Mexican territories threatened to destroy the political power of the slave states. To solve the problem caused by the abolition of slavery in Mexico, Southern leaders needed to restore the sectional balance, and they were prepared to do so by any means necessary.

ON MARCH 4, 1853, A CARRIAGE PROCESSED TOWARD THE CAPItol. Crowds lined Pennsylvania Avenue. Flags whipped against the hickory pole that had been raised for the occasion at the *Union* newspaper offices. From nearly every window and balcony in the city, people pushed for a view. By the time the carriage reached the Senate building, women had "entire possession" of the galleries above the chamber where the president-elect would take the oath of office. Franklin Pierce was notable for winning a majority of the popular vote in both the North and the South (the last president to do so, until 1932), but something else drew the public to Washington, DC, for his inauguration. By all accounts, the president-elect was "the most handsome man to ever serve as president of the United States."[7]

Pierce's looks might have been his greatest asset. Although he was a compromise candidate who was supposed to unite the Northern and Southern factions of the Democratic Party, the new president would help turn the slow burn of sectionalism into a blaze. Pierce felt "a profound sense of responsibility" when he took the oath of office, knowing that he was assuming the presidency at a difficult time. The seizure of lands from Mexico where slavery was abolished had shifted the balance of power in favor of the North. And Southern politicians were denouncing the Compromise of 1850 as a betrayal. The Democratic Party was meanwhile showing signs of fracture, as politicians in Georgia, Alabama, and Mississippi established new Southern Rights parties. Talk of secession was in the air. In his inaugural address, Pierce outlined a solution. To restore balance, Pierce proposed annexing additional slave-holding territories. From the East Portico of the Capitol, Pierce made the case that expansion "has not only shown itself compatible with the harmonious action of the States and Federal Government in their respective constitutional spheres, but has afforded an additional guaranty of the strength and integrity of both." Indeed, he believed that "our attitude as a nation and our position on the globe render the acquisition of certain possessions not within our jurisdiction eminently important for our protection, if not in the future essential for the preservation of the rights of commerce and the peace of the world."[8]

Pierce did not have to say which possessions he wanted to acquire. The US government had long trained its sights on Cuba, which remained under Spanish control, and where slavery was deeply entrenched. After the US-Mexican War, the Polk administration offered $100 million for the island. When the Spanish Crown refused to negotiate, *norteamericanos* directed their annexationist energies toward nominally unauthorized military expeditions aimed at the "liberation" of Spanish Cuba. Between 1849 and 1851, US citizens, under the direction of the Venezuelan adventurer Narciso López, mounted three major filibuster invasions of the island.[9]

Pierce's inaugural address alarmed foreign leaders. Spain clung desperately to what remained of its empire. England and France resented the growing power of the United States. Mexican leaders believed that control of Cuba determined the future of the Gulf. In 1829, Spain had launched its invasion of Mexico from Cuba, and annexation of the island by the United States threatened, in the words of the Mexico City newspaper *El Universal*, to open "the door of our nationality to those who had as much ambition to take possession of our fertile territories as the wild lands of the opulent Antilles."[10]

To stop the Pierce administration from annexing Cuba, the nations of England, France, and Spain discussed forging an offensive and defensive alliance, in which the three powers would retaliate in the event that the United States Army invaded the island. European officials did not think to include Mexico in the proposed alliance. Mexico's treasury was in dire financial straits, and the government was so desperate to raise revenues that, at one point, it levied a tax on dogs. To make matters worse, the political system in Mexico remained so unstable that in 1853, Mexican leaders invited none other than Antonio López de Santa Anna to return from exile in Colombia and rule over the country as a dictator.[11]

Nonetheless, Mexico's diplomats doubted that the proposed alliance between Spain, England, and France would succeed without their country's participation. Mexico was "the neighbor of this invasory people," as Mexico's minister to France put it. This proximity exposed the "weak side of the United States—slavery." If Mexican forces, "backed by a French and English squadron, entered the Southern states of the Union and proclaimed the liberty of the blacks," a war with the United States would be "of short duration," and Cuba would remain in Spanish hands. The Mexican Army with an antislavery decree was, according to Mexico's minister to France, "the stone that could shatter the clay foot of the giant."[12]

When Antonio López de Santa Anna stopped in Havana en route to Mexico in 1853, Buenaventura Vivó, the Mexican minister to Cuba, raised the possibility of invading the Southern states in the event that the Pierce administration annexed Cuba. Santa Anna was not an abolitionist. Not long after hearing Vivó's proposal, Santa Anna granted to a former adjutant a plum concession—exporting Mayan captives from Yucatán to Cuba to work under labor contracts that were so unfavorable as to amount to slavery. But Mexico's leader did not have to be committed to abolition to advance an antislavery policy that both served his interests and undermined those of the United States. After running the proposal by the captain general of Cuba and the Spanish minister to Mexico, Santa Anna appointed Vivó to the Mexican legation in Madrid with instructions to carry out the agreed upon plan.[13]

BUENAVENTURA VIVÓ ARRIVED IN MADRID TO FIND THE STREETS crowded with women in mantillas hurrying to mass and men smoking cigarettes on their stoops. *Rigoletto* seemed to be playing from every hand organ in Madrid. The tenor aria's jovial refrain matched the diplomat's mood. Vivó was optimistic that he would be able to convince the Spanish authorities to include Mexico in the alliance to prevent the annexation of Cuba.[14]

Not long after arriving in Madrid, Vivó met with the Spanish Secretary of Foreign Relations. Vivó explained that an alliance with Mexico would avoid a "mercantile imbalance," preserve the "Latin race," and, in general, advance "the interests of humanity." But his Spanish counterpart did not seem interested in what he was saying. Instead of discussing the offensive and defensive alliance, the Spanish Secretary of Foreign Affairs pontificated on literature, physics, and chemistry. Baffled, Vivó asked his contacts in Madrid for insights. They informed him that the Spanish authorities agreed that an alliance would be "convenient," but did not believe that the Mexican government was "stable enough" to negotiate on such a "grave subject." A treaty between Mexico and Spain would alarm the *norteamericanos*, who would use the alliance as "pretext" for intervention.[15]

For his plan to succeed, Vivó needed to convince another European power to join the alliance, and so he instructed his secretary to arrange for visits to Mexico's legations in France and England. Mexico's minister in London tried to convince the British authorities to stop "the expansion of the United States towards the South of the continent." The annexation of Cuba, he argued, would bring about "the unleashing of these new Vandals and Goths in the hemisphere of Columbus, and from thence to the Old World." The British, however, refused to act "in the name of justice and the necessity of conserving the political balance." Mexico's minister in London reported that British interests were too closely aligned with the United States—a people "who came from her breast and represented her race and ideals in America."[16]

Mexico's minister in Paris, J. R. Pacheco, made a stronger case to the French emperor, Louis Napoleon, the nephew of Napoleon Bonaparte. Louis Napoleon had taken power in 1851, and in 1852 he declared himself the emperor of France. In a meeting with Louis Napoleon's foreign minister, Pacheco outlined the plan. If the United States invaded Cuba, Mexican forces would march across the US South, while the French Navy patrolled the Gulf of Mexico. To protect the "zone of blacks in its own territory, &c., &c.," the Pierce administration would have to divert troops from Cuba to Texas and Louisiana, just as Spanish commanders had recalled troops from Mexico to Cuba in 1829. Pacheco handed his French counterpart a map of Mexico in order to give him a more detailed sense of its "geographical area and location" with respect to the United States. The French foreign minister promised to study it.[17]

Buenaventura Vivó remained cautiously optimistic about the prospects of an alliance with Louis Napoleon. "France is of a more generous character, somewhat less attached to the material interests of the moment, and representative of the first order in Europe of the Latin race," Vivó wrote. Moreover, she "has greater sympathies for Mexico and the Hispanic American nations and could better than any other nation fulfill these sentiments." France was powerful enough that even England would "respect her decision" to join an alliance with Mexico and Spain.

But Vivó's optimism proved to be misplaced. The French authorities, however "generous," could not ultimately justify the costs of promoting the cause of Hispanic America. Without the support of France, the Spanish government would not commit men or ships to the cause. "Neither philanthropy nor humanity—empty words in European politics—will move them to action," lamented Mexico's minister in Berlin.[18]

Even though the European powers refused to take part in any alliance with Mexico, rumors of Mexico's diplomacy spread anyway. The French legation in Madrid reported that General Santa Anna "has offered to conquer the . . . Port of San Domingo and deliver it over to Spain provided Spain . . . agrees to give Mexico a sort of general support (this is so vague I do not understand what it can mean) in any future disputes with the United States." The Mexican minister in Washington recounted that rumors were circulating of a European alliance to "maintain a political balance" in the Americas. "It is also known that the cooperation of Mexico is counted upon for the development of these plans," he wrote. The US minister to Mexico confirmed that "Santa Anna is drifting into an alliance with England, France, and Spain on the Cuba issue." "It becomes repulsive to the high responsibilities of the American Federation," he complained, "when European powers threaten and stimulate in Santa Anna alliances hostile to the American system." As Spanish diplomats feared, the Pierce administration resolved to act decisively before any alliance formed.[19]

By temperament, Senator Pierre Soulé of Louisiana was more a revolutionary than a statesman. Born in 1801 in France, he was locked in prison at age nineteen for inciting insurrection. After escaping from jail, he fled first to Haiti and then to Louisiana. He practiced law in New Orleans until 1849, when the Louisiana state legislature appointed him, a fugitive from justice, to the United States Senate. His colleagues in the capital did not know what to make of him, with his dark, deep-set eyes and his hair in the style of old French Republicans—long in the back, and parted far to the right. He was "impetuous" and "proud" with a "vast fund of knowledge and a deposit of vanity which was never exhausted." But he had a "tropical charm." As James G. Blaine of Maine put it, he sounded "eloquent even in a language he could not pronounce."[20]

Soulé adamantly opposed the Compromise of 1850. As a senator, he voted against the admission of California as a "free" state, and after the measure passed he added his name to a letter of protest that was signed by ten Southern senators. Admitting California, the letter read, was "destructive of the safety and liberties of those whose rights have been committed to our care, fatal to the peace and equality of the States which we represent, and must lead if persisted in, to the dissolution of that confederacy, in which the slaveholding States have never sought more than equality, and in which they will not be content to remain with less."[21]

To Soulé, the only way to right the balance of power was to annex Cuba and bring the number of slave and "free" states to an even sixteen. As he saw it, the Northern public had ample reason to support annexation. The Northern economy depended on exports to the Caribbean. Annexing the island to the United States would eliminate the tariffs, sometimes in excess of 200 percent, that the Spanish imposed on the flour, lumber, fish, and meat that Northern producers shipped to Cuba. *La Verdad*, a newspaper published by Cuban exiles in New York, estimated that annexation would increase US exports of flour from less than five thousand barrels in 1846 to more than two million a year.[22]

In 1853, Franklin Pierce appointed Soulé the United States minister to Spain. On the eve of his departure for Madrid in the late summer of 1853, Cuban exiles in New York marched by torchlight up Broadway, carrying transparencies that read "Free Thought and Free Speech for the Cubans" and "Cuba Must and Shall Be Free." Soulé greeted them from his balcony at the New York Hotel, saying, "I could not believe that we were eternally to be encircled within the narrow limits described as the space assigned to us at the dawn of the Republic." He promised the five-thousand-strong crowd that he would "carry where he [went] the throbbing of that people that speak out such tremendous truths to the tyrants of the old continent."[23]

With Pierce in the White House, and an unabashed expansionist at the US Embassy in Madrid, the United States only needed an excuse to seize Cuba. On February 28, 1854, a US-owned ship named the *Black Warrior* arrived at the port of Havana. The captain did not declare the nine hundred bales of cotton in the steamer's hold, and when customs officials discovered the cargo, they seized it. Though the captain had plainly violated Spanish customs regulations, *norteamericanos* were indignant at his punishment. "It only remains to be seen," the proslavery New Orleans *Daily Picayune* wrote, "whether our Government and people will submit to this, or make it a cause of war." A Mississippi newspaper predicted that the United States government would soon tear that jewel from the Spanish crown."[24]

The Pierce administration had what it needed—an excuse. On May 15, 1854, the president asked Congress to adopt "provisional measures" for war. But with majorities in both houses, Northerners refused to honor the president's request. Pierce was not deterred. On March 16, the New York and Atlantic Steamship Company paid a six-thousand-dollar fine, and Spanish authorities released the *Black Warrior*. The next day, the Pierce administration instructed Soulé to demand that Spain supply a three-thousand-dollar indemnity for the "flagrant wrong" of having seized the steamship and her cargo. Soulé received further instructions two weeks later to "agree, treat, consult, and negotiate" for the purchase of Cuba. The United States government would offer up to $130 million. If Spain refused to negotiate, Secretary of State William Marcy instructed Soulé to direct his efforts "to the next desirable object which is to detach that island from the Spanish dominion."[25]

The Pierce administration was determined to restore the balance of power, and the annexation of Cuba was only one means of doing so. At the same time that the Pierce administration was preparing to seize

Cuba by force, congressional Democrats were pushing to overturn the Missouri Compromise and open the unorganized territories of the Louisiana Purchase to slavery.

THE CHAIRMAN OF THE SENATE COMMITTEE ON TERRITORIES WAS Illinois Senator Stephen Douglas. Douglas had a strong interest in organizing the Kansas and Nebraska Territories, the only unorganized territories that remained from the Louisiana Purchase. The senator owned land in northwestern Illinois, and building a railroad from Chicago to San Francisco was projected to increase its value fourfold. But the territories needed to be organized before the railroad could be built, and the terms of their organization were proving controversial.[26]

The earlier debates over the incorporation of the former Mexican territories had destroyed any semblance of a consensus about how to organize the territories. During the US-Mexican War, Northern Democrats invoked the principle of noninterference to argue that Congress could neither restrict slavery where it existed nor reestablish it where it did not. The territories, as Senator John Adams Dix of New York explained in 1847, should be "taken as they were found." But Southern moderates, fearful of losing political power, took the extreme position of firebrands like John C. Calhoun, arguing that Congress could not interfere with slavery *anywhere*. According to this interpretation, the antislavery provisions of the Northwest Ordinance and the Missouri Compromise were unconstitutional.[27]

Now Southern politicians swore to oppose any measures to organize the remaining territories of the Louisiana Purchase in accordance with the Missouri Compromise. The prohibition on slavery north of 36°30' was a "festering thorn" in "the side of the South," as Senator Andrew P. Butler of South Carolina put it, because it decreased the chances that another slave state would join the Union. Senator David Atchison of Missouri crowed that Southern politicians would prefer Kansas to "sink into hell" than become a "free" state. "If we can't all go there on the same [s]tring, with all our property of every kind, I say let the Indians have it *forever*," wrote another Missouri politician. "They are better neighbors than the abolitionists, *by a damn sight*."[28]

Douglas knew that overturning the thirty-four-year-old compromise would cause "a hell of a storm" in the North, but he saw no alternative. On January 23, 1854, Douglas proposed to organize the Kansas and Nebraska Territories in accordance with what was known as the doctrine of popular sovereignty. According to this doctrine, the territorial legislatures—not Congress—had the power to decide whether or not to permit slavery. As such, the Kansas-Nebraska Act declared the prohibition of slavery north of 36°30' "inoperative and void."[29]

Northerners were outraged. The Missouri Compromise was, to them, a sacred compact. They had only agreed to admit Missouri as a slave state in exchange for the prohibition against slavery north of 36°30'. Now that it had come time to organize those territories, Southern politicians were reneging on the bargain. Douglas tried to reassure Northerners that the doctrine of popular sovereignty would have no effect on the status of slavery in Kansas or Nebraska. No law on slavery would exist in the region until the territorial legislatures voted on one, and slaveholders would never risk bringing their slaves to a territory without any legal protections. The first territorial legislature of Kansas, no doubt made up of merchants and yeoman farmers, would cast their votes against slavery. As in California, Douglas predicted that these territories would join the Union as "free" states.[30]

Despite Douglas's assurances, Northern congressmen feared that popular sovereignty would not work in the unorganized territories of the Louisiana Purchase as it had in California. In California, Mexican law abolished slavery, and the local courts ruled on two separate occasions that these statutes remained in effect until the US Congress overturned them. Since Congress had not modified those laws, Southern planters risked forfeiting their slaves by relocating to the former Mexican territories. Moving to Kansas or Nebraska did not carry the same risk, because the previous laws passed by the French in Louisiana *had* recognized slavery. To address this concern, Northerners proposed adding an article to the Kansas-Nebraska Act, clarifying that it would not revive any previous law "establishing, prohibiting, or abolishing slavery." The article passed, 35 to 6.[31]

On May 22, 1854, the House of Representatives called the Kansas-Nebraska Act to a vote. Forty-four Northern Democrats voted for the bill, convinced by the argument that popular sovereignty would conciliate the South without reestablishing slavery in the remaining territories of the Louisiana Purchase. The bill passed, 113 to 110. Three days later, the Senate adopted the Kansas-Nebraska Act by a vote of 35 to 13.[32]

A day after the Kansas-Nebraska Act passed, the *New York Times* noted "a growing and profound determination among the masses of the free states that slavery shall not extend itself." On January 22, 1854, Senator Salmon Chase of Ohio denounced the bill in the abolitionist *National Era* as a "plot against humanity" to extend the "blight of slavery" across the free territories. A week later, former Representative David Wilmot of Pennsylvania organized a public meeting to write a political platform based on Chase's letter. This new coalition of Northern Whigs and discontented Democrats would come to call itself the Republican Party, and its purpose was to repeal the Kansas-Nebraska Act. "The Nebraska question has sadly shattered our party in all the free states," Democrat William Marcy acknowledged in a letter to Senator James Mason of Virginia. As Northern Democrats left their party in droves, the need to restore the balance of power became even more pressing. Northerners enjoyed majorities in both the House and the Senate. If Southern politicians failed to annex Cuba, nothing would stop Northerners from imposing their views on the nation.[33]

ON AUGUST 1, 1854, THE PIERCE ADMINISTRATION ASKED CONGRESS for $10 million to negotiate the purchase of Cuba. The Senate Committee on Foreign Relations, which fielded the request, decided to postpone debate until the December session of Congress. But Pierce was not inclined to wait. The president instructed the US ministers to Spain, France, and England to work out a plan for the annexation of Cuba.[34]

In October, the three ministers convened in Ostend, Belgium. The document that they drafted listed a number of reasons for the Spanish government to cede the island to the US. They noted that Spain had given the United States no satisfaction after the *Black Warrior* incident. Moreover, the annexation of Cuba was essential to "the internal peace and the existence of our cherished Union." In Ostend, the ministers concluded that by the laws of "self-preservation," the United States "shall be justified in wresting [Cuba] from Spain."[35]

The document that became known as the Ostend Manifesto unleashed a political maelstrom. European newspapers predicted that the United States would go to war over Cuba. Horace Greeley, the antislavery editor of the *New-York Tribune*, skewered the Pierce administration for returning the world to "the days of Attila or Genghis Kahn." The *New-York Evening Post* concluded that as US minister to Spain, Pierre Soulé deserved no more confidence "than any patient taken at random from the Bloomingdale Insane Asylum."[36]

The president and his cabinet desperately tried to distance themselves from the Ostend Manifesto. The midterm elections had already delivered a humiliating defeat to the Democratic Party, which lost its majority in the House of Representatives for the first time since 1846. With only seven of the forty-five Northern Democrats who voted for the Kansas-Nebraska Act reelected, the Pierce administration was in no position to force the annexation of Cuba. When Congress asked for all documents relating to the Ostend meeting, the administration decided against including the letter instructing Soulé to "detach" Cuba from Spain. But the damage was already done. On November 13, Secretary Marcy rejected the ministers' recommendation to seize Cuba, and Soulé resigned.[37]

The seizure of Mexican territories where slavery was abolished tilted the balance of power in favor of the North, and none of the efforts to right it had succeeded. Cuba had slipped Pierce's grasp. The Kansas-Nebraska Act gave rise to a political party determined to halt the expansion of slavery. To make matters worse, the Fugitive Slave Act had gone unenforced in several high-profile cases. In 1850, two bounty hunters were arrested in Boston for attempted kidnapping and public smoking while the fugitive slaves that they had been hired to return escaped to Canada. A year later, as a fugitive slave named Shadrach Minkins was awaiting trial at the Boston courthouse, several men barged through the door, overpowered the federal marshals, and carried him down the stairs into a carriage. Minkins never returned to slavery in Virginia.[38]

President Franklin Pierce could not stand for such disregard of the law under his watch. On May 24, 1854, Deputy Marshal Asa O. Butman arrested an escaped slave named Anthony Burns as he was leaving the clothing store on Brattle Street in Boston where he worked. But when a group of black and white abolitionists took a battering ram to the courthouse door in an effort to free Burns, Pierce dispatched the US Marines to Boston. On June 2, soldiers led Burns through the streets of the city. The buildings were draped in black. A United States flag was hanging upside down. At the wharf, a revenue cutter waited to take Burns back to Virginia. The air was electric. "We went to bed one night old fashioned, conservative Compromise Union Whigs," wrote the textile magnate Amos A. Lawrence, "& waked up stark mad Abolitionists." At the cost of $100,000, and Northern public opinion, President Pierce had defended slaveholders' rights.[39]

Yet slavery in the United States was far from secure. Enslaved people were escaping to the Northern states and Canada, as well as to Mexico. A dozen slaves reached Matamoros, in Mexico, each month. In a single year, 270 arrived at Laredo, Tamaulipas, a border town on the Rio Grande. In 1860, six of the nine slaves that the census takers tallied in Brownsville, Texas, were "fugitives from the state." Not only was the institution of slavery under threat. Slaveholders were convinced that their very lives were in danger. Residents of Washington-on-the-Brazos feared that runaways were "lurking" in the canebrakes. Rumors circulated of

Mexican troops assembling on the border to drive every *norteamericano* "over the Nueces." Local authorities set to work negotiating extradition treaties with the governments of Coahuila and Nuevo León. Bounty hunters searched the ranches and haciendas of northeastern Mexico for runaways. But the problem only seemed to be getting worse. "The frequent occurrence of the running off of our negroes is becoming so great an evil that it calls for a remedy," wrote a concerned citizen to the governor of Texas. Something had to be done—and soon.[40]

ELEVEN

CITIZENSHIP

In the town of Minatitlán, one hundred miles south of Veracruz, a *norteamericano* named Lucien Matthews was arrested in 1853 for having "uttered words" against His Serene Highness Antonio López de Santa Anna. A. C. Allen, the consul in Minatitlán, often interceded on behalf of detained US citizens, but in this case, he hesitated. Lucien Matthews was "a colored man." In the United States, the status of African Americans was unclear. Federal statutes excluded people of color from the rights and privileges of citizenship, while state governments had passed conflicting legislation on the subject. Free blacks could claim citizenship in some Northern states, but many Southern states denied them even the most basic civil rights.[1]

Not knowing "what kind of protection if any could be given to American free negroes," Allen asked the US Secretary of State for guidance. When he received no reply, he wrote again. The closest he got to an answer was when a diplomat in Matamoros forwarded a copy of another communication from Washington, which, while purporting to define "the relations of Free Persons of Color to Representatives of the U. States abroad," simply advised consuls to exercise judgment based on the circumstances. After some consideration, Allen decided to help Matthews. The diplomatic corps, he reasoned, had a "sacred duty" to protect *norteamericanos*, "whether they be citizens in their full rights or natives."[2]

The consular dispatches from Minatitlán caught the attention of James Gadsden, the US minister to Mexico. A land speculator, railroad promoter, and slaveholder, Gadsden was above all a showman: he bluffed, blustered, and, according to one historian, "uniformly employed high-sounding and redundant phrases whose meaning he did not fully comprehend." As US minister to Mexico, Gadsden used "insulting" language, excited "incessant" disputes on "trifling" grounds, and insisted on referring to the Republic of Mexico as a "kingdom." His aim was to further the political interests of the Southern states. To that end, he negotiated the purchase of twenty-nine million acres of what would become southern Arizona and New Mexico in the spring of 1853, clearing the way for the construction of a railroad from El Paso to San Diego that would link the former Mexican territories to the South. Railroad boosters hoped that a stronger Southern influence would transform New Mexico and perhaps even California into slave states.[3]

After doing what he could to help restore the balance of power between North and South, Gadsden turned his attentions to undercutting the emancipatory policies of Mexico. For years, diplomats from the United States had been trying without success to undermine the promise of freedom in Mexico. Negotiations for an extradition treaty repeatedly failed. Attempts to kidnap runaways from across the Rio Grande fared no better. But the correspondence from the consuls in Minatitlán seemed to offer another way to undercut Mexico's antislavery laws. Each year, foreigners in Mexico had to apply for a visa known as a *carta de seguridad* or face a twenty-dollar fine. (The indigent could, alternatively, spend ten days in prison.) To apply for *cartas de seguridad*, foreigners had to submit documentation from their local consul proving that they were citizens of the nation from which they claimed to have come. US consuls certified the citizenship of eighty-two African Americans applying for *cartas* between 1831 and 1857—a number that James Gadsden suspected included fugitive slaves.[4]

Gadsden believed that he had at last found a way to stop the Mexican government from granting freedom and citizenship to African Americans. If foreigners could live safely in Mexico only by being granted a *carta de seguridad*, then refusing to certify the citizenship of African Americans would deliver a death blow to Mexico's emancipatory policies.

On June 28, 1854, James Gadsden distributed a circular that "strongly" discouraged the US diplomatic corps from acknowledging the citizenship of African Americans in Mexico. People of African descent were not "recognized as Citizens at home," and so they could not "claim abroad what would be denied to them in the States from which they have absconded." Recognizing African Americans as citizens, the circular continued, "acted as a strong encouragement to increase the number of fugitives" from the United States. A growing number of African Americans applied for *cartas de seguridad* in the wake of the US-Mexico War, but as United States consuls carried out Gadsden's instructions, the number of *cartas* issued to African Americans plummeted. "As the State Department at Washington does not grant passports to such," the US consul in Veracruz wrote, "I, as an officer of the General Government of the US, which is essentially a 'white government,' cannot recognize such authority in the premises." The average number of African Americans applying for *cartas* each year dropped from about twenty-six between 1850 and 1854 to twelve between 1855 and 1859 (Table 2).[5]

TABLE 2: BLACK APPLICANTS FOR CERTIFICATES OF CITIZENSHIP

YEAR	NUMBER OF APPLICANTS
1840	6
1841	23
1842	8
1843	20
1844	49
1845	20
1846	16
1847	11
1848	15
1849	16
1850	14
1851	18
1852	23
1853	31
1854	47
1855	20
1856	8
1857	22
1858	8
1859	3

This table lists the number of US citizens, by year, who applied for certificates of citizenship from the US consuls in Mexico, and whose skin color was described as black, mulatto, or *trigueño* (swarthy). (I have included *trigueño* because some applicants identified one year as *trigueño* were identified in other years as blacks or mulattos.) The number of applicants plummeted after Gadsden's circular in 1854. The uptick in 1857 might have resulted from the Mexican Constitution of 1857 (which did not restrict citizenship on the basis of color) or the *Dred Scott* decision (which denied citizenship to people of color in the United States).

Mexican officials criticized Gadsden's circular. President Antonio López de Santa Anna rejected it as "contradictory to the principles, sentiments, and acts of this government." Mexican newspapers mocked the circular. "It does not stop being strange and to a certain point scandalous this exclusion in a Christian country where every status and every race has equal right to and protection under the laws," wrote the *Eco del Comercio* in Veracruz. The *Diario Oficial* took Gadsden's directive as additional proof that the United States' "beautiful theories" were nothing but "shameful" lies. "The United States did not have orders of knights nor titles of nobility, but every one of her citizens believed himself a king who disdained those of another race."[6]

The charge that Gadsden's instructions violated the founding principles of the United States struck a nerve. The US diplomatic corps defensively insisted that people of African descent did, in fact, enjoy protections abroad after leaving the United States. John T. Pickett, the US consul at Veracruz, who regarded African Americans not as "citizens" or "subjects" but "minors under tutelage," remarked in 1855 that he would nonetheless "protect them if imposed on." Even James Gadsden decided to intervene in Lucien Matthews's case in Minatitlán in 1855, arguing that "the African born under that protection and who has been recognized and respected as such on a foreign soil will find that his claim to be shielded from personal violence and abuse will be respected as much by an accredited minister and consul or official as that of the recognized citizens of the Federal States who they represent." Though not a US citizen, Matthews continued to enjoy "the protection which nativity, long allegiance, and good conduct had secured for him in the state of his birth." According to Gadsden, it was Mexico, not the United States, that had failed to live up to its founding principles, for the same government that promised "asylum," "protection," and "milder treatment" to blacks had imprisoned a "simple African" from Louisiana without due process.[7]

Even if the diplomatic corps had refused to intercede on behalf of African Americans, fugitive slaves would have continued to enjoy freedom and citizenship in Mexico. Gadsden fundamentally misunderstood the purpose of *cartas de seguridad*. These documents did not extend the citizenship rights or permanent residence status that many people of African descent sought. Instead, *cartas de seguridad* granted them political protections while in Mexico for limited periods of time. These protections were important for African Americans who intended to return to the United States. Gadsden's instructions made it more difficult for African American travelers like Edward Wright, a free black seaman from Philadelphia, whose work often took him from Veracruz to Minatitlán to Tehuantepec, to apply for *cartas de seguridad*. But these instructions did not stop African Americans from applying for citizenship in Mexico—a process in which consuls played no role. Gadsden's circular was not an example of the United States government exercising extraterritorial authority: this episode tells not of power but the illusion of it. In spite of Gadsden's efforts, diplomats could not return fugitive slaves by bureaucratic obstruction, any more than slaveholders could by brute force.[8]

FOREIGNERS COULD BECOME CITIZENS OF MEXICO IN ONE OF TWO ways. The first was to request a *carta de naturalización*, or "letter of naturalization." To embark on this path to citizenship, foreigners had to submit affidavits proving their Catholic faith and their "good conduct." They also had to swear to obey Mexican laws and to renounce allegiance to other nations. Their naturalization had to be voted on by a state legislature or the Congress, then it finally had to be approved by the governor or the president. Black foreigners took advantage of this option. In 1850, twenty-eight African Americans who fought with an artillery company in Tampico submitted a request for citizenship. The president himself approved their application, on the recommendation of two high-ranking military men, and issued the *cartas* free of charge.[9]

The second route to citizenship was simpler and, as a result, more common. Foreigners who owned property, joined the military, or performed "some honest and useful industry" became citizens by default. No formal applications or approvals were required. African Americans often became Mexican citizens without putting pen to paper. They simply fulfilled their obligations and then exercised the rights of citizenship. They asked for and received land from the government (at the time, foreigners could not become landowners in Mexico). They were placed on municipal juries and were appointed as deputies to local magistrates, both duties reserved for citizens. Their names were not included on the list of foreigners that local authorities sent each year to the Department of Foreign Relations.[10]

Exercising the rights of citizenship was neither easy nor assured. Foreigners who became naturalized by joining the military and performing other "useful" services never received documentation of their citizenship. As a result, Mexican authorities often struggled to distinguish between these naturalized citizens and foreign residents who had neglected to apply for the required *cartas de seguridad*. To prove that they were loyal citizens rather than negligent foreigners, black émigrés had to rely on witnesses. In 1852, after the authorities arrested an African American coachman named Enrique Van Scoit for not having a *carta*, his baptismal godfather testified that Van Scoit did not need such documentation because he was "considered to be Mexican" for having converted to Catholicism.[11]

Even those who formally applied for naturalization were hardpressed to prove their citizenship when it was called into question. In 1850, an African American man named Francisco Dupuis applied for a *carta de naturalización* on the grounds that he had fought with an artillery company in Tampico during the US-Mexican War. The president himself approved the application, but Dupuis left Tampico before receiving his naturalization papers. Far from the military commanders who could serve as witnesses, and without any record of his naturalization, Dupuis was detained in 1853 in San Juan del Rio, Querétaro, for having failed to apply for a *carta de seguridad*. Dupuis petitioned for the fines to be waived and his naturalization papers reissued, but his application was forwarded to the Department of Foreign Relations, which issued *cartas de seguridad*, instead of the executive branch, which issued *cartas de naturalización*. The administrator who processed Dupuis's application assumed that he had "mistakenly" asked for a *carta de naturalización*, and issued him a *carta de seguridad* instead.[12]

The difficulties of proving their legal status when it was called into question undercut the rights of African Americans in Mexico, but these obstacles were not bureaucratic ruses designed to deny citizenship to people of African descent. Dozens of white foreigners also mistakenly applied to the Department of Foreign Relations for naturalization papers, when instead they needed to apply to their state legislature or the Congress. In 1834, the Department of Foreign Relations approved Jaime Castellano's request for a "letter of naturalization and citizenship" but as with Francisco Dupuis, delivered a *carta de seguridad* instead. Fifteen years later, Joseph Purnell explained that he had no passport from his "native country" of Florida, because he intended to "subsist in this town as a citizen." Although Purnell hoped to become naturalized, the Department of Foreign Relations sent the only document it was authorized to issue: a *carta de seguridad.* Their naturalization requests were denied, not because the Mexican government was conspiring against them, but because they had misfiled their applications.[13]

Even when white applicants secured naturalization papers, their citizenship rights were not secure. In 1853, a Spaniard was charged a fine for not having a *carta*—a fine that he disputed by calling witnesses to testify that he had become a citizen after living in Mexico for forty-two years, marrying a Mexican woman, and serving in the Mexican military. Five years later, the Mexican government refused to compensate a *norteamericano* named John Long for a forced loan on the grounds that as a foreigner he was not entitled to repayment. The town council of Múzquiz, Coahuila, interceded on his behalf, explaining that Long had immigrated from the United States, married the daughter of the governor of Coahuila y Téjas, and with his father-in-law's help, applied for a letter of citizenship in 1832. The town council of Múzquiz informed the national authorities that Long was a Mexican citizen because he had "lived in the town for almost thirty years and never with a *carta de seguridad*, as was required of foreigners."[14]

Becoming a citizen of Mexico was not a straightforward process. Some African Americans applied for *cartas de naturalización*. Others proved themselves worthy of citizenship by their actions. Neither option stopped their status from being called into question. But in contrast to the United States, where naturalization was limited to "any alien, being a white person," foreigners could and did become Mexican citizens, regardless of race. For former slaves who sought not just personal freedom but political belonging, this possibility was significant. For their masters, it underscored the danger that Mexico's policies posed to slavery in the United States.[15]

On August 25, 1855, ten slaveholders from San Antonio wrote to the subinspector of the military colonies in Chihuahua, threatening to recover their runaway slaves by force if no "friendly agreement" could be reached. The subinspector was a Danish émigré named Emilio Langberg, who had remade himself when he arrived in Mexico at the age of twenty-four. He boasted that he had fought in "various battles" in Europe, although he had never served in the military. Nonetheless Langberg's claims were enough to secure him a professorship at the Heroico Colegio Militar, a military academy in Mexico City. During the US-Mexican War, he fought for his adopted country, winning a special commendation for his service. After the war, he was appointed subinspector of the military colonies in Chihuahua. But his career stalled on the Mexican frontier. During the six years that he attacked Comanche strongholds and trained field pieces on *norteamericano* filibusters, he did not receive a single promotion.[16]

Discontented with his years of "fruitless frontier duty," Langberg whiled away as much of his "virtual exile" as possible in Texas. He took his cavalrymen to the dress parades at Fort Fillmore, thirty miles north of Paso del Norte. He even celebrated his birthday by drinking with his friends in the US officer corps. Increasingly, he found himself sympathizing with slaveholders in Texas. Although he had, on at least one occasion, asked the Seminoles and their black allies to join him on an expedition, he insisted that fugitive slaves were more "burdensome" than "useful." He also came to believe that Southern planters treated their slaves "with greater consideration than we do our peons." On August 31, 1855, when the ten slaveholders from San Antonio requested the return of their slaves, Langberg forwarded their petition to his superiors, with a note of support. Texans, he felt, had as much right to pursue their slaves in Mexico as Mexicans had to reclaim their indentured servants in the United States. Better to negotiate, he argued, than to "expose the entire frontier to an invasion."[17]

Northern Mexicans immediately rebuked Emilio Langberg for recommending the extradition of fugitive slaves. The townspeople of Guerrero, Coahuila, accused Langberg of treason. The military colonists at the Presidio de Rio Grande and Piedras Negras demanded an investigation, decrying his "despotic character" and "airs of a sultan." Two weeks later, the governor of Nuevo León formally rejected Langberg's recommendation, stating that "it is not considered in the authority of a few residents of Béxar to settle this business." The Mexican minister of war agreed that if these Texans "resolve to invade our frontier with the aim of recovering their runaway slaves and their stolen horses, in this case you will with regret be compelled to repel force with force." Langberg lamented that "this business of the extradition has encountered much opposition in the government" and feared that he would "not be able to arrange anything on this subject."[18]

Negotiations having failed, slaveholders prepared to make good on their threats to invade Mexico. In the late summer of 1855, Ranger Captain James Calhoun Callahan marched with eighty men from San Antonio to the Rio Grande. By the time they reached Eagle Pass at the end of September, Callahan's forces numbered over one hundred. On October 2, the men began swimming their horses across the Rio Grande. The next day, they rode toward the military colony where the Seminoles and their black allies had settled.[19]

On October 3, the soldiers at Fort Duncan, Texas, were just finishing their evening duties, when a "badly wounded" man stumbled into their midst and told them what had happened to Callahan's men earlier that day. At Rio Escondido, twenty miles from the military colony, a force of Mexicans, Seminoles, and—fittingly—"Negroes" ambushed the Texans. According to the wounded man, "the Mexicans had attacked the Texans with such an overwhelming force that he feared they had all been killed." Major Sidney Burbank, the commander at Fort Duncan, received "repeated messages" that Callahan's forces "were pursued by the Mexicans and Indians, and expected to be attacked every minute." Burbank "immediately placed several heavy guns in such position as to command the ferry and crossing." But instead of returning to the United States under the cover provided by Burbank, Callahan's men occupied Piedras Negras, the Mexican town across the river from Fort Duncan. Callahan issued a proclamation claiming that his men had defeated a superior force of Mexicans, Seminoles, and Lipan Apaches, and urging all able-bodied men to join the fight.[20]

On October 6, Mexican forces advanced on Piedras Negras. Callahan dispatched a message to Fort Duncan, asking for protection as his men crossed the river. Captain Sidney Burbank sent a "decided refusal." Later that evening, Callahan wrote again, explaining that his men were deserting him, and that the seventy or so Texans who remained did not stand a chance against the Mexican forces. Burbank replied "that they had deliberately come to the determination to make a stand against the Mexican forces, and after what had transpired, they must abide by their determination." Outnumbered, the Texans set fire to the town to cover their retreat. By the next morning, Piedras Negras was nearly burned to the ground. Seven Mexicans had died, and twenty-three were injured in the conflagration. The commandant general of Coahuila warned that "the enemies of our national integrity will repeat the same or greater insults as they perpetrated recently in Piedras Negras."[21]

SOUTHERN WHITES FOUND IT DIFFICULT TO BELIEVE THAT EN-slaved people preferred to live in Mexico as free and indentured laborers than in the United States as slaves. In 1854, the proslavery *New Orleans*

Daily Crescent claimed that Mexican landowners were making runaways into slaves "after the Mexican fashion" by forcing them to sign indenture contracts. Three years later, the *San Antonio Texan* reported that runaways in Mexico were "ragged," "starving," and "destitute of the comforts of life." The banner of liberty bandied by the Mexican government was, to one Texas slaveholder, as "false as hell itself."[22]

Texas newspapers even asserted that the conditions in Mexico were so poor that runaways were returning to the United States of their own accord. Noah Smithwick, a gunsmith who had lived in Texas since 1827, recalled that a slave named Moses had grown tired of living off "husks" in Mexico and returned to his master's "lenient rule" along the San Bernard River. Another came back from his "Mexican tour" in 1852, according to the proslavery *Northern Standard*, with a "supreme disgust" for Mexicans. The *Benton Independent* reported that three runaways turned back before they even reached the Rio Grande.[23]

Some fugitive slaves did return to Texas, though not for the reasons that slaveholders assumed. In 1854, Texas authorities arrested a slave "formerly belonging to a Mr. Gordon of Texas" who escaped to Mexico two years earlier. "Like all others who live there he has a poor opinion of the country and laws," reported the *Independent Press*. "Many negroes are leaving Mexico and coming to Texas to keep from starvation." The runaway, Albert Gordon, was whipped for having escaped. As his wounds crusted and knitted together, he worked diligently at his master's cotton plantation near Matagorda, Texas, where the Brazos River emptied into the Gulf, leaving a red plume of mud. But Albert had not come back to stay. Six months later, he was gone—this time, with his brothers, Henry and Isaac.[24]

Other fugitive slaves returned to the United States for the same reason as Albert Gordon. After escaping from Texas, Peter Saens secured a contract with the state government of Coahuila. For twenty-five pesos a month, he worked as a blacksmith, repairing arms and agricultural tools for the Seminole military colony near Múzquiz. In the spring of 1856, Saens decided to rescue his brother from across the Rio Grande. With the permission of the state authorities in Saltillo, Saens slipped across the Rio Grande and returned some time later with his brother.[25]

Larger political developments in Mexico would only strengthen the claims of escaped slaves like Albert Gordon and Peter Saens to freedom and citizenship. In the late summer of 1854, His Serene Highness Antonio López de Santa Anna was ousted from power. The politicians who took his place sought to eliminate the parts of Mexico's colonial heritage that they believed prevented the rise of a stable, republican political system. The series of reforms that they enacted took aim at the special privileges granted to religious figures and indigenous peoples. Monasteries were seized. Indians' communal lands were divided. To inaugurate what many hoped would be the modern political era, Mexico's government convened a special congress that was tasked with drafting a new constitution—one that would finally make good on the promise that all were equal before the law.[26]

MEXICO'S CONSTITUENT CONGRESS HAD A YEAR TO WRITE A CONstitution. Beginning on February 14, 1856, the delegates met every day on the second floor of the National Palace in Mexico City. Francisco Zarco attended every debate. The representative from Durango was unmistakable, with his curly black hair, parted at the side, and a thick mustache that curved downward, accentuating his already severe demeanor. But what most distinguished him was that he was taking notes.[27]

Recording what was being said at the Constituent Congress was not one of his official duties, although for Zarco it was an important way to fulfill the oath he had taken as a new congressman to defend the "good and prosperity of the nation." Zarco believed that the people had a right to know what was going on in the National Palace, and as the editor of the newspaper *El Siglo Diez y Nueve*, he had a way to tell them. And so every night, after leaving the National Palace, Zarco strode to his office on the Calle de Rebeldes. There, he began to set type.[28]

The changes that the delegates proposed to Mexico's political system were drastic. The new constitution guaranteed the right to education and the right to bear arms, the freedom of speech and the freedom of conscience; it also abolished the death penalty in most cases, and it prohibited the Roman Catholic Church from owning more real estate than strictly necessary for religious purposes—an open attack on ecclesiastical power in Mexico. These changes promised to transform Mexican society, but to former slaves, the most important guarantees of the new constitution had to do with freedom and citizenship.[29]

After discussing the "rights of man" upon which the Republic of Mexico had been founded, the delegates voted unanimously on July 18, 1856, to write the "freedom principle" into the national constitution. Everyone born in Mexico was free. No fugitive slaves would be extradited. Enslaved people would "recover their liberty" from the moment they "set foot on the national territory." Forced labor of any kind was prohibited. Citizenship was granted not just to children born to Mexican parents but also to any foreigner who acquired property, married a Mexican citizen, or became naturalized. Every Mexican, no matter how poor, could vote and serve in public office. When the constitution was ratified on February 5, 1857, the delegates exalted that "equality, as of today, is the great law of the Republic."[30]

In the United States, Southern whites noted this development with alarm. Their own government had just proposed a very different vision of citizenship. On March 6, 1857, eight months after Mexico's Constituent Congress promised freedom and citizenship to people of African descent, the United States Supreme Court issued its ruling in *Dred Scott v. Sandford*. The plaintiff, a slave named Dred Scott, sued for his freedom in Missouri on the grounds that he had lived with his master, John Sanford, in the Wisconsin territory, as well as in the "free" state of Illinois. The question before the Court, as Chief Justice Roger Taney put it, was whether "a negro, whose ancestors were imported into this country, and sold as slaves, [could] become a member of the political community formed and brought into existence by the Constitution of the United States, and as such become entitled to all of the rights, and privileges, and immunities, guaranteed by that instrument to the citizens." The Supreme Court answered in the negative.[31]

In the majority opinion, Chief Justice Taney denied that people of African descent had been or ever could be citizens of the United States. To Taney, it was "too clear for dispute that the enslaved African race were not intended to be included" in the opening lines of the Declaration of Independence. In 1821, Attorney General William Wirt had ruled that "free persons of color were not citizens." Taney himself had prepared an opinion while serving as attorney general under Andrew Jackson in the early 1830s. In that opinion, Taney held that the African race was a "degraded class" not entitled to the guarantees of the Constitution. In the 1850s, Attorney General Caleb Cushing prohibited African Americans from obtaining passports as citizens of the United States. From these precedents, Chief Justice Taney concluded that Dred Scott was not a citizen and therefore could not bring a civil suit in federal court. Nor could any other African American. The decision, as the Massachusetts legislature noted, "virtually denationalized" people of African descent, even those living in the Northern states that recognized them as citizens.[32]

The contrast between Mexico's Constitution of 1857 and the *Dred Scott* decision was stark. Mexico's Constitution did not restrict citizenship on the basis of race as the *Dred Scott* decision did. Mexico's Constitution emancipated enslaved people from the moment they set foot on free soil. Taney ruled that Dred Scott remained in bondage even after being taken to jurisdictions that had abolished slavery.[33]

The difference between these two approaches, articulated so close in time, did not pass without notice. "We, by annexation, compelled Mexico to acknowledge our independence; they, in turn presented this new constitution to rob us of our property," protested one Texan. The Mexican Constitution, as the antislavery *New-York Tribune* noted, "wholy [sic] repudiated the Taney interpretation of the rights of man" and "completely block[ed] that game of slave-hunters in recovering fugitive slaves under the character of fugitive criminals." Five hundred *norteam-ericanos* signed a petition criticizing Mexico's Constitution as a "great grievance" and an insult to "the institutions and national honor, dignity and interests of the whole confederation." These rival visions of who was entitled to citizenship and who was not would soon come into violent conflict on the Rio Grande.[34]

THE TEXAS STATE CAPITOL BUILDING STOOD ON A HILL OVERLOOK-ing Austin—a burgeoning town of three thousand, which Frederick Law Olmsted, who traveled in Texas on assignment from the *New York Times*, described as having "a remarkable number of drinking and gambling shops, but not one bookstore." To the south was the Colorado River, and to the west, the hill country. Though Austin was the capital of Texas, its buildings were "smaller in number and meaner in appearance" than Eastern visitors expected. Austin was a town in the wilderness, with its capitol upon a hill.[35]

Built of white limestone mined from nearby quarries, the neoclassical building, with its rotunda and portico, reminded Easterners of the United States Capitol. "Washington, *en petit*," wrote Frederick Law Olmsted, "seen through a reversed glass." The state legislators impressed visitors with their "honest eloquence" and "respect for the working of Democratic institutions." Only once during Olmsted's visit did a "gentleman, in a state of intoxication," attempt to address the House. "But," Olmsted was quick to add, "that happens everywhere."[36]

On December 10, 1857, Representative Thomas Freeman McKin-ney, a sober man in every sense of the word, rose to speak. In his hand was the draft of an act that would encourage the capture of slaves escaping "beyond the limits of the U. States" by granting one-third of the runaway's value to any person securing the slave's return from outside the US. To the representatives, Texans were entitled to recover runaways, not only from the Northern states but from foreign countries. "Property is property," insisted one citizen, whether it be African slaves, porcelain vases, cotton cloth, or spermaceti candles. "The Alligator of the one is the Crocodile of the other." By a nearly unanimous vote, McKinney's Act to Encourage the Reclamation of Slaves, Escaping beyond the Limits of the Slave Territories of the United States passed into law.[37]

Soon Texans began to claim their rewards under the new law. On September 15, 1860, John Lerens captured a mulatto slave, appraised at twelve hundred dollars. Two months later, Leanobra Zabar and José María López brought before the clerk of Uvalde County "a certain negro man" whom they "captured as a fugitive slave beyond the limits of the slave territory of the United States." Two appraisers valued the "quick spoken and very polite" man at $1,000, of which Zabar and López received one-third.[38]

The noticeable uptick in kidnapping attempts did not stop local Mexican authorities from defending people of African descent as their constitution required. On February 1, 1859, Anastacio Elua was tending his fields in Northern Tamaulipas when a Texas slaveholder named Francis Cameron seized him, tied his wrists, and slung him over a horse. Cameron insisted that Elua was a fugitive slave, until the governor of Tamaulipas produced evidence that he was the son of a black Louisiana creole who had purchased freedom for himself and his family in the 1820s. "Owing to the measures of the Mexican authorities," a report later recounted, "the aggressors found themselves compelled to set Elua at liberty."[39]

Civilians also took up arms in defense of their African American neighbors. On July 5, 1859, "a party of eight armed Americans" seized a "free Mexican negro servant" near Paso del Norte. (It is unclear whether the man was free from birth or whether he freed himself by escaping to Mexico.) As the kidnappers fled, they drew their revolvers and fired several shots. Local citizens ducked into their houses, only to reappear, moments later, with rifles. A running fight ensued. By the time they reached the riverbank, the Texans surrendered, too exhausted to cross. They would not be released until they paid a hefty fine, surrendered their arms, and pledged never to return to Mexico.[40]

Ordinary citizens and local authorities defended fugitive slaves, but sometimes neither succeeded. On June 26, 1859, a black woman named Merlley traveled from Brownsville to bring a crime to the attention of the mayor of Reynosa, Tamaulipas. She reported that a family of fugitive slaves—Henderson, Terme, and their four children—had been working on Juan Longoria Tijerina's ranch near Reynosa for several years when they suddenly reappeared on the US side of the Rio Grande in the possession of their former owner. Merlley must have known of Mexico's freedom principle, because she asked that the authorities investigate. They did. Their investigation revealed that five *norteamericanos*, aided by a local named Manuel Muñoz, searched for the fugitive slaves while pretending to buy livestock. For guiding the party back to the Rio Grande, Muñoz received "a great deal of money." On the basis of this information, the judge of Reynosa indicted Muñoz for his involvement in the kidnapping.[41]

Mexican authorities prosecuted wrongdoers like Muñoz—even when the wrong could not be undone. This commitment is significant, because it suggests that Mexico's emancipatory promise was not empty. Rarely, if ever, did laws produce lockstep compliance. Any single violation is less informative than the response to it. Disregarding a law that is routinely ignored might not merit comment, while disregard for a foundational legal principle would provoke outrage. And in Mexico, the response to violations was telling. A Mexican citizen who aided an expedition to kidnap runaways living "under the protection of the laws" was convicted of treason in 1854. Two others served a four-year sentence for helping a Texas slaveholder kidnap a free black man. By order of the governor of Coahuila, any property belonging to these accomplices was auctioned off, and the proceeds were used to buy the freedom of kidnapped slaves whose owners refused to return them to Mexico.[42]

IN 1857, A CIVIL WAR BROKE OUT IN MEXICO OVER THE PROVISIONS of the new constitution that expropriated church property. The devout in Jalisco and Michoacán rebelled. The Mexican Army seized Mexico City, dissolved Congress, and shortly thereafter installed General Félix Zuloaga as president. But Zuloaga's authority was tenuous. According to the Constitution of 1857, if the duly elected president could not serve, the chief justice of the Supreme Court would take his place. The man who served in that position was a full-blooded Zapotec Indian from Oaxaca named Benito Juárez. In the early months of 1858, Juárez declared himself—not Zuloaga—the legitimate leader of the Republic of Mexico. Juárez's insurgent government quickly took control of the far northern states, along with those bordering the Gulf of Mexico.[43]

Mexico's civil war made the northern frontier even more vulnerable to attack from the United States. Ramón Múzquiz, the prefect of the Monclova district, complained that the "principal object" of such incursions was to recover African Americans who had "succeeded in placing themselves under the protection of the laws of Mexico in order to escape from slavery." Now, more than ever before, local authorities like Múzquiz lacked the men and resources to stop kidnappers from crossing the Rio Grande.[44]

To make matters worse, the Seminoles at the military colony were turning against their former allies, the Black Seminoles. In the winter of 1856, Seminole warriors returning from their latest campaign discovered rashes on their faces and arms that began spreading to their chests. They began to sweat with fever and shake with chills. By the time they reached their camp at Alto, near Múzquiz, the sick had begun to perish. As smallpox spread to the military colony, John Long, a doctor from the United States living in Múzquiz, inoculated the Seminoles and their black allies. But the Seminoles continued to die. In January, the Seminoles fled for the hills. By the time they returned in March, smallpox had claimed the lives of twenty-eight women and twenty-five men, including the Seminole leader Wild Cat. By contrast, only two Black Seminoles had died.[45]

The Seminoles blamed their losses on their black allies, whom they accused of slaughtering their animals, stealing their irrigation water, and refusing to take up arms against the "wild" Indians. The result, they claimed, was that the Black Seminoles owned more horses and spent more time tending their fields, while the Seminoles faced a grinding poverty that culminated in the fifty-three deaths during the smallpox epidemic. The mayor of Santa Rosa reported that the Seminoles were threatening to return to the United States if matters did not improve. "We cannot subject ourselves to such thieves as these Negroes," asserted a new Seminole leader named Lion. Some Mexican officials agreed that the Black Seminoles displayed "bad propensities" that made them "not very beneficial" to the state. Still, the commanders of the military colony, who suspected the Seminoles of conspiring with Texas slave catchers, remained skeptical.[46]

In 1859, state authorities decided to placate the Seminoles and discourage invasions from the United States by relocating the Black Seminoles to the town of Parras in southern Coahuila. There, the Black Seminoles would defend against Lipan Apache raids, which were launched from a nearby desert basin known as the Bolsón de Mapimí. To deny the Texans any excuse to cross into Mexico, the local authorities had to remove not just the runaways who had joined the military colony but also the former slaves who worked on nearby ranches. "This measure will save these poor wretches from falling prey to the rapacity of those men without souls, who contrary to natural law, wish to traffic in these men, only because of a difference in their color," wrote Ramón Múzquiz, the prefect of the Monclova district.[47]

The order to move south reached the Black Seminoles after the fields had already been cleared and planted. The timing could not have been worse, but the outcome could have been. The Mexican authorities might have decided to return escaped slaves to the United States. Instead they continued to protect runaways. At the beginning of May 1859, a young "snub-nosed" runaway of a "not very dark color" arrived in Santa Rosa from San Antonio. When he asked for the Black Seminoles, the mayor directed him toward Parras. A month later, another escaped slave named Albert Julian crossed the Rio Grande. The mayor of Santa Rosa issued him a pass to join the Black Seminoles to the south.[48]

As Mexican officials tried to uphold the principle of equality, Southern politicians continued to deny that all men were created equal, as the Declaration of Independence stated. As early as 1826, the doctrine of equal rights was discounted. Representative John Randolph of Virginia claimed the doctrine was a "fanfaronade of metaphysical abstractions." Eleven years later, Governor James Henry Hammond of South Carolina explained that the Founders were "much excited, nay, rather angry" when they drafted the opening lines of the Declaration of Independence. "The phrase was simply a finely sounding one." Chief Justice Roger Taney endorsed this interpretation when he ruled in the *Dred Scott* decision that African Americans were not citizens. Southern politicians were determined to uphold that viewpoint in Congress, particularly now that they were on the verge of restoring the balance of power between the two sections.[49]

In the spring of 1858, Kansas petitioned to join the Union as a slave state. President James Buchanan declared that the territory was "as much a slave State as Georgia or South Carolina," but Northern politicians balked at the irregular process by which Kansas had applied for statehood. The referendum on the state constitution only allowed the people of Kansas to choose between the "Constitution With Slavery" or the "Constitution Without Slavery." Both options guaranteed "the right of property in slaves now in this Territory." No matter the results of the referendum, the two hundred slaves in the state would remain in bondage, and so would their children. Four-fifths of eligible voters boycotted the election, and on December 21, 1857, the "Constitution With Slavery" passed, 6,226 to 526. The territorial governor was so appalled that he ordered a vote on the *entire* constitution two weeks later. This time, over ten thousand citizens cast ballots against the constitution. To Northern Democrats, the two elections made clear that a majority of Kansas voters were in favor of joining the Union as a "free" state. On April 1, the House of Representatives defeated the bill to admit Kansas, 120 to 112.[50]

To avoid outright defeat, the Buchanan administration proposed a compromise. The constitution of Kansas claimed twenty-three million acres of public land, six times the average amount granted to new states. Congress had reduced the land grant, which gave the Buchanan administration an excuse to submit the constitution to the people of Kansas a second time. If Kansans rejected the land grant, they could only petition for admission once their population equaled the target population for a House district—approximately ninety thousand. The president hoped that the people of Kansas would take a proslavery constitution over delayed admission. To his disappointment, they voted overwhelmingly against the constitution on August 2.[51]

After popular sovereignty failed to make Kansas into a slave state, many Southern Democrats dismissed the doctrine in favor of a more extreme position. Insisting that the territories were common property of all of the states, Southern politicians argued that all citizens could enter the territories with whatever property they possessed under the laws of the places from which they came. If the Fifth Amendment protected life, liberty, and property, then Congress should draft a federal slave code that would guarantee those rights in these territories. As Senator John Berrien of Georgia asserted, "the Constitution of this country recognizes my title to the slave within my State, beyond my State, and within a sovereign State that inhibits slavery." By encouraging slaveholders to move west, a federal slave code would transform the remaining territories into slave states and, at long last, restore the sectional balance.[52]

Northern Democrats, however, refused to accept this argument. The disagreement threatened to divide the party. On April 23, 1860, Democratic delegates assembled in Charleston, South Carolina, to nominate a candidate for the upcoming presidential election. When the convention refused to endorse a platform that called on Congress to adopt a territorial slave code, the delegates from Alabama, Mississippi, Louisiana, Arkansas, Texas, Florida, and South Carolina walked out. The remaining delegates continued to vote. But even after fifty-seven rounds, no candidate had secured the required two-thirds majority. There was no choice but to hold another convention. If the Democrats failed to agree on a candidate, the Republican Party stood a chance of carrying the "free" states—and winning the election.[53]

TWELVE

WAR

F OR SIX WEEKS, NOTHING COULD BE HEARD FROM THE VACANT
lot at the corner of Lake and Market Streets except the staccato of
hammers. The Republican Party was holding its convention in Chicago
and the local committee had decided to build a hall for the occasion.
With a capacity of ten thousand, the hall was among the largest in the
city. The inclined floor space permitted even the shortest delegates to see
the stage. For the first time in United States history, journalists watched
from a press box rather than the galleries. Decorated with evergreen
boughs, and illuminated by gaslight, the convention hall was, according
to a reporter from the *Cincinnati Commercial*, "a small edition of the
New York Crystal Palace."[1]

The convention hall was only just completed by the time the delegates assembled on May 16, 1860. David Wilmot, the former representative from Pennsylvania, opened the convention with a speech. In
it he accused Democrats of plotting to reestablish slavery where it did
not exist in order to maintain the balance of power between North and

South. Republicans opposed the expansion of slavery not because they necessarily sympathized with African Americans, but because they believed that a slave-based labor system posed a threat to white citizens and the democracy they had founded. "Whose rights are safe where slavery has the power to trample them underfoot?" Wilmot demanded. "Who to-day is not more free to utter his opinions within the Empire of Russia, or under the shade of despotism of Austria, than he is within the limits of the slave States of this Republic?" The former representative from Pennsylvania, whose proviso helped to unleash the forces that gave rise to the Republican Party, finished his speech and stepped down from the speaker's platform to thunderous applause.[2]

The frontrunner for the Republican nomination was William H. Seward of New York, who served one term as state senator and another as governor before joining the United States Senate. But the electoral map posed a significant obstacle to his candidacy. Given that California, Oregon, and New Jersey were Democratic bastions, the Republican nominee had to win Pennsylvania and either Illinois or Indiana, and Seward was disliked in all three. Other candidates, including Governor Salmon P. Chase of Ohio, Senator Simon Cameron of Pennsylvania, former Representative Edward Bates of Missouri, and former Representative Abraham Lincoln of Illinois, argued that they stood a better chance of winning the election.[3]

On the first round of voting, Seward led with 137½ votes. Abraham Lincoln came in second with 102. Because none of the candidates had won a majority—233 votes—the convention took a second ballot. Lincoln won 179 votes, Seward 184½. Still, Seward's supporters did not expect Lincoln's candidacy to succeed. Newspapers routinely misspelled his name as Abram. Few pundits listed him among the potential nominees. The candidate himself acknowledged his lack of experience. When the publisher of Pennsylvania's *Chester County Times* requested biographical information, Lincoln composed a "little sketch" of 606 words. "There is not much of it," he confessed, because "there is not much of me."[4]

At the third ballot, however, Lincoln surged to 231½ votes, 1½ votes shy of a majority. The chairman was preparing for another vote when the leader of the Ohio delegation elbowed his way toward the stage. "I rise, Mr. Chairman, to announce the change of four votes of Ohio . . . to Mr. Lincoln," he said. For a moment, no one spoke, and then, a wave of cheers broke across the floor. "Fire the salute," someone shouted. "Old Abe is nominated!" From the roof, a cannon boomed. Black powder smoke began to fill the hall. But the crowd did not stop cheering.[5]

A month after Lincoln secured the nomination, Democratic delegations arrived at the Front Street Theater in Baltimore to decide on their nominee for the upcoming election. On June 18, 1860, a dispute broke out over which delegates would be seated—the hardliners who walked out of the previous convention, or the moderates from the lower South who organized rival delegations. The credentials committee voted to admit most of the delegates who had bolted from the first convention, but when it seated the moderates from Alabama and Louisiana, the hardliners from the lower South walked out again, and this time most of the delegates from the upper South joined them. Declaring themselves the legitimate representatives of the Democratic Party, the bolters nominated the current vice president, John C. Breckinridge of Kentucky. The delegates who remained in the Front Street Theatre nominated Senator Stephen Douglas of Illinois for president.[6]

The breaking apart of the Democratic Party transformed the electoral landscape. If Republicans carried all—or nearly all—of the "free" states, Lincoln would win the Electoral College and become the first president ever elected on a platform to stop the expansion of slavery. In Washington, DC, Matias Romero, Mexico's chargé d'affaires to the United States, rejoiced that Lincoln's election would commit the United States to fighting for "one of the most philanthropic principles in which humanity can be occupied"—the same principle that the Mexican government had defended for more than two decades.[7]

Southern hardliners began to prepare for the likelihood that a Republican opposed to the expansion of slavery would become president.

If that happened, the only option, as they saw it, would be to leave the Union. To coordinate a secession movement, a low-country planter and two Charleston lawyers established what they called the 1860 Association. Every Thursday, the fifteen members of the executive committee met over wine to plan. By November 1860, the association had printed two hundred thousand copies of a set of pamphlets, with titles ranging from *The Doom of Slavery in the Union* to *The South Alone Should Govern the South*.[8]

THROUGHOUT THE NIGHT OF NOVEMBER 6, 1860, THE TELEGRAPHS in Charleston, South Carolina, clicked. Pencils scratched against paper, as the operators tallied election totals. Early the next morning, Charleston residents took to the streets. Despite the rain, crowds cheered and waved flags. Fireworks streaked the gray sky. "The tea has been thrown overboard," exclaimed the *Charleston Mercury*. "The Revolution of 1860 has been initiated."[9]

Lincoln won the popular vote with 1,865,908 votes, or 39.8 percent of the total. Carrying every county in New England and every Northern state except New Jersey, he beat his nearest rival, John C. Breckinridge, by half a million votes. His victory was even more decisive in the Electoral College, where he secured 180 votes, far more than the 152 needed to win. The other candidates collectively secured only 123 votes. Southern newspapers printed the election results with the black border usually reserved for obituaries.[10]

Southern politicians weighed whether or not to make good on their threats to secede. South Carolina's state legislature scheduled a convention to vote on secession in mid-January, but in the face of public pressure, moved up the date to December 17. The *Charleston Daily Courier* argued that disunion was the only defense against a Republican administration that supported "negro equality, the only logical *finale* of which is emancipation." In Charleston, the Young Men's Secessionist

Association organized a parade, lit by lanterns and lightwood torches, and punctuated by the explosion of rockets and Roman candles. One of the banners depicted a shroud, with the words: "Here lies the Union, Born 4th July 1776, Died 7th Nov. 1860."[11]

On December 17, 1860, the South Carolina legislature called their convention to order. On December 20, they voted to secede. Within six weeks, Mississippi, Florida, Alabama, Georgia, Louisiana, and Texas all followed suit. The *Charleston Mercury* declared that Lincoln's election would lead to "the loss of liberty, property, home, country—everything that makes life worth having." The rebels played on these fears. "Will you consent to be robbed of your property," Jefferson Davis asked in 1861, or will you "strike back bravely for liberty, property, honor and life?"[12]

Lincoln repeatedly promised to recognize and protect slavery where it existed. But in his view, the "assumption about the equality of races," expressed in the opening lines of the Declaration of Independence, was not "an error." The leaders of the Confederate States of America disputed this point, and their disagreement lay at the heart of the controversy between North and South. If Thomas Jefferson meant it when he wrote that "all men are created equal," then the Republican Party was correct to insist in its platform that "the normal condition of all the territory of the United States was freedom." But if the opening lines of the Declaration of Independence were a rhetorical abstraction, as Southern politicians claimed, then the federal government had no obligation to restrict slavery in the territories.[13]

Some members of Congress made one final attempt to reconcile these competing views. In the late winter of 1861, Senator John J. Crittenden of Kentucky proposed seven amendments to the Constitution, designed to restore and maintain the balance of power. The final and most controversial amendment extended the Missouri Compromise line to the Pacific, prohibiting slavery north of 36°30', while permitting it in all territories "now held, or hereafter acquired" south of the line. This was the compromise that had kept sectional controversy at bay for nearly thirty years—until the United States seized territory from Mexico where slavery was abolished. In 1847, Congress voted down Representative Henry Washington Hilliard's proposal to extend the line to the Pacific. Now Crittenden proposed the same solution, urging Congress to permit slavery to exist in the Southwest "until the Territory becomes a State, and decides for itself whether slavery shall continue longer or not."[14]

Republicans rejected Crittenden's argument. "A compromise!" harrumphed Senator Henry Wilson of Massachusetts. "It is, sir, a cheat! A delusion! A snare! It is an unqualified concession, a complete surrender of all practical issues concerning slavery in the Territories, to the demands of slave propagandism." Representative James Campbell of Pennsylvania doubted that the people would ever "ratify the idea of extending slavery to free soil." The public reaction to the Crittenden Compromise seemed to prove him right. Horace Greeley, the editor of the *New-York Tribune*, feared that the compromise was an invitation to adventurers "to readjust the equilibrium of the Union" by warring against every people from the Baja Peninsula to Tierra del Fuego. In Pittsburgh, Republicans put an end to one unionist meeting by shutting off the gas, destroying seats, and crying 'God d—n John J. Crittenden and his compromise!" On February 26, the Senate rejected Crittenden's proposed constitutional amendment by a vote of 11 to 8. Northerners continued to oppose extending slavery where it did not exist, as had been the case a decade earlier. But this time, no compromise seemed likely. War appeared imminent, and Abraham Lincoln had not even left Springfield.[15]

WHEN THE STATE LEGISLATURE WAS OUT OF SESSION, THE HOTELS of Springfield, Illinois, were vacant. No one crowded around the billiard tables. The small town near the Sangamon River was "indescribably dull," according to the *New York Herald*, "like one grand Quaker meeting house." But by the second week of November 1860, the capital of Illinois took on a new aspect. Every car on the Chicago and Alton Railroad was packed. The people seeking appointments—the "groveling tide waiters, fawners, sycophants, and parasites," as one reporter put it—overwhelmed the hotels in Springfield. Those who could not book a room spent the night on sleeping cars reserved for the purpose at the station.[16]

Among the passengers who stepped onto the platform in Springfield on January 18, 1861, was Matias Romero, a young man with a full beard and a large, square forehead that would only grow larger as his hairline receded into baldness. It had taken him eleven days to travel to central Illinois from Washington, DC. From the train station, the unpaved streets into the town were nearly impassable from the rain and snow that winter. Romero hardly noticed. A native of Oaxaca, Mexico, he had experienced rains so heavy that the mules drawing the stagecoaches drowned in the mud.[17]

Romero had not come to Springfield to ask for a position in the incoming administration. As Mexico's chargé d'affaires, he had been instructed to congratulate the president-elect. A day after he arrived in Springfield, Romero carried out his instructions. Sitting across from Lincoln, he commended "the triumph of republican ideals" in the United States. Romero went on to note that Mexico had recently celebrated a similar victory. The civil war that had erupted over the Constitution of 1857 was over. In 1860, Benito Juárez's forces defeated the clergy and the army, which had taken up arms against the principle of equality before the law. Neither could raise "the standard of rebellion" again. Mexico's "constant revolutions" were over.[18]

Romero expressed the hope that Mexico and the United States could at last forge a "truly fraternal" relationship. The two countries shared the "same principles of liberty and progress." The "unanimous sentiment" of the people of Mexico was against slavery. The US drive to extend slavery to the Pacific had cost Mexico half of its territory. Now those same "egotistical and antihumanitarian" principles threatened to destroy the Union, too. This was the "point of contact with the politics and principles of Mr. Lincoln" that the Mexican government hoped would consolidate "the friendship of both countries."[19]

Lincoln was hesitant. Although the president-elect wanted to place slavery on a course of ultimate extinction, he feared that imposing abolition on the South would cause even more states to leave the Union. The most that Lincoln was prepared to do at that point was "to defend and maintain the supremacy of the Constitution and to preserve the Union with all the dignity, equality, and rights of the several States unimpaired." To Lincoln, the best way to save the Union was to avoid the issue of slavery altogether. Romero doubted that he would be able to. "If the civil war in this country goes on," Romero predicted on June 6, 1861, "it will become a servile war, and that a great number, if not all, of the blacks in the Southern States will obtain their liberty." Lincoln doubted that the war would last as long as Romero suspected, but the victories that the Confederate Army scored in the opening months of the conflict soon tested the president's confidence.[20]

ON JULY 21, 1861, NEAR A LANGUID, TREE-CHOKED RIVER NORTH of Manassas, Virginia, the Union and Confederate armies clashed for the first time. The Civil War had broken out three months earlier, when Confederate forces at Charleston opened fire on the transport ships sent to resupply the United States garrison at Fort Sumter. As the Lincoln administration called for seventy thousand volunteers to enlist in the Union Army, four more states—Virginia, Arkansas, North Carolina, and Tennessee—seceded. At the end of July, Union forces marched into northern Virginia, where Confederate commanders were assembling their army.[21]

No one expected the ninety-day Union volunteers to hold out for long. They had never been under fire. They had not yet been given even the rudimentary training in how to make an orderly retreat. And yet after marching through the night to flank the Confederate forces, the men were steadily gaining ground. Their uniforms were dark with sweat. Their lips were black with powder from biting off cartridges in battle. They had been fighting for fourteen hours, with little food and water, when, at dusk, the Confederates surged forward, as eerie, blood-curdling screams pierced the summer air.[22]

The sound did not carry to the outcropping two miles away where journalists, congressmen, and members of the public had come to watch the battle. But the spectators did not need to hear what became known as the rebel yell to see its immediate and unmistakable effect. The Union soldiers turned and ran. They threw away guns, packs, and anything else that would slow their escape, as a "cruel, crazy, mad, hopeless panic" spread down the line.[23]

One of the civilians who came to watch the battle was the Mexican conservative Rafael Rafael. What he saw at Manassas convinced him that the Civil War would continue for years. This was the opportunity that Mexican conservatives had been waiting for. Ever since Agustín de Iturbide sailed into exile, they had wanted to return Mexico to monarchical rule. But the threat of war with the United States always stymied their plans. Now that neither the Union nor the Confederacy could enforce the Monroe Doctrine, they could at last install a European monarch on the Mexican throne. This plan ignited the ambitions of the French emperor, Louis Napoleon. President Benito Juárez of Mexico seemed unprepared to prevent a royalist takeover. Developments in Europe provided a convenient cover for Louis Napoleon's schemes. Mexico's recent civil war had bankrupted its treasury, and when Juárez suspended foreign debt payments on July 17, 1861, France, Spain, and Great Britain agreed to invade Mexico.[24]

Now, all Mexican conservatives needed was a monarch. Louis Napoleon suggested Archduke Maximilian, the younger brother of Franz Joseph, Emperor of Austria and King of Hungary. As the second-born son, Maximilian had limited prospects of ruling over anything in Europe. He spent his days at a castle he had built overlooking the Adriatic, with distant views of Trieste, and a winter garden stocked with exotic birds. He was restless, and so was his ambitious wife, Carlotta. They wanted to *do* something. On October 10, 1861, an agent of Louis Napoleon explained to the couple that they had the opportunity to rule an empire. Maximilian listened closely. The archduke was nearly six feet tall with a fair complexion and thinning hair. His sideburns grew so long that they hung below his jawline, giving him the long-jowled look of a walrus. Maximilian wanted to accept Napoleon's offer to become the emperor of Mexico. "I shall always and in every circumstance of life be found ready to make every sacrifice, however heavy it may be, for Austria and the power of my house," he said. But he considered himself a liberal and, as such, could only accept if he were sure that he was acting according to the will of the Mexican people. Louis Napoleon's agent assured him that he was and promised that the French emperor would soon provide proof.[25]

Delighted, Maximilian prepared to embark for Mexico. He practiced Spanish. He drafted a code of courtly etiquette. He studied the geography and the history of his new empire. Maximilian's younger brother nicknamed him Montezuma. Those who knew better called the archduke of Austria the archdupe of France. The people of Mexico did not want a European monarch, and they would not submit to colonial rule as easily as Louis Napoleon expected.

Maximilian and Carlotta remained in Europe while on December 8, 1861, French, Spanish, and British forces landed at Veracruz. It did not take long for Louis Napoleon's allies to realize that the French emperor had invaded Mexico for another reason beyond securing compensation for unpaid creditors. In early 1862, the British and Spanish armies withdrew from Mexico, while the French forces continued on toward Mexico City. On May 5, 1862, the Mexican Army under President Benito Juárez routed the professionally trained French soldiers at the Battle of Puebla. It would take another year of heavy fighting before Juárez retreated north to San Luis Potosí and French forces finally took Mexico City. Even then, the French Army controlled less than a third of the country's territory. France's hold over Mexico was tenuous, and it would only become more so as the tide of war in the United States turned in favor of the Union and *norteamericanos* shifted their attention from the sectional crisis to Mexico.[26]

AS THE FIGHTING DRAGGED ON, THE STAKES OF THE CIVIL WAR changed. Northerners were beginning to realize that the only way to end the conflict was to confront what lay at its heart. To restore the Union, slavery had to end. The turning point for some came on the night of April 5, 1862, when thirty thousand Confederates set out from Corinth, Mississippi, under cover of darkness. To dampen any sound, they tied clothing to their boots. They cinched burlap to the wheels of their wagons and caissons. By daybreak, they had nearly reached a small wooden church in a village called Shiloh, just across the border in Tennessee.[27]

At the Union camp nearby, thousands of soldiers were milling around their tents, making coffee, and dressing, when the Confederate forces came screaming out of the woods. The Union soldiers were caught unaware, most without weapons, some with only one foot through the legs of their blue trousers. After hours of brutal fighting, the Confederates drove them two miles back, to the banks of the Tennessee River. Some of the Union officers wanted to retreat. "Retreat?" asked their commander, Ulysses S. Grant. "No. I propose to attack at daylight and whip them." And that was exactly what he did.[28]

The next morning, the Union forces counterattacked, taking back the ground they had lost. This bold offensive prevented the Confederates from regaining the initiative in the Mississippi Valley. Between the two sides, 23,741 had died in forty-eight hours. Grant had never seen anything like it. He remembered an open field "so covered with dead that it would have been possible to walk across the clearing in any direction, stepping on dead bodies without the foot touching the ground." The sight of it transformed his view of the war. After the

Battle of Shiloh, he "gave up all idea of saving the Union except by complete conquest."[29]

Northern politicians were slowly coming to the same view. In the summer of 1862, several months after the Battle of Shiloh, one hundred thousand soldiers landed on the peninsula in Virginia between the York and James Rivers, along with three hundred cannon; twenty-five thousand horses, mules, and cattle; and tons of equipment. It was an awesome demonstration of the North's logistical capacities. But the "administrative genius" of the "New England race," one Confederate noted, did not make up for "its sterility in Generals." Union General George B. McClellan moved his troops forward with caution. Confederate commanders played on his fears of being outnumbered by marching their infantry and moving their artillery as often and with as much racket as possible. After two months, McClellan's army finally reached the outskirts of Richmond. The men were so close to the city that they could hear the church bells ringing. But then Confederate General Robert E. Lee launched a counterattack. For seven unrelenting days the Confederate Army drove McClellan's forces back. Thirty thousand men were killed or wounded, more than in all the battles that year in the western theater combined.[30]

The high casualty rates troubled Northern politicians as much as larger diplomatic concerns. After the Battle of the Seven Days, British and French leaders debated an offer of mediation, which would have represented a de facto recognition of the Confederate States of America. This development convinced Lincoln that the war could no longer be fought "with elder-stalk squirts, charged with rose water." The time for "white kid-glove warfare" was over, as Senators John Sherman and William Pitt Fessenden put it. To keep the British government from recognizing the Confederacy, Lincoln needed to raise the stakes of the war.[31]

On September 22, 1862, the president issued the preliminary Emancipation Proclamation, which gave the seceded states until the end of the year to return to the Union. If they continued to rebel, Lincoln would declare their slaves "then, thenceforward, and forever free" on January

1, 1863. The border states and the Union-occupied areas of Louisiana and Virginia were exempt, because Lincoln did not think he had the power to interfere with slavery in places loyal to the Union. However, he argued that his war powers *did* authorize him to seize enemy resources, including enslaved people who escaped to Union lines. Twenty-six years after General Antonio López de Santa Anna ordered his generals to free enslaved people during the Texas Revolution, Lincoln threatened to use the same policy against the rebels in the United States.[32]

The Confederate states did not return to the Union by the end of the year, and on January 1, 1863, Abraham Lincoln signed the Emancipation Proclamation, which not only freed enslaved people who escaped from Confederate-held territory, but also permitted "such persons of suitable condition" to enroll in "the armed service of the United States." Nearly 180,000 black men enlisted, most of them former slaves, and they quickly distinguished themselves on the field of battle. On June 7, 1863, Union forces composed almost entirely of black troops drove off a Confederate advance at Milliken's Bend near Vicksburg, Mississippi. Five weeks later, on July 18, the Fifty-Fourth Massachusetts, one of the first units made up of black men, courageously fought their way onto the parapets of Fort Wagner near Charleston, South Carolina, although half the regiment was killed in the process. The president wrote in the late summer that "the emancipation policy, and the use of colored troops, constitute the heaviest blow yet dealt to the rebellion."[33]

Lincoln justified emancipation as a military necessity, but it was also an act of justice. On the day that the Emancipation Proclamation went into effect, Philadelphia's black community gathered in their churches. Cannon sounded at the navy yard in Washington, DC. At Hilton Head, South Carolina, which had been under Union control since 1861, Colonel Thomas Wentworth Higginson organized a ceremony to celebrate the Emancipation Proclamation. After one of the speakers finished reading the text of the decree, one man, a former slave, started to sing: "My country 'tis of thee, sweet land of liberty, of thee I sing." The song was not on the program. The white people in the audience looked at one another, unsure of what was going on. As "the quavering voices sang on verse after verse," others "of the colored people" joined in. This was the first day that the country to which they belonged recognized their place within it. "I never saw anything so electric," Higginson wrote in his diary. "It made all words cheap."[34]

Norteamericanos were not the only ones to celebrate the Emancipation Proclamation. The Mexican chargé d'affaires Matias Romero commended "its intrinsic justice." A Mexico City newspaper looked hopefully toward the North and predicted that "the great republic will purify itself with revolution." The shift in policy signaled that the United States and Mexico were at last fighting for the common "glorious cause of liberty and self government." Even before Maximilian ascended to the throne, Lincoln and Juárez seemed to be united against him.[35]

IN THE SPRING OF 1864, MAXIMILIAN EMBARKED FOR MEXICO. In the United States, a minor Confederate victory made it clear that black Union soldiers were in a fight for their lives. At Fort Pillow in west Tennessee, in April, hundreds of African American troops, most of them recently escaped slaves, were gunned down as they attempted to surrender. Then, as Maximilian's ship entered the Gulf of Mexico, all hell broke loose in Virginia, where weeks of heavy fighting—the Battle of the Wilderness, Spotsylvania Court House, and Cold Harbor—left tens of thousands dead and wounded. But the heavy guns of Grant's Overland Campaign could not be heard on the Mexican coast.[36]

All that greeted the Emperor Maximilian and the Empress Carlotta when their vessels reached Veracruz on May 28, 1864, was silence. The eighty-five members of the royal entourage proceeded through the nearly deserted streets. No one cheered. No bands played. Someone, finally, thought to set off a couple of rockets, as workmen loaded over five hundred pieces of luggage onto rickety carriages for the journey to Mexico City. The emperor's reception was only slightly better in the capital. "Few curtains were hung out during the day," the United States minister, Thomas Corwin, noted, "and the illumination in the evening was a miserable failure."[37]

This was not what Maximilian and Carlotta had envisioned. Louis Napoleon led them to believe that they were assuming the leadership of Mexico with "the clear and distinctly expressed will of the country itself." A number of towns issued "acts of adhesion" to the new empire, but those towns, according to the British minister Charles Wyke, were inhabited, at most, "by two Indians and a monkey." Most of Mexico supported Benito Juárez, whose determination to drive out the French remained undiminished even as his men were forced to retreat toward the Rio Grande. The churchmen, conservative generals, and indigenous leaders who supported Maximilian were in the minority. The French had engineered much, but they could not produce a suitable ground-swell of popular support.[38]

If Maximilian was disappointed, so were the conservatives who had invited him to rule over Mexico. The new emperor filled his cabi-net with liberals. He refused to wear a crown emblazoned with a cross. Rather than restore the property that Juárez expropriated, Maximilian confirmed the transfers and drafted a constitution that guaranteed the free exercise of religion. The Emperor told his Secretary of State that he wished "to be before all things a Mexican and to place the interests of his people above all others." The people of Mexico might not have wanted an Austrian archduke to rule over them, but Maximilian hoped that his liberal policies would win them over.[39]

The main problem that Mexico faced, as Maximilian saw it, was a labor shortage. The obvious solution seemed to be immigration. To convince Europeans to settle in Mexico rather than the war-torn United States, the imperial government issued contracts for two colonies near Veracruz—one for French immigrants and another for Germans. On March 28, 1865, the Emperor established a junta that would issue more contracts. It did not take long for the junta to take up the question of whether the imperial authorities should permit slavery and other forms of coerced labor in order to encourage immigration.[40]

In the summer of 1865, the junta considered a petition from a railroad magnate named Abdón Morales Montenegro, asking to bring one hundred thousand "African and Chinese colonists" to Mexico. The junta's more liberal members did not approve of Morales Montenegro's proposal. One of these members, Manuel Piña y Cuevas, asked what would happen if Morales Montenegro's laborers refused to work after arriving in Mexico. It seemed obvious that the only way to force them back into the fields would be to take away their freedom. And it did not matter that the term of their contract was limited to a certain number of years. Ultimately, it was an arrangement that struck Piña y Cuevas as little more than slavery by another name. Maximilian's empire, he argued, should promote immigration by other means—restoring peace, promoting industry, and establishing a functioning judicial system. This "would inevitably win over the European population," who would flock to Mexico "without exclusive privileges, without compromises for our government, without violating the rules of humanity and justice, and without altering the good principles upon which the Empire is founded."[41]

Most of the other members of the junta agreed. Urbano Fonseca noted that "the conversion of men into simple machines" was not only unjust but carried with it "the latent germ of its destruction and annihilation," as the Civil War in the United States seemed to prove. The tragic assassination of President Lincoln on April 15, 1865, a mere six days after Lee's surrender at Appomattox, offered added confirmation of the chaos this germ could cause. Francisco Pimentel warned that even so "disguised," slavery would degrade individuals and divide society. On June 14, 1865, two months after Lincoln's assassination, the emperor's junta in Mexico City rejected Morales Montenegro's proposal by a vote of 7 to 5.[42]

The junta, though divided, wanted to limit—not recognize—forced labor. On July 12, 1865, it issued legislation to protect peons, day workers, and indentured laborers. The law required Mexican employers to pay their workers cash wages—a quarter of which would be deposited in government bonds to encourage savings. The term of an indentured labor contract could not exceed ten years, during which time workers would be fed and housed, their health tended to, and their children cared for.[43]

At the same time that the junta sought to protect the rights of workers, it extended guarantees to those who hired them. On September 5, 1865, Maximilian signed a colonization law that included provisions to enforce labor contracts. If employees broke their contracts, the law stated that they would be put to work without pay on the public works. If they died, their children would complete the terms of their contract "until reaching the age of majority." The junta was careful to make clear that these provisions were not intended to reestablish slavery. The first line of the new statute reiterated that "all people of color are free by the sole act of stepping on the Mexican territory." But this provision did not stop thousands of former Confederates, desperate to avoid the consequences of their defeat, from making their way to Mexico.[44]

In the spring of 1865, three Confederate ambulances, a number of wagons, and about a thousand head of stolen cattle descended from the mountains of western Arkansas. The Civil War had ended, and the Confederacy was no more. Rather than give up his slaves—two girls, Amalia and Amanda; Burrill and Mariana Daniel and their children; and a mixed-race woman named Rany Willoughby—Colonel Joel M. Bryant decided to leave his home for Mexico.[45]

Colonel Joel Bryant was a difficult man—proud, impatient, and violent. He fought with Braxton Bragg at Chickamauga and with John B. Hood in the Atlanta Campaign. The weeks spent walking with no shoes and eating nothing but hardtack had made him angry and volatile.

The defeat of the Confederate Army only depressed him further. Bryant probably did not tell his slaves that the war was lost, although they must have presumed as much from the fact that they were "forced to walk day and night" toward Mexico. Bryant rode a horse, driving the cattle and mules that he stole as they went. By early summer, Bryant arrived at the southern limits of the Choctaw Nation, where he sold several of his slaves. He was nervous and irritable, suspecting, perhaps, that his slaves would escape or be taken from him.[46]

After crossing the Rio Grande, Bryant grew calmer. The pace slowed. Bryant must have hoped that he would be able to keep his enslaved people in bondage in Mexico. A Confederate agent, William M. Gwin, was already in Mexico City, petitioning the French bureaucrats to reinstitute slavery. Public reports were hopeful. An unsigned letter (probably from Gwin) to the *New Orleans Times* reported that the Mexicans "seriously proclaim that they can only save the empire by the emigration of Southerners, who rally by the thousands at the call of Gwin." But Gwin was more circumspect in private. "I am learning to exercise the admirable quality of patience," he wrote to his mother in 1865. It is "the best thing a man can do in Mexico, where the object of the community is to approach as nearly as possible to a state of vegetation."[47]

Joel Bryant would soon come to understand the precarious future of slavery in Maximilian's Mexico. In the fall of 1865, his wagon train came to a ranch two miles outside of Chihuahua, the capital of the state of the same name. Not long after his arrival, the US consul in Chihuahua, Reuben Creel, sent a black servant to Bryant's residence to inform his slaves that "no one had the right to call himself their master." On learning that they were free, the Daniel family fled.[48]

MATIAS ROMERO COULD HARDLY KEEP TRACK OF THE CORRESPONDENCE that arrived at his office in Washington, DC. Union soldiers wrote to the Mexican chargé d'affaires from the army-issue tents pitched outside of Petersburg, Virginia; from Lovejoy's Hotel on the corner of Park Row and Beekman Street in New York City; and from the many small towns that had recently welcomed them home. All of them wanted to "drive Jonny Napoleon and the Austrian double-headed buzzard back to their 'petit vin' and 'sour Kraut.'" Their enthusiasm was pervasive. "I know many young men here who have the 'fever,'" wrote a man in Louisville, Kentucky, "and have no doubt but it might be made 'contagious.'"[49]

And it was not just young, able-bodied men who had the "fever." Anna Tellez of St. Louis, Missouri, volunteered to raise money and men for the cause. A New York businessman offered fifty-five thousand pairs of "the best quality army shoes." An inventor from Massachusetts promised a machine that would place a rifleman "twenty feet in the air" for firing, while still protecting him "from the rifle balls of the enemy." Even Lieutenant Colonel Horace G. Thomas of Buffalo, New York, who had not recovered the use of his left arm after being shot in the shoulder and both thighs at the Second Battle of Bull Run, wanted to fight for Juárez.[50]

Their indignation owed, in no small part, to the new colonization law that Maximilian's government had passed that sought to encourage immigration by including provisions to enforce labor contracts. In September 1865, the US minister to Mexico, Thomas Corwin, reported that Maximilian's decree had been "drawn up solely (though not ostensibly) with the view of inducing our Southern planters to emigrate with their slaves." Corwin informed the Department of State that the system of indenture that the law established was "but slavery disguised." When Secretary of State William Seward raised Corwin's concerns before the cabinet, Attorney General James Speed drafted a report on the substance of the decree. He found that the law permitted laborers to be sold and their debts transferred to their children at their deaths. If slavery was "a law by which one man asserts dominion over the conduct of another, either for a specified time, or for life," then the regulations established "a grinding and odious form of slavery."[51]

Maximilian immediately sent an envoy to Washington to counter the charges that his government was trying to reestablish slavery. The archduke was strongly opposed to human bondage. Several years earlier, he visited sugar plantations on a botanical expedition to Brazil. What he witnessed convinced him that slavery contained "within it the seed of a state's ruin." As emperor, he insisted that the "abominable" practice had no place in Mexico. In Washington, Maximilian's agent explained that former slaves who accompanied their masters to Mexico would not remain in bondage. Instead, they would serve out the terms of any contract and then receive forty-five acres of farmland from the Office of Colonization. Maximilian's envoy noted that in the US, the new Freedmen's Bureau provided former slaves with only a fraction of what Mexico gave to newly released indentured servants.[52]

But *norteamericanos* remained convinced that the law was a ploy to persuade former Confederates to immigrate to Mexico with their slaves, and Matias Romero did everything that he could to stoke their fears. He met with congressmen; he distributed copies of Maximilian's colonization law; he made statements to the press; he lobbied influential members of the Republican Party; he answered questions from students assigned to write essays about the French intervention in Mexico. And his efforts had their intended effect. At the end of 1865, two senators introduced a resolution against a policy so "directly hostile" to the interests of the United States as Maximilian's colonization law. An anonymous pamphlet published in 1866 railed against the "forced introduction" of slavery on "our next neighbor."[53]

The pressure against Maximilian was mounting. Since the French Army's invasion of Mexico in 1861, the United States had maintained a policy of strict neutrality. This was done in order to keep Louis Napoleon from recognizing the Confederacy. But now that the Civil War was over, *norteamericanos* saw no reason to withhold support for Juárez, who had never wavered in his support for the Union. In 1861, Juárez negotiated an extradition treaty with the Lincoln administration, which explicitly prohibited the return of fugitive slaves. That same year, Juárez rejected a proposed alliance with the Confederate States of America. Instead, he gave Union forces permission to land at the Pacific port of Guaymas and march across northern Mexico so that they could turn back a Confederate attack in Arizona. In 1865, Secretary of State William Seward finally reciprocated Juárez's support by taking a firmer stance against the French intervention. "The presence and operations of a French army in Mexico, and its maintenance of an authority there, resting upon force and not the free will of the people of Mexico, is a cause of serious concern to the people of the United States," he wrote on November 6, 1865.[54]

"This turn of events has come to greatly serve the interests of our cause," Matías Romero wrote, "because nothing could have put Maximilian in a worse light before this nation, than to reestablish an institution that rebels against the feelings of this century and that this people has just destroyed with a costly war of four years." *Norteamericanos* wanted to prevent the reestablishment of slavery in the Americas as much as they hoped to stop European nations from interfering in the affairs of the Western Hemisphere. The letters kept arriving at Romero's office. On November 3, 1865, a Prussian-born lieutenant wrote from Nashville on behalf of the "four hundred good, well drilled colored soldiers" that he commanded in the Thirteenth US Colored Heavy Artillery. These men wanted to fight against France, just as they had fought against the Confederacy, and the lieutenant urged Romero to accept their offer. "Negroes are the best soldiers," the lieutenant wrote, "for they will fight."[55]

LOUIS NAPOLEON REGRETTED HIS DECISION TO INVADE MEXICO. Now that the Civil War ended, United States forces were being sent to the Rio Grande. Moreover, their commander, General Philip Sheridan, was giving the liberals in Mexico "as much back bone" as he could. On January 22, 1866, Napoleon informed the *corps législatif* that he decided to withdraw French troops from Mexico. Maximilian did not stand a chance without the French Army. He had 21,700 men of his own. Juárez had 69,700. "I believe also (entre nous) that the Emperor is finding out that he is in a horrible mess here," wrote a British diplomat. As Juárez's forces advanced toward Mexico City, Maximilian fled to Querétaro, about a hundred twenty miles northwest. He lived, under siege, at the Convento de la Santa Cruz. In the early morning hours of May 15, 1867, he woke in the darkness to find his headquarters overrun by Juárez's men.[56]

If Maximilian, as an emperor, was a target for scorn, he became, as a prisoner, an object of pity. His lawyers pleaded for mercy, pointing to the French revolutionaries who spared the life of Charles X in 1830. Even Victor Hugo urged Juárez to pardon Maximilian. But Juárez refused. He could not risk Maximilian setting up a court in exile and, after a year or two, returning to Mexico at the head of another, even larger army. A court martial sentenced him to death by firing squad.[57]

On June 19, 1867, Maximilian stood at attention, his back to the wall of a cemetery on the outskirts of Querétaro, the brim of his sombrero turned down to block the early morning sun. The soldiers stood five paces away, each dressed in a gray uniform, with a white leather belt cinched tightly at the waist. At seven o'clock, they raised their rifles and, at the signal, fired in unison. After the first volley, Maximilian sunk to the ground, writhing in pain. A soldier stepped forward and fired again, placing his muzzle so close that Maximilian's vest caught on fire. After another shot, his body, at last, fell still. The *Boletín Republicano* reported that "the Archduke Ferdinand Maximilian of Austria ceased to exist." His death ended any conjecture that Mexico would once again reestablish slavery.[58]

IN 1871, BURRILL DANIEL PETITIONED TO CLAIM 125,000 PESOS before a US-Mexico Claims Commission for having been "subjected to the condition of slavery against the laws of both nations." Daniel accused his former master, Joel Bryant, of holding his family in bondage in Mexico. And he argued that his enslavement continued even after he and his family escaped from Bryant's custody.[59]

After the Daniels fled, Joel Bryant tried to reclaim them. He insisted that he did not wish to deprive his former slaves of their liberty, but having paid the expenses of their journey to Mexico, Bryant claimed that the family owed him service. The US consul in Chihuahua, Reuben Creel, flatly denied this claim. The former slaves had more than paid the costs of travel with their labor. Creel told Burrill Daniel not to sign any contract with Bryant, but Daniel, whether because he had been threatened or because he did not know whom to trust, ignored the advice and signed a contract. Not long thereafter, Bryant transferred the contract to the governor of Chihuahua, Luis Terrazas.[60]

During the five years that the Daniels worked on Terrazas's hacienda, their employer paid them "well and punctually," according to Mariana. But while Mariana Daniel and her children were valued as diligent workers, Burrill Daniel often came to blows with Terrazas over accusations that he was not working hard. In November 1869, the governor had had enough. He transferred the Daniels' debts—and by extension, their labor—to a Prussian émigré named Jacobo Hamburg whose wife did not understand Spanish and who needed servants who spoke English. The Daniel family met his requirements, but not, as it turned out, his standards. To Hamburg, Burrill Daniel seemed "lazy and useless," while his sons shirked their duties "like deserters."[61]

In the spring and summer of 1870, the claims commissioners interviewed Burrill Daniel and his family, their employer Jacobo Hamburg, the US consul in Chihuahua, Reuben Creel, and a former Cherokee slave named Thomas, whose master had joined Colonel Joel Bryant on his march to Mexico. Reuben Creel argued that the Daniel family had not been treated as slaves, because they received the "same salary" and the "same treatment" as Mexican servants. Likewise, to Burrill's wife, Mariana, freedom was the ability to earn a wage; unlike in Arkansas, she was paid for her work in Mexico. It is striking that Mariana defined freedom in the same terms as Reuben Creel—as the ability to earn a salary. And yet she insisted that her claims were her own. "She considered herself to be free," the commissioners wrote, "and *was* free to that very moment."[62]

To Burrill Daniel, however, a contract was a manacle and his status no different in Mexico than it had been in the United States. As evidence, he testified that shortly after arriving in Chihuahua, his former master, Colonel Joel Bryant, opened a "true slave market." Of the "many citizens of that City" who perused its wares was Governor Luis Terrazas. Burrill claimed that Bryant sold him and the rest of his family to the governor for a reduced price to earn his support for "this barbarous traffic." But Burrill's son contradicted his father's claim, asserting that the only market that Bryant set up was for the livestock he had stolen in Arkansas. A local merchant also confirmed that Bryant sold "some horses to the French and also livestock to various people," but never slaves. Still, Burrill insisted that he had been treated like a slave. His debts had been transferred to a new master without his consent. He had been whipped and put in irons. His salary, such as it was, could barely "clothe himself and his family with decency." To Burrill, real freedom was not a wage, counted against a debt he should not have owed, but the power to govern himself.[63]

The US-Mexico Claims Commission never awarded damages to Burrill Daniel. But his claim shows that even within the black community, even within the same family, African Americans disputed the meaning of freedom in the wake of the US Civil War and the French intervention in Mexico. Mariana Daniel found liberation in wages. She was paid for performing domestic chores, the same kind of work that the wives of white men continued to do across the United States without any form of compensation. But her husband saw wage labor as slavery. Like so many freedmen, he must have seen land ownership as the only way to secure real independence. Neither Mariana nor Burrill, however, disputed the right that they had been denied as slaves in Arkansas—the right to define freedom for themselves.[64]

EPILOGUE

I N THE SUMMER OF 1942, AN OLD SCHOOL BUS MADE ITS WAY
toward the small town of Nacimiento de los Negros in northeastern
Mexico, passing through endless scrublands dotted with dense stands of
prickly pear. By the time the bus heaved to a stop, the sun was setting
behind the limestone peaks of the nearby Santa Rosa Mountains, and
Nacimiento was growing dark. The closest that the town had come to
electricity was when the mayor installed a wind generator to power the
lights in his house, but now the generator was broken, its turbine spin-
ning listlessly in the hot, dry wind.[1]

As the driver unwound the bailing wire that held the bus door shut,
a man in his mid-thirties stood up from the wood plank balanced atop
two milk crates that served as his seat. Born in 1905 on a farm near Ster-
ling, Kansas, Kenneth Wiggins Porter spent his childhood ninety miles
from the line—36°30'—that divided the slaveholding South from the
nonslaveholding North during the nineteenth century. While pursuing
his doctorate in history at Harvard University, he found himself thinking about slavery's other border, the border between the United States

and Mexico, nine hundred miles to the south of his hometown. Porter knew that free blacks and runaway slaves had escaped to Mexico with the Seminole Indians in the decade before the Civil War, and when he learned that their descendants still lived in Nacimiento, he decided to interview them.[2]

Porter was no stranger to small towns, but he soon realized that Nacimiento was nothing like the other rural places he had known. After shouldering his bag and climbing down from the bus, Porter walked toward the town center, passing a jail, two churches, and a general store until he found a restaurant. He opened the door, and a young black woman waved him in. As he stepped inside and looked up, he saw something that he had never seen in Kansas. Hanging from a hook was a goat carcass, draped with a gunnysack to keep off the flies. "I got meat, but it's goat," the woman said, noticing his expression. "I 'speck I better kill you a chicken."[3]

For the next several days, Porter conducted interviews in juke joints and drinking shacks, in adobe houses with thatched roofs, and in backyards under huisache trees. As his interviewees talked, he took notes in shorthand. Afterward he would type a complete transcript of the interview, almost always on the same day, and often within an hour or two. The stories that the descendants told him described an existence that, to Porter, seemed as different from slavery "as swimming, even against a strong current, is from floundering in quicksand."[4]

To Porter, this history showed that the frontier was not the exclusive purview of white pioneers. At a time when African Americans were as invisible from history textbooks as they were from the whites-only restaurants of the Jim Crow South, this point struck him as important. Although academic presses were eager to publish Porter's research on provincial assemblies during the French Revolution and the sandalwood trade in the Hawaiian Islands, editors did not express interest in his current subject. Porter's seven-hundred-page manuscript was filed away, unpublished.[5]

KENNETH WIGGINS PORTER SPENT THE REST OF HIS CAREER RE-
searching and writing about the role of African Americans in the
western United States. In 1971, he published *The Negro on the American Frontier*, which showed that African Americans worked and lived
alongside whites and native peoples in the West. In the decades that
followed, historians continued to document the significance of African
Americans in the West, from the enslaved Africans who accompanied
Spanish explorers in the sixteenth century to the black pioneers who
followed the Overland Trail in the nineteenth.[6]

For all of the scholarship on African Americans on the frontier, the
fugitive slaves who fled to Mexico have largely escaped notice. Part of
the reason is the sources themselves. No slaveholder could deny that
enslaved people were escaping to Mexico. But most struggled to believe
that "an offset of degenerate Spain" had adopted such liberal policies.
Norteamericanos considered Mexicans an "uncivilized heterogeneous
people, constantly divided by petty personal feuds and ambitions; always
engaged unmaking pronunciamientos; entirely wanting in patriotism
and high-toned sentiments; altogether unfitted for self-government."[7]

To square what they observed with what they believed, *norteamericanos* credited Mexico's antislavery policies to Great Britain. After
the Texas Revolution, *norteamericanos* blamed Britain for trying to establish "a negro nation, a sort of Hayti on the continent," even though
Mexico was the only nation trying to end slavery in Texas. The following decade, US slaveholders lived in dread of British agents unfurling
the "banner of abolition" as a "signal of servile insurrection," when it
was Mexican authorities who proposed inciting a slave revolt in the US
South in response to US efforts to annex Cuba. Crediting Mexico's antislavery diplomacy to Great Britain allowed Southern whites to invoke
the Monroe Doctrine, which prohibited European interference in the
Americas. It also proved easier to recognize the humanitarian sentiments of a mother country than those of a "semi-barbarous" neighbor.[8]

Norteamericanos also dismissed Mexico's antislavery policies as inevitable or hypocritical. Some credited abolition not to moral convictions or political principles but to Mexico's declining slave population. "Negro slavery never existed in Mexico, to an extent worth notice," wrote the *Charleston Courier* in 1837. Others discredited Mexico's policies because forced labor continued in other forms. "It is a fact well known to all persons who have travelled through Mexico, that half of the population are in a state of slavery intolerable compared with that of most southern negroes," the *Telegraph and Texas Register* reported in 1837.[9]

US historians, immersed in US sources, accepted the claim that neither Mexico's government nor its citizenry was committed to antislavery. They argued that abolition was the inevitable result of a declining slave population and that Mexico's supposedly half-hearted policies buckled easily under pressure from the United States. They accused Mexico's leaders of hypocrisy for abolishing slavery while allowing coercion to continue in the form of debt peonage. Like the sources upon which they drew, scholars acknowledged that British abolitionism contributed to a growing sense of embattlement among slaveholders, even though the most proximate threat to the US South was not England or even Haiti but Mexico.[10]

I FIRST LEARNED ABOUT ENSLAVED PEOPLE ESCAPING TO THE south during an early research trip to northern Mexico. This was 2012—at the height of a war between the Zetas and the Sinaloa cartels over control of the drug corridors to the United States. Bodies were being exhumed from mass graves. Without warning major thoroughfares would empty, the sudden quiet broken by the sound of a black pickup careening down the road, carrying men in flak jackets and ski masks, automatic rifles slung over their shoulders.

At the time, I was studying the violence on the US-Mexico border in the early nineteenth century. I found reams of documents about cattle rustlers and Lipan Apaches. But I also came across a different and unexpected kind of violence. I learned about Jean Antoine, who tried to escape to Campeche in the hold of a ship and killed himself rather than return to bondage in Louisiana. I read about Manuel Luis del Fierro, who threatened to shoot two slaveholders trying to kidnap a young woman named Mathilde Hennes. I came across correspondence from the four town councilmen in Guerrero, Coahuila, who shot a slaveholder rather than permit him to return a runaway to the United States. After that early research trip, I became preoccupied with a number of questions. Why were enslaved people escaping to Mexico? Why would ordinary Mexicans risk their lives to protect them? And why had scholars overlooked this history?

It is easy to discount the laws that abolished slavery in both Mexico and the United States, because coercion continued in so many other forms. Across the South, state legislatures passed vagrancy laws and enacted convict leasing programs that kept people of African descent in conditions not unlike slavery. In Mexico, particularly on the Yucatán Peninsula, debt peons labored for long hours in horrific conditions for insignificant wages. To overlook these shortcomings is triumphalism. But to make them the entire story results in a different kind of distortion. Even hypocritical, self-interested, or unenforced policies could have profound significance. These unexpected consequences should not be ignored because they arose amid unfulfilled promises.

The abolition of slavery across North America did not end coercion, but it was a momentous achievement nonetheless. Only by abolishing human bondage was it possible to extend the debate over the full meaning of universal freedom. As the poet Walt Whitman put it: "It is provided in the essence of things, that from any fruition of success, no matter what, shall come forth something to make a greater struggle necessary."[11]

Their work—our work—is not over.

Acknowledgments

WRITING THIS BOOK WAS THE HARDEST THING I HAVE EVER DONE, and it exists because of the people who helped me, in both large and small ways, on the way.

The research for this book would not have been possible without the help of Christina Bryant at the New Orleans Public Library, Peter Blodgett at the Huntington Library, George Miles at the Beinecke Rare Book & Manuscript Library, Abel Juárez Lavios at the Archivo General de la Nación, Gricelda Hernández at the Archivo Municipal de Monclova, María de los Ángeles Corral Rodríguez and María de Lourdes Ángel Torras at the Archivo Histórico del Congreso del Estado de Coahuila, Sonia Estrada at the Archivo del Congreso del Estado de Nuevo León, Cesar Morado at the Archivo General del Estado de Nuevo León, and Hilda Amalia Rodríguez, Linda Rosa Castillo, Elizabeth Ramírez, and José Luis Reyes at the Archivo General del Estado de Coahuila.

Generous institutional support came from the Beinecke Rare Book & Manuscript Library, the Huntington Library, the MacMillan Center for International and Area Studies, the Department of History at Yale University, the Gilder Lehrman Center for the Study of Slavery,

Resistance, and Abolition, the American Historical Association, the Andrew W. Mellon Foundation, the Council of Library and Information Resources, the Dolph Briscoe Center for American History, the Center of the American West at the University of Colorado Boulder, the Mahindra Humanities Center at Harvard University, and the Society of Fellows at the University of Southern California.

Many thanks to Bobby Gibbs, Nicole Deziel, Jane and Dave Maher, Janie Robbins, Gabriel Martínez Serna, Luis Garcia, and Martha Rodríguez and her husband Lalo, who made my research trips both enjoyable and productive. Thanks also to Jorge Delgadillo, Greg Downs, Caitlin Fitz, Tatiana Seijas, Karl Jacoby, Grace Tiao, Marcela Echeverri, Gil Joseph, Ed Russell, Dave McCollum, Amy Greenberg, and the Center of the American West Book Club, who provided helpful comments on this manuscript. Roni Iris, Kurt Gutjahr, Honey Ashenbrenner, Nicoli Bowley, Brooke Neeley, and Kerri Clements made my year at the University of Colorado Boulder among my happiest and most productive. At Harvard, Sam Dolbee, Andrea Volpe, and Allie Beizer provided thoughtful feedback and good company. At the University of Southern California, I learned so much from my colleagues in the Department of History, especially Bill Deverell, Jason Glenn, Paul Lerner, Richard Fox, Phil Ethington, Nathan Perl-Rosenthal, Lindsay O'Neill, Amy Watson, and Julia Lewandowski. Special thanks to Steve Ross, who took time away during his sabbatical to read the penultimate draft of this manuscript.

Putting the pieces of this book together felt, at times, like wandering through a maze. Brian Distelberg always managed to find the thread that led me out. I could not have asked for a better editor. Katie Lambright and Mike van Mantgem expertly guided the manuscript through the final stages of editing. Kate Blackmer was a joy to work with on the maps. James Shinn's sharp eye and encyclopedic knowledge of US history corrected many errors of interpretation and fact.

My greatest debts are some of my oldest. My high school English teacher, Alice Price, taught me to pay attention to sentences. Andrew

Ehrgood read almost everything I wrote in college, providing thoughtful feedback about style and structure. Spending an hour every other week editing my writing with Anne Fadiman was a valuable apprenticeship in the craft. Taylor Spence made me love history and continues to show me what it means to be a teacher of it. Jay Gitlin took me on at the eleventh hour as his eleventh advisee, when he had every right to say that he was too busy. It is thanks to him that I became a historian. At Oxford, Alan Knight encouraged me to ask big questions and to turn every page in the archives—both invaluable gifts. In the PhD program at Yale, John Mack Faragher agreed to advise my dissertation, despite being on the eve of retirement. He understood from a very early stage what this project was about and helped me to put that argument into words. David Blight, who chaired my dissertation committee along with Johnny, was a model of intellectual generosity, talking through my ideas with patience, curiosity, and enthusiasm.

When I was applying for academic jobs, search committees would often ask me what kind of historian I was. The answer is that I want to be the same kind of historian as Patty Limerick—humorous, brilliant, curious, generous, spirited, and public-minded. Her careful edits on an earlier draft of the manuscript were pivotal. The time that I spent with her (and her inimitable cat, Yofi) changed not only how I wrote this book but also how I teach and think about the West.

Peter Wood has played an equally important and transformative role in my life. The conversations we had over our weekly lunches helped me to think about this book, as well the responsibilities of being a historian. He edited the complete manuscript twice, and in the process he taught me so much about how to craft a historical narrative. The best parts of this book are thanks to him. He is a mensch among mensches, and my debts to him are beyond repayment. *Dios se lo pague.*

My friend Jake Huzenis was never far from my mind while writing this book, which is, in so many ways, the answer that I wish I had been able to give to his question in the last conversation we had—that ordinary people, doing ordinary things, can change the world that they live in even when they can see no evidence of it changing. He was never my teacher in any formal way, but he is among the teachers to whom this book is dedicated.

I owe so much to my family, both given and chosen. Jody Reimer, Helen Jack, Sarah Piazza, and Liz Losch helped in more ways than they know. Their friendship means everything to me. While researching and writing this book, I enjoyed the generous hospitality of Emma Baumgartner and Brian Schwartz, as well as that of Brian's parents, Mark and Shelly Schwartz. Andrea Baumgartner is the reason I wanted to write books in the first place. Bill Baumgartner has edited almost everything I have ever written, including multiple drafts of this manuscript. I would not be who I am without them.

With this much help, this book should be a masterpiece. Inevitably, it is not. But it is the absolute best that I could do. I hope that this is enough to make it worthy of the time and effort that everyone—whether archivists or colleagues, anonymous reviewers or close mentors—poured into it. Whatever is beautiful, clarifying, and truthful here belongs to them.

PASADENA, CALIFORNIA
FEBRUARY 2020

Abbreviations Used in the Notes

ACEC: Archivo del Congreso del Estado de Coahuila
ACENL: Archivo del Congreso del Estado de Nuevo León
AEMEUA: Archivo de la Embajada de México en los Estados Unidos
    de América
AGEC: Archivo General del Estado de Coahuila
AGENL: Archivo General del Estado de Nuevo León
AGN: Archivo General de la Nación
AHS: Archivo Histórico del H. Senado
AHSDN: Archivo Histórico de la Secretaría de Defensa Nacional
AMG: Archivo Municipal de Guerrero
AMGuad: Archivo Municipal de Guadalajara
AMM: Archivo Municipal de Monclova
AP: *Austin Papers*, Eugene Barker, ed. (Washington: Government
    Printing Office, 1924)
BA: Bexar Archives
BCAH: Dolph Briscoe Center for American History
BLAC: Benson Latin American Center
BRBML: Beinecke Rare Book & Manuscript Library
CG: *Congressional Globe*

CGA: *Congressional Globe Appendix*

CONDUMEX: Centro de Estudios Históricos de México

DoC: *Abridgment of the Debates of Congress, from 1789 to 1856,* Thomas Hart Benton, ed. (New York: D. Appleton, 1860–1867)

DUSC: Despatches from the US Consuls

DUSM: Despatches from the US Ministers

FJBP: Fondo Jefatura Política de Béxar

FSXIX: Fondo Siglo XIX

HEH: Henry E. Huntington Library

HSP: Historical Society of Pennsylvania

JLBP: Jean Louis Berlandier Papers

LoC: Library of Congress

LSU: Louisiana State University Archives

NA: Nacogdoches Archives

NAFW: National Archives, Fort Worth

NA-K: National Archives of Great Britain, Kew

NARA-CP: National Archives and Records Administration, College Park

NARA-DC: National Archives and Records Administration, DC

NOPL: New Orleans Public Library

NYPL: New York Public Library

PCRCT: *Papers Concerning Robertson's Colony in Texas*, Malcom D. McLean, ed. and comp., (Fort Worth: Texas Christian University, 1974–1976)

PO: Periódico Oficial

PTR: John H. Jenkins, ed., *Papers of the Texas Revolution, 1835–36*, 10 vols. (Austin: Presidial Press, 1973)

SCRBC: Schomburg Center for Research in Black Culture

SRE: Archivo Histórico de la Secretaría de Relaciones Exteriores

SWHQ: *Southwestern Historical Quarterly*

TSA: Texas State Archives

UCLA: University of California, Los Angeles Library Special Collections

WHQ: *Western Historical Quarterly*

Notes

INTRODUCTION

1. John Forsyth to Sebastián Lerdo de Tejada, July 27, 1857, vol. 20, reel 21, DUSM-Mexico.

2. For Mexico's laws, see "Proyecto de la ley constitucional de garantías individuales," *El Siglo Diez y Nueve* (February 14, 1849); Francisco Zarco, *Crónica del Congreso Extraordinario Constituyente* (Mexico City: El Colegio de Mexico, 1957), 274. For George and James Frisby's fates, see Juan Lainé to Ministerio de Guerra y Marina, August 10, 1857, vol. 20, reel 21, DUSM-Mexico.

3. Forsyth to Lerdo de Tejada, July 27, 1857.

4. For free blacks, see *The State v. Leonide Clair*, November 26, 1823, vol. 1, reel #89-219, Decisions of the Mayor in Criminal Cases, 1823–1832, AA370, NOPL. For ship captains, see "Petition of Francois Barthelmey LeBeau, July 18, 1840," *F. B. LeBeau v. Captain and Owners of the Ship Tecumseh*, no. 18773, reel 34, VMA290, First Judicial District Court Case Records, NOPL. For Mexicans, see "More Negro Stealing," *Texas Monument* (September 26, 1854), 2. For Germans, see "The Advertiser," *Colorado Citizen* (August 14, 1858), 2. For preachers, see "Colonel I. R. Lews," *State Gazette* (September 5, 1857), 2. For gamblers and lurking scoundrels, see "Negroes," *Telegraph and Texas Register* (September 15, 1851), 2. For mail rider, see "A Negro Man,"

Civilian and Gazette (December 21, 1858), 1. For forged slave passes, see "Runaway Negroes," *Texas Republican* (January 28, 1854), 2. *State v. Thomas Mason*, April 13, 1829, volume 2, reel #89-219, Decisions of the Mayor in Criminal Cases, 1823–1832, AA370, NOPL. For firearms, see "By a Communication," *Texas State Gazette* (February 24, 1851), 1. For skiffs, see "Sixty Dollars Reward," *Louisiana Advertiser* (November 8, 1830), 2. For horses, see "Two Negroes Shot," *Texas Ranger and Lone Star*, vol. 4, no. 42 (April 25, 1853), 2. For jewelry, see "Petition of Francois Barthelmey LeBeau," July 18, 1840, *F. B. LeBeau v. Captain*. For boats, see "Eight Negroes," *Civilian and Galveston City Gazette* (June 8, 1844), 1. For dirk knives, see "A Gang of Negroes," *State Gazette* (October 3, 1857), 2. For fur hats, see "Taken," *Dallas Herald* (September 22, 1858), 2. For oysters, see "Runaway Negro," *Telegraph and Texas Register* (November 5, 1845), 2. For camp meeting, see "Stampede of Slaves," *Colorado Citizen* (September 12, 1857), 2.

5. For debt peonage in Yucatán, see Moisés González Navarro, *Raza y tierra: La guerra de castas y el henequén* (Mexico City: El Colegio de Mexico, 1970), 58. For Chiapas, see Merced Olivera Bustamante and Maria Dolores Palomo Infante, eds, *Chiapas: De la Independencia a la Revolución* (Mexico City: Centro de Investigaciones y Estudios Superiores en Antropología Social, 2005), 78–79; Sarah Washbrook, "'Una Esclavitud Simulada': Debt Peonage in the State of Chiapas, Mexico, 1876–1911," *Journal of Peasant Studies* 33 (July 2006): 395–401. For an overview of debt peonage in Mexico, see Alan Knight, "Debt Bondage in Latin America," in *Slavery: And Other Forms of Unfree Labor*, ed. Leonie Archer (New York: Routledge, 2013), 103, 116. Andrés Reséndez suggests that coercion was the norm, though he also acknowledges in a footnote that "it goes without saying that conditions varied from place to place." Andrés Reséndez, *The Other Slavery: The Uncovered Story of Indian Enslavement in America* (Boston: Houghton Mifflin Harcourt, 2016), 397.

6. For recent works on the Underground Railroad, see Eric Foner, *Gateway to Freedom: The Hidden History of the Underground Railroad* (New York: W. W. Norton, 2014), and Richard Blackett, *The Captive's Quest for Freedom: Fugitive Slaves, the 1850 Fugitive Slave Law, and the Politics of Slavery* (Cambridge: Cambridge University Press, 2018). The lower estimate comes from Eric Foner, *Gateway to Freedom*, 122. The higher estimate comes from Fergus Bordewich, *Bound for Canaan: The Epic Story of the Underground Railroad* (New York: Harper Collins, 2006), 16. For scholarship on fugitive slaves to Mexico, see Rosalie Schwartz, *Across the Rio to Freedom: U.S. Negroes in Mexico* (El Paso: University of Texas Press, 1975), 40; Sarah Cornell, "Citizens of Nowhere: Fugitive Slaves and Free African Americans in Mexico, 1833–1857," *Journal*

of American History (September 2013): 351–374; James David Nichols, "The Line of Liberty: Runaway Slaves and Fugitive Peons in the Texas-Mexico Borderlands," *WHQ* 44 (Winter 2013): 413–433; Mekala Shadd-Sartor Audain, "Mexican Canaan: Fugitive Slaves and Free Blacks on the American Frontier, 1804–1867 (unpublished PhD diss., Rutgers, The State University of New Jersey, 2014); James David Nichols, *The Limits of Liberty: Mobility and the Making of the Eastern U.S.-Mexico Border* (Lincoln: University of Nebraska Press, 2018), 57–79, 125–146; Gerardo Gurza-Lavalle, "Against Slave Power? Slavery and Runaway Slaves in Mexico-United States Relations, 1821–1857," *Mexican Studies/Estudios Mexicanos* 35:2 (Summer 2019): 143–170. For the experience of runaway slaves in the "free" states, see Frederick Douglass, *Narrative of the Life of Frederick Douglass, an American Slave* (New York: Webb and Chapman, 1846), 86; "Fugitive Slave Act of 1793," *Proceedings and Debates of the House of Representatives*, 2nd Congress, 2nd Session (November 5, 1792 to March 2, 1794), 1414–1415; Stephen Middleton, *The Black Laws: Race and Legal Process in Early Ohio* (Athens: Ohio University Press, 2005), 51; Eric Foner, *The Fiery Trial: Abraham Lincoln and American Slavery* (New York: Norton, 2010), 8.

7. For the decline of slavery in New Spain, see Dennis N. Valdés, "The Decline of Slavery in Mexico," *The Americas* 44:2 (October 1987), 168. Recent scholarship has argued that the decline in slavery was not as pronounced as Valdés suggests. See: Tatiana Seijas and Pablo Miguel Sierra Silva, "The Persistence of the Slave Market in Seventeenth-Century Central Mexico," *Slavery and Abolition* 37:2 (2016): 307–333. For the number of African slaves imported to New Spain, see Frank Proctor III, "Slave Rebellion and Liberty in Colonial Mexico," *Black Mexico: Race and Society from Colonial to Modern Times* (Albuquerque: University of New Mexico Press, 2009), 23. For people of African descent in New Spain, see Gonzalo Aguirre Beltrán, *La Población Negrá de México, 1519–1810: Estudio Etnohistórico* (Mexico City: Ediciones Fuente Cultural, 1946), 210; Rina Cáceres Gómez, *Rutas de Esclavitud en África y América Latina* (San José: Editorial de la Universidad de Costa Rica, 2001), 115–144, 177–194, 211–222, 223–250, 289–304; Matthew Restall, *The Black Middle: Africans, Mayas, and Spaniards in Colonial Yucatan* (Stanford, CA: Stanford University Press, 2009), 238; Ben Vinson III, *Bearing Arms for His Majesty: The Free-Colored Militia in Colonial Mexico* (Stanford, CA: Stanford University Press, 2001), 35–202; Patrick J. Carroll, "Black-Native Relations and the Historical Record," *Beyond Black and Red: African-Native Relations in Colonial Latin America* (Albuquerque: University of New Mexico Press, 2005), 246–255; Colin A. Palmer, *Slaves of the White God: Blacks in Mexico,*

1570–1650 (Cambridge, MA: Harvard University Press, 1976), 21–188; Javier Villa-Flores, "'To Lose One's Soul': Blasphemy and Slavery in New Spain, 1596–1669," *Hispanic American Historical Review*, LXXXII (2002), 435–468; Herman L. Bennett, *Africans in Colonial Mexico: Absolutism, Christianity, and Afro-Creole Consciousness, 1570–1640* (Bloomington: University of Indiana Press, 2003), 3–35.

8. For estimates on the number of slaves in New Spain in 1810, see Guadalupe Jiménez, *México: su tiempo de nacer, 1750–1821* (Mexico City: Fondo Cultural Banamex, 2001), 62. This represented a sharp decrease from 1742, when Gonzalo Aguirre Beltrán estimates that there were 286,327 slaves in Mexico.

9. Jaime Olveda Legaspi, "La abolición de la esclavitud en México, 1810–1917," *Signos Historicos* 29 (January–June 2013), 8–34; Marcela Terrazas y Basante y Gerardo Gurza Lavalle, *Imperios, repúblicas y pueblos en pugna por el territorio, 1756–1867* (Universidad Nacional Autónoma de México, Instituto de Investigaciones Históricas/Secretaría de Relaciones Exteriores, 2012), 148.

10. For the abolition of slavery in Mexico in 1837, see Law of April 5, 1837, vol. 96, Justicia Archivo, AGN. For the ways in which Mexico used antislavery to serve its political purposes, see Gurza-Lavalle, "Against Slave Power?," 143–170.

11. Nicholas Trist to James Buchanan, December 6, 1847, vol. 14, roll 15, DUSM-Mexico.

12. Mark Wasserman, *Everyday Life and Politics in Nineteenth Century Mexico: Men, Women, and War* (Albuquerque: University of New Mexico Press, 2000), 46; James McPherson, *Battle Cry: The Civil War Era* (Oxford: Oxford University Press, 1988), 9–10.

13. For the origins of the term "America," see Felipe Fernández-Armesto, *Amerigo: The Man Who Gave His Name to America* (New York: Random House, 2008), 3, 94–132.

CHAPTER 1: DEFENDING SLAVERY

1. Frank M. Flinn, *Campaigning with Banks in Louisiana, '63 and '64, and with Sheridan in the Shenandoah Valley in '64 and '65* (Boston: W. B. Clarke, 1889), 77; John D. Winters, *The Civil War in Louisiana* (Baton Rouge: Louisiana State University Press, 1991), 281. For more on Port Hudson during the Civil War, see Lawrence L. Hewitt, *Port Hudson, Confederate Bastion on the Mississippi* (Baton Rouge: Louisiana State University Press, 1987).

2. "A Noble Woman," *Fort Worth Morning Register* (October 15, 1899), 10; Company Muster Roll for December 10, 1862, to February 28, 1863, First

Texas Battalion Sharp Shooters; Regimental History file, First Texas Sharp-shooters, Texas Heritage Museum; Burnet's Battalion First Texas Sharpshoot-ers, National Archive Microfilm Series 323, Roll #260–261. Confederate troops at Vicksburg had subsisted on shoe leather during the siege, and their fellow soldiers at Port Hudson likely would have resorted to the same desper-ate tactics if the siege continued. James McPherson, *Battle Cry of Freedom: The Civil War Era* (Oxford: Oxford University Press, 1988), 634, 638.

3. For "darkest day," see John B. Jones, *A Rebel War Clerk's Diary*, ed., John B. Jones (Urbana, IL: Sangamore Press, 1958), 238–239. For "your negroes," scc *Dallas Herald*, September 30, 1863.

4. 1790 United States Census, Wake County, North Carolina, Series M637, Roll 7, page 254, image 152, Ancestry.com. 1820 United States Census, Natchitoches, Louisiana, Series M33, roll 31, image 92, Ancestry.com.

5. Sven Beckert, *Empire of Cotton: A Global History* (New York: Alfred A. Knopf, 2014), 67, 85–86; Edward E. Baptist, *The Half Has Never Been Told: Slavery and the Making of American Capitalism* (New York: Perseus Books, 2014), 113; Andrew J. Torget, *Seeds of Empire: Cotton, Slavery, and the Trans-formation of the Texas Borderlands, 1800–1850* (Chapel Hill: The University of North Carolina Press, 2015), 4–7.

6. Beckert, *Empire of Cotton*, 102–103; Stuart Weems Bruchey, *Cotton and the Growth of the American Economy* (New York: Harcourt, 1967), 45–46; Angela Lakwete, *Inventing the Cotton Gin: Machine and Myth in Antebellum America* (Baltimore: Johns Hopkins University Press, 2004), 21–46.

7. For the three-fifths clause, see US Constitution, art. I, § 2. For the fu-gitive slave clause, see US Constitution, art. IV, § 2. For the international slave trade, see US Constitution, art. I, § 9. Beckert, *Empire of Cotton*, 112; Adam Rothman, *Slave Country: American Expansion and the Origins of the Deep South* (Cambridge, MA: Harvard University Press, 2005), 55–56; Baptist, *Half Has Never Been Told*, 228.

8. John Craig Hammond, *Slavery, Freedom, and Expansion in the Early American West* (Charlottesville: University of Virginia Press, 2004), 3; Randall M. Miller and John David Smith, *Dictionary of Afro-American Slavery* (West-port, CT: Greenwood Publishing, 1997), 53.

9. Peter Onuf, *Statehood and Union: A History of the Northwest Ordinance* (Bloomington: Indiana University Press, 1987), 111–147; David Brion Davis, "The Significance of Excluding Slavery from the Old Northwest in 1787," *In-diana Magazine of History*, vol. 84, no. 1 (March 1988): 75–89; Paul Finkelman, "Slavery and Bondage in the 'Empire of Liberty,'" in *Northwest Ordinance: Es-says on Its Formulation, Provisions, and Legacy*, Frederick D. Williams, ed. (East

Lansing: Michigan State University Press, 1988), 61–95. For earlier visions on how to organize the territories, see Arthur Bestor, "Constitutionalism and the Settlement of the West," in *The American Territorial System*, John Porter Bloom, ed. (Athens: Ohio University Press, 1969), 15–30.

10. For the existence of slavery in the Northwest Territory, see Matthew Salafia, *Slavery's Borderland: Freedom and Bondage Along the Ohio River* (Philadelphia: University of Pennsylvania Press, 2013), and Tiya Miles, *The Dawn of Detroit: A Chronicle of Slavery and Freedom in the City of the Straits* (New York: The New Press, 2017). For the interpretation of the antislavery provision of the Northwest Ordinance, see St. Clair to George Washington, May 1, 1790, in Clarence Edwin Carter, ed., *The Territorial Papers of the United States* (Washington, DC, 1934), II, 248; Francis Samuel Phillbrick, *Laws of Illinois Territory, 1809–1818* (Springfield: Illinois State Historical Library, 1950), ccxxiii–ccxl; Don E. Fehrenbacher, *The Dred Scott Case: Its Significance in American Law and Politics* (Oxford: Oxford University Press, 1978), 32.

11. Hammond, *Slavery, Freedom, and Expansion*, 10; Richard L. Forstall, ed., *Population of States and Counties of the United States: 1790–1990* (Washington: US Department of Commerce, 1996), 4.

12. March 23, 1798, *DoC*, 2:222, 224; D. Clayton James, *Antebellum Natchez* (Baton Rouge: Louisiana State University Press, 1993), 45, 52. "An Act for the Amiable Settlement of Limits with the State of Georgia, and Authorizing the Establishment of a Government in the Mississippi Territory," April 7, 1798, in Richard Peters, ed., *Public Statutes at Large of the United States of America* (Boston: Little and Brown, 1850), 1:550.

13. Lacy K. Ford, *Deliver Us from Evil: The Slavery Question in the Old South* (Oxford: Oxford University Press, 2009), 64–65; Salafia, *Slavery's Borderland*, 108–136; William W. Freehling, *The Road to Disunion: Secessionists at Bay, 1776–1854* (2 vols., New York: Oxford University Press, 1990), 1:13–24; Graham Hodges, *Root and Branch: African Americans in New York and East Jersey, 1613–1863* (Chapel Hill: University of North Carolina Press, 2005), 162–186; James J. Gigantino, *The Ragged Road to Abolition: Slavery and Freedom in New Jersey, 1775–1865* (Philadelphia: University of Pennsylvania Press, 2014), 64–94; Graham Hodges, *Slavery and Freedom in the Rural North: African Americans in Monmouth County, New Jersey, 1665–1865* (Lanham, MD: Rowman & Littlefield, 1997), 113–146; Shane White, *Somewhat More Independent: The End of Slavery in New York City, 1770–1810* (Athens: University of Georgia Press, 2012), 24–55; David N. Gellman, *Emancipating New York: The Politics of Slavery and Freedom, 1777–1827* (Baton Rouge: Louisiana State University Press, 2006), 153–188.

14. Ronald Seavoy, *An Economic History of the United States* (New York: Routledge, 2013), 27. The United States paid $15 million for preemption rights to the territory, but over $2.6 billion to native peoples living in Louisiana for their soil rights. Robert Lee, "Accounting for Conquest: The Price of the Louisiana Purchase of Indian Country," *Journal of American History* (March 2017): 922–923. For Kirkham's departure from North Carolina, see John G. Belisle, *History of Sabine Parish, Louisiana* (Natchitoches: Sabine Banner Press, 1912), 69; Gifford E. White, *Character Certificates in the General Land Office of Texas* (Baltimore, MD: Genealogical Publishing Company, 2009), 104.

15. For the description of Natchitoches, see January 3–6, 1829, "Journal de Voyage aux limites N.E. de la Republique Mexicaine," JLBP, vol. 30, f. 122, BRBML; Texas por Terán, f. 20, JLBP, BRBML; *A Visit to Texas: Being the Journal of a Traveller Through Those Parts Most Interesting to American Settlers*, 2nd ed. (New York: Van Nostrand and Dwight, 1836), 180–181. For the pronunciation of Natchitoches, see Edward Warren to Henry Warren, December 25, 1835, folder 293, box 5, Streeter Collection, BRBML. For the population of Natchitoches, see William Darby, *The Emigrant's Guide to the Western and Southwestern States and Territories* (New York: Kirk and Mercein, 1818), 102.

16. For Kirkham's plantation, see John Belisle, *History of Sabine Parish: From the First Explorers and Settlers to the Present* (Many, LA: Daughters of the Revolution, 2006), 69–70; US Congress, *American State Papers: Documents, Legislative and Executive, of the Congress of the United States* (Washington: Gales and Seaton, 1859), 135; "Report of the Register and Receiver of the Land District South of Red River in Louisiana," Document No. 50 (January 13, 1826), *House Documents, 19th Congress, 1st Session* (Washington: Gales and Seaton, 1826), 111. For Kirkham's slaves, see "Declaración del Negro Esclavo Martin," f. 222, "Declaración del Negro Esclavo Ricardo Moran," f. 225, "Declaración de la Negra Esclava Fivi," f. 227, April 20, 1820, vol. 776, box 2Q238, Ramsdell Transcripts, BCAH.

17. For slavery in the Louisiana Territory, see Patricia Reid-Merrit, ed., *A State-by-State History of Race and Racism in the United States* (New York: ABC-CLIO, 2018), 2:356; Jennifer M. Spear, "Liberty, Slavery, and the Louisiana Purchase of 1803: The Incorporation of the Territory of Orleans," *Oxford Research Encyclopedia of American History* (Oxford: Oxford University Press, 2018), 10; Sanford Levinson and Bartholomew Sparrow, eds., *The Louisiana Purchase and American Expansion, 1803–1898* (New York: Rowman & Littlefield, 2005), 169.

18. "The Remonstrance of the Representatives Elected by the Freemen of Their Respective Districts in the District of Louisiana," *American State Papers*,

Class X, Misc., 1:401–404; Governor W.C.C. Claiborne to James Madison, March 10, 1804, in Dunbar Rowland, ed., *Official Letter Books of W.C.C. Claiborne, 1801–1816* (6 vols., Jackson: University of Mississippi Press, 1917), 2:25; "The Remonstrance of the People of Louisiana against the Political System Adopted by Congress for Them," *Annals of Congress*, 8th Congress, 2nd Session, 727–728.

19. John W. Gurley to the Postmaster General, July 14, 1804, in Clarence E. Carter, ed., *The Territorial Papers of the United States* (28 vols., Washington, DC: Government Printing Office, 1934–1975), 9:262; Daniel Clark to James Madison, April 27, 1803, in "Despatches from the United States Consul in New Orleans, 1801–1803," II, *American Historical Review*, 33 (1928), 340; Hammond, *Slavery, Freedom, and Expansion*, 57.

20. John Sibley to Governor Claiborne, March 8, 1805, William C. Claiborne Letters and Depositions, Mss. 5018, LSU.

21. Alexander von Humboldt, *Political Essay on the Kingdom of New Spain*, John Black, trans. (New York: I. Riley, 1811), 118; Timothy Anna, "The Independence of Mexico and Central America," in *The Cambridge History of Latin America*, ed. Leslie Bethell (12 vols., Cambridge: Cambridge University Press, 1985), 3:51; Victor Bulmer Thomas, *Economic History of Latin America* (Cambridge: Cambridge University Press, 2014), 510; Tatiana Seijas and Jake Frederick, *Spanish Dollars and Sister Republics: The Money That Made Mexico and the United States* (Lanham, MD: Rowman & Littlefield, 2017), 1.

22. Von Humboldt, *Political Essay*, 25. For the population of Mexico City, see Mark Wasserman, *Everyday Life and Politics in Nineteenth Century Mexico: Men, Women, and War* (Albuquerque: University of New Mexico Press, 2000), 199. For the population of New York, see 1800 United States Census, New York City, Ancestry.org.

23. Lesley Byrd Simpson, *Many Mexicos* (Berkeley: University of California Press, 1971), 4, 8.

24. Simpson, *Many Mexicos*, 10; Douglas R. Cope, *The Limits of Racial Domination: Plebeian Society in Colonial Mexico City, 1660–1720* (Madison: University of Wisconsin Press, 1995), 19; Andrew B. Fisher and Matthew D. O'Hara, eds., *Imperial Subjects: Race and Identity in Colonial Latin America* (Durham: Duke University Press, 2009), 1–38; María Elena Martínez, *Genealogical Fictions: Limpieza de Sangre, Religion and Gender in Colonial Mexico* (Stanford, CA: Stanford University Press, 2008), 1–21; Patricia Seed, "Social Dimensions of Race: Mexico City, 1753," *Hispanic American Historical Review* 62:4 (November 1982): 569–606; Timothy J. Henderson, *A Glorious Defeat:*

Mexico and Its War with the United States (New York: Farrar, Straus and Giroux, 2007), 9–11.

25. For the importance of Catholicism in Mexican society, see Matthew D. O'Hara, *A Flock Divided. Race, Religion, and Politics in Mexico, 1749–1857* (Durham, NC: Duke University Press, 2010), 236; D. A. Brading, *Mexican Phoenix: Our Lady of Guadalupe: Image and Tradition Across Five Centuries* (Cambridge: Cambridge University Press, 2001), 74. For Congress seeking spiritual aid, see Charles Bankhead to Earl of Aberdeen, December 31, 1844, f. 149–150, FO 50/177, NA-K. For divine approval of a treaty, see H. G. Ward to George Canning, June 2, 1825, f. 28, FO 50/13, NA-K. For religious processions, see H. G. Ward to George Canning, July 12, 1825, f. 146, FO 50/13, NA-K.

26. Brading, *Mexican Phoenix*, 74; Javier Villa Flores, "On Divine Persecution: Blasphemy and Gambling," in *Religion in New Spain*, eds. Susan Schroeder and Stafford Poole (Albuquerque: University of New Mexico Press, 2007), 243; Magali M. Carrera, *Imagining Identity in New Spain: Race, Lineage, and the Colonial Body in Portraiture and Casta Paintings* (Austin: University of Texas Press, 2010), 118–119.

27. The scholarly consensus has long held that slavery disappeared by the seventeenth century as the indigenous population of New Spain recovered from a series of devastating epidemics. But recent demographic studies have shown that the indigenous population did not recover until the nineteenth century. Peter Gerhard, *A Guide to the Historical Geography of New Spain* (Cambridge: Cambridge University Press, 1972), 23–25; Norma Angélica Castillo Palma, *Cholula: sociedad mestiza en ciudad india, un análisis de las consecuencias demográficas, económicas y sociales del mestizaje en una ciudad novohispana, 1649–1796* (Mexico City: Universidad Autónoma Metropolitana, 2001), 445–454; Elsa Malvido, *La población, siglos XVI al XX* (Mexico City: UNAM, 2006), 233–236. For the black population of Mexico City, see Herman L. Bennett, *Colonial Blackness: A History of Afro-Mexico* (Bloomington: Indiana University Press), 5; Rebecca Horn, *Postconquest Coyoacán: Nahua-Spanish Relations in Central Mexico, 1519–1650* (Stanford, CA: Stanford University Press, 1997), 223–225; Frank Proctor, "Afro-Mexican Slave Labor in the Obrajes de Paños of New Spain, Seventeenth and Eighteenth Centuries," *The Americas* 60:1 (2003): 42; John C. Super, "Querétaro Obrajes: Industry and Society in Provincial Mexico, 1600–1810," *Hispanic American Historical Review* 56:2 (May 1976), 197–216. For the black population of Guadalajara, see Arturo Chávez Hayhoe, *Guadalajara en el Siglo XVI* (Guadalajara: Ayuntamiento de Guadalajara, 1991), 123.

For the San Cosme plantation, see Tatiana Seijas and Pablo Miguel Sierra Silva, "The Persistence of the Slave Market in Seventeenth-Century Central Mexico," *Slavery and Abolition* 37:2 (2016): 31. For the black population of Béxar, see Phillip Thomas Tucker, *Exodus from the Alamo: The Anatomy of the Last Stand Myth* (Philadelphia: Casemate, 2009), 12.

28. For orders to whip runaways, see Manuel de Salcedo to Audiencia de Guadalajara, November 8, 1811, box 1, Wagner Collection, BRBML. For examples of slaves being branded, see José Javier Ezquerra González, coord., *Los Esclavos en la Nueva Galicia: Testamentos, lentos y donaciones hasta la abolición de la esclavitud* (Guadalajara: Gobierno de Jalisco, 2003), 15. For slaves being put in chains, see "Juicio Promovido por Manuela de Arciniega en Favor de su hijo Juan de Segura, como Esclavo de Don Pablo Coronel," November 15, 1730, Fondo Colonial, Archivo Municipal de Guadalajara. At the same time, the legal protections that enslaved people enjoyed were not a dead letter. In 1807, a twenty-one-year-old mulatto complained to the authorities in Monclova, Coahuila, that he was given too much work, though he did not give any details about what he was forced to do. Luis de la Garza to Sr. Gov. D. Juan Ignacio de Arizpe, March 17, 1807, folder 4, box 10, Fondo Colonial, AMM. In 1803, a slave named José Flores complained to the authorities of Monclova, Coahuila, that his owner did not give his family enough to eat. S.f. to Sr. Subdelegado de Saltillo, November 10, 1803, folder 11, box 4, Fondo Colonial, AMM.

29. Colin A. Palmer, *Slaves of the White God: Blacks in Mexico, 1570–1650* (Cambridge, MA: Harvard University Press, 1976), 86; Alejandro de la Fuente, "Slave Law and Claims-Making in Cuba: The Tannenbaum Debate Revisited," *Law and History Review* 22:2 (Summer, 2004), 339–369. For the status of slaves in Spanish law, see Emily Berquist, "Early Anti-Slavery Sentiment in the Spanish Atlantic World, 1765–1817," *Slavery and Abolition* 31:2 (June 2010): 181–205; Herman L. Bennett, *Africans in Colonial Mexico*, 4, 33–34; Frank Tannnbaum, *Slave and Citizen* (New York: Knopf, 1946), 48–55; David Brion Davis, *The Problem of Slavery in Western Culture* (Ithaca, NY: Cornell University Press, 1966), 29–121, 165–261; Eugene Genovese, *The World the Slaveholders Made* (New York: Pantheon, 1969), 3–113.

30. The policy proved so useful that Spanish authorities reiterated their commitment to protect fugitive slaves in 1733, 1740, 1750, and 1789; Manuel Lucena Salmoral, ed. *Regulación de la esclavitud negra en las colonias de America Española: documentos para su estudio* (Alcalá de Henares: Universidad de Alcalá-Universidad de Murcía, 2005), 268; Jane Landers, *Black Society in Spanish Florida* (Chicago: University of Illinois Press, 1999), 25; Jane Landers, "Spanish Sanctuary: Fugitives in Florida, 1687–1790," *Florida Historical Quarterly*

62:3 (January 1984): 296–313; John J. TePaske, "The Fugitive Slave: Inter-colonial Rivalry and Spanish Slave Policy, 1687–1764" in *Eighteenth Century Florida and Its Borderlands*, ed. Samuel Proctor (Gainesville: University Press of Florida, 1975), 6. We know that these decrees were circulating because enslaved people invoked them. On February 8, 1823, a fugitive slave from the United States named Andrés Dortola petitioned for his freedom in Mexico by expressing his desire "to continue the exercise of the Catholic religion which he professes." In his petition, Dortola cites the royal decree of September 24, 1750, that promised freedom to slaves who converted to Catholicism. See Solicitud del esclavo Andrés Dortola, f. 28–29, doc. 5, exp. 12, box 85, Gober-nación sin sección, AGN. For the circulation of news among slaves more gen-erally, see Julius Sherrard Scott, *The Common Wind: Currents of Afro-American Communication in the Era of the Haitian Revolution* (New York: Verso, 2018), 38–158; Linda M. Rupert, "'Seeking the Water of Baptism,' Fugitive Slaves and Imperial Jurisdiction in the Early Modern Caribbean" in *Legal Pluralism and Empires, 1500–1850*, eds. Lauren Benton and Richard J. Ross (New York: New York University Press, 2013), 206.

31. Claiborne to Secretary of State James Madison, January 1, 1809, Dunbar Rowland, ed., *Official Letter Books of Claiborne* (Jackson, MS: State Department of Archives and History, 1917), 4:282–285.

32. "El Grito de Dolores en 1810," *Diario del Gobierno de los Estados Unidos Mexicanos* (September 16, 1835), 3; Henderson, *A Glorious Defeat*, 20–21. For ears as epaulets, see *Colección de documentos para la historia de la guerra de inde-pendencia de México de 1808 a 1821* (Mexico City: J. M. Sandoval, 1882), 408. For the independence movement in New Spain, see Eric Van Young, *The Other Rebellion: Popular Violence, Ideology, and the Mexican Struggle for Independence* (Stanford, CA: Stanford University Press, 2001), and Peter Guardino, *Peas-ants, Politics, and the Formation of Mexico's National State: Guerrero, 1800–1857* (Stanford, CA: Stanford University Press, 1996). For the independence move-ments in the Spanish colonies, see Jeremy Adelman, *Sovereignty and Revolution in the Iberian Atlantic* (Princeton, NJ: Princeton University Press, 2006); D. A. Brading, *The First America* (Cambridge: Cambridge University Press, 1991); Jordana Dym, *From Sovereign Villages to Nation States: City, State, and Federa-tion in Central America, 1759–1839* (Albuquerque: University of New Mexico Press, 2006); François Xavier Guerra, *Modernidad e Independencias* (Mexico City: Fondo de Cultura Económica, 1993); Tamar Herzog, *Defining Nations: Immigrants and Citizens in Early Modern Spain and Spanish America* (New Ha-ven: Yale University Press, 2003); Jaime Rodríguez, *The Independence of Spanish America* (Cambridge: Cambridge University Press, 1998).

33. Donald R. Hickey, *The War of 1812: A Forgotten Conflict* (Champaign: University of Illinois Press, 2012), 1–2; Nicole Eustace, *War and the Passions of Patriotism* (Philadelphia: University of Pennsylvania Press, 2012), xi; Robert V. Remini, *The Life of Andrew Jackson* (New York: Harper Collins, 2001), 7, 8, 19, 32, 45, 86–104. For the Seminoles, see Kevin Mulroy, *Freedom on the Border: The Seminole Maroons in Florida, the Indian Territory, Coahuila, and Texas* (Lubbock: Texas Tech University Press, 1993), 7; James Leitch Wright, *Creeks & Seminoles: The Destruction and Regeneration of the Muscogulge People* (Lincoln: University of Nebraska Press, 1986), 4; Landers, *Black Society in Spanish Florida*, 72–73; Haggard, "Neutral Ground," 1026–1027.

34. Jackson to Monroe, January 6, 1818, in Harold D. Jackson, ed., *Papers of Andrew Jackson: 1816–1820* (Knoxville: University of Tennessee Press, 1980), 1:167; Andrew Jackson to Calhoun, March 25, 1818, in *American State Papers, Military Affairs*, 1:698. For Jackson's invasion of Florida, see Remini, *Life of Andrew Jackson*, 116–128; Deborah Rosen, *Border Law: The First Seminole War and American Statehood* (Cambridge, MA: Harvard University Press, 2015), 11–39.

35. John Quincy Adams, *Memoirs of John Quincy Adams*, ed. Charles Francis Adams (12 vols., Philadelphia: J. B. Lippincott, 1874), 1:103–114.

36. David Bushnell, "The Wars of Independence in Spanish America" in *Cambridge History of Latin America*, 3:128; Rafe Blaufarb, "The Western Question: The Geopolitics of Latin American Independence," *American Historical Review* 112 (June 2007), 742–763.

37. Haggard, "The Neutral Ground," 1023; William Earl Weeks, *John Quincy Adams and American Global Empire* (Lexington, KY: University Press of Kentucky, 1992), 107–199.

38. For the prohibition on carrying arms, see section 20, "Black Code: An Act Prescribing the Rules and Conduct to Be Observed with Respect to Negroes and Other Slaves of This Territory," approved, June 7, 1806, Louis Moreau Lislet, ed. *A General Digest of the Acts of the Legislature of Louisiana* (New Orleans: B. Levy, 1828), 1:104. For the prohibition on riding horses, see section 25, ibid., 105. For restrictions on mobility, see section 30, ibid., 107. For intoxicating liquors, see section 24, ibid., 105. For dancing at night, see "An Act to Amend the Act Entitled 'An Act Prescribing the Rules and Conduct to Be Observed with Respect to Negroes and Other Slaves of This Territory,'" April 14, 1807, ibid., 120. For bans on slaves owning property, see section 38, ibid., 110. Section 15, ibid., 103. For branding, see John Sibley to Governor Claiborne, March 8, 1805, William C. Claiborne Letters and Depositions,

Mss. 5018, LSU. For slave codes, see Sally Hadden, "The Fragmented Laws of Slavery in the Colonial and Revolutionary Eras," in Michael Grossberg and Christopher Tomlins, eds., *Cambridge History of Law in America* (Cambridge University Press, 2008), 253–287; Vernon V. Palmer, *Through the Codes Darkly: Slave Law and Civil Law in Louisiana* (Clark, NJ: Lawbook Exchange, 2012).

CHAPTER 2: THE MEANING OF LIBERTY

1. For how the escape was planned, see "Declaration of the Black Slave Ricardo Moran," April 25, 1820, f. 225–226, box 2Q238, vol. 776, Ramsdell Transcripts, BCAH.

2. For British promises of emancipation, see Donald R. Hickey, *The War of 1812*, 213. For Martin's branding, see "Declaration of the Black Slave Martin," April 25, 1820, f. 224, box 2Q238, vol. 776, Ramsdell Transcripts, BCAH. For enslaved people escaping from the Lower Mississippi Valley, see S. Charles Bolton, *Fugitivism: Escaping Slavery in the Lower Mississippi Valley, 1820–1860* (Fayetteville: University of Arkansas Press, 2019), 30–32, 85–87.

3. For alligators, see Edward Warren to Henry Warren, December 25, 1835, box 5, Streeter Collection, BRBML. For "astonomical instruments," January 3–6, 1829, "Journal de Voyage aux limites N.E. de la Republique Mexicaine," f. 127, vol. 30, JLBP, BRBML. For "dark, somber aspect," see Jean Louis Berlandier, "Considerations generales sur le Departement de Texas," 1828, f. 18, vol. 36, JLBP, BRBML.

4. "Declaration of the Black Slave Martin," April 25, 1820, f. 224, box 2Q238, vol. 776, Ramsdell Transcripts, BCAH; Testimony of George B. Little, April 8, 1820, f. 226, vol. 187, Provincias Internas, AGN.

5. For the process of planting and harvesting cotton, see "Plantation Diary," 1825, vol. 3, box 15, Stirling (Lewis and Family) Papers, LSU; "Declaración de Xacobo Querkham," December 23, 1820, Provincias Internas, AGN. Temporary absenteeism was the most common kind of escape. John Hope Franklin and Loren Schweninger, *Runaway Slaves: Rebels on the Plantation* (New York: Oxford University Press, 1999), 98–109.

6. "Memorandum of Property Taken from Little Rock," *AP*, 1:368.

7. Gregg Cantrell, *Stephen F. Austin: Empresario of Texas* (New Haven: Yale University Press, 1999), 26, 28, 70.

8. For population of Alabama, Mississippi, and Louisiana, see Richard L. Forstall, ed., *Population of States and Counties of the United States: 1790–1990* (Washington, DC: US Department of Commerce, 1996), 4. For land

prices, see "Speech of Mr. Ewing Before the Senate," March 15, 1836, *Register of Debates in Congress* (Washington, DC: Gales and Seaton, 1836), 12:817; Cantrell, *Stephen F. Austin*, 70.

9. For slaveholders in Missouri defending their "property" rights, see William E. Foley, *The Genesis of Missouri: From Wilderness Outpost to Statehood* (Columbia: University of Missouri Press, 1989); John Mack Faragher, "'More Motley than Mackinaw': From Ethnic Mixing to Ethnic Cleansing on the Frontier of the Lower Missouri, 1783–1833," in Andrew R. L. Cayton and Fredrika J. Teute, eds., *Contact Points: American Frontiers from the Mohawk Valley to the Mississippi, 1750–1830* (Chapel Hill: University of North Carolina Press, 1998), 304–326. For the letter from Kaskaskia, see John Edgar to John Fowler, September 25, 1803, in Clarence E. Carter, ed., *The Territorial Papers of the United States* (28 vols., Washington, DC: Government Printing Office, 1934–1975), 13:5–7. For the letter from Vincennes, see Thomas T. Davis to John Breckinridge, October 17, 1803, ibid., 7:124. For the controversy over Missouri, see Glover Moore, *The Missouri Controversy, 1819–1821* (Lexington: University of Kentucky Press, 1953), 32; John R. Van Atta, *Wolf by the Ears: The Missouri Crisis, 1819–1821* (Baltimore: Johns Hopkins University Press, 2015); Matthew Mason, "The Maine and Missouri Crisis: Competing Priorities and Northern Slavery Politics in the Early Republic," *Journal of the Early Republic* 33 (Winter 2013), 675–700; Robert Pierce Forbes, *The Missouri Compromise and Its Aftermath: Slavery and the Meaning of America* (Chapel Hill: University of North Carolina Press, 2007); John Craig Hammond, "President, Planter, Politician: James Monroe, the Missouri Crisis, and the Politics of Slavery," *Journal of American History* (March 2019): 843–867.

10. February 15, 1819, *DoC*, 6:345, 352.

11. Ibid., 334, 340, 357.

12. February 15, 19, 1819, *DoC*, 6:344, 367; "From the Pittsburgh Gazette," *City of Washington Gazette* (April 17, 1820), 3; Sean Wilentz, "Jeffersonian Democracy and the Origins of Political Antislavery in the United States: The Missouri Crisis Revisited," *Journal of the Historical Society* IV:4 (Fall 2004), 379.

13. Forbes, *Missouri Compromise*, 47; Don E. Fehrenbacher, *The Dred Scott Case: Its Significance in American Law and Politics* (Oxford: Oxford University Press, 1978), 106. For Cobb and Tallmadge's exchange, see February 16, 1819, *DoC*, 4: 351.

14. *Petersburg Intelligencer*, quoted in *New-York Daily Advertiser*, March 18, 1820; *Louisville Public Advertiser*, February 14, 1821.

15. *New-York Daily Advertiser*, November 13, 1819, June 7, 1820; *Boston Columbian Centinel*, February 26, 1820, *Annals of Congress*, 16th Congress, 1st Session, 71, 80; *St. Louis Enquirer*, February 5, 1820.

16. Forbes, *Missouri Compromise*, 62–84; Fehrenbacher, *Dred Scott*, 107.

17. March 2, 1819, *DoC*, 4:371; January 28, 1820, *DoC*, 4:485.

18. February 17, 1819, *DoC*, 4:357; "The Hon. Jonathan Mason," Boston *Christian Watchman* (April 1, 1820), 3. For this vision of limited government, see Michael F. Holt, *Political Parties and American Political Development from the Age of Jackson to the Age of Lincoln* (Baton Rouge: Louisiana State University Press, 1992), 33–87.

19. Moore, *Missouri Controversy*, 88, 92, 102; Adams, *Memoirs of John Quincy Adams*, 5:13; Matthew W. Hall, *Dividing the Union: Jesse Burgess Thomas and the Making of the Missouri Compromise* (Carbondale: Southern Illinois University Press, 2015), 117.

20. Holt, *Political Parties*, 33–87.

21. E. M. Sanders, "The Natural Regions of Mexico," *Geographical Review* 11:2 (April 1921), 213, 223–224; Diary of General Whiting's Tour of Inspection in Texas, May 2–August 22, 1851, Streeter Collection, BRBML; February 6, July 25–28, 1829, "Journal de Voyage aux limites N.E. de la Republique Mexicaine," f. 205, vol. 30, JLBP, BRBML; Cantrell, *Stephen F. Austin*, 86–87; Andrew J. Torget, *Seeds of Empire: Cotton, Slavery, and the Transformation of the Texas Borderlands, 1800–1850* (Chapel Hill: The University of North Carolina Press, 2015), 1–3.

22. "Independence of Texas: Declaration by the Supreme Council of the Province of Texas," *The Courier*, London (October 18, 1819). For hunting, see Testimony of John Gordon, April 7, 1820, f. 217, vol. 187, Provincias Internas, AGN; Testimony of Marshal Smith, April 8, 1820, f. 224, ibid.; Testimony of Simeon Manuel, f. 225, ibid. For horses, see Testimony of James Hail, April 11, 1820, f. 230, ibid. For land, see Testimony of Michael Brake, April 8, 1820, f. 219, ibid. For more on James Long's expedition, see Ed Bradley, "Fighting for Texas: Filibuster James Long, the Adams-Onís Treaty, and the Monroe Administration," *SWHQ* 102 (Jan. 1999): 323–342; William C. Davis, *Lone Star Rising* (New York: Simon and Schuster, 2004), 46–50.

23. H. W. Brands, *Lone Star Nation: The Epic Story of the Battle for Texas Independence* (New York: Anchor, 2005), 20; Torget, *Seeds of Empire*, 49.

24. Cantrell, *Stephen F. Austin*, 86; Austin to the Governor of Texas, December 26, 1820, in Mattie Hatcher, *The Opening of Texas to Foreign Settlement* (Austin: University of Texas Press, 1927), 355; Antonio Martínez to Joaquín

de Arredondo, December 26, 1820, in *PCRCT*, 1:301. For the military budget, see Torget, *Seeds of Empire*, 50.

25. Cantrell, *Stephen F. Austin*, 86–87.

26. Moses Austin to Stephen F. Austin, May 22, 1821, in *AP*, 1:393; Moses Austin to Martínez, January 26, 1821, in *AP*, 1:377–378; Moses Austin to Baron de Bastrop, January 26, 1821, in *AP*, 1:379–380; Moses Austin to Felix Trudeaux, February 3, 1821, in *AP*, 1:381–382; Guy M. Bryan, "Hardships of Travel," n.d., *AP*, 1:377; Cantrell, *Stephen F. Austin*, 87–89.

27. Christopher Schmidt-Nowara, *Slavery, Freedom, and Abolition in Latin America and the Atlantic World* (Albuquerque: University of New Mexico Press, 2011), 110; Clara Álvarez Alonso, "Libertad y propiedad; El primer liberalismo y la esclavitud," *Anuario de Historia del Derecho Español*, núm. 65 (1995): 559–583; Timothy Anna, *Forging Mexico, 1821-1835* (Lincoln: University of Nebraska Press, 1998), 74–75; Amy S. Greenberg, *A Wicked War: Polk, Clay, Lincoln, and the 1846 U.S. Invasion of Mexico* (New York: Knopf, 2012), 56.

28. Peter Guardino, *Peasants, Politics, and the Formation of Mexico's National State: Guerrero, 1800–1857* (Stanford, CA: Stanford University Press, 1996), 77; Theodore G. Vincent, *The Legacy of Vicente Guerrero: Mexico's First Black Indian President* (Gainesville: University Press of Florida, 2001), 8–12.

29. Nettie Lee Benson, "Iturbide y los planes de independencia," *Historia Mexicana* 2:3 (January–March 1953): 439–446; William Spence Robertson, *Iturbide of Mexico* (Westport, CT: Greenwood Press, 1968), 67–71; Jaime E. Rodríguez O., "The Transition from Colony to Nation: New Spain, 1810–1821," in *Mexico in the Age of Democratic Revolutions, 1750–1850*, ed. Jaime E. Rodríguez O. (Boulder, CO: Lynne Rienner, 1994), 97–132; Alfredo Ávila, *En nombre de la nación. La formación del gobierno representativo en México* (Mexico City: CIDE/Taurus, 2002), 196–201; Ivana Frasquet, *Las caras del águila. Del liberalismo gaditano a la república federal Mexicana (1820–1824)* (Castelló: Universitat Jaume I, 2008), 29–88; Ivana Frasquet and Manuel Chust, "Agustín de Iturbide: From the Pronunciamiento of Iguala to the Coup of 1822," in *Forceful Negotiations: The Origins of the Pronunciamiento in Nineteenth-Century Mexico*, ed. Will Fowler (Lincoln: University of Nebraska Press, 2010), 22–46; Timothy E. Anna, *The Mexican Empire of Iturbide* (Lincoln: University of Nebraska Press, 1990), 1–26; Anna, *Forging Mexico*, 85; Treaty of Cordoba, in Lic. Roberto Olagaray, ed., *Colección de Documentos Históricos Mexicanos* (Mexico City: Antigua Imprenta de Murguia, 1924), 2:170.

30. Agustín Iturbide, February 24, 1821, "Plan e indicaciones pa. el gobierno," in *Colección de Documentos Historicos Mexicanos*, 2:8; Testimony of José Trinidad Martínez, January 16, 1823, vol. 22, folder 3, Justicia, AGN; Un-

signed extract, St. Martinsville, July 9, 1822, box 1, Slavery Collection, LSU; "Mexico, An Empire," *Courrier de la Louisiana* (July 29, 1822), 1.

31. David Brion Davis, *The Problem of Slavery in Western Culture* (Ithaca, NY: Cornell University Press, 1966), 82; David M. Potter, *The Impending Crisis, 1848-61* (New York: Harper & Row, 1976), 44.

32. "Declaración del Negro Esclavo Juan Pedro," April 24, 1820, f. 220, vol. 776, box 2Q238, Ramsdell Transcripts, BCAH. "Declaración del Negro Esclavo Martin," April 25, 1820, f. 222, ibid.; "Declaración del Negro Esclavo Ricardo Moran," f. 225, ibid.; "Declaración de la Negra Esclava Fivi," f. 228, ibid.

CHAPTER 3: THE RIGHT TO PROPERTY

1. Stephen F. Austin, "Journal of Stephen F. Austin on His First Trip to Texas, 1821," *Quarterly of the Texas State Historical Association* 7:4 (April 1904), 288–291.

2. Andrew J. Torget, *Seeds of Empire: Cotton, Slavery, and the Transformation of the Texas Borderlands, 1800–1850* (Chapel Hill: The University of North Carolina Press, 2015), 63–64; Gregg Cantrell, *Stephen F. Austin: Empresario of Texas* (New Haven: Yale University Press, 1999), 94.

3. "Census of the Residents of the Real Presidio of La Bahía del Espíritu Santo," December 31, 1804, reel 1, frames 1487–1494, and "Census Report of the Presidial Company of La Bahía del Espíritu Santo," December 31, 1804, reel 1, frames 1499–1504, in Carmen Leal, ed., *Translations of Statistical and Census Reports of Texas* (San Antonio: University of Texas at San Antonio, 1979). For a general history of La Bahía, see Kathryn Stoner O'Connor, *The Presidio La Bahía del Espíritu Santo de Zúñiga, 1721 to 1846* (Austin: Von Boeckmann-Jones, 1966); Austin, "Journal," 298, 300, 302.

4. Austin, "Journal," 303, 306.

5. Cantrell, *Stephen F. Austin*, 89, 109; Austin to Antonio Martínez, October 13, 1821, *AP*, 1:419.

6. Cantrell, *Stephen F. Austin*, 110.

7. Austin to J. H. Hawkins, May 1, 1822, *AP*, 1:504–505; Austin to James E. B. Austin, March 23, 1822, *AP*, 1:487; Austin to J.E.B. Austin, July 8, 1822, *AP*, 1:530.

8. Francisco Laborda, "Catecismo Político," October 24, 1821, f. 11–32, folder 3, vol. 21, Justicia, AGN; Secretary of War to Mexican Consul in New Orleans, August 11, 1828, f. 185, L-E-1055, SRE; H. G. Ward to George Canning, June 3, 1825, f. 32, FO 50/13, NA-K.; H. G. Ward to George Canning,

May 21, 1825, f. 8, ibid.; Rafael González to Señores Diputados, January 8, 1825, exp. 100, leg. 2, ACEC; Benedict Anderson, *Imagined Communities: Reflections on the Origin and Spread of Nationalism* (London: Verso, 1983), 49; David Brading, *The Origins of Mexican Nationalism* (Cambridge: Cambridge University Press, 1985), 3–23.

9. "Congreso General: Cámara de Diputados, Sesión del día 8 de enero," *El Sol* (January 17, 1827), 1–2; *El Amigo del Pueblo* (September 3, 1828): 713–714. For how US citizens celebrated their independence, see Simon P. Newman, *Parades and the Politics of the Street: Festive Culture in the Early American Republic* (Philadelphia: University of Pennsylvania Press, 1997), 83–119. For examples of slave owners offering up their slaves, see José San Martin to Pablo La Llave, f. 155, exp. 32, vol. 22, Justicia, AGN; Report, December 15, 1825, f. 55, exp. 7, vol. 26, Justicia, AGN.

10. For eliminating distinctions of caste, see Timothy Henderson, *The Mexican Wars for Independence* (New York: Farrar, Straus and Giroux, 2009), 219. For "we cannot," see *Diario de las Sesiones de la Soberana Junta . . . del Imperio Mexicano* (Mexico City: Imprenta de A. Valdés, 1821), 126.

11. Austin to James E. B. Austin, May 22, 1822, *AP*, 1:517–518; Timothy Anna, *The Mexican Empire of Iturbide* (Lincoln: University of Nebraska Press, 1990), 68–72; Manuel Ferrer Muñoz, *La formación de un estado nacional en México: el Imperio y la República federal, 1821–1835* (Mexico City: Universidad Nacional Autónoma de México, 1995), 120–127.

12. William Taylor to John Quincy Adams, August 4, 1822, vol. 1, DUSC-Veracruz; Stanley Green, *The Mexican Republic: The First Decade, 1823–1832* (Pittsburgh: University of Pittsburgh, 1987), 31; Will Fowler, *Santa Anna of Mexico* (Lincoln: University of Nebraska Press, 2007), 79.

13. Juan Antonio Mateos, *Historia Parlamentaria de los Congresos Mexicanos* (Mexico City: J. V. Villada, 1877), 1:812, 815–817, 820.

14. Hugh McGuffin to Austin, September 13, 1822, *AP*, 1:546; Timothy Anna, *Forging Mexico, 1821–1835* (Lincoln: University of Nebraska Press, 1998), 11, 95.

15. Austin to José Felix Trespalacios, January 8, 1823, *AP*, 1:567; Debates of November 23 and 26, 1822, quoted in Torget, *Seeds of Empire*, 75; Wyly Martin, Jefe Político of San Felipe de Austin, to D. C. Barrett and E. Gritten, July 21, 1835, folder 128, box 3, Wagner, BRBML.

16. "Bando sobre colonización publicado el día 7 del corriente," *Gaceta del Gobierno Imperial de México*, 7:1 (January 16, 1823); Austin to José Felix Trespalacios, January 8, 1823, *AP*, 1:567.

17. Ira Berlin, *The Long Emancipation: The Demise of Slavery in the United States* (Cambridge, MA: Harvard University Press, 2015), 193.

18. Henderson, *A Glorious Defeat*, 26; N. P. Trist to James Buchanan, October 25, 1847, f. 196, folder 4, vol. VI, box 2, Justin H. Smith Collection, BLAC; Fowler, *Santa Anna*, 171–173, 191, 224, 256, 301.

19. Austin to Gaspar Flores [answering letter of December 6, 1824], in *AP*, 1:984–985.

20. Raymond Buve, "Ayuntamientos and Pronunciamientos during the Nineteenth Century: Examples from Tlaxcala Between Independence and the Reform War," in *Malcontents, Rebels, and Pronunciados: The Politics of Insurrection in Nineteenth-Century Mexico*, ed. Will Fowler (Lincoln: University of Nebraska Press, 2012), 129; Anna, *Forging Mexico*, 139.

21. Jaime E. Rodríguez O., "La Constitución de 1824 y la formación del estado mexicano," *Historia Mexicana* 40:3 (January–March 1991): 518; Timothy Anna, "Inventing Mexico: Provincehood and Nationhood after Independence," *Bulletin of Latin American Research* 15:1 (1996): 7–17; Ivana Frasquet, "De la autonomía provincial a la República Federal. México, 1820–1824," *Ayer* 74 (2009): 49–76; Mexican Constitution of 1824, Article 3, Title 1; Anna, *Forging Mexico*, 148–150.

22. Guadalupe Victoria's real name was José Miguel Fernández. During the wars of independence, he christened himself Guadalupe, after the Virgin, and Victoria, for victory. Anna, *Forging Mexico*, 179. For the running joke about Guadalupe Victoria, see Stanley C. Green, *The Mexican Republic: The First Decade, 1823–32* (Pittsburgh: University of Pittsburgh Press, 1987), 87; George Bancroft, *History of Mexico* (San Francisco: The History Company, 1887), V:656.

23. Torget, *Seeds of Empire*, 80; Sesión del Dia 25 de Agosto de 1824, vol. 1, Actas del Congreso Constituyente del Estado Libre de Coahuila y Texas, ACEC.

24. "Proclamation," *AP*, 1:781.

25. "Concluye la sesión del 14 de enero de 1824, *Aguila Mexicana*, no. 277 (January 16, 1824), 1–2. The provision was not without precedent in Mexico. In 1821, the head of a group of delegates from New Spain at the Cortes in Madrid proposed and succeeded in passing a law abolishing the slave trade and promising freedom to illegally imported slaves. (This law remained in effect until 1824.) See Will Fowler, "The Texan Revolution of 1835–36 and Early Mexican Nationalism," in Sam W. Haynes, ed., *Contested Empire: Rethinking the Texas Revolution* (College Station: Texas A&M University Press, 2015),

116. For the US Act, see Paul Finkelman, "Slavery in the United States: Persons or Property?," in Jean Allain, ed., *The Legal Understanding of Slavery: From the Historical to the Contemporary* (Oxford: Oxford University Press, 2012), 122; David Brion Davis, "The Rocky Road to Freedom—Crucial Barriers to Abolition in the Antebellum Years," in Alexander Tsesis, ed., *The Promises of Liberty: The History and Contemporary Relevance of the Thirteenth Amendment* (New York: Columbia University Press, 2010), xvii. For British prohibition, see Rosanne Marion Adderley, *"New Negroes from Africa": Slave Trade Abolition and Free African Settlement in the Nineteenth-Century Caribbean* (Bloomington: Indiana University Press, 2006), 25–26.

26. "Concluye la sesión del 14 de enero de 1824," *Aguila Mexicana*, no. 277 (January 16, 1824), 1–2; Erasmo Seguin to A. Bexar, July 24, 1825, 2B115, Barker Collection, BCAH.

27. Consulta del jefe político de Texas sobre la prohibición de la esclavitud y las concesiones de los colonos americanos en Texas, October 11, 1824, f. 217, vol. 3, Justicia Archivo, AGN; Congress to jefe político de Texas, October 18, 1824, ibid.

28. Miguel Soto, "Politics and Profits: Mexican Officials and Land Speculation in Texas, 1824–1835," in *Contested Empire*, 82–83; *Laws and Decrees of the State of Coahuila and Texas: In Spanish and English*, J. P. Kimball, trans. (Houston: Telegraph Power Press, 1839), 22.

29. John Martin Davis Jr., *Texas Land Grants, 1750–1900: A Documentary History* (New York: McFarland), 12–13; Torget, *Seeds of Empire*, 85; "Census of the District of Colorado for the Year 1825," *AP*, 2:1, 244; Mary Crownover Rabb, *Travels and Adventures in Texas In the 1820's* (Waco: Morrison, 1962), 1–2; Rosa Groce Bertleth, "Jared Ellison Groce," *SWHQ* 20 (April 1917): 358–368; Cantrell, *Stephen F. Austin*, 203.

30. Torget, *Seeds of Empire*, 71, 122, 125–126.

31. José Manuel Zozaya, December 26, 1822, in Secretario de Relaciones Exteriores, *La diplomacia mexicana* (2 vols., Mexico City, 1910–1912), 1:101–103; J. A. Torrens to the Mexican government, January 26, 1824, ibid., 2:74; Statement of Thomas Hart Benton, February 10, 1825, in *St. Louis Missouri Republican*, March 14, 1825.

32. Sesión del día 30 de Noviembre de 1826, Vol. 3, Actas del Congreso Constituyente del Estado Libre de Coahuila y Texas, ACEC.

33. Austin to José Antonio Saucedo, September 11, 1826, *AP*, 1:1452.

34. Austin to Coahuila y Tejas State Legislature, August 11, 1826, in *AP*, 1:1406–1409; Sesión del día 30 de Noviembre de 1826, vol. 3, Actas del Congreso Constituyente del Estado Libre de Coahuila y Texas, ACEC.

35. Antonio Saucedo to Victor Blanco, September 17, 1826, DCX-LIX-5.51.1, CONDUMEX; Coahuila y Téjas Congress to Vice-Governor, October 16, 1826, El Libro de Decretos y Ordenes de 1824 a 1826, Hacienda, ACEC.

36. "Governor's Opinion Concerning Slavery," November 30, 1826, in *AP*, 1:1523–1525.

37. Jaime del Arenal Fenochio, "La utopia de la libertad: la esclavitud en las primeras declaraciones mexicanas de derechos humanos," semanario la tradición indiana y el origen de las declaraciones de derechos humanos (Comisión Nacional de Derechos Humanos y el Instituto de Investigaciones Jurídicas de la UNAM, 23 y 24 de septiembre de 1933), 20; Sesión del día 30 de noviembre de 1826, vol. 3, Actas del Congreso Constituyente del Estado Libre de Coahuila y Texas, ACEC.

38. Ayuntamiento de Santa Rita de Morelos to Honorable Congress, March 25, 1825, fondo Comisiones, Segundo Congreso Constitucional, Primer Periodo Ordinario, ACEC. The nine states were Chihuahua, Coahuila y Téjas, Estado de México, Michoacan, Nuevo León, Oaxaca, Puebla, Veracruz, Yucatán. The constitutional congresses of Jalisco, Durango and Estado de Occidente (Sinaloa/Sonora) abolished slavery with the promise of indemnification. In Chihuahua, Querétaro, and Chiapas, the representatives declared the end of slavery but instructed the legislature to establish a process by which slaves would be freed. The constitution of both Tabasco and San Luis Potosí promised freedom and citizenship. For an excellent summary of this legislation, see Jaime Olveda Legaspi, "La abolición de la esclavitud en Mexico, 1810–1917," Signos Históricos 29 (January–June 2013), 8–34.

39. "Congreso del Estado, Cámara de Diputados, Sesión del día 19 de julio," *El Oriente* (September 29, 1826), 2–3.

40. Entry of March 31, 1828, in Barker, "Minutes of the Ayuntamiento of San Felipe de Austin, 1828–1832," *SWHQ* 21:3 (January 1918), 311; Tijerina and Navarro, April 30, 1828, expediente 15, leg. 4, dec. num. 56, Primero Congreso Constitucional, Segundo Periodo Ordinario, Comisión de Gobernación, ACEC; Sesión del 3 de mayo de 1828, Actas del Primer Congreso Constitucional del Estado Libre de Coahuila y Tejas, vol. IV (June 28, 1827–September 30, 1829), 900. An English translation of the law can be found: https://texashistory.unt.edu/ark:/67531/metapth217328. Austin to Richard Ellis, June 16, 1830, Eugene C. Barker, *AP*, 2:422; Torget, *Seeds of Empire*, 133.

41. Francisco Pizarro Martinez to Manuel de Mier y Terán, February 5, 1832, folder 9, file 20, AEMEUA, SRE; Franklin Chase to John Appleton, Assistant Secretary of State, October 13, 1857, vol. 4, reel 4, DUSC-Tampico.

42. Will Fowler, "The Texan Revolution of 1835–36 and Early Mexican Nationalism," in *Contested Empire*, 113; Henderson, *A Glorious Defeat*, 50.

CHAPTER 4: AN ANTISLAVERY REPUBLIC

1. Juan Bautista Elguézabal, "A Description of Texas in 1803," trans. Odie Faulk, *SWHQ* 66:4 (April 1963): 513–515; Terán to President of Mexico, June 30, 1828, in Jack Jackson, ed., *Texas by Terán: The Diary Kept by General Manuel de Mier y Terán on His 1828 Inspection of Texas* (Austin: University of Texas Press, 2000), 97; Timothy J. Henderson, *A Glorious Defeat: Mexico and Its War with the United States* (New York: Farrar, Straus and Giroux, 2007), 50–53; Will Fowler, "The Texan Revolution of 1835–36 and Early Mexican Nationalism," in *Contested Empire*, 104; David J. Weber, *The Mexican Frontier, 1821–1846: The American Southwest Under Mexico* (Albuquerque: University of New Mexico Press, 1982), 167.

2. Jackson, *Texas by Terán*, 99, 178; Miguel Soto, "Politics and Profits: Mexican Officials and Land Speculation in Texas, 1824–1835," in *Contested Empire*, 83.

3. Manuel Mier y Terán, *Reflexiones que hago sobre cada articulo de la Ley de 6 de Abril de este año*, June 6, 1830, f. 123, exp. 30, leg. 5, vol. 312, Archivo de la Secretaria de Fomento, Colonización y Terrenos Baldios, Elizabeth H. West Transcripts, BCAH; Jackson, *Texas by Terán*, 57, 101.

4. C. E. Castañeda, trans., "Statistical Report on Texas by Juan N. Almonte," *SWHQ* 27 (January 1925): 179; Will Fowler, *Santa Anna of Mexico* (Lincoln: University of Nebraska Press, 2007), 162; Jackson, *Texas by Terán*, 98; Gregg Cantrell, *Stephen F. Austin: Empresario of Texas* (New Haven: Yale University Press, 1999), 219; Andrés Reséndez, *Changing National Identities at the Frontier: Texas and New Mexico, 1800–1850* (Cambridge: Cambridge University Press, 2005), 22–23; Manuel Mier y Terán, *Reflexiones que hago sobre cada articulo de la Ley de 6 de Abril de este año en cumplimiento de lo q. me ordena S.E. el ciudadano Ministro de Relaciones*, June 6, 1830, f. 123, exp. 30, leg. 5, vol. 312, Archivo de la Secretaria de Fomento, Colonización y Terrenos Baldios, West Transcripts, BCAH.

5. Mier y Terán, *Reflexiones*, f. 123, exp. 30, leg. 5, vol. 312, West Transcripts, BCAH.

6. Joel Roberts Poinsett to Henry Clay, April 26, 1827, folder 6, vol. 4, Poinsett Papers, HSP.

7. Sean Wilentz, *Andrew Jackson* (New York, Henry Holt, 2007), 4, 86; Nettie Lee Benson, "Texas as Viewed from Mexico, 1820–1834," SWHQ 90:3

(January 1987), 270; William Forrest Sprague, *Vicente Guerrero, Mexican Liberator: A Study in Patriotism* (Chicago: Pr. by R. R. Donnelley & Sons, 1939), 91–96. For general biographies of Vicente Guerrero, see Maria Lafragua, *Vicente Guerrero* (Mexico City: PRI, Comisión Nacional Editorial, 1976); Vicente Fuentes Díaz, *Revaloración del Gral. Vicente Guerrero: Consumador de la Independencia* (Chilpancingo, MX: Universidad Autónoma del Estado, 1989); Silvia Martínez del Campo, *Vicente Guerrero* (Mexico City: Planeta Mexicana, 2005).

8. Robert V. Remini, *The Life of Andrew Jackson* (New York: Harper Collins, 2001), 168–169; "Editorial," *Correo de la Federación*, December 1, 1828, 1. For an overview of the riots, see Silvia M. Arrom, "Popular Politics in Mexico City: The Parián Riot, 1828," in *Hispanic American Historical Review* 68 (1985): 245–270; Leslie Bethell, ed., *Mexico Since Independence* (Cambridge: Cambridge University Press, 1991), 11.

9. Stanley Green, *The Mexican Republic: The First Decade, 1823–1832* (Pittsburgh: University of Pittsburgh Press, 1987), 165; Timothy Anna, *Forging Mexico, 1821–1835* (Lincoln: University of Nebraska Press, 1998), 224.

10. José María Sánchez, "A Trip to Texas in 1828," trans. Carlos Castañeda, *SWHQ* XXIX:4 (April 1926), 279; Cantrell, *Stephen F. Austin*, 219; Andrés Reséndez, *Changing National Identities at the Frontier: Texas and New Mexico, 1800–1850* (Cambridge: Cambridge University Press, 2005), 22–23.

11. Crawford to Richard Pakenham, July 25, 1829, f. 19, FO 50/57, NA-K. For a description of Tampico, see Benjamin Moore Norman, *Rambles by Land and Water, or Notes of Travel in Cuba and Mexico* (Boston: Paine & Burgess, 1845), 99; Cañedo to Secretary of War, August 9, 1828, f. 93, 481.3/654, AHSDN; Cañedo to Secretary of Guerra y Marina, July 30, 1828, f. 95, 481.3/654, AHSDN. For Campeche, see H. Bell to Commanding Officer of H. M's Ships & Vessels in the Pacific, August 7, 1829, f. 9, FO 50/57, NA-K. For Yucatán, see William Taylor to Martin Van Buren, July 1, 1829, reel 1, DUSC-Veracruz. For reports of a US invasion by way of Louisiana, *Sesión del día 17 de Agosto de 1829*, ADRP X, AHS; *Sesión del dia de 18 de Agosto de 1829*, ADRP X, AHS. "Texas," July 19, 1829, *El Correo*, 3. For the Spanish invasion, see Ivana Frasquet, "Milicianos y soldados: la problemática social Mexicana en la invasión de 1829," *Las ciudades y la guerra, 1750–1898*, ed. Salvador Broseta Peralles (Castelló de la Plana, ES: Universitat Jaume, 2002): 115–132; Harold Sims, *The Expulsion of Mexico's Spaniards, 1821–1836* (Pittsburgh, PA: University of Pittsburgh Press, 1990), 139–159; Nettie Lee Benson, "Texas as Viewed from Mexico," *SWHQ* 90 (January 1987): 264–265; Jesús Ruiz de Gordejuelo Urquijo, "El brigadier Barradas y la reconquista de México, 1829," *Revista de historia militar* 113 (2012): 162–166.

12. Richard Pakenham to Earl of Aberdeen, August 26, 1829, f. 60–66, FO 50/55, NA-K; Jaime F. Rodriguez O., "Oposición a Bustamante," *Historia Mexicana* (1999): 199–234. For Mexico State's militia, see Joaquin Lebrija a todos sus habitantes, August 5, 1829, folder 5.1, Decrees, Wagner, BRBML. For the ladies of Monclova, see Maria Roberta Barrera, Maria Josefa Valde de Garza, and Juana de la Fuentes to Gobierno del Estado, August 9, 1829, folder 3, box 3, series 1, FSXIX, AMM. For Anahuac's offer, see Committee of Citizens to Ramon Muzquiz, Jefe Político de Texas, September n.d., 1829, folder 5, box 2S243, BA, BCAH.

13. Pakenham to Earl of Aberdeen, August 26, 1829, f. 60–66, FO 50/55, NA-K; Harold Sims, *La reconquista de México: la historia de los atentados españoles, 1821–1830* (Mexico City: Fondo de Cultura Económica, 1984), 79, 82; George Prager to Martin Van Buren, December 4, 1829, vol. 1, roll 1, DUSC-Tampico; Crawford to Pakenham, September 5, 1829, f. 171, FO 50/55, NA-K; Crawford to Pakenham, August 1, 1829, f. 92, ibid.

14. Benson, "Texas as Viewed from Mexico," 262; Feliciano Montenegro a Guerrero, June 16, 1829, *Buletín del Archivo General Nacional*, 22:2 (1951): 333–335; José María Bocanegra, *Memorias para la historia de México independiente, 1822–1846* (Mexico City: Imprenta del Gobierno Federal en el Ex-Arzobispado, 1892), 2:41.

15. On Barradas's plan, see Feliciano Montenegro to Vicente Guerrero, August 6, 1829, L-E-2129, SRE. For Guerrero, see Benson, "Texas as Viewed from Mexico," 270; Discurso pronunciado por el ciudadano Presidente de la República Vicente Guerrero, August 27, 1829, folder 27.1, Decrees, Wagner Collection, BRBML.

16. Decree abolishing slavery, September 15, 1829, folder 15.1, Decrees, Wagner, BRBML. For an English language version, see "Abolition of Slavery," *The American Annual Register for the Year 1829–30* (Boston: Gray and Bowen, 1832), 147. For "great injustice," see Charles O'Gorman to Bidwell, Foreign Office, September 17, 1829, f. 121–122, FO 50/57, NA-K.

17. Juan Estrada, Juan Luis Macgregor y Esteban Panalladas to Minister of Justice, October 18, 1829, folder 1, box 293, Gobernación sin Sección, AGN.

18. Ayuntamiento de Córdoba to Despacho de Justicia, n.d. [1829?], f. 129, folder 11, box 246, Gobernación sin Sección, AGN; Ayuntamiento de Córdoba to President, December 10, 1829, f. 305, folder 34, vol. 48, Justicia, AGN; Iniciativa que la legislatura del estado libre y soberano de Yucatán hace a las cámaras del Congreso, October 10, 1829, DUSC-Veracruz. For the "cruel attack on property," see F. G. Cicero, *Demostración de la Legalidad del Pronun-*

ciamiento en Favor del Sistema de República Central en Yucatán (Campeche, MX: Imprenta del Gobierno, 1830), 7–8.

19. "Letter from Alabama," *Constitutional Advocate and Texas Public Advertiser* 1:28 (June 19, 1830), 3. Laviña was originally from New Orleans, and had been living in Allende for eight months. It is unclear whether he had escaped from slavery in Téjas, or whether he was free. His wife's name was María Regina Rodríguez. José Maria Felán to Gov. de Coahuila y Téjas, October 16, 1829, exp. 15, folder 1, box 11, FSXIX, AGEC. The men from the De León Colony were reported to be from Guinea; Judge of Guerrero to J. M. Viescas, October 18, 1829, folder 63, box 6, Múzquiz Collection, BRBML; Luis Lombraña to Governor of Coahuila y Téjas, December 19, 1829, exp. 11, folder 8, box 12, FSXIX, AGEC.

20. Lorenzo de Zavala, *Ensayo crítico de las revoluciones de México desde 1808 hasta 1830* (Paris, 1831–1832, Reprint, Mexico City: Editorial Porrúa, 1969), 2:101; José María Tornel, *Breve reseña histórica de los acontecimientos más notables de la nación Mexicana* (Mexico City: Imprenta de Cumplido, 1852), 85. For Tornel's speech in the Cámara de Diputados against slavery in 1827, see "Congreso General: Cámara de Diputados, Sesión del día 8 de enero," no. 1311, *El Sol* (January 17, 1827), 1–2.

21. Ohland Morton, "Life of General Don Manuel de Mier y Terán: As It Affected Texas-Mexican Relations," *SWHQ* 48:1 (July 1944): 60; Felipe de la Garza to Minister of War, July 23, 1829, f. 7–9, folder 741, collection 481.3, AHSDN; Eugene C. Barker, *Mexico and Texas, 1821–35* (New York: Russel & Russell, 1965), 78–79.

22. Eduardo de Gorostiza to Secretary of Foreign Relations, February 20, 1830, f. 177–183, L-E-2128, SRE; Francisco Tacón to Francisco Vives, January 19, 1830, January 25, 1830, April 9, 1830, in José Luciano Franco, *Revoluciones y Conflictos Internacionales en el Caribe, 1789–1854* (Havana: Instituto de Historia Academia de Ciencias, 1965), 2:147; Jaime Delgado, *España y Mexico en el Siglo XIX*, vol. 1 (Madrid: Instituto Gonzalo Fernández de Oviedo, 1950), 377.

23. Benson, "Texas as Viewed from Mexico," 264; Sprague, *Vicente Guerrero*, 87; Michael Costeloe, *La respuesta a la independencia: la España imperial y las revoluciones hispanoamericanas, 1810–1840* (Mexico City: Fondo de Cultura Económica, 1989), 235–241; Frasquet, "Milicianos y soldados," 115–132.

24. Guillermo Prieto, *Memorias de mis tiempos, 1828 á 1840* (Paris, Mexico City: Librería de Bouret, 1906), 1:35; Ayuntamiento de Guadalajara to Senate, September 1, 1829, AY 1/1829, Ant. Paq. 50, leg. 97, AMGuad; Addington to Earl of Aberdeen, February 10, 1830, FO 72/367, NA-K; H. U. Addington to Foreign Office, March 3, 1830, f. 327, FO 50/64, NA-K; Sr. Comandante Gral

de estos Estados to Governor Viesca, July 12, 1830, folder 65, box 6, Múzquiz Collection, BRBML; Pakenham to Earl of Aberdeen, September 30, 1829, f. 205, FO 50/55, NA-K.

25. William DePalo, *The Mexican National Army, 1822–1852* (College Station: Texas A&M Press, 1997), 39; Stanley C. Green, *The Mexican Republic: The First Decade, 1823–1832* (Pittsburgh: University of Pittsburgh Press, 1987), 190–191; Mark Wasserman, *Everyday Life and Politics in Nineteenth Century Mexico: Men, Women, and War* (Albuquerque: University of New Mexico Press, 2000), 56; Michael P. Costeloe, *La primera República Federal de México (1824–1835): un estudio de los partidos políticos en el México independiente* (Mexico City: Fondo de Cultura Económica, 1983), 183–187; Anna, *Forging Mexico*, 227–228; Henderson, *A Glorious Defeat*, 68.

26. Henderson, *A Glorious Defeat*, 67; James Smith Wilcocks to Joel Roberts Poinsett, June 27, 1831, Poinsett Papers, HSP; Anthony Butler to Martin Van Buren, August 26, 1830, DUSM-Mexico.

27. Lucas Alamán to José María Tornel, May 20, 1830, f. 55, folder 2, file 17, AEMEUA, SRE; Secretary of Foreign Relations to Manuel de Gorostiza, May 5, 1830, f. 186–188, L-E-2128, SRE; Delgado, *España y Mexico*, 379.

28. Agentes confidenciales en Nassau to Angel Laborde in Franco, *Revoluciones y Conflictos*, 147; Francisco Tacon to Vives, April 9, 1830, José Franco, *Documentos para la historia de México existentes en el Archivo Nacional de Cuba* (Havana: Archivo Nacional de Cuba, 1961), 494–495; Acta de la Junta, La Habana, May 7, 1830, Franco, *Documentos*, 495–497; "Careo entre D. Manuel Roxo y Don José Julian Solis," March 16, 1830, *Boletín del Archivo Nacional* (Havana: Imprenta Siglo XIX, September to December 1913), 255; Circular del Gobernador de Matanzas a los Capitanes de Partido, June 16, 1830, ibid., 209; 5a Declaración de D. José Julian Solis, "Copia fiel de la primera pieza de la causa principal seguida por la conspiración titulada 'Gran Legión del Águila Negra,' que instruyó la Comisión militar española en 1830," *Boletín del Archivo Nacional*, XIII:1 (Havana: Imprenta El Siglo XX, 1914), 98; "The Cuba Conspiracy," *Louisiana Advertiser*, April 22, 1830, 2; Adrian del Valle, *Historia documentada de la conspiración de la Gran legión del águila negra* (Havana: Imprenta El Siglo XX, 1929), 21.

29. Sims, *La reconquista de Mexico*, 124–125; F. M. Dimond to Martin Van Buren, January 30, 1830, vol. 6, roll 6, DUSC-Cap Haitian.

30. John Witt, *Lincoln's Code: The Laws of War in American History* (New York: Free Press, 2012), 16–17.

31. Emer de Vattel, *The Law of Nations* (Philadelphia: T. & J. W. Johnson, 1849, 7th edition), 65, 352; Jennifer Pitts, *Boundaries of the International: Law*

and Empire (Cambridge, MA: Harvard University Press, 2018), 71–78; Lauren Benton and Lisa Ford, *Rage for Order: The British Empire and the Origins of International Law, 1800–1850* (Cambridge, MA: Harvard University Press, 2016), 20, 87.

32. Gorostiza to Secretary of Foreign Relations, February 20, 1830, f. 177–183, L-E-2128, SRE; Dale W. Tomich, *Through the Prism of Slavery: Labor, Capital, and World Economy* (New York: Rowman & Littlefield, 2004), 56–94; Anthony E. Kaye, "The Second Slavery: Modernity in the Nineteenth-Century South and the Atlantic World," *Journal of Southern History* 75, no. 3 (2009): 627–650.

33. Gorostiza to Secretary of Foreign Relations, February 20, 1830, f. 177–183, L-E-2128, SRE; *Cuba; or the Policy of England, Mexico, and Spain with Regard to that Island by an Englishman* (London: James Rideway 169, Picadilly, 1830), 8, 12–13, 16; Manuel Ortuño Martínez, "Manuel Eduardo de Gorostiza, hispano-mexicano, romántico y liberal," *Asociación Cultural de Amistad Hispanoamericana* (1991), 106–117.

34. Anglo American Mining Association to Earl of Aberdeen, August 4, 1829, f. 184–186, FO 50/58, NA-K.

35. Gorostiza to "my dear friend," February 9, 1830, L-E-2128, SRE; Tornel, the Mexican Minister to Washington, reported what Van Buren had told him; Tornel to Secretary of Foreign Relations, October 10, 1830, f. 140, folder 1, file 17, AEMEUA, SRE; Tornel to Secretary of Foreign Relations, March 16, 1830, Washington, f. 17–18, folder 1, file 17, AEMEUA, SRE; Gorostiza to Secretary of Foreign Relations, February 20, 1830, f. 147, L-E-2128, SRE.

36. Alamán to Tornel, Instrucciones, May 24, 1830, f. 19, folder 2, file 17, AEMEUA, SRE.

37. Constantino de Tarnava to Minister of War, January 6, 1830, Correspondence and Papers Relating to Mexico and Texas, BRBML. A translation of this document is available in Alleine Howren, "Causes and Origin of the Decree of April 6, 1830," *SWHQ* 16, no. 4 (April 1913), 407–413.

38. Green, *The Mexican Republic*, 11, 192; D. A. Brading, *The First America: The Spanish Monarchy, Creole Patriots, and the Liberal State, 1492–1867* (New York: Cambridge University Press, 1991), 642; Charles A. Hale, *Mexican Liberalism in the Age of Mora, 1821–1853* (New Haven, CT: Yale University Press, 1968), 16–17; Anna, *Forging Mexico*, 242–243; Salvador Méndez Reyes, *El hispanoamericanismo de Lucas Alamán, 1823–53* (Mexico City: Universidad Autónoma del Estado de México, 1996), 85–155.

39. Alamán to President, January 14, 1830, in Howren, "Causes and Origin of the Decree of April 6," 413; Report of the Secretary of State to the

Congress of Mexico, encl. Butler to Department of State, March 9, 1830, DUSM-Mexico.

40. Ibid.; Howren, "Causes and Origin," 416.

41. Acuerdo: Se pasa una comisión especial el Decreto expedido últimamente sobre Colonización, March 10, 1834, leg. 6, exp. 9, Cuarto Congreso Constitutional, ACEC; Ayuntamiento de Bexar, "Representación Dirijida por el Ilustre Ayuntamiento de la Ciudad de Bexar al Honorable Congreso del Estado" [Personal copy of Stephen F. Austin, Mexico 1835], Zc52 833sa, BRBML; Ramon Múzquiz to Stephen F. Austin, November 8, 1832, folder 197, box 4, Streeter Collection, BRBML; Brian DeLay, *War of a Thousand Deserts: Indian Raids and the U.S.-Mexican War* (New Haven: Yale University Press, 2009), 72; Austin to Richard Ellis, June 16, 1830, in *AP*, 2:422.

42. Anna, *Forging Mexico*, 242.

43. For the law repealing Guerrero's executive decrees, see Law of February 15, 1831, "Declaraciones Relativas a los Actos del Gobierno General en Virtud de Facultades Extraordinarias," in Arrillaga, *Leyes, Decretos, Bandos, Reglamentos, Circulares y Providencias de los Supremos Poderes y Otras Autoridades de la República Mexicana*, tomo de 1831, 37–38; "Resumen comparativo, o paralelo, entre la pasada y presente administración," *El Gladiador* (May 2, 1831), 4. For evidence that slavery continued legally in Mexico, see Decision of Manuel de los Santos Coy, November 24, 1831, f. 112, vol. 57, NA, TSA; *John M. Dor & Blake v. O. D. Oaks*, August 16, 1835, f. 118, vol. 79, NA, TSA; Petition of Naomi Mackey, March 25, 1835, f. 195–196, vol. 79, NA, TSA; Samuel Stadium to Constitutional Alcalde of District of Nacogdoches, April 1, 1833, f. 53, vol. 69, NA, TSA; Actas de la Villa de Nacogdoches, January 10, 1835, f. 145, vol. 71, NA, TSA.

CHAPTER 5: "IN ACCORDANCE WITH THE LAWS, THEY ARE FREE"

1. Louis Elie Laroque Tourgeau, "Declaration," 12-12-31, Reclamaciones, SRE; "A Sketch of the Mississippi River," *Farmer's Cabinet* (Amherst, New Hampshire), October 8, 1831, 2; "Extract of a letter from New Orleans," *New-York Evening Post* (February 11, 1831), 2.

2. In 1830, there were 3,567 slaves out of a total population of 5,426. United States Census of 1830, Ascension Parish, Louisiana.

3. "Trois negres," *The Bee* (February 24, 1831), 3. For violence between enslaved people, see Jeff Fornet, *Slave Against Slave: Plantation Violence in the*

Old South (Baton Rouge: Louisiana State University Press, 2015), 2. My understanding of resistance is shaped by James Scott, *The Weapons of the Weak: Everyday Forms of Peasant Resistance* (New Haven, CT: Yale University Press, 1985) and Eugene Genovese, *Roll, Jordan, Roll: The World the Slaves Made* (New York: Vintage Books, 1972). For a skeptical view of everyday forms of resistance, see Jeffrey Rubin, "The Ambiguity of Resistance," *Studies in Law, Politics and Society*, 15 (1996): 237–260 and Walter Johnson, "On Agency," *Journal of Social History* 37:1 (Autumn 2003), 113–124.

4. Tourgeau, "Declaration," 12-12-31, Reclamaciones, SRE; Ernest Obadele-Starks, *Freebooters and Smugglers: The Foreign Slave Trade in the United States after 1808* (Fayetteville: University of Arkansas Press, 2007), 84.

5. Tourgeau, "Declaration," 12-12-31, Reclamaciones, SRE.

6. City Council to Mayor, June 28, 1806, folder 13a, box 4, New Orleans Municipal Records, LSU; Contract for the framing of all sidewalks, April 15, 1805, folder 12, box 3, ibid.; City Council to Mayor, November 5, 1805, folder 12c, box 3, ibid. A plan for improving the health of the city of New Orleans, October 11, 1833, no. 760, f. 189, vol. 2, reel #90-156, AB320, Letters, petitions, and reports, Conseil de ville, NOPL; "A Rat Battle," *Telegraph and Texas Register* (December 4, 1839), 4; *Marchall A. Mathis v. W. Talbot*, box 190, General Case Files of the Eastern District of Louisiana, NAFW.

7. Francisco Pizarro Martínez to Sr. Camacho, July 29, 1826, L-E-1169, SRE; Francisco Pizarro Martínez to Juan José Espinosa de los Monteros, March 22, 1827, L-E-1169, SRE; Francisco Pizarro Martínez to Secretary of State, January 26, 1833, f. 11, 379/27, Gobernación sin sección, AGN; Francisco Pizarro Martínez to Presidente y Vocales de la Dirección del Banco para Fomento de la Industria Nacional, January 26, 1833, f. 32, ibid.; Francisco Pizarro Martínez to Presidente de la Dirección del Banco de Avío para Fomento de la Industrial Nacional, April 3, 1833, f. 49, ibid.; Articles of Agreement made and entered between William Archer of Philadelphia and Francisco Pizarro Martínez, August n.d., 1833, f. 77, folder 27, box 379, Gobernación sin Sección, AGN.

8. J. M. Guerra to Ramón Múzquiz, October 13, 1831, folder 6, box 2S278, BA, BCAH; Deliberations of Council, August 25, 1812, folder 19, box 5, New Orleans Municipal Records, LSU; Francisco Pizarro Martínez to Manuel de Mier y Terán, September n.d., 1831, f. 3, 12-12-31, Reclamaciones, SRE.

9. Francisco Pizarro Martínez to Encargado de Negocios, September 10, 1831, exp. 9, leg. 18, AEMEUA, SRE; Eugene C. Barker, *The Life of Stephen F. Austin: A Chapter in the Westward Movement of the Anglo-American People* (Nashville and Dallas: The Cokesbury Press, 1925), 257; May 1829, Memorandum

Book in ed. Moser, *Papers of Andrew Jackson*, 194; "The Purchase of Texas," *Hampshire Gazette* (September 30, 1829), 2.

10. Secretario del Estado to Pizarro Martínez, November 26, 1831, 12-12-31, Reclamaciones, SRE.

11. For how the mail was transported, see Thomas Clark, *The Old Southwest, 1795–1830* (Norman: University of Oklahoma Press, 1996), 175–176.

12. Anthony Butler to Martin Van Buren, December 31, 1829, roll 6, DUSM-Mexico. For Butler's Mexican mission, see Robert Arthur Carter, *Anthony Butler and His Mission to Mexico* (Austin: University of Texas at Austin, 1952); Irene Zea Prado, *Gestión diplomática de Anthony Butler en México, 1829–1836* (Mexico City: Secretaría de Relaciones Exteriores, 1982); Gerald D. Saxon, "Anthony Butler: A Flawed Diplomat," *East Texas Historical Journal* 24:1 (1986): 3–14; Quinton Curtis Lamar, "A Diplomatic Disaster: The Mexican Mission of Anthony Butler, 1829–1834," *The Americas* (July 1988): 1–17. For Wilcocks' complaint, see James Smith Wilcocks to Edward Livingston, February 15, 1833, vol. 2, DUSC-Mexico City; Wilcocks to Secretary of State, April 27, 1836, ibid.; Butler to Livingston, January 3, 1833, vol. 7, DUSM-Mexico.

13. Butler to Van Buren, March 9, 1830, vol. 6, DUSM-Mexico; Butler to Jackson, June 23, 1831, reel 39, General Correspondence, Jackson Papers, LoC.

14. Miguel Soto, "Texas en la mira: política e intereses al iniciarse la gestión de Anthony Butler," *Política y negocios. Ensayos sobre la relación entre México y los Estados Unidos en el siglo XIX*, eds. Ana Rosa Suárez Arguello y Marcela Terrazas Basante (Mexico City: UNAM, 1997), 32.

15. Butler to Livingston, October 25, 1831, roll 6, DUSM-Mexico; "A Treaty of Amity, Commerce, and Navigation Between the United States of America and the United Mexican States," *Treaties and Conventions Concluded Between the United States of America and Other Powers* (Washington, DC: US Government Printing Office, 1871), 544.

16. Butler to Livingston, November 13, 1830, roll 6, DUSM-Mexico; Extract from a debate in the Mexican Senate, October 10, 11, and 13, 1828, enclosed with Poinsett to Henry Clay, November 15, 1828, DUSM-Mexico.

17. Butler to Van Buren, November 2, 1830, ibid.; Butler to Jackson, May 25, 1831, ibid.; Butler to Livingston, October 25, 1831, DUSM-Mexico.

18. I have not been able to find a transcript or summary of these debates in any of the Mexico City newspapers that reported on the national Congress or in the Archivo Histórico del Senado. I have relied on the account of the Senate Committee on Foreign Relations, which reported on what the deputies

argued, in order to respond to their concerns. See Senate Committee on Foreign Relations, December 7, 1831, f. 24, folder 5, file 23, AEMEUA, SRE; Senate Committee on Foreign Relations, December 7, 1831, f. 24, folder 5, file 23, AEMEUA, SRE; Butler to Livingston, November 23, 1831, roll 6, DUSM-Mexico.

19. Notes of Consejo de Gobierno, October 21, 1831, folder 5, file 23, AEMEUA, SRE.

20. Ibid.

21. Butler to Livingston, October 24, 1831, vol. 6, DUSM-Mexico; Butler to Livingston, December 24, 1831, no. 351, *House Documents, Otherwise Publ. as Executive Documents* (25th Congress, 2nd Session), 12:413.

22. Butler to Alamán, December 14, 1831, ibid., 411; Butler to Livingston, December 24, 1831, ibid., 414; Committee on Foreign Relations, December 18, 1831, f. 18, folder 5, file 23, AEMEUA, SRE; Francisco Pizarro Martínez to Encargado de Negocios, April 7, 1832, folder 9, file 20, AEMEUA, SRE.

23. M. Santos Coy to José de las Piedras, January 13, 1831, f. 49, vol. 57, NA, TSA. The Commander of the Port of Veracruz returned two slaves in 1831 who had escaped from New Orleans by concealing themselves on board a ship. Consejo de Gobierno to Senate, October 21, 1831, f. 15, folder 5, file 23, AEMEUA, SRE and Consejo de Gobierno to Senate, December 2, 1831, f. 24, ibid.; Jefatura de Béxar to Alcalde de Nacogdoches, March 26, 1832, f. 192, vol. 63, NA, TSA.

24. M. Fiske, *A Visit to Texas: Being the Journal of a Traveller Through Those Parts Most Interesting to American Settlers,* 2nd ed. (New York: Van Nostrand and Dwight, 1836), 90–91. (Fiske reached Anahuac on March 26, 1831.)

25. Margaret Swett Henson, *Juan Davis Bradburn: A Reappraisal of the Mexican Commander of Anahuac* (College Station: Texas A&M University Press, 1982), 19–47.

26. Report to Comandante General, Estados Internos de Oriente, 1832, f. 99, folder 91, box 3, Wagner, BRBML; Austin to Mary Austin Holley, January 4, 1832, *AP*, 2:732.

27. Report to Comandante General, Estados Internos de Oriente, 1832, folder 91, box 3, Wagner, BRBML.

28. Thomas Tucker, *Exodus from the Alamo: The Anatomy of the Last Stand Myth* (Philadelphia: Casemate, 2009), 30–31; Michael R. Green, "To the People of Texas & All Americans in the World," *SWHQ* 91:4 (April 1988): 484; William C. Davis, *Three Roads to the Alamo: The Lives and Fortunes of David Crockett, James Bowie, and William Barret Travis* (New York: Harper Collins, 2009), 189–206, 259–286, 365–388, 445–470, 503–530.

29. H. W. Brands, *Lone Star Nation: The Epic Story of the Battle for Texas Independence* (New York: Anchor, 2005), 164–165.

30. P. C. Jack, Notes Regarding Disturbances at Anahuac, *The Papers of Mirabeau Buonaparte Lamar*, eds., C. A. Gulick and K. Elliott (Austin: Von Boecmann-Jones, Co., 1921–1927), 3:233–235.

31. Alcalde of Nacogdoches to the Political Chief of Texas, June 29, 1832, NA, TSA.

32. Barker, *Life of Stephen F. Austin*, 348–369.

33. Pizarro Martínez to Mier y Terán, February 5, 1832, folder 9, file 20, AEMEUA, SRE; H.P.N. Gammel, comp., *Laws of Texas, 1822–1897* (Austin: Gammel Book Company, 1898), 1:303.

34. Ramón Múzquiz to Governor of Texas, June 3, 1832, folder 55, box 22, FJBP, AGEC; Pizarro Martínez to Mexico's Chargé d'Affaires in Washington, March 23, 1832, exp. 9, leg. 20, AEMEUA, SRE.

35. Will Fowler, *Santa Anna of Mexico* (Lincoln: University of Nebraska Press, 2007), 133–135; Stanley C. Green, *The Mexican Republic: The First Decade, 1823-1832* (Pittsburgh: University of Pittsburgh Press, 1987), 193; Jan Bazant, "Mexico from Independence to 1867," in Leslie Bethell, ed., *The Cambridge History of Latin America, c. 1870–1930*, vol. IV (Cambridge: Cambridge University Press, 1986): 4:452–455; Timothy Anna, *Forging Mexico, 1821–1835* (Lincoln: University of Nebraska Press, 1998), 246–248.

36. Fowler, *Santa Anna of Mexico*, 141–142; Raúl Mejía Zúñiga, *Valentín Gómez Farías, hombre de México* (Mexico City: Fondo de Cultura Económica, 1981); Michael Costeloe, *The Central Republic in Mexico, 1835–1846: "Hombres de Bien" in the Age of Santa Anna* (Cambridge: Cambridge University Press, 2002), 26; Josefina Zoraida Vázquez, *Don Antonio López de Santa Anna: Mito y Enigma* (Mexico City: Centro de Estudios de Historia de México, 1987), 21.

37. Timothy J. Henderson, *A Glorious Defeat: Mexico and Its War with the United States* (New York: Farrar, Straus and Giroux, 2007), 88; "Confidential Instructions" in Juan Almonte, *Almonte's Texas: Juan N. Almonte's 1834 Inspection, Secret Report & Role in the 1836 Campaign*, Jack Jackson, ed. (Austin: Texas State Historical Association, 2005), 40.

38. Fowler, *Santa Anna of Mexico*, 146; Anna, *Forging Mexico*, 259.

39. Austin to James F. Perry, March 10, 1835, *PTR*, 1:33–36; Barrett Travis to Domingo de Ugartechea, July 31, 1835, f. 87–88, folder 1100, collection XI/481.3, AHSDN.

40. Jessica M. Lepler, *The Many Panics of 1837: People, Politics, and the Creation of a Transatlantic Financial Crisis* (Cambridge: Cambridge Univer-

sity Press, 2013), 13; Scott P. Marler, *The Merchants' Capital: New Orleans and the Political Economy of the Nineteenth-Century South* (Cambridge: Cambridge University Press, 2013).

41. Libro que registra las entradas de embarcaciones mexicanas al Puerto de Nueva Orleans, 1831–40, fs. 1–22, folder 1, box 32, Relaciones Exteriores, AGN.

42. It is likely that Jean Antoine was imported illegally to New Orleans from Cuba on the *General Santa Anna*. The ship and its cargo belonged to Cucullu, Lapeyre, and Co., a New Orleans firm known to act as an agent of the largest slaving outfit in Havana. See "Cleared," *New Orleans Bee* (June 3, 1835), 2; H. W. Macaulay to W. W. Lewis to Right Hon. Viscount Palmerston, May 13, 1839, *Correspondence with the British Commissioners, at Sierra Leone, the Havana, Rio de Janeiro, and Surinam: From May 11th to December 31st, 1840, inclusive* (London: William Clowes, 1841), 62. Though Francisco Pizarro Martínez's logs never noted Cuba as an intermediate stop, the US Consul in Campeche noted in a dispatch that the *General Santa Anna* tacked a route between New Orleans, Havana, and the Mexican coast. Henry Perrine to Secretary of State Henry Clay, July 11, 1828, vol. 1, DUSC-Campeche. For "animal and vegetable substances," see John Fincham, *An Outline of Ship-building* (London: Whittaker, 1852), 39.

43. Testimony of William Cantarell, October 9, 1835, f. 210, folder 1, file 25, AEMEUA, SRE; List of Vessels that Entered Campeche during the Year 1835, vol. 2, DUSC-Campeche.

44. For the population of Campeche, see Terry Rugeley, *Yucatán's Maya Peasantry and the Origins of the Caste War* (Austin: University of Texas Press, 2010), 79. The earliest instance I have found of a runaway slave escaping to Campeche in the hold of a ship and being returned is from 1811. See: Charles Trudeau to William C. C. Claiborne, November 29, 1811, reel 1, vol. 1, Letter books, 1811–1827, roll #90-144, AA530, Records of the Mayor, NOPL. Francisco Pizarro Martínez's ship logs never list Cantarell as the captain of the *General Santa Anna*, making it possible that he was the master of the ship, not its captain. (The captain, according to the consul's list, was a man named Pedro Rexach.) See Returns of Ships Arriving in the Year 1835, vol. 3, DUSC-Campeche. Pizarro Martínez to Secretary of Foreign Relations, October 26, 1835, exp. 1, leg. 25, AEMEUA, SRE.

45. Pizarro Martínez to Joaquín María del Castillo y Lanzas, December 8, 1834, folder 14, file 22, AEMEUA, SRE; Pizarro Martínez to Joaquín María del Castillo y Lanzas, January 15, 1835, f. 11, folder 1, file 25, ibid.; Testimony of Alejandro Duque de Estrada, October 9, 1835, f. 210, folder 1, file 25, ibid.;

Pizarro Martínez to Mexico's Chargé d'Affaires in Philadelphia, October 26, 1836, folder 1, file 25, ibid.

46. Francis W. Johnson to William Martin, May 6, 1835, *PTR*, 1:100; William B. Travis to David Burnet, May 21, 1835, ibid., 1:122.

47. Travis to D. G. Burnet, May 21, 1835, *PTR*, 1:132–133; Ron J. Jackson Jr. and Lee Spencer White, *Joe, the Slave Who Became an Alamo Legend* (Norman: University of Oklahoma Press, 2015), 128; Paul D. Lack, *The Texas Revolutionary Experience: A Political and Social History, 1835-1836* (College Station: Texas A&M University Press, 1992), 25; Mina Resolutions, July 4, 1835, *PTR*, 1:191–194; Committee of Columbia to citizens, July 15, 1835, *PTR*, 1:242.

48. Samuel May Williams to Don Carlos Barrett, January 2, 1836, *PTR*, 3:407; Sworn statement of A. J. Yates, I. N. Moreland, and A. C. Allen, August 29, 1835, *PTR*, 1:376–378; *Telegraph and Texas Register* (October 17, 1835), 1; B. J. White to S. F. Austin, October 17, 1835, *AP*, 3:190; Herbert Aptheker, *American Negro Slave Revolts* (New York: Columbia University Press, 1943), 93.

CHAPTER 6: THE TEXAS REVOLUTION

1. Ethel Zivley Rather, *DeWitt's Colony* (Austin: University of Texas Press, 1905), 134; John Henry Brown, *History of Texas* (St. Louis: Becktold, 1893), 1:126–127; Will Fowler, *Santa Anna of Mexico* (Lincoln: University of Nebraska Press, 2007), 131–157; Michael Costeloe, *The Central Republic in Mexico, 1835–1846: "Hombres de Bien" in the Age of Santa Anna* (Cambridge: Cambridge University Press, 2002), 36–45; Michael P. Costeloe, "Federalism to Centralism in Mexico: The Conservative Case for Change, 1834–1835," *The Americas* 45 (1988): 173–185.

2. Alwyn Barr, *Texans in Revolt: The Battle for San Antonio, 1835* (Austin: University of Texas Press, 1990), 4; H. W. Brands, *Lone Star Nation: The Epic Story of the Battle for Texas Independence* (New York: Anchor, 2005), 260; Vicente Filisola's testimony, September 23, 1836, f. 116, 200/2020, Archivo de Guerra, AGN.

3. Andrew Jackson Sowell, *Early Settlers and Indian Fighters of Southwest Texas* (Austin: Ben C. Jones, 1900), 4; Andrew Ponton to Ramón Múzquiz, September 26, 1835, f. 816, roll 166, BA.

4. Rather, *DeWitt's Colony*, 35. Historians have argued that "protecting slavery was not the primary cause of the Texas Revolution." Randolph B. Campbell, *An Empire for Slavery: The Peculiar Institution in Texas, 1821–1865* (Baton Rouge: Louisiana State University Press, 1989), 48–49. See also: Eugene

Barker, "The Influence of Slavery in the Colonization of Texas," *Mississippi Valley Historical Review* 11:1 (June 1924), 3–36. Some scholars have recognized the importance of slavery in the rebellion. Josefina Zoraida Vázquez, "The Texas Question in Mexican Politics, 1836–1845," *SWHQ* 89:3 (January 1986): 309–344; Fowler, *Santa Anna of Mexico*, 163; Josefina Zoraida Vázquez, "The Colonization and Loss of Texas: A Mexican Perspective," in eds., Jaime E. Rodríguez O. and Kathryn Vincent, *Myths, Misdeeds, and Misunderstandings: The Roots of Conflict in U.S.-Mexican Relations* (Wilmington, DE: SR Books, 1997), 76; Quintard Taylor, *In Search of the Racial Frontier: African Americans in the American West, 1528–1990* (New York: W. W. Norton, 1998), 37–45; Andrew J. Torget, *Seeds of Empire: Cotton, Slavery, and the Transformation of the Texas Borderlands, 1800–1850* (Chapel Hill: The University of North Carolina Press, 2015), 57–178. Although this scholarship understands slavery as being wrapped up in larger questions of federalism, it does not acknowledge the immediate threat that Mexico's ban on the importation of slaves posed to slavery in Téjas.

5. For the Battle of Gonzales, see Miles S. Bennet, "The Battle of Gonzales, the 'Lexington' of the Texas Revolution," *Quarterly of the Texas State Historical Association* 2:4 (April 9, 1899): 313–316.

6. "Minutes of Procedings of the Consultation of the chosen delegates of all Texas, in General Convention assembled," *Telegraph and Texas Register* (November 7, 1835), 4–5; James Kerr to Ira B. Lewis, August 3, 1835, *PTR*, 1:303.

7. Henry Bruce, *Life of General Houston, 1793–1863* (New York: Dodd, Mead, 1891), 93; Marquis James, *The Raven: A Biography of Sam Houston* (Austin: University of Texas Press, 1929), 162–167, 194–196; Llerena Friend, *Sam Houston, the Great Designer* (Austin: University of Texas Press, 2010), 38–40; "Ensayo Sobre la Revolución de Téjas," *Siglo XIX* (July 1, 1843), 2; Jos. J. Crawford to Richard Pakenham, April 4, 1837, f. 153, FO 50/106, NA-K; Anthony Butler to Andrew Jackson? January n.d., 1849, folder 5, Anson Jones Papers, BCAH; David Burnet to Mary Austin Holley, April 25, 1844, folder 135, box 3, Wagner, BRBML.

8. Paul D. Lack, *The Texas Revolutionary Experience: A Political and Social History, 1835-1836* (College Station: Texas A&M University Press, 1992), 13, 17; Sam Haynes, "'Imitating the Example of Our Forefathers': The Texas Revolution as Historical Reenactment," in *Contested Empire*, 50–51.

9. David Pantoja Morán, *El supremo poder conservador: el diseño institucional en las primeras constituciones mexicanas* (Michoacán, MX: El Colegio de Michoacán, 2005), 165–184; Josefina Zoraida Vázquez, *El Primer Liberalismo Mexicano: 1808–1855* (Mexico City: Museo Nacional de Historia, 1995), 31, 66, 93;

Timothy Anna, *Forging Mexico, 1821–1835* (Lincoln: University of Nebraska Press, 1998), 261.

10. Edwin Legrand Sabin, *With Sam Houston in Texas* (Philadelphia: J. P. Lippincott, 1916), 157; Will Fowler, "Valentín Gómez Farías: Perceptions of Radicalism in Independent Mexico, 1821–1847," *Bulletin of Latin American Research* 15:1 (1996): 44; Gail Borden to Stephen F. Austin, November 5, 1835, *AP*, 3:238; James E. Crisp, *Sleuthing the Alamo: Davy Crockett's Last Stand and Other Mysteries of the Texas Revolution* (New York: Oxford University Press, 2005), 32; Declaration of the People of Texas, In General Convention Assembled, November 7, 1835, *PTR*, 2:346–348; Paul D. Lack, *The Texas Revolutionary Experience: A Political and Social History, 1835–1836* (College Station: Texas A&M University Press, 1992), 49; David J. Weber, *The Mexican Frontier, 1821–1846: The American Southwest Under Mexico* (Albuquerque: University of New Mexico Press, 1982), 246.

11. W. Roy Smith, "The Quarrel Between Governor Smith and the Council of the Provisional Government of the Republic," *Quarterly of the Texas State Historical Association* 5 (April 1902), 269–346.

12. Noah Smithwick, *The Evolution of a State; or, Recollections of Old Texas Days* (Austin: Gammel Book Company, 1900), 109–110; Austin to President of Consultation, November 5, 1835, *AP*, 3:241.

13. Eugene Campbell Barker, ed., *The Writings of Sam Houston* (Austin: University of Texas Press, 1938), 1:313.

14. Barr, *Texans in Revolt*, 41–59.

15. Brands, *Lone Star Nation*, 297.

16. Randy Roberts and James S. Olson, *Line in the Sand: The Alamo in Blood and Memory* (New York: Free Press, 2001), 58–59; Lois A. Garver, "Benjamin Rush Milam," *SWHQ* 38 (October 1934): 79–121, 38 (January 1935): 173–202.

17. Henry C. Dance to an unidentified editor, April 25 [?], 1836, *PTR*, 6:62.

18. Crisp, *Sleuthing the Alamo*, 35.

19. James L. Batson, *James Bowie and the Sandbar Fight* (Madison, AL: Batson Engineering and Metalworks, 1992), 1–88; Walter W. Bowie, *The Bowies and Their Kindred: A Genealogical and Biographical History* (Washington, DC: Cromwell Brothers, 1899), 270–277; A. R. Kilpatrick, "Early Life in the Southwest—The Bowies," *DeBow's Southern and Western Review* 1 (October 1852), 21; Raymond W. Thorp, *Bowie Knife* (Albuquerque: University of New Mexico Press, 1948), 6, 13, 77; Randy Roberts and James S. Olson, *Line*

in the Sand: The Alamo in Blood and Memory (New York: Free Press, 2001), 45, 110.

20. James Bowie to Governor Henry Smith, February 2, 1835, *PTR*, 4:237.

21. William Barret Travis to Henry Smith, January 28, 1836, *PTR*, 4:176.

22. Stephen L. Hardin, *Texian Iliad* (Austin: University of Texas Press, 1994), 117; Michael R. Green, "To the People of Texas & All Americans in the World," *SWHQ*, 490; Roberts and Olson, *A Line in the Sand*, 113; Ron J. Jackson Jr. and Lee Spencer White, *Joe, the Slave Who Became an Alamo Legend* (Norman: University of Oklahoma Press, 2015), 98; William Barret Travis to President of the Convention, March 3, 1836, "Proceedings of the Convention at Washington," in H.P.N. Gammel, *Laws of Texas, 1822–1897* (Austin: Gammel Book Company, 1898), 1:845.

23. Roberts and Olson, *A Line in the Sand*, 66–67; Hardin, *Texian Iliad*, 54.

24. John A. Cameron to General Andrew Jackson, February 14, 1831, vol. 1, reel 1, DUSC-Veracruz; W. S. Parott to Secretary of State, December 14, 1835, DUSC-San Luis Potosí; Barr, *Texans in Revolt*, 56–57; Fowler, Santa Anna of Mexico, 163.

25. Legación Mexicana en EEUU to Despacho de Relaciones, July 24, 1836, f. 41, folder 19, box 51, Relaciones Exteriores, AGN; Michael Muldoon to Stephen Austin, April 29, n.d., folder 193, box 4, Streeter Collection, BRBML; "F. W. Johnson's Letter, January 10th, 1836," *Telegraph and Texas Register* (January 16, 1836), 2; William Harris Wharton to Henry Smith, Memphis, January 27, 1836, folder 301, box 5, Streeter Collection, BRBML.

26. Fowler, *Santa Anna of Mexico*, 165.

27. Green, "To the People of Texas," 491.

28. Quoted in Roberts and Olson, *A Line in the Sand*, 60; James, *The Raven*, 235; Torget, *Seeds of Empire*, 168–169; "The Unanimous Declaration of Independence Made by the Delegates of the People of Texas in General Convention at the Town of Washington on the 2nd Day of March 1836," http://avalon.law.yale.edu/19th_century/texdec.asp; George C. Childress to Sam Houston, February 13, 1836, no. 253, folder 150, box 2-22, Andrew Jackson Houston Collection, TSA.

29. William Barret Travis to President of the Convention, March 3, 1836, "Proceedings of the Convention at Washington," in Gammel, *Laws of Texas*, 1:845; William F. Gray, *Virginia to Texas* (Houston: Gray, Dillate, 1909), 136–137.

30. Brands, *Lone Star Nation*, 369; Roberts and Olson, *A Line in the Sand*, 2.

31. Brands, *Lone Star Nation*, 370.

32. Ibid., 374–376.

33. José Enrique de la Peña, *With Santa Anna: A Personal Narrative of the Revolution* (College Station: Texas A&M University Press, 2010), 47–51; Brands, *Lone Star Nation*, 372.

34. De la Peña, *With Santa Anna*, 54.

35. *El mosquito mexicano*, April 5, 1836, and in *La lima de volcano*, April 5, 1836; Thomas Tucker, *Exodus from the Alamo: The Anatomy of the Last Stand Myth* (Philadelphia: Casemate, 2009), 31–32, 34; Amy S. Greenberg, *A Wicked War: Polk, Clay, Lincoln, and the 1846 U.S. Invasion of Mexico* (New York: Knopf, 2012), 9.

36. Santa Anna to Joaquín Ramírez y Sesma, March 8, 1836, vol. 1, *Documentos para la historia de la guerra de Texas*, NYPL; Santa Anna to José Urrea, March 23, 1836, ibid.; F. M. Díaz Noriega to Santa Anna, February 29, 1836, Guerra y Marina, AGN.

37. *El Cosmopólito*, March 9, 1836; David Barnet Edward, *The History of Texas, or the Emigrant's Guide* (Reprint, ed., Austin: Pemberton Press, 1967), 248; D. C. Barrett, Chairman, L. C. Mason, S. Bowen, F. C. Gray, Gowin Harris, Citizens of Brazoria, March 1836, Mexican Broadsides, BRBML; James Morgan to [Sam P. Carson], March 24, 1836, reel 1, Executive Record Books, TSA; José Urrea, *Diario de las operaciones militares de la división que al mando del general José Urrea hizo la campaña de Tejas* (Victoria de Durango, MX: Imprenta del gobierno a cargo de M. Gonzalez, 1838), 24; José Enrique de la Peña, *With Santa Anna in Texas: A Personal Narrative of the Revolution* (College Station: Texas A&M University Press, 1975), 104, 179; "Reminiscences of Ann Raney Thomas Coleman," Ann Raney Thomas Coleman Papers, BCAH; Sean Kelley, "'Mexico in His Head': Slavery and the Texas-Mexico Border, 1810–1860," *Journal of Social History* 37:3 (Spring 2004), 716; Campbell, *An Empire for Slavery*, 44.

38. Creed Taylor, *Tall Men with Long Rifles* (San Antonio: Naylor, 1935), 107.

39. Edmund Gaines to Lewis Cass, March 29, 1836, *Register of Debates in Congress* (Washington, DC: Gales & Seaton, 1836), 12:3513; *New York Herald*, April 28, 1836.

40. For the Battle of San Jacinto, Hardin, *Texian Iliad*, 175–218; Stephen L. Moore, *Eighteen Minutes: The Battle of San Jacinto and the Texas Independence Campaign* (Lanham, MD: Rowman & Littlefield, 2004), 222–368.

41. Manuel Crecencio Rejón to Wilson Shannon, October 31, 1844, f. 174–175, FO 50/176, NA-K; Legación Mexicana en los Estados Unidos to

Despacho de Relaciones, July 12, 1836, f. 34, folder 19, box 51, Relaciones Exteriores, AGN.

42. Henry M. Morfit to John Forsyth, September 12, 1836, *US Public Documents*, 297, Doc. 20, 26–29.

43. Harry L. Watson, *Liberty and Power: The Politics of Jacksonian America* (New York: Hill & Wang, 1990), 232; Ted Widmer, *Martin Van Buren* (New York: Macmillan, 2005), 14; Ben Epstein, *The Only Constant Is Change: Technology, Political Communication, and Innovation Over Time* (Oxford: Oxford University Press, 2018), 34; Jessica Lepler, *The Many Panics of 1837: People, Politics, and the Creation of a Transatlantic Financial Crisis* (Cambridge: Cambridge University Press, 2013), 14.

44. Lepler, *The Many Panics of 1837*, 8, 12, 15; Donald B. Cole, *Martin Van Buren and the American Political System* (Princeton, NJ: Princeton University Press, 1984), 257.

45. Torget, *Seeds of Empire*, 184. For the antislavery movement in the United States, see W. Caleb McDaniel, *The Problem of Democracy in the Age of Slavery: Garrisonian Abolitionists and Transatlantic Reform* (Baton Rouge: Louisiana State University Press, 2013), 260; "To the public," *The Liberator*, January 1, 1831; for Garrison, see Louis Filler, *Crusade Against Slavery: 1830–1860* (New York: Routledge, 2017), 67. For British abolition, see Seymour Drescher, "European Antislavery: From Empires of Slavery to Global Prohibition," *Cambridge History of World Slavery* 4:385; Gelien Mattthews, *Caribbean Slave Revolts and the British Abolitionist Movement* (Baton Rouge: Louisiana State University Press, 2013); Edward B. Rugemer, *Slave Law and the Politics of Resistance in the Early Atlantic World* (Cambridge, MA: Harvard University Press, 2018), 251; Richard Huzzey, *Freedom Burning: Anti-Slavery and Empire in Victorian Britain* (Ithaca, NY: Cornell University Press, 2012), 121–122. For Child's offer, see D. L. Child to Joaquín María del Castillo, Philadelphia, December 26, 1835, folder 1, file 24, AEMEUA, SRE. For Lundy, see Greenberg, *A Wicked War*, 9.

46. Benjamin Lundy, *The War in Texas* (Philadelphia: Merrihew and Gunn, 1837), 56; *Debates in Congress* (24th Congress, 2nd Session), 4041–4043.

47. "Constitution of Republic of Texas," *Laws of the Republic of Texas, in Two Volumes* (Houston: Printed at the Office of the Telegraph, 1838), 1:9–25; "From the Pawtucket Chronicle," *The Liberator*, July 28, 1837.

48. Robert V. Reimini, *Andrew Jackson and the Course of American Democracy, 1833–1845* (New York: Harper & Row, 1984), 352–368; John M. Belohlavek, *"Let the Eagle Soar!": The Foreign Policy of Andrew Jackson* (Lincoln: University of

Nebraska Press, 1985), 218–238; José María Ortiz Monasterio to US Secretary of State, March 31, 1837, f. 22, FO 50/111, NA-K; Comandancia del Ejército del Norte (?) to Governor of Nuevo León and Tamaulipas, May 15, 1837, box 69, Fondo Militares, AGENL; Joseph Eve to Daniel Webster, December 10, 1842, no. 31, folder 4, box 2, Justin H. Smith Collection, BLAC; Consul Kennedy to the Earl of Aberdeen, June 14, 1844, f. 76, FO 701/29, NA-K; G. W. Terrell to Charles Elliott, October 15, 1842, f. 105, FO 75/4, NA-K.

49. This description of Mexico City comes from "The Journal of a Volunteer Officer in the Mexican War," f. 229, folder 84, box 7, W.W.H. Davis Papers, BRBML.

50. "Parte Oficial: Congreso General," *Diario del Gobierno de la República Mexicana* (April 15, 1837), 1; Manuel Larranizas, November 12, 1836, f. 1, folder 9, box 471, Gobernación sin sección, AGN. If there was debate when the law was first proposed, it was not recorded: "Parte Oficial," *Diario del Gobierno de la República Mexicana* 560:4 (November 10, 1836), 2; "Congreso General: Sesión del día 10 de febrero de 1837, *Diario del Gobierno de la República Mexicana* (February 18, 1837), 1. Nor could I find any documentation of any debates at the committee level in the Archivo Histórico del Senado.

51. Decree of April 5, 1837, vol. 96, Justicia Archivo, AGN. The government in Yucatán did make claims for compensation on behalf of their constituents, see Hacienda del Departamento de Yucatán to Minister of Interior, August 26, 1837, f. 23, vol. 104, Justicia Archivo, AGN.

52. Timothy J. Henderson, *A Glorious Defeat: Mexico and Its War with the United States* (New York: Farrar, Straus and Giroux, 2007), 115, 128.

53. José María Tornel, *Tejas y los Estados Unidos de América, en sus Relaciones con la República Mexicana* (Mexico City: Ignacio Cumplido, 1837), 65–69.

54. "Mexico, Agosto 25 de 1842," *El voto de Coahuila* (September 24, 1842), 3; "Proposition presentada a la asamblea departamental de Mexico por el vocal de ella ciudadano José María Franco," *El Siglo Diez y Nueve* (August 15, 1844), 2; J. M. de Castillo y Lanzas to John Forsyth, March 8, 1837, roll 2, vol. 4, Notes from the Mexican Legation in the United States to the Department of State; Manuel Crecencio Rejón to Wilson Shannon, October 31, 1844, f. 174–175, FO 50/176, NA-K.

55. *Journal des Debats*, Paris, June 22, 1836, L-E-1061, SRE and "La Prensa," Paris, July 5, 1836, L-E-1062, SRE; Discusión en la Cámara de los Comunes sobre la Cuestión de Texas, n.d., f. 98, L-E-1062, SRE; Foreign Office to Mr. Bankhead, September 30, 1844, f. 75, FO 50/172, NA-K; Charles Elliot to Foreign Office, n.d. (1845?), f. 11–26, FO 75/13, NA-K; H. Martin to Sir Robert Peel, July 1, 1842, f. 92–93, FO 50/158, NA-K.

56. Luis de la Rosa to Cámara de Diputados, July 21, 1845, L-E-1169, SRE; Legación de México en los Estados Unidos to SRE, May 5, 1844, f. 317, folder 1, file 29, AEMEUA, SRE.

57. Marguerite Johnston, *Houston, The Unknown City, 1836–1946* (College Station: Texas A&M University Press, 1991), 3–12; David G. McComb, *Houston, a History* (Austin: University of Texas Press, 1981), 9–30.

58. Jackson and White, *Joe*, 217–218.

59. I have taken this description from the runaway notice that John Rice Jones published a month after Joe's disappearance; "Fifty Dollars," *Telegraph and Texas Register* (May 26, 1837), 2:18. Joe was caught before he reached Mexico, though he escaped again in 1838 to the plantation of William Barret Travis's brother, Nicholas Travis, in Alabama. Jackson and White, Joe, 224–238.

CHAPTER 7: ANNEXATION

1. For the proposal of annexation, see, *House Executive Document* 40 (25th Congress, 1st Session), 2–11. For biographies of Van Buren, see Denis Tilden Lynch, *An Epoch and a Man: Martin Van Buren and His Times* (New York: Liveright, 1929); James C. Curtis, *The Fox at Bay: Martin Van Buren and the Presidency, 1837–1841* (Lexington: University Press of Kentucky, 1970); John Niven, *Martin Van Buren and the Romantic Age of American Politics* (New York: The Easton Press, 1986); Donald Cole, *Martin Van Buren and the American Political System* (Princeton, NJ: Princeton University Press, 1984); Joel H. Sibley, *Martin Van Buren and the Emergence of American Popular Politics* (Lanham, MD: Rowman & Littlefield, 2002); Major L. Wilson, *The Presidency of Martin Van Buren* (Lawrence: University of Kansas Press, 1984); Ted Widmer, *Martin Van Buren* (New York: Macmillan, 2005); Jessica Lepler, *The Many Panics of 1837: People, Politics, and the Creation of a Transatlantic Financial Crisis* (Cambridge, MA: Cambridge University Press, 2013), 20.

2. Widmer, *Martin Van Buren*, 101; Ralph Waldo Emerson, *Journals of Ralph Waldo Emerson* (Cambridge, MA: Harvard University Press, 1965), 304.

3. For Martin Van Buren and the Whigs, see William J. Cooper Jr., *The South and the Politics of Slavery, 1828–1856* (Baton Rouge: Louisiana State University Press, 1978), 141–143; Michael F. Holt, *The Political Crisis of the 1850s* (New York: John Wiley & Sons, 1978), 30. For the states-rights faction of the Whig Party, see Charles Sellers Jr., "Who Were the Southern Whigs?," *American Historical Review* 59:2 (January 1954): 335–346; Joel H. Silbey,

Storm over Texas: The Annexation Controversy and the Road to Civil War (Oxford: Oxford University Press, 2005), 28. For the Nullification Crisis, see William Freehling, *Prelude to Civil War: The Nullification Controversy in South Carolina, 1816–1836* (Oxford: Oxford University Press, 1965), 232–293. The best book on the Whig Party remains Daniel Walker Howe, *The Political Culture of the American Whigs* (Chicago: University of Chicago Press, 1979).

4. Torget, *Seeds of Empire*, 184.

5. *Journal of the House of Representatives of the State of Ohio* (Columbus: Samuel Medary, 1837–1838), 146, 312; Clay to Crittenden, December 5, 1843, in Chapman Coleman, ed., *The Life of John J. Crittenden* (Philadelphia: J. B. Lippincott, 1873), 1:208; D. F. Caldell to Daniel Barringer, April 10, 1844, quoted in Rachel A. Shelden, "Not So Strange Bedfellows: Northern and Southern Whigs and the Texas Annexation Controversy, 1844–1845," in *A Political Nation: New Directions in Mid-Nineteenth Century American Political History*, eds. Gary W. Gallagher and Rachel A. Shelden (Charlottesville: University of Virginia Press, 2012), 16.

6. William Ellery Channing, *A Letter to the Hon. Henry Clay, on the Annexation of Texas to the United States* (Boston: J. Munroe, 1837), 17, 44.

7. "Texas," *United States Telegraph*, January 17, 1837; Calhoun's Resolutions, December 27, 1837, *DoC*, 13:568; J. Mills Thornton, *Politics and Power in a Slave Society: Alabama, 1800–1860* (Baton Rouge: Louisiana State University Press, 1978), 167.

8. Norman E. Tutorow, "Whigs of the Old Northwest and Texas Annexation, 1836–April, 1844," *Indiana Magazine of History*, 60–61; *Cong Globe*, 25 Congress, 2nd Session, 453 Justin Smith, *Annexation of Texas* (New York: Macmillan, 1919), 67.

9. J. N. Almonte to A. P. Upshur, Washington, November 3, 1843, roll 2, vol. 4, Notes from the Mexican Legation in the United States to the Department of State; Anson Jones to Aaron Vail, October 12, 1838, *US Public Documents*, 344, no. 2, p. 33.

10. Widmer, *Martin Van Buren*, 102–106; Cole, *Martin Van Buren*, 331–333.

11. Widmer, *Martin Van Buren*, 138; Steven E. Woodworth, *Manifest Destinies: America's Westward Expansion and the Road to the Civil War* (New York: Knopf, 2010), 16–17.

12. Svend Petersen, *A Statistical History of the American Presidential Elections* (Westport, CT: Greenwood Press, 1981), 18–27; Gary May, *John Tyler* (New York: Henry Holt, 2008), 1–8.

13. Woodworth, *Manifest Destinies*, 11; May, *John Tyler*, 3; George W. Julian, *Political Recollections, 1840 to 1872* (Chicago: Jansen, McClur, 1884), 12–13.

14. May, *John Tyler*, 5, 98; Quoted in Edward P. Crapol, *John Tyler: The Accidental President* (Chapel Hill: University of North Carolina Press, 2012), 5.

15. Duff Green to Robert Peel, June 6, 1843, Green Papers, LoC; Frederick Merk, *Slavery and the Annexation of Texas* (New York: Knopf, 1972), 14; Thomas R. Hietala, *Manifest Design: American Exceptionalism and Empire* (Ithaca: Cornell University Press, 2003), 15–16; Stephen W. Belko, *The Invincible Duff Green: Whig of the West* (Columbia: University of Missouri Press, 2006), 356–381.

16. Belko, *Invincible Duff Green*, 79–167. For violence in Southern culture, see Elliott J. Gorn, "'Gouge and Bite, Pull Hair and Scratch': The Social Significance of Fighting in the Southern Backcountry," *American Historical Review* 90:1 (February 1985): 18–43; Felther M. Green, "Duff Green, Militant Journalist of the Old School," *American Historical Review* 52:2 (January 1947), 251–252.

17. Duff Green to Abel Upshur, October 17, 1843, in Merk, *Slavery and the Annexation of Texas*, 14; Abel Upshur to W. S. Murphy, August 8, 1843, in Sen. Doc., 28 Congress, 1st Session. (Ser. 435), no. 341, 18–19; Duff Green to Abel Upshur, November 16, 1843, quoted in Hietala, *Manifest Design*, 20.

18. Matthew Karp, *This Vast Southern Empire: Slaveholders at the Helm of American Foreign Policy* (Cambridge, MA: Harvard University Press, 2016), 32–34; Woodworth, *Manifest Destinies*, 114; May, *John Tyler*, 105.

19. Richard Pakenham to Charles Bankhead, September 30, 1844, f. 84–87, FO 75/20, NA-K; Jeff Green to David G. Burnet, April 1, 1836, folder 21, box 401-1216, Army Correspondence, TSA; William Kennedy to Earl of Aberdeen, October 20, 1845, in Ephraim Douglass Adams, ed., *British Diplomatic Correspondence Concerning the Republic of Texas, 1838–46* (Austin: Texas State Historical Association, 1918), 46; Memorandum from Minister Plenipotentiary of Great Britain in Mexico, August 12, 1839, folder 12, box 390, Gobernación sin sección, AGN. For the argument that the primary aim of British diplomacy in Texas was to check US expansion, see Ephraim D. Adams, *British Interests and Activities in Texas, 1838–1846* (Ann Arbor, MI: University Microfilms International, 1978); Kenneth Bourne, *Britain and the Balance of Power in North America, 1815–1908* (London: Longmans, 1967); Wilbur Devereux Jones, *Aberdeen and the Americas* (Athens: University of Georgia Press, 1958); Wilbur Devereux Jones, *The American Problem in*

British Diplomacy, 1841–1861 (London: Macmillan, 1974); David Pletcher, *The Diplomacy of Annexation: Texas, Oregon, and the Mexican War* (Columbia: University of Missouri Press, 1973); Paul Varg, *United States Foreign Relations, 1820–1860* (East Lansing: Michigan State University Press, 1979); Charles Bankhead to Earl of Aberdeen, May 30, 1844, f. 93–94, FO 50/174, NA-K.

20. Why not circulate the more recent law abolishing slavery? Texans had no reason to comply with laws passed after they had declared independence from Mexico, like the law abolishing slavery. But they could not deny that the slave trade had been abolished in 1824. By virtue of this law, the slaves imported from the United States were undeniably free. Almonte to SRE, April 27, 1841, L-E-1795, SRE.

21. "Mexican emissaries," *Telegraph and Texas Register*, 10:40 (October 1, 1845), 2; Pizarro Martínez to SRE, January 24, 1836, folder 12, file 27, AEMEUA, SRE; "Negro Stealing," *Red-Lander* (July 7, 1842), 4. This same episode was reported on in the Mexican press. "Noticias de Tejas," *El Voto de Coahuila* (July 16, 1842), 3, PO, AGEC.

22. Wilson Shannon to W. J. Murphy, November 25, 1843, folder 4, box 2, United States Diplomatic Records for Texas, NARA-CP; Charles Elliott to Earl of Aberdeen, July 28, 1845, f. 170, FO 75/13, NA-K; Timothy J. Henderson, *A Glorious Defeat: Mexico and Its War with the United States* (New York: Farrar, Straus and Giroux, 2007), 127; *New Orleans Commercial Bulletin*, March 18, 1842; "Congress," April 23, 1842, *Niles' National Register*, Jeremiah Hughes, ed. (Baltimore: Exchange Place, 1842), 124; A. Upshur to W. J. Murphy, August 8, 1843, folder 6, box 1, United States Diplomatic Records for Texas, NARA-CP.

23. Abel P. Upshur, Secretary of State, to Edward Everett, US Minister to Great Britain, Washington, September 28, 1843, William R. Manning, ed., *Diplomatic Correspondence of the United States, Inter-American Affairs* (Washington, DC: Carnegie Endowment for International Peace, 1936), 2:6–11. For how Southern politicians hijacked the Monroe Doctrine to their own purposes, see Jay Sexton, *The Monroe Doctrine: Empire and Nation in Nineteenth-Century America* (New York: Hill & Wang, 2011), 85–122.

24. "Interesting Correspondence on the Texas Question," *The Globe* (March 20, 1844), f. 61, FO 75/10, NA-K; William Kennedy to Earl of Aberdeen, June 15, 1842, f. 96, FO 75/3, NA-K; "Woodworth, *Manifest Destinies*, 120–121; *Pennsylvanian*, March 9, 1844; *Philadelphia Ledger*, March 26, 29, 1844.

25. A Treaty of Annexation, concluded between the United States of America and the Republic of Texas, April 12, 1844, *Treaties and Other International Acts of the United States of America* (Washington, DC: Government Printing Office, 1934), 4:697–699.

26. George Sykes to Ann Sykes, March 20, 1844, in St. George L. Sioussat, "The Accident on Board the U.S.S. Princeton, February 28, 1844: A Contemporary Newsletter," *Pennsylvania History* 4:3 (July 1937): 170.

27. Woodworth, *Manifest Destinies*, 115.

28. George Sykes to Ann Sykes, March 20, 1844, 171.

29. Ibid., 171–173.

30. Woodworth, *Manifest Destinies*, 118; George Sykes to Ann Sykes, March 20, 1844, 177.

31. Richard Kenner Crallé, ed., *The Works of John C. Calhoun* (New York: D. Appleton, 1864), 632.

32. Hietala, *Manifest Design*, 24.

33. Lord Aberdeen to Abel P. Upshur, December 26, 1843, forwarded February 26, 1844, No. 271, *House Documents* (28th Congress, 1st Session), 332.

34. Charles Sellers, *James K. Polk: Continentalist, 1843–1846* (Princeton, NJ: Princeton University Press, 1987), 2:58–60; John C. Calhoun to Richard Pakenham, April 18, 1844, in Crallé, ed., *Works of John C. Calhoun*, 333–334.

35. Sellers, *James K. Polk*, 2:60; Francis Preston Blair to Martin Van Buren, March 18, 1844, Van Buren Papers, quoted in Sellers, *James K. Polk*, 2:58; Merk, *Slavery and the Annexation of Texas*, 76; *CGA* (28 Congress, 1st Session), 482. Twenty-eight of the twenty-nine Whigs voted against the treaty, as did seven Northern Democrats. Shelden, "Not So Strange Bedfellows," 20.

36. Amy S. Greenberg, *A Wicked War: Polk, Clay, Lincoln, and the 1846 U.S. Invasion of Mexico* (New York: Knopf, 2012), 28.

37. James K. Polk, "Letters of James K. Polk to Cave Johnson, 1833–1848," *Tennessee Historical Magazine* (September 1915): 240.

38. Sean Wilentz, *The Rise of American Democracy* (New York: W. W. Norton, 2005), 581.

39. Henry Clay to Stephen Miller, July 1, 1844, *The Papers of Henry Clay* (Lexington: University of Kentucky Press, 2015), 10:79; Reinhard O. Johnson, *The Liberty Party, 1840–1848: Antislavery Third-Party Politics in the United States* (Baton Rouge: Louisiana State University Press, 2009), 22–49; Corey M. Brooks, *Liberty Power: Antislavery Third Parties and the Transformation of American Politics* (Chicago: University of Chicago Press, 2016), 77–104.

40. Brian DeLay, *War of a Thousand Deserts: Independent Indians and the U.S.-Mexican War* (New Haven, CT: Yale University Press, 2009), 220; James Richardson, ed., *A Compilation of the Messages and Papers of the Presidents*, 10 vols., (Washington, DC: Bureau of National Literature, 1917), 1896–1898, 4:344.

41. Edmund Thornton Miller, *A Financial History of Texas* (University of Texas Bulletin 37, Austin, 1916), 59; *CGA* (28th Congress, 1st Session), 482.

42. January 13, 1845, *DoC*, 15:187; January 24, 1845, *DoC*, 15:195; Woodworth, *Manifest Destinies*, 140.

43. May 8, 1850, *DoC*, 16:196; Shelden, "Not So Strange Bedfellows," 28; Greenberg, *A Wicked War*, 100.

44. Woodworth, *Manifest Destinies*, 140; Smith, *Annexation of Texas*, 327–337; David Pletcher, *The Diplomacy of Annexation: Texas, Oregon, and the Mexican War* (Columbia: University of Missouri Press, 1973), 180–182; Arthur Cole, *Whig Party in the South* (Washington, DC: American Historical Association, 1913), 117–118.

45. J. M. de Bocanegra to Daniel Webster, May 12, 1842, roll 2, vol. 4, Notes from the Mexican Legation in the United States to the Department of State; Resolution of June 4, 1845, copied in John Black to James Buchanan, June 10, 1845, vol. 8, reel 4, DUSC-Mexico City; Franklin Chase to James Buchanan, January 20, 1846, vol. 3, roll 3, DUSC-Tampico.

46. Alleine Howren, "Causes and Origin of the Decree of April 6, 1830," *SWHQ* 16, no. 4 (April 1913), 414.

47. Mexican Legation in USA to Secretaría de Relaciones Exteriores, September 22, 1844, no. 1265, f. 64, folder 1, file 29, AEMEUA, SRE; Buenaventura Vivó to Minister of Foreign Relations, April 23, 1854, folder 5, file 44, AEMEUA, SRE; Bocanegra, "Decree Relating to Passports," *Diario del Gobierno* (July 27, 1844), encl. Benjamin E. Green to John C. Calhoun, July 30, 1844, vol. 12, reel 13, DUSM-Mexico; "Revista de Periódicos," *El Siglo Diez y Nueve* (January 2, 1844), 3; *El Amigo de Pueblo*, August 21, 1845; "Interesantísimo Historia de Tejas," *El Monitor Constitucional* (March 25, 1845), 3.

48. Anthony Butler describes the procedure for closing the US Legation in Butler to Forsyth, July 1, 1835, vol. 6, reel 7, DUSM-Mexico.

CHAPTER 8: COMPROMISE LOST

1. Darwin Payne, "Camp Life in the Army of Occupation: Corpus Christi, July 1845 to March 1846," *SWHQ* 73:3 (January 1970), 327; John

W. Dodd to "my dear wife," June 3, 1847, folder 4, box 1, John W. Dodd Papers, BRBML.

2. John J. Peck to Editors, *New York Tribune*, September 18, 1845, box 1, Peck Papers, BRBML; Peck to Sister, October 11, 1845, ibid.; Brian DeLay, *War of a Thousand Deserts: Indian Raids and the U.S.-Mexican War* (New Haven, CT: Yale University Press, 2009), 141–252; Pekka Hamalainnen, *The Comanche Empire* (New Haven, CT: Yale University Press, 2008), 181–291; Timothy J. Henderson *A Glorious Defeat: Mexico and Its War with the United States* (New York: Farrar, Straus and Giroux, 2007), 165; Pedro Santoni, *Mexicans at Arms: Puro Federalists and the Politics of War, 1845–48* (Fort Worth, TX: Christian University Press, 1996), 101; Miguel Soto, *La conspiración monárquica en México* (Mexico City: Editorial Offset, 1988), 49–52; Jaime Delgado, *La monarquía en México, 1845–1847* (Mexico City: Editorial Porrúa, 1990); Frank N. Samponaro, "Mariano Paredes y el movimeinto monarquista mexicano en 1846," *Historia Mexicana* 32:1 (July–September 1982), 39–54.

3. John J. Peck to Father, February 3, 1846, box 1, Peck Papers, BRBML; Amy S. Greenberg, *A Wicked War: Polk, Clay, Lincoln, and the 1846 U.S. Invasion of Mexico* (New York: Knopf, 2012), 95.

4. Peck to Father, November 7, 1845, f. 24, box 1, Peck Papers, BRBML; Peck to [?], August 26, 1845, ibid.; Henderson, *A Glorious Defeat*, 163–164; *The Cleveland Herald*, May 22, 1846.

5. Sven Beckert, *Empire of Cotton: A Global History* (New York: Alfred A. Knopf, 2014), 89. Alexander von Humboldt, *Political Essay on the Kingdom of New Spain*, John Black, trans. (New York: I. Riley, 1811), 44.

6. Letters of Lieut. Thomas Williams to his father, May 14, 1846, folder 5, vol. XV, box 5, Smith Collection, BLAC.

7. Don E. Fehrenbacher, *The Dred Scott Case: Its Significance in American Law and Politics* (Oxford: Oxford University Press, 1978), 131; August 8, 1846, *CG* (29th Congress, 1st Session), 1214. For scholars who have claimed that Wilmot did not author his proviso, see Charles Eugene Hamlin, *The Life and Times of Hannibal Hamlin* (Cambridge, MA: Riverside Press, 1899), 156–157; Henry Wilson, *History of the Rise and Fall of the Slave Power in America* (3 vols., Boston: J. R. Osgood, 1872–1877), 2:16.

8. August 8, 1846, *CG*, 29th Congress, 1st Session, 1214.

9. Ibid., 1217.

10. Fehrenbacher, *Dred Scott*, 131.

11. August 10, 1846, *DoC*, 15:649.

12. Ibid., 15:650.

13. This account comes from August 10, 1846, *DoC*, 15:650–651.

14. "At the next session of Congress we shall hear more of this grave matter," a newspaper in New Orleans predicted; "President Dew," *Jeffersonian Republican* (September 17, 1846), 2. For "gratuitous," see Richard R. Stenberg, "The Motivation of the Wilmot Proviso," *Mississippi Valley Historical Review*, XVIII (March 1932), 535–541. For "attempt to exclude," see Clark E. Persinger, "The 'Bargain of 1844' as the Origin of the Wilmot Proviso," *Annual Report of the American Historical Association for the Year 1911* (2 vols., Washington, 1913), I, 189–195. For "defensive movement," see Eric Foner, "The Wilmot Proviso Revisited," *Journal of American History* 56:2 (September 1969), 265–279.

15. Roberts' Diary, December 15, 1846, f. 196, folder 11, vol. X, box 3, Justin H. Smith Collection, BLAC; John Prickett Diary, September n.d., 1846, f. 148, folder 13, vol. XIV, box 5, ibid.

16. John J. Peck to sister, October 3, 1845, box 1, Peck Papers, BRBML; John to Eliza, September 9, 1847, folder 9, box 1, John W. Dodd Papers, BRBML; "Adventures of a Dragoon Officer," HM 4021, Merrill Collection, HEH.

17. John Stilwell Jenkins, *History of the War Between the United States and Mexico* (Auburn, NY: Derby, Miller, 1849), 163, 166; for the Battle of Monterrey, see Cesar Morado Macías, *El emplazamiento de los cuerpos; Elementos para una interpretación sobre la Batalla de Monterrey durante la guerra México-Estados Unidos en 1846* (Monterrey, MX: Consejo para la Cultura y las Artes de Nuevo León, 2011) and Christopher D. Dishman, *A Perfect Gibraltar: The Battle for Monterrey, Mexico, 1846* (Norman: University of Oklahoma Press, 2010), 150–151.

18. Henderson, *A Glorious Defeat*, 163.

19. John J. Peck to n.d., Camp near Matamoros, April 17, 1846, box 1, Peck Papers, BRBML; *El Estandarte Nacional*, April 5, 1845.

20. *Eco del Norte de Tamaulipas*, October 15, 1845; José Ignacio Guerrero to Foreign Minister, January 25, 1844, f. 75, vol. 37, Cartas de Seguridad, AGN; Rómulo Díaz de la Vega to Mariano Arista, August 18, 1849, fs. 43–45, vol. 3072, AHSDN; Arista to de la Vega, August 29, 1849, ibid.

21. John Peck to Hon. S. Edwards, November 28, 1846, Peck Papers, BRBML; Maj. Gen. Worth, Circular, June 16, 1847, f. 81, folder 4, vol. X, box 3, Justin H. Smith Collection, BLAC.

22. *Message from the President of the United States to the Two Houses of Congress, December 8, 1846* (Washington, DC: Ritchie and Hermes, 1846), 8; February 2, 1847, *CG* 29 (29th Congress, 2nd Session), 275.

23. David I. Durham, *A Southern Moderate in Radical Times: Henry Washington Hilliard, 1808–1892* (Baton Rouge: Louisiana State University Press, 2008), 83.

24. January 5, 1847, *CGA* (29th Congress, 2nd Session), 229.

25. Michael F. Holt, *Political Parties and American Political Development from the Age of Jackson to the Age of Lincoln* (Baton Rouge: Louisiana State University Press, 1992), 33–87; Richard R. Stenberg, "The Motivation of the Wilmot Proviso," *Mississippi Valley Historical Review*, XVIII (March 1932), 535–541; Clark E. Persinger, "The 'Bargain of 1844' as the Origin of the Wilmot Proviso," *Annual Report of the American Historical Association for the Year 1911* (2 vols., Washington, DC: American Historical Association, 1913), 1:189–195; Foner, "The Wilmot Proviso Revisited," 265–279.

26. "To the Whigs of the State of New York," *Niles National Register* (October 16, 1847), 108–109.

27. *CGA*, February 9, 1847 (29th Congress, 2nd Session), 333–334; *CGA*, June 22, 1848 (30th Congress, 1st Session), 716.

28. *CGA*, February 8, 1847 (29th Congress, 2nd Session), 316; Fehrenbacher, *The Dred Scott Case*, 134.

29. Arthur Styron, *The Cast-Iron Man: John Calhoun and American Democracy* (New York: Longmans, Green, 1935), iii; February 19, 1847, *DoC*, 16:56; February 19, 1847, *CG* (29 Congress, 2 Session), 453–455; Speech on introduction of his resolutions, February 19, 1847, *Works of John C. Calhoun*, 4:343, 348.

30. Congress had not yet seated the two senators from Iowa, the most recently admitted state, giving the South a slim majority. February 19, 1847, *CG* (29th Congress, 2nd Session), 454–455.

31. Norman A. Graebner, "James K. Polk: A Study in Federal Patronage," *Mississippi Valley Historical Review* 38:4 (March 1952): 613–614; Daniel Walker Howe, *The Political Culture of the American Whigs* (Chicago: University of Chicago Press, 1979), 24.

32. August 8, 1846, *CG*, 29th Congress, 1st Session, 1215–1216.

33. Emer D. Vattel, *The Law of Nations* (Philadelphia: T. & J. W. Johnson, 1849, 7th edition), 65.

34. February 8, 1847, *DoC*, 16:55–56.

35. Rudolph M. Lapp, *Blacks in Gold Rush California* (New Haven, CT: Yale University Press, 1995), 8–9; "Slavery in California," *Daily Commercial Register* (November 27, 1849), 2.

36. Charles Buxton Going, *David Wilmot Free-Soiler: A Biography of the Great Advocate of the Wilmot Proviso* (New York: D. Appleton, 1924), 242;

February 9, 1847, *CGA* (29th Congress, 2nd Session), 331; February 10, 1847, *CG* (29th Congress, 2nd Session), 380.

37. *Semi-weekly Union* (July 10, 1849), 2; *Coldwater Sentinel* (July 13, 1849), 1.

38. Baylies to John E. Wool, November 5, 1849, box 1, Francis Baylies Correspondence, HEH.

39. Journal of Albert G. Brockett, f. 44, folder 14, vol. XIV, box 5, Justin H. Smith Collection, BLAC; Roberts' Diary, December 4, 1846, f. 196, folder 11, vol. X, box 3, ibid. March 27, 1847, Peck Papers, BRBML.

40. Letters of Lieut. Thomas Williams to his father, April 21, 1847, folder 5 vol. XV, box 5, Justin H. Smith Collection, BLAC; April 19, 1847, Peck Papers, BRBML.

41. March n.d., 1847, July 15, 1847, August 9, 1847, August 20, 1847, Peck Papers, BRBML; K; Jack Bauer, *The Mexican War, 1846–48* (Lincoln: University of Nebraska Press, 1992), 295.

42. August 20, 1847, Peck Papers, BRBML; "A Battery in Action," *Cincinnati Commercial Gazette*, n.d., f. 19, folder 5, vol. XIV, box 5, Justin H. Smith Collection, BLAC; Bauer, *The Mexican War*, 301.

43. Albert G. Brockett Journal, f. 122, folder 14, vol. XIV, box 5, Justin H. Smith Collection, BLAC; N. C. Miller to Lizzie, November 30, 1847, f. 189, folder 11, vol. X, box 3, ibid.; D. H. Hastings, "With Doniphan in Mexico," f. 1, folder 1, vol. XV, box 5, ibid.; Alexander Watkins Terrell Reminiscences, f. 46, Box 1947/5, TSA; "Later from Vera Cruz," *Richmond Enquirer* (June 25, 1847), 2; Louisiana Governor to Veracruz Governor, May 21, 1848, folder 1, Winder Papers, UNC Special Collections. My thanks to Tatiana Seijas for this document. One historian claims that Domingo Otero was "allegedly a former slave from New Orleans named Abraham," who was still living in Veracruz in 1865, but I have found no evidence in either document cited to connect Domingo Otero to Abraham. The only reference to an Abraham in William Marshall Anderson's diary is to the late president. See Sarah Cornell, "Citizens of Nowhere: Fugitive Slaves and Free African Americans in Mexico, 1833–1857," *Journal of American History* (September 2013), 366. For more on Domingo Otero, see Diary of William Marshall Anderson, July 26, 1865, folder 378, box 7, Anderson Family Papers, 1810–1948, HEH.

44. Trist to Buchanan, September 4, 1847, roll 15, DUSM-Mexico; "Esposición [sic] con que el Ministro de Relaciones presenta al Congreso nacional el tratado de paz celebrado entre Megico [sic] y los Estados Unidos de America," *Órgano Oficial del Gobierno del Estado de Nuevo León*, 1:8 (May 28, 1848), 18; Memorandum of M. Esteva y Ulibarri, April 25, 1854, exp. 5, leg.

44, AEMEUA, SRE. The best book on the treaty remains, Richard Griswold del Castillo, *The Treaty of Guadalupe Hidalgo: A Legacy of Conflict* (Norman: University of Oklahoma Press, 1992).

45. "Slavery in Mexico," *Trenton State Gazette* (August 18, 1848), 2; *Coldwater Sentinel* (July 13, 1849), 1.

46. "Free Soil, Free Speech, Free Men, Free Labor," *Vermont Gazette* (August 29, 1848), 2; "Free Soil Meeting," *Berkshire County Whig* (August 10, 1848), 2.

47. Peck to father, December 23, 1847, Peck Papers, BRBML.

48. Fergus M. Bordewich, *America's Great Debate: Henry Clay, Stephen A. Douglas, and the Compromise that Preserved the Union* (New York: Simon & Schuster, 2012), 18, 22, 29.

49. General Zachary Taylor to General Jefferson Davis, July 27, 1847, Series 6, Additions, 1820–1863; Zachary Taylor Papers, Manuscripts Division, LoC.

50. Zachary Taylor quoted in "Mr. Slidell's Mission to Mexico," *American Whig Review* (April 1847), 331.

51. John Ross Browne, ed., *Report of the Debates in the Convention of California, on the Formation of the State Constitution, in September and October, 1849* (Washington, DC: J. T. Towers, 1850), 140–141, 149, 420, 445, 479; Fergus Bordewich, *America's Great Debate: Henry Clay, Stephen A. Douglas, and the Compromise that Preserved the Union* (New York: Simon & Schuster, 2013), 56.

52. "Journal and Proceedings of a Convention of Delegates," Miscellaneous Doc., No. 39 (31st Congress, 1st Session), 11–12; Article I, Section 1, Constitution of the State of New Mexico, Ex. Doc. No. 74 (31st Congress, 1st Session), 3; "To the people of N. Mexico," Ex. Doc. No. 74 (31st Congress, 1st Session), 16–17; "Digest of the votes given for and against the constitution of the State of New Mexico," ibid., 74.

CHAPTER 9: LIBERTY FOUND

1. "An Act Regulating the Sale of Runaway Slaves," February 5, 1841, H.P.N. Gammel, *Laws of Texas, 1822–1897* (Austin: Gammel Book Company, 1898), 2:649. A runaway taken up in 1858 near Williamson, Texas, "was interrogated as to his master's name, his whereabouts, &c. He (the negro) evaded answers, saying he was sick." Later "he told several tales as to where he came from, his masters, &c." See "The Freesoilers of Williamson," *State Gazette* (July 24, 1858), 2. Another runaway said she belonged to Jack Malone of Nacogdoches, but a J. H. Arnold claimed that she had been sold to Captain Scott

of Harrison County. See "In Jail," *Texas Republican* (July 13, 1861), 3. Of the 781 runaways, 588 who were "taken up" were heading toward Mexico. The next most popular directions were toward Houston, Indian Territory, and Louisiana.

2. Luis de la Rosa to John M. Clayton, received July 8, 1850, reel 3, Notes from the Mexican Legation in the United States; Luis de la Rosa to Mexico's vice consul in Brownsville, March 4, 1850, f. 179, folder 8, file 58, AEMEUA, SRE; Instrucción para la celebración de un tratado de extradición de criminales, June 8, 1849, exp. 1, leg. 31, AEMEUA, SRE; Peones fugitivos, 1842–68, 7-12-63, SRE; Mexican Consul in Brownsville to Minister Plenipotentiary in Washington, November 25, 1850, 7-11-18, SRE; Ayuntamiento de N. Laredo to Jefatura Política del Norte de Tamaulipas, June 12, 1850, 7-11-34, SRE; Ayuntamiento de Reynosa to SRE, April 20, 1850, ibid.; Ayuntamiento de Camargo, April 28, 1850, ibid.

3. Luis de la Rosa to minister of relations, December 21, 1848, 7-11-36, SRE; De la Rosa to Clayton, receive July 8, 1850, reel 3, Notes from the Mexican Legation in the United States; Instrucción para la celebración de un tratado de extradición de criminales, June 8, 1849, exp. 1, leg. 31, AEMEUA, SRE; De la Rosa to Secretary of Foreign Relations, February 8, 1850, folder 2, file 32, AEMEUA, SRE; De la Rosa to Clayton, received July 8, 1850, reel 3, Notes from the Mexican Legation in the United States.

4. Mexico's ban on the slave trade included similar language, but only applied to illegally imported slaves. Now all enslaved people were free from the moment they reached Mexico. "Proyecto de la ley constitucional de garantías individuales," *El Siglo Diez y Nueve* (February 14, 1849). The state of Nuevo León passed a similar law shortly thereafter. Sr. Garza y Melo, October 4, 1849, Actas del Congreso Constituyente, ACENL.

5. For the runaway who stole the beaver overcoat, see Karolyn Smardz Frost, *I've Got a Home in Glory Land: A Lost Tale of the Underground Railroad* (New York: Farrar, Strauss and Giroux, 2008), 222. For the runaway ordered back to the United States, see Robin W. Winks, *The Blacks in Canada: A History* (Montreal: McGill-Queen's Press, 1997), 172. The public outcry was so great that the slave, John Anderson, was permitted to stay in Canada. David Murray, *Colonial Justice: Justice, Morality, and Crime in the Niagara District, 1791–1849* (Toronto: University of Toronto Press, 2003), 214.

6. For the freedom principle in Haiti, see Ada Ferrer, "Haiti, Free Soil, and Antislavery in the Revolutionary Atlantic," *American Historical Review* 117:1 (2012): 40–66. For the effects of the Haitian Revolution on other slaveholding societies in the Americas, see David Geggus, ed., *The Impact of the Haitian Revolution in the Atlantic World* (Columbia: University of South Carolina Press,

2001); Edward Bartlett Rugemer, *The Problem of Emancipation: The Caribbean Roots of the American Civil War* (Baton Rouge: Louisiana State University Press, 2008); Carla Calarge, *Haiti and the Americas* (Jackson: University Press of Mississippi, 2013).

7. Loring Moody, *Facts for the People Showing the Relations of the United States Government to Slavery, Embracing a History of the Mexican War, Its Origin and Objects* (Boston: Anti-Slavery Office, 1827), 34; Baron de Bastrop to Señores Diputados, March 6, 1829, exp. 18, leg. 1, Segundo Congreso Constitucional, Primer Periodo Ordinario, ACEC.

8. David J. Weber, *Mexican Frontier, 1821–1846: The American Southwest Under Mexico* (Albuquerque: University of New Mexico Press, 1982), 114; José Maria Villareal to Governor of Nuevo León, September 18, 1842, box 79, Fondo Militares, AGENL; Ramón Múzquiz to Ayuntamiento de Monclova, June 3, 1859, folder 9, box 6, series 4, FSXIX, AMM; Minister of War to Governor of Coahuila y Téjas, August 22, 1825, exp. 26, leg. 2, ACEC; Peña, Aragon, Valdez, Sender, and García to Congreso, May 9, 1829, exp. 12, leg. 1, Fondo Comisiones, Segundo Congreso Constitucional, Primer Periodo Ordinario, ACEC; "Indios de Nuevo León," n.d., 7-12-20, box 2, SRE; "Reglamento de la Dirección de Colonización (Mexico City: Imprenta de Vicente Garcia Torres, 1846), 10–11, f. 55, folder 2, box 1, Mexican proclamations issued during the Mexican-American War, Collection 997, UCLA.

9. Juan Manuel Maldonado to Antonio María Jáuregui, July 13, 1850, E7, F1, C8, FCMO, AGEC. Deborah Rosen, *Border Law: The First Seminole War and American Statehood* (Cambridge, MA: Harvard University Press, 2015), 102–122; Kenneth W. Porter, "Relations Between Negroes and Indians Within the Present Limits of the United States," *Journal of Negro History*, 321, 323; Gopher John to General Augur, n.d., folder 3, box 23, Porter Papers, Schomburg; "An Indian War Brewing on Our Frontier," *Choctaw Intelligencer* (July 25, 1850), 2; "Runaway negroes," *Morning Star* (February 10, 1844), 3; Major B.L.E. Bonneville, writing what Gopher John dictated, June 10, 1848, folder 3, box 23, Porter Papers, SCRBC; Rosalie Schwartz, *Across the Rio to Freedom: U.S. Negroes in Mexico* (El Paso: University of Texas Press, 1975), 40. For Coacoochee's statement, see John Rollins to Peter Hansborough Bell, October 30, 1850, folder 2, box 301–318, Peter Hansborough Bell Papers, TSA.

10. Oral History of Sarah Daniels and "various informants," folder 3, box 23, Porter Papers, SCRBC; Juan Manuel Maldonado to Subinspector de las Colônias de Oriente, July 24, 1850, N. 261, exp. 27, folder 2, box 8, FCMO, AGEC; Anastasio Santos to Gobierno del Estado, July 20, 1850, *Siglo XIX*

(August 26, 1850), 2. For the text of the letter, see Letter of Recommendation from Don Bernardo de Valdez, June 30, 1780, *La Patria* (August 3, 1850), 2, L-E-1593, SRE.

11. Vice Governor, "Contestación al oficio que inserta del Jefe de Téjas participando el pronto aviso de un considerable número de indios extranjeros," November 3, 1826, Leyes, Decretos, y Acuerdos, 1824–1826, Comisión de Hacienda, ACEC; Ley de Colonización, no. 16, March 24, 1825, ibid.; Solicitud de tierras hecha por los Indios Sabanó, November 26, 1824, Legajo 1, Expediente 76, Comisiones de Gobernación, Hacienda, Justicia, puntos Constitucionales, Comercio y Colonización, Congreso Constituyente, Primer Periodo Ordinario (1824–1827), ACEC; Stephen F. Austin to Francisco Madero, November 14, 1827, expediente 12, legajo 4, Primero Congreso Constitucional, Segundo Periodo Ordinario, Comisión de Gobernación, ACEC; May 4, 1835, f. 290–291 and May 8, 1835, f. 298, Journal, Coahuila and Texas (Mexico) Congreso, WA MSS S-266, BRBML; Antonio Gaona to Antonio López de Santa Anna, March 22, 1826, vol. 1, *Documentos Para La Historia de Texas*, NYPL; José Urrea to Minister of War, June 27, 1836, f. 21–24, XI/481.3/1150, AHSDN.

12. Juan Manuel Maldonado to Subinspector de las Colonias de Oriente, July 24, 1850, N. 261, exp. 27, folder 2, caja 8, FCMO, AGEC; Justin Smith, *War with Mexico* (New York: Macmillan, 1919), 55–56. For more on the organization of Mexico's military colonies, see Ana María Alonso, *Thread of Blood: Colonialism, Revolution, and Gender on Mexico's Northern Frontier* (Tucson: University of Arizona Press, 1995), 35; Manuel Chust Calero, "Milicia, milicias y milicianos: nacionales y cívicos en la formación del Estado nación Mexicana, 1812–1835," in Juan Ortiz Escamilla, ed., *Fuerzas militares en "Iberoamérica," siglos XVIII y XIX* (Mexico City: El Colegio de Mexico, 2005); Luis Garcia, "A Medieval Frontier: Warfare and Military Culture in Texas and Northeastern Mexico, 1686–1845" (unpublished PhD dissertation: Southern Methodist University, 2015); Bárbara Corbett, "Las fibras del poder: la guerra contra Texas (1835–1836) y la construcción de un estado físico militar en San Luis Potosí," in Jorge Silva Riquer, Juan Carlos Grosso, and Carmen Yuste, *Circuitos mercantiles y mercados en latinoamérica* (Mexico City: Instituto de Investigaciones Históricos José María Luis Mora, 1995); José Antonio Serrano Orteca, "Los estados armados: milicias cívicas y sistema federal en México, 1824–1835," in Alberto Carrillo Cazares, ed., *La Guerra y la paz. Tradiciones y costumbres* (Morelia, Michoacán, MX: El Colegio de Michoacán, 2002).

13. Kevin Mulroy, *Freedom on the Border: The Seminole Maroons in Florida, the Indian Territory, Coahuila, and Texas* (Lubbock: Texas Tech University Press, 1993), 61–106.

14. Various Informants, folder 3, box 23, Porter Papers, SCRBC; Gerónimo Cardona to Minister of Gobernación, December 11, 1853, *La Union* (December 1853), 3, PO, AGEC. For schoolteacher, see Juan F. Valdez, "Estado que manifiesta el N. de niños de la tribu mascogo y seminole que reciben educación," July 1, 1856, box 175, Fondo Militares, AGENL; for tools, see Juan Manuel Maldonado to Antonio María Jáuregui, April 12, 1851, E25, F5, C13, FCMO, AGEC. The Mexican government also supplied the Seminoles and their black allies with rifles. See Jesus Garza González to Sr. Presidente del Ayuntamiento de Monclova, February 26, 1856, folder 3, box 1, series 4, Fondo Siglo XIX, AMM. In 1855, the Seminoles received 17 gourds, 3 bushels of corn, 3 bushels of sweet potatoes, four pounds of piloncillo, and three steers. See Alcalde de Villa de Rosas to Francisco Maldonado (?), November 1, 1855, box 168, Fondo Militares, AGENL. In 1856, they received 200 pesos and tools. See Tomás Talantes to Sr. Secretaría de la Comandancia General del Estado de Coahuila, January 7, 1856, box 169, ibid.; Juan Manuel Maldonado to Antonio Maria Jáuregui, October 22, 1851, E43, F7, C13, FCMO, AGEC.

15. Juzgado de Guerrero to Juzgado de Rosas, April 23, 1849, exp. 2, folder 8, caja 2, FSXIX, AGEC; Juan Manuel Maldonado to Antonio Maria Jáuregui, November 1, 1850, E1, F1, C10, FCMO, AGEC; Oral History of Adam McClain, 1941, 1943, folder 3, box 23, Porter Papers, SCRBC. These men might have been among those illegally imported to Texas from Africa by way of Cuba. For more on the illegal slave trade to Texas, see Eugene C. Barker, "The African Slave Trade in Texas," *The Quarterly of the Texas State Historical Association* 6:2 (October 1902), 145–158; Obadele-Starks, *Freebooters and Smugglers*, 83. "La total población es de 76 hombres de tropa y ocho vecinos, contando por todo, incluso los negros que entonces existían all 440 personas." I arrived at these calculations by subtracting the number of soldiers (76) and *vecinos* (8) from the total population. See Día 10, folder 2, "Itinerario de la expedición de San Carlos a Monclova el Viejo hecha por el Coronel D. Emilio Langberg, Inspector interino de las Colonias militares de Chihuahua . . . en el año de 1851," WA MSS S-1496, BRBML.

16. Oral history of Molly Perryman, 1941, Enrique Galan Long, 1942, and Dindie Factor, 1943, folder 3, box 23, Porter Papers, SCRBC; Oral history of Rosa Fe, 1942, and Penny Factor, 1943, ibid.; Oral history of Jane Phillips, 1943, ibid.

17. Ramón Múzquiz to Alcalde de Múzquiz, January 27, 1859, folder 127, box 11, Múzquiz Collection, BRBML; Jesus de la Garza to (?), July 3, 1858, folder 115, box 10, ibid.; Francisco Treviño to Secretary of War of the Northern Army, June 1, 1856, box 175, Fondos Militares, AGENL; Oral history of Julia Payne, Molly Perryman, and Penny Factor, folder 3, box 23, Porter Papers, SCRBC; Don Francisco de Castañeda to Inspector General de las Colonias, June 21, 1853, exp. 123, folder 14, caja 21, FCMO, AGEC.

18. Julia Payne, 1944, folder 3, box 23, Porter Papers, SCRBC; "Mexico was a land of freedom," folder 3, box 23, Porter Papers, SCRBC.

19. Manuel Flores to the Ayuntamiento of Guerrero, September 27, 1851, E3, F5, C9, FSXIX, AGEC; Ayuntamiento de Guerrero to Presidencia de Guerrero, September 24, 1851, f. 54, exp. 25, AMG, AGEC; Ayuntamiento to Presidencia, November 8, 1851, f. 54, exp. 25, AMG, AGEC.

20. Manuel Maldonado to the Ayuntamiento of Guerrero, no. 1, September 23, 1851, expediente 3, folder 5, box 9, FSXIX, AGEC; Marcos Arronil, "El Esclavo Negro: A Mi Amigo Francisco Zarco," *Demócrata* (July 9, 1850), 2; "Esclavitud," *Religion y la Sociedad* (January 1, 1865), 241; "A nuestro amigo," *Universal* (December 14, 1853), 3; James Sanders, *Vanguards of the Atlantic World: Creating Modernity, Nation, and Democracy* (Durham, NC: Duke University Press, 2014), 39–63.

21. For "hardworking men," Antonio Jauregui to Juan Manuel Maldonado, October 29, 1850, f. 9, exp. 9, folder 10, box 6, FSXIX, AGEC. For "very bellicose," see Antonio de Jáuregui to Governor of Nuevo Leon, July 18, 1850, Solicitudes de terrenos para que las tribus Seminoles, Quikapus y Mascogos, procedentes de los Estados Unidos, puedan establecerse en Territorio Mexicano, CL-36/620, Sección Concluidos, AGENL; Juan Manuel Maldonado to Antonio María Jáuregui, August 15, 1851, *La Patria* (August 1851), 2–3; Andrés de la Garza to Gobierno del Estado, June 13, 1851, *La Patria* 2:46 (June 1851), PO, AGEC; Francisco Treviño to Ejército del Norte, March 25, 1856, box 171, Fondo Militares, AGENL.

22. José Antonio de Arredondo to Chief Justice of Bexar, September 21, 1851, no. 3, folder 17, box 301–319, Peter Hansborough Bell Papers, TSA; Manuel Maldonado to ?, September 23, 1851, exp. 3, folder 5, caja 9, FSXIX, AGEC; Sub. Inspector de las Colonias de Oriente to el Comité de la Colonia de Guerrero, September 26, 1851, exp 3, ficha 5, caja 9, SXIX, AGEC; Manuel Maldonado to the Ayuntamiento of Guerrero, no. 2, September 23, 1851, exp. 3, folder 5, caja 9, FSXIX, AGEC. Wild Cat seems to have left the two hundred pesos at Fort Duncan. Capitan of the Guerrero Colony to Juan Manuel Maldonado, October 6, 1851, exp. 8, folder 2, caja 15, FCMO, AGEC. Oral

tradition has it that the coins were covered in blood. Jesse Sumpter, folder 3, box 23, Porter Papers, Schomburg.

23. For runaway slaves going to Matamoros, see Testimony of John Jefferson, 1941, folder 3, box 23, Porter Papers, SCRBC. For the black population in Matamoros, see Government of Tamaulipas to Sebastián Camacho, August 23, 1841, f. 212–226, vol. 29, Cartas de Seguridad, AGN. For Northern Mexicans hiring African Americans, see "Mexico," *Texas State Times* (October 6, 1855), 2; "Liquidación formada a los Negros Mascogos," June 4, 1856, box 175, Fondos Militares, AGENL; Juan Manuel Maldonado to Manuel Leal, February 8, 1850, C5, F4, E62, 14F, FCMO, AGEC; Pablo Espinoza to Mayor of Guerrero, September 12, 1859, exp. 11, folder 1, caja 4, FSXIX, AGEC; First Judge of the District of Northern Tamaulipas to Justo Treviño, August 20, 1850, 3-5-13, SRE; Investigation of the First Mayor of Reynosa, June 25, 1859, ibid.

24. Felix Haywood, *Slave Narratives: A Folk History of Slavery in the United States from Interviews with Former Slaves* (Washington, DC: Works Progress Administration, 1941), 2:132; Cora Montgomery, *Eagle Pass; or, Life on the Border* (New York: George P. Putnam, 1852), 132; Luis Lombraña to Governor of Coahuila y Tejas, December 19, 1829, exp. 11, folder 8, caja 12, FSXIX, AGEC.

25. Gilbert M. Joseph, *Revolution from Without: Yucatan, Mexico, and the United States, 1880–1924* (Durham, NC: Duke University Press, 1988), 84; Andrés Reséndez, *The Other Slavery: The Uncovered Story of Indian Enslavement in America* (Boston: Houghton Mifflin Harcourt, 2016), 238–239; "Esclavonia en el Estado de Veracruz," *El Siglo Diez y Nueve* (August 25, 1849), 2; "La Raza Indígena," *El Monitor Republicano* (October 20, 1857), 1.

26. Charles Gibson, *The Aztecs Under Spanish Rule: A History of the Indians of the Valley of Mexico, 1519–1810* (Palo Alto, CA: Stanford University Press, 1964), 25; Alan Knight, "Mexican Peonage: What Was It and Why Was It?," *Journal of Latin American Studies* 18:1 (May 1986), 55; Harry E. Cross, "Living Standards in Rural Nineteenth-Century Mexico: Zacatecas, 1820–80," *Journal of Latin American Studies* 10:1 (May 1978), 2, 16–17; François Chevalier, "The North Mexican Hacienda: Eighteenth and Nineteenth Century," in *The New World Looks at Its History*, ed.; Archibald R. Lewis and Thomas F. McGann (Austin: University of Texas Press, 1963), 101–106; and Harry E. Cross, "Debt Peonage Reconsidered: A Case Study in Nineteenth-Century Zacatecas, Mexico," *Business History Review* 53 (Winter 1979): 473–495; Jan Bazant, "Peones, arrendatarios y aparceros en México, 1851–53," *Historia Mexicana* 23:3 (1973): 330–357.

27. Testimony of Pablo Sains, December 30, 1850, Suprema Tribunal de Justicia, AGENL; Testimony of María Desideria Flores, June 29, 1856, Sección Concluidos, CL-43/804, AGENL; Judgment of José María Garza, Alcalde 2o Constitucional de Galeana, no. 2301, Leg. 94, April 9, 1860, Suprema Tribunal de Justicia, AGENL.

28. Testimony of María Desideria Flores, June 29, 1856, Sección Concluidos, CL-43/804, AGENL; Decisión, July 18, 1856, Sección Concluidos, CL-43/804, AGENL.

29. Testimony of C. Guadalupe García, 3-5-13, SRE.

30. Cheney's father had founded the town in 1811, when he moved from South Carolina to start a sugar plantation on the banks of a stream called Bayou Boeuf. For more on Cheneyville, see Workers of the Writers' Program of the Work Projects Administration in the State of Louisiana, eds., *Louisiana: A Guide to the State* (New York: Hastings House, 1941), 667. Solomon Northup, *Twelve Years a Slave*, ed. Sue Eakin and Joseph Logsdon (Baton Rouge, 1996), 188. Sarah Cornell, "Citizens of Nowhere: Fugitive Slaves and Free African Americans in Mexico, 1833–1857," *Journal of American History* (September 2013), 351. Herbert Aptheker, *American Negro Slave Revolts* (New York: Columbia University Press, 1943), 93.

31. Testimony of Manuel Luis del Fierro, Case against William Henry brought before Lic. Justo Treviño, Judge of Northern Tamaulipas, 3-5-13, SRE. Cheney remained in jail at least until September 14, 1850. See "Diligencias sobre encarcelación bajo de fianza de Don Eduardo Cheney," folder 911, box 35, Justicia, Archivo Municipal de Matamoros. I'm grateful to James David Nichols for sharing this document with me.

32. Emilio Langberg, October 10, 1851, Itinerario de la expedición, folder 2, BRBML; Juan Manuel Maldonado to Emilio Langberg, November 3, 1851, *La Patria* (November 1851), 1–2, PO, AGEC; November 1–18, Langberg, "Itinerario de la Expedición," BRBML; Manuel Flores to secretario de gobierno, March 18, 1851, C3-F8-E8-7F, FSXIX, AGEC; Ayuntamiento de Guerrero to Presidencia de Guerrero, March 20, 1851, f. 54, exp. 25, AMG, AGEC; Testimony of Jesus Flores, March 18, 1851, C3-F8-E8-7F, FSXIX, AGEC.

33. Oral History of Adam McClain, 1941, 1943, folder 3, box 23, Porter Papers, SCRBC; Roselle Kibbits and Julia Payne, "Freedom Over Me: A Folk-History of the Wild Cat John Horse Band of Seminole Negroes 1848–1882," unpublished typescript based on interviews and correspondence with the Seminole maroons in Texas and Coahuila during the 1930s and 1940s, folder 3, box 23, Porter Papers, SCRBC; Ignaz Pfefferkorn and Theodore E.

Treutlein, *Sonora, a Description of the Province* (Albuquerque: University of New Mexico Press, 1949), 145.

34. John L. Brooke, *"There Is a North": Fugitive Slaves, Political Crisis, and Cultural Transformation in the Coming of the Civil War* (Amherst: University of Massachusetts Press, 2019), 23–64, 89–115; Borrego, Decreto sobre organización y arregla de una campaña anual contra los indios bárbaros, August 24, 1843, exp. 38, leg. 2, Congreso Constitucional (1849), ACEC; Juan Martín de Vera Mendi to Governor of Nuevo León, January 21, 1833, box 1, Correspondencia con Coahuila y Téjas, AGENL; "Mexican Operations," *Niles National Register* (May 15, 1847); "Manifesto," *Martinsburg Gazette* (May 28, 1846), 2; "Mexico," *Niles National Register* (August 7, 1847).

35. Baylies to John E. Wool, May 14, 1848, box 1, Francis Baylies Correspondence, HEH; *CGA*, February 13, 1847, 372; "From Washington," *New York Daily Tribune* (January 18, 1859), 3.

36. William S. Withers to Mssr. Coleman, Putnam, Jackson, Mississippi, March 10, 1857, folder 3, file 50, AEMEUA, SRE.

37. Arrangoiz to Almonte, March 27, 1854, New Orleans, f. 39, no. 39, folder 4, file 43, AEMEUA, SRE; Warren Moise to William Marcy, April 20, 1854, folder 1, file 44, AEMEUA, SRE. In 1855, Texans kidnapped another Mexican named Enrique Sánchez, claiming him as a fugitive slave, until the Mexican consul in Brownsville, Texas, produced documents proving Sánchez's freedom. Javier Erdozain to Minister Plenipotenciary of Mexico in the United States, 1855, no. 28, f. 45–46, folder 2, file 46, AEMEUA, SRE.

38. A. M. Green to Secretary of State, May 19, 1844, folder 1, box 2, Justin H. Smith Collection, BLAC; José Y. Morgan to Vice Consul of the United States in Matamoros, May 19, 1836, folio 19/29, box 17, Correspondencia Ministerio de Relaciones Exteriores, Fondo Correspondencia Ministerios, AGENL.

39. Pickett to Gadsden, July 10, 1854, vol. 6, reel 6, DUSC-Veracruz. Underlining in original. "Texas not a Paradise," *Richmond Whig and Advertiser* (May 5, 1846), 4; "Editorial Correspondence," *American Flag* (January 6, 1858), DUSC-Matamoros, reel 281. Underlining in original. Viscount Palmerston to Consul Lyon, December 5, 1851, FO 701/27, NA-K; Alfred Conkling to Clement Vann, April 22, 1853, vol. 16, reel 17, DUSM-Mexico.

CHAPTER 10: THE BALANCE OF POWER

1. For more on Henry Clay, see Merrill D. Peterson, *The Great Triumvirate: Webster, Clay, and Calhoun* (New York: Oxford University Press, 1987); Robert

V. Remini, *Henry Clay: Statesman for the Union* (New York: Norton, 1991); Maurice G. Baxter, *Henry Clay and the American System* (Lexington: University Press of Kentucky, 2015).

2. Speech in Senate, January 29, 1850, *Papers of Henry Clay*, 10:655; January 28, 1850, *DoC*, 16:395.

3. March 4, 1850, *DoC*, 16:404–405, 411; May 15, 1850, *CG* (31st Congress, 1st Session), 1003; John M. Berrien, "Slavery in the Territories," *CGA* (31st Congress, 1st Session), 207. This was a variation on an argument that Southern politicians had been making since war broke out with Mexico. In 1847, Congressman Brockenbrough of Florida pointed out that "servitude of poor debtors of all races to the wealthy" continued in Mexico. February 13, 1847, *CGA* (29th Congress, 2nd Session), 375. Two years later, Senator Joseph Underwood of Kentucky denied that the abolition of slavery had any practical effect on a territory as unpeopled as the northwestern reaches of Mexico. "How does it operate in the construction of society *ab ovo*, if I may be permitted the expression?" he asked. *CG*, February 26, 1849 (30th Congress, 1st Session), 323.

4. April 5, 1850, *CGA*, 482. Benton read from the *Colección de las leyes y decretos expedidos por el Congreso General de los Estados Unidos Mexicos en los años de 1829 y 1830* (Mexico City: Galván, 1831), 150. Baylies to John Wool, January 24, 1851, box 1, Francis Baylies Correspondence, HEH; February 27, 1850, *CG*, 401; May 15, 1850, *CG* (31st Congress, 1st Session), 1003.

5. Select Committee Report, May 8, 1850, *DoC*, 16:549; Don E. Fehrenbacher, *The Dred Scott Case: Its Significance in American Law and Politics* (Oxford: Oxford University Press, 1978), 161; Carl Schurz, *The Reminiscences of Carl Schurz* (2 vols., New York: Doubleday, 1917), 2:30; Damon Wells, *Stephen Douglas: The Last Years, 1857–1861* (Austin: University of Texas Press, 1971), 7; quoted in Fergus Bordewich, *America's Great Debate: Henry Clay, Stephen A. Douglas, and the Compromise that Preserved the Union* (New York: Simon & Schuster, 2012), 30.

6. Bordewich, *America's Great Debate*, 34; Andrew Delbanco, *The War Before the War: Fugitive Slaves and the Struggle for America's Soul from the Revolution to the Civil War* (New York: Penguin, 2018), 5.

7. "Inauguration of President Pierce," *Weekly Union* (March 12, 1853), 3; David Potter, *The Impending Crisis, 1848–61* (New York: Harper and Row, 1976), 231; Michael F. Holt, *Franklin Pierce* (New York: Macmillan, 2010), 1.

8. Holt, *Franklin Pierce*, 37; Franklin Pierce, Inaugural Address, in Robert V. Remini and Terry Golway, eds., *Fellow Citizens: The Penguin Book of U.S. Presidential Inaugural Addresses* (New York: Penguin, 2008), 146, 148.

9. Matthew Karp, *This Vast Southern Empire: Slaveholders at the Helm of American Foreign Policy* (Cambridge, MA: Harvard University Press, 2016), 186–187.

10. "Slavery Extension," *DeBow's Review*, July 1853, 1–14; "La cuestión de Cuba," *The Universal*, n.d. (1855?), Encl. Gadsden to Marcy, April 3, 1855, vol. 19, reel 20, DUSM- Mexico.

11. Will Fowler, *Santa Anna of Mexico* (Lincoln: University of Nebraska Press, 2007), 294–299.

12. J. R. Pacheco to Drowyn de Lhuys, October 24, 1853, 16-3-47, SRE; Legation of Mexico in France to Minister of Foreign Relations, October 10, 1853, f. 64, folder 2, file 41, AEMEUA, SRE; "Gestaciones y Documentos sobre la Concertación de Suizas," 1855, f. 10, 6-2-22, SRE; J. R. Pacheco to Drowyn de Lhuys, Minister of Foreign Relations, October 24, 1853, 16-3-47, SRE.

13. Buenaventura Vivó, *Memorias de Buenaventura Vivo* (Madrid: M. Rivadeneyra, 1856), 3; William L. Marcy to James Buchanan, March 11, 1854, *Diplomatic Correspondence*, 2:102–104; Percy W. Doyle to Earl of Clarendon, October 3, 1853, f. 1, FO 50/261, NA-K; Testimony of Pedro Estrada and Juan Chan, June 7, 1853, f. 5–12, FO 50/261, NA-K; José Vicente Relles to General Peck, May 16, 1853, f. 21, FO 50/261, NA-K. Percy Doyle to Earl of Clarendon, August 2, 1853, f. 136–137, FO 50/260, NA-K.

14. Madame Calderón de la Barca, *The Attaché in Madrid, Or Sketches of the Court of Isabella H.* (D. Appleton, 1856), vii, 97; Vivó, *Memorias*, 55.

15. Ibid., 56, 70; Buenaventura Vivó to Secretary of Foreign Relations, September 10, 1853, 16-3-47, SRE; Buenaventura Vivó to Secretary of Foreign Relations, April 23, 1854, f. 94-54, folder 5, file 44, AEMEUA, SRE.

16. J. R. Pacheco to Drowyn de Lhuys, October 24, 1853, 16-3-47, SRE; Pacheco to Secretary of Foreign Relations, October 31, 1853, 16-3-47, SRE; Memorandum of M. Esteva y Ulibarri, April 25, 1854, exp. 5, leg. 44, AEMEUA, SRE.

17. J. R. Pacheco to Secretary of Foreign Relations, Paris, October 31, 1853, 16-3-47, SRE; Pacheco to Secretary of Foreign Relations, October 10, 1853, exp. 2, leg. 41, AEMEUA, SRE.

18. Buenaventura Vivó to Secretary of Foreign Relations, April 23, 1854, f. 94-54, folder 5, file 44, AEMEUA, SRE; J. L. Uraga to Almonte, December 21, 1853, f. 209, exp. 2, leg. 41, AEMEUA, SRE.

19. Lord Howden to Earl of Clarendon, February 1, 1854, FO 72/842, NA-K; Alamán to Minister to Spain, May 2, 1853, 16-3-47, SRE; James Gadsden to William Marcy, May 18, 1855, vol. 19, roll 20, DUSM-Mexico.

20. *Concord New Hampshire Patriot and State Gazette*, October 27, 1852, p. 2, citing the *New York Home Journal*; Calderón de la Barca, *The Attaché in Madrid*, 72–73; John Forney, *Anecdotes of Public Men* (New York: Harper & Brothers, 1873), 57; G. W. Julian, *Political Recollections, 1840–1872* (Chicago: Jansen, McClurg, 1884), 108–109; James G. Blaine, *Twenty Years of Congress* (Norwich, CT: Henry Bill Publishing Company, 1884), 1:90.

21. August 12, 1850, *DoC*, 16:591.

22. *Louisville Daily Courier*, January 11, 1859; John H. Coatsworth, "American Trade with European Colonies in the Caribbean and South America, 1790–1812" (PhD Diss.: University of Wisconsin Madison, 1967), 248; Rodrigo Lazo, *Writing to Cuba: Filibustering and Cuban Exiles in the United States* (Chapel Hill: University of North Carolina Press, 2005), 77.

23. Amos A. Ettinger, *Mission to Spain of Pierre Soulé, 1853–55* (New Haven, CT: Yale University Press, 1932), 176.

24. *New Orleans Daily Picayune*, March 11, 1854; *Natchez Daily Courier*, March 10, 1854.

25. "Presidential message with report on seizure of steamer Black Warrior," March 15, 1854, *CG* (33rd Congress, 1st Session), 601, 636–637; Robert May, *The Southern Dream of a Caribbean Empire, 1854–1861* (Athens: University of Georgia Press, 1989), 58; Marcy to Pierre Soulé, July 23, 1853, March 17, April 3, 1854, in Manning (ed.), *Diplomatic Correspondence*, 11:160–165, 174–175; Ettinger, *Mission to Spain of Pierre Soulé*, 246–247.

26. Nicole Etcheson, *Bleeding Kansas: Contested Liberty in the Civil War Era* (Lawrence: University Press of Kansas, 2004), 9–10.

27. P. Orman Ray, The Repeal of the Missouri Compromise (Cleveland, OH: The Arthur H. Clark Company, 1909), 20; "The Three Million Bill," March 1, 1847, *John Adams Dix's Speeches and Occasional Addresses*, vol. 1 (New York: D. Appleton, 1864), 181.

28. *CGA* (33rd Congress, 1st Session, 1309), 240; *St. Louis Missouri Democrat*, January 11, 1854, quoted in Etcheson, *Bleeding Kansas*, 11; C. F. Jackson to D. R. Atchison, January 18, 1854, quoted in ibid.

29. *CGA* (33rd Congress 1st Session), 299. Douglas Egerton, *Year of Meteors: Stephen Douglas, Abraham Lincoln, and the Election that Brought on the Civil War* (New York: Bloomsbury Press, 2010), 27–29. For popular sovereignty, see Potter, *The Impending Crisis*, 174, 192; Fehrenbacher, *The Dred Scott Case*, 145–146, 182–183; Christopher Childers, "Interpreting Popular Sovereignty: A Historiographical Essay," *Civil War History* 57:1 (March 2011): 48–70; Christopher Childers, *The Failure of Popular Sovereignty: Slavery, Manifest Des-*

tiny, and the Radicalization of Southern Politics (Lawrence: University Press of Kentucky, 2012), 9–21.

30. Robert R. Russel, "The Issues in the Congressional Struggle over the Kansas-Nebraska Bill, 1854," *Journal of Southern History* 29:2 (May 1963), 191, 197.

31. *CGA* (33rd Congress, 1st Session, 520), 289–296, 836; Russel, "The Issues in the Congressional Struggle," 191.

32. Russel, "The Issues in the Congressional Struggle," 208.

33. *New York Times*, May 26, 1854; Marcy to John Y. Mason, quoted in James A. Rawley, *Race & Politics: "Bleeding Kansas" and the Coming of the Civil War* (Lincoln: University of Nebraska Press, 1969), 135; *New York Herald*, July 4, 1854; James A. Rawley, "Stephen A; Douglas and the Kansas-Nebraska Act," in John R. Wunder and Joann M. Ross, eds., *The Nebraska-Kansas Act of 1854* (Lincoln: University of Nebraska Press, 2008), 73–74; The best history of the Republican Party remains Eric Foner, *Free Soil, Free Labor, Free Men: The Ideology of the Republican Party Before the Civil War* (Oxford: Oxford University Press, 1995).

34. *CG* (33rd Congress, 1st Session), 2178; May, *Southern Dream*, 68.

35. Ettinger, *Mission to Spain*, 363–364.

36. May, *Southern Dream*, 69; Horace Greeley, *The American Conflict* (Hartford, CT: O. D. Case, 1866), 1:275; *New-York Evening Post*, March 6, 1855.

37. Etcheson, *Bleeding Kansas*, 23; May, *Southern Dream*, 70.

38. Delbanco, *The War Before the War*, 269; Gordon S. Barker, *Fugitive Slaves and the Unfinished American Revolution* (New York: McFarland, 2013), 39–40.

39. Charles Stevens, *Anthony Burns: A History* (Boston: John P. Jewett, 1856), 16; James McPherson, *Battle Cry of Freedom: The Civil War Era* (Oxford: Oxford University Press, 1988), 119–120.

40. An escaped slave in Matamoros counted forty arrivals in the past three months. Frederick Law Olmsted, *A Journey Through Texas; or a Saddle-Trip on the Southwestern Frontier: with a Statistical Appendix* (New York: Dix, Edwards, 1857), 188–189; "Mr. W. Secrest," *Telegraph and Texas Register* August 29, 1851, 2; Slave Schedule for Brownsville, Texas, Ancestry.com. *1860 U.S. Federal Census—Slave Schedules* [database on-line], Provo, UT. According to the instructions given to census takers, "fugitives from the state" referred to "the fugitives who, having escaped within the year, have *not been returned* to their owners." See United States Department of the Interior, *Eighth Census, U.S., Instructions, &c.* (Washington: George W. Bowman, 1860), 18; "If something

is not done," *The Washington American* (April 14, 1857), 2; Francis J. Parker to Governor H. Bell, May 16, 1852, folder 33, box 301–318, Peter Hansborough Bell Papers, TSA; J. F. Welsh to Department of Texas, April 18, 1853, Register of Letters Received by Department of Texas, NARA-DC; Santiago Vidaurri to presidente de la junta directiva del estado de Texas, July 28, 1855, box 164, Fondo Militares, AGENL. The legislature of Louisiana also tried to negotiate its own treaty. J. M. Montoya to Consul in New Orleans, March 23, 1832, exp. 2, caja 2, Relaciones Exteriores, AGN; "Invasion of Mexico," *Daily National*, August 15, 1855, vol. 8, reel 4, Notes from the Mexican Legation in the United States; Gideon Lincecum to Peter Bell, February 13, 1851, folder 18, box 301-20, Peter Hansborough Bell Papers, TSA.

CHAPTER 11: CITIZENSHIP

1. A. C. Allen to Captain Larragriti, n.d., vol. 1, reel 1, DUSC-Minatitlán; A. C. Allen to J. M. Monterde, January 26, 1857, ibid.; Allen to Marcy, February 10, 1855, ibid.; Allen to Marcy, February 17, 1853, ibid.; Leon Litwack, "The Federal Government and the Free Negro, 1790–1860," *Journal of Negro History* 43:4 (October 1958): 261.

2. Allen to Marcy, February 10, 1855, vol. 1, reel 1, DUSC-Minatitlán; A. C. Allen to Wm. L. Marcy, February 17, 1853, ibid.; Gadsden to Marcy, March 19, 1855, vol. 19, reel 20, DUSM-Mexico; For his attempts to help Luciano, see Allen to J. M. Monterde, February 9, 1857, ibid.; A. C. Allen to James Gadsden, February 16, 1855, ibid.; James A. Pleasants to Marcy, October 1, 1855, ibid.; A. C. Allen to J. M. Monterde, February 9, 1857, ibid.

3. "A Fugitive Slave in Mexico," *Alexandria Gazette* (August 21, 1854), 2; J. Fred Rippy, "Negotiation of the Gadsden Treaty," *SWHQ* 27:1 (July 1923), 3; Manuel Díez de Bonilla to Juan Almonte, October 3, 1854, vol. 7, reel 4, Notes from the Mexican Legation in the United States. For the importance of the railroad to Southern plans, see Robert R. Russel, *Improvement of Communication with the Pacific Coast as an Issue in American Politics* (New York: Torch Press, 1948); Jere W. Roberson, "The South and the Pacific Railroad, 1845–55," *WHQ* 5:2 (April 1974): 173–174; Robert Spencer Cotterill, "Improvement of Transportation in the Mississippi Valley, 1845–1850" (PhD dissertation, University of Wisconsin, 1919), and Kevin Waite, *West of Slavery: The Continental Crisis of the Civil War Era* (Chapel Hill: University of North Carolina Press, 2021).

4. John T. Pickett to William Marcy, June 25, 1854, vol. 6, reel 6, DUSC-Veracruz.

5. James Gadsden to Consuls of the United States in Mexico, June 28, 1854, ibid.; J. T. Pickett to C. Cushing, January 25, 1855, ibid.; James Gadsden, Circular to the consuls of the United States, June 28, 1854, ibid.; John McCall to Powhattan Ellis, September 9, 1839, vol. 9, roll 10, DUSM-Mexico; Gadsden to Marcy, July 3, 1854, vol. 18, reel 19, ibid.

6. Manuel Díez de Bonilla to Gadsden, November 7, 1854, vol. 18, reel 19, DUSM-Mexico. "Anuncio," *Eco del Comercio* (January 21, 1855), 3; "Una de tantas inconsecuencias," *Diario Oficial* (January 15, 1855), vol. 19, reel 20, DUSM-Mexico.

7. Pickett to William Marcy, February 21, 1855, vol. 6, reel 6, DUSC-Veracruz. Gadsden to Manuel Díez de Bonilla, March 25, 1855, vol. 19, reel 20, DUSM-Mexico. Gadsden to William Marcy, July 3, 1855, ibid.

8. Miguel Palacio to José María Ortiz Monasterio, August 21, 1851, f. 151, vol. 98, Cartas de Seguridad, AGN. Edward Wright's certificate described him as having "black woolly hair and light Sambo complexion." This description comes from *Proofs of Citizenship Used to Apply for Seamen's Certificates for the Port of Philadelphia, Pennsylvania, 1792–1861*, US Customs Service, NARA Microfilm publication M1880, record group 36, roll 36, f. 514. For his travels in Mexico, see Carta de Seguridad de Eduardo Wright, Veracruz, May 1852, f. 217, vol. 101, Cartas de Seguridad, AGN; Carta de Seguridad de Eduardo Wright, Tehuantepec, February 1855, f. 254, vol. 164, ibid.; A. C. Allen to W. L. Marcy, December 19, 1854, vol. 1, reel 1, DUSC-Minatitlán.

9. Naturalization Law, 1826, Bandos publicados por el gobierno en los que se da a conocer el contenido de los decretos, folder 17, box 155, Gobernación sin Sección, AGN. Naturalization Law, April 14, 1828, f. 138–145, folder 39, box 4, Laredo Archives, TSA; Erika Pani, *Para pertenecer a la gran familia mexicana: Procesos de naturalización en el siglo XIX* (Mexico City: Colegio de México, 2015), 32–42; Lista que continene filiaciones de ciudadanos originarios de Nueva Orleans, August 14, 1850, f. 438, vol. 86, Cartas de Seguridad, AGN.

10. Tamar Herzog, *Defining Nations: Immigrants and Citizens in Early Modern Spain and Spanish America* (New Haven: Yale University Press, 2003), 4; Julio César Guanche, "Populismo, ciudadanía y nacionalismo; La cultura política republicana en Cuba hacia 1940 (PhD dissertation, Facultad Latinoamericana de Ciencias Sociales Ecuador, 2017), 2–3; "Reglamento de la Direccíon de Colonización" (Mexico City: Imprenta de Vicente Garcia Torres, 1846), 10–11, f. 55, folder 2, box 1, Mexican proclamations issued during the Mexican-American War, Collection 997, UCLA; Ministro de la Guerra to Antonio Maria Jauregui, November 18, 1850, *Siglo XIX*; Declaration of Thom Ysobel, January 11, 1866, folder 125, box 11, Múzquiz Collection, BRBML;

Secretaría del Gobierno de Coahuila to Ayuntamiento de Múzquiz, August 18, 1852, ibid.; Mayor of Múzquiz to Prefect of Monclova, February 26, 1859, folder 113, box 10, ibid.; List of the citizens who were elected to the jury of this municipality, December 1858, folder 115, ibid.; Testimony of Miguel Shields, July 3, 1858, folder 114, ibid.; Miguel Castro to Secretaría de Gobierno, January 12, 1853, exp. 6, folder 2, box 1, FSXIX, AGEC.

11. Pickett to Marcy, June 25, 1854, vol. 6, reel 6, DUSC-Veracruz; Raul Barrio to José Aroyo, October 4, 1852, f. 5, vol. 103, Cartas de Seguridad, AGN. When examining this same case, historians have suggested that Barrio understood conversion to Catholicism as equivalent to a *carta*, when conversion actually made such paperwork unnecessary. Sarah Cornell, "Citizens of Nowhere: Fugitive Slaves and Free African Americans in Mexico, 1833–1857," *Journal of American History* (September 2013), 368.

12. Lista que contiene filiaciones de ciudadanos originarios de Nueva Orleans, August 14, 1850, f. 438, vol. 86, Cartas de Seguridad, AGN; Francisco Dupuis to Prefecto de San Juan del Río, July 22, 1853, f. 178, vol. 130, ibid.; Ignacio Rayón to Prefecto de San Juan del Río, July 29, 1853, f. 180, ibid.

13. For his application, see Vicente Yerno por parte de Jayme Castellano to Gobernador del Estado, f. 240, December 31, 1833, vol. 7, Cartas de Seguridad, AGN. For approval, see Minister of Foreign Relations to Governor of Yucatán, March 1, 1834, f. 243, vol. 7, Cartas de Seguridad, AGN. Eduardo González to Luis G. Cuevas, January 29, 1849, vol. 78, Cartas de Seguridad, AGN.

14. Francisco Pérez to Manuel Díez de Bonilla, November 19, 1853, vol. 127-2, Cartas de Seguridad, AGN; Solicitud de Juan Braun and Juan Long, February 7, 1832, exp. 11, leg. 3, Tercer Congreso Constitucional, Segundo Periodo Ordinario, Comisiones, ACEC; minutes from the meeting of the town council, June 19, 1858, Folder 115, Box 10, Múzquiz Collection, BRBML.

15. Leon Litwack, "The Federal Government and the Free Negro, 1790–1860," *Journal of Negro History*, 261–278; Stephen Kantrowitz, *More Than Freedom: Fighting for Black Citizenship in a White Republic, 1829–1889* (New York: Penguin, 2012), 1–9.

16. Citizens of San Antonio to Emilio Langberg, August 25, 1855, box 165, Fondo Militares AGENL; "Proceedings of Bexar County in Regard to Runaway Slaves," *Texas State Gazette* 6:4 (September 16, 1854), 4; Santiago Vidaurri to W. L. Marcy, October 18, 1855, box 167, Fondo Militares, AGENL; Bob Cunningham and Harry P. Hewitt, "A 'Lovely Land Full of Roses and Thorns': Emil Langberg and Mexico, 1835–1866," *SWHQ* 98, no. 3 (1995): 406, 411; Manuel Robles Pezuela to Inspector of Colonias Militares, February 26, 1852, E69, F7, C16, FCMO, AGEC.

17. Cunningham and Hewitt, "A 'Lovely Land Full of Roses and Thorns,'" 406–407; Emilio Langberg to Military Commander of Nuevo León, August 30, 1855, 3-5-10, SRE; Emilio Langberg to Ejército Libertador del Norte, September 1, 1855, box 165, AGENL; For Langberg's request that the Seminole and Mascogo join him on an expedition, see Robles to Inspector of Colonias Militares, February 26, 1852, E69, F7, C16, FCMO, AGEC; Langberg to Vidaurri, September 1, 1855, box 18, Primera Seccion, Fondo Vidaurri, AGENL; Langberg to Secretary of War, August 31, 1855, *El Siglo Diez y Nueve* (November 12, 1855), 3; Langberg to Secretary of War, August 31, 1855, box 165, Fondo Militares, AGENL.

18. Typescript, box 7, box B, Guajardo Papers, BRBML; Secretary of War to Langberg, September 11, 1855, *El Siglo Diez y Nueve* (November 12, 1855), 3; Langberg to Vidaurri, February 23, 1856, no. 5806, caja 18, Primera Sección, Fondo Vidaurri, AGENL.

19. Diary of J. S. McDowell, *Galveston Daily News*, January 8, 1893.

20. Langberg to Primera autoridad de la villa de Múzquiz, September 3, 1855, folder 3, BRBML; Juan y Galán to Ayuntamiento de Monclova, October 21, 1855, folder 4, box 12, series 3, FSXIX, AMM; J. Burbank to Asst. Adj. General, October 4, 1855, folder 1153, box 401, Adjutant General Ranger Records, TSA; W. R. Henry to Captain Manchaca, October 5, 1855, Box 166, Fondo Militares, AGENL; "Capt. Callahan," *The Times-Picayune* (October 17, 1855), 6; Persifor F. Smith to S. Cooper, October 10, 1855, f. 12, exp 4, leg 48, AEMEUA, SRE; Kenneth Wiggins Porter, "The Seminole in Mexico, 1850–1861," *Hispanic American Historical Review* 31:1 (February 1951), 18–20; Ronnie C. Tyler, "The Callahan Expedition of 1855: Indians or Negroes?," *SWHQ* 70:4 (April, 1967), 574–585.

21. Burbank to Asst. Adj. Gen., October 8, 1855, 401–1153, Adjutant General Ranger Records, TSA; Emilio Langberg to Secretary of War, October 18, 1855, box 167, Fondo Militares, AGENL; Testimony of Manuel Menchaca, 3-5-10, SRE; Juan y Galán to Ayuntamiento de Monclova, October 21, 1855, folder 4, box 12, series 3, FSXIX, AMM.

22. "Negro-Stealing," *New Orleans Daily Crescent* (August 9, 1854), 2; "The San Antonio Texan," *Weekly Telegraph* (February 11, 1857), 2; H. M'Bride Pridgen, *Address to the People of Texas on the Protection of Slave Property* (Austin, 1859), 10, BRBML.

23. Noah Smithwick, *The Evolution of a State; Or, Recollections of Old Texas Days* (Austin: Gammel Book Company, 1900), 37; "The Return of Willis," *Northern Standard*, 10:8 (December 25, 1852), 1; "It seems like," *Benton Independent* (June 19, 1858), 2.

24. "RUNAWAY CAUGHT," *Independent Press* (October 13, 1854), 3; "Runaway Negro Caught," *The Matagorda Gazette* (July 31, 1858); Oral history of Priscilla Dixey, 1943, and Curley Jefferson, 1950, folder 3, box 23, Porter Papers, SCRBC.

25. The contract with the military colony stipulated that Saens could bring his brother from Texas to help him with his work. See Jesús García Gonzáles to 1a Autoridad Política de la Villa de Múzquiz, May 24, 1856, folder 125, box 11, Múzquiz Collection, BRBML. Free blacks were not permitted in Texas, except if given a dispensation by the state legislature, but no one by the name of Saens had been granted such an allowance. For laws against free blacks coming to and living in Texas, see "An ordinance and decree to prevent the importation and emigration of free negroes and mulattoes into Texas," January 1, 1836, H.P.N. Gammel, *The Laws of Texas, 1822–1897* (Austin: Gammel Book Company, 1898), 1:721; Section IX, Constitution of the Republic of Texas, 1836, ibid., 2:19; "An Act," February 5, 1840, ibid., 2:325–327. Not long after their return, a gang of men descended on Long's ranch, killing one of the brothers. Jesus Garza to 1a Autoridad Política de Múzquiz, December 22, 1856, folder 107, box 10, Múzquiz Collection, BRBML. The mayor of Múzquiz informed the governor that "Don Pedro Saens" had been killed, but it is unclear whether he had just been injured, or whether it was his brother who had been shot, because Pedro Saens continued to appear in the local records.

26. Jan Bazant, "Mexico from Independence to 1867," in Leslie Bethell, ed., *Cambridge History of Latin America, 1870-1930* (Cambridge: Cambridge University Press, 1986): 4:452–455; Will Fowler, *Santa Anna of Mexico* (Lincoln: University of Nebraska Press, 2007), 311–316; Richard Johnson, *The Mexican Revolution of Ayutla, 1854–55: An Analysis of the Evolution and Destruction of Santa Anna's Last Dictatorship* (Wastport, CT: Greenwood Press, 1974), 33–35; María del Carmen Vázquez Mantecón, *Santa Anna y la encrucijada del estado: La dictadura, 1853–1855* (Mexico City: Fondo de Cultura Económica, 1986), 184–186; Anselmo de la Portilla, *Historia de la revolución de México contra la dictadura del General Santa Anna, 1853–1855* (Mexico City: Fondo de Cultural Económica, 1993), 65–93, 187–200; Edmundo O'Gorman, "Precedentes y sentido del plan de Ayutla," in *Plan de Ayutla: Conmemoración de su primer aniversario* (Mexico City: Universidad Nacional Autónoma de México, 1954), 169–204.

27. Catalina Sierra Casasús, "Estudio Preliminar," in Francisco Zarco, *Crónica del Congreso Extraordinario Constituyente* (Mexico City: El Colegio de Mexico, 1957), xv.

28. Francisco Zarco, *Historia del Congreso Extraordinario Constituyente de 1856 y 1857* (Mexico City: Imprenta de Ignacio Cumplido, 1898), 1:29; Sierra Casasús, "Estudio Preliminar" in Zarco, Crónica, x, xi, xv.

29. Erika Pani, "Entre transformar y gobernar; La Constitución de 1857," in *Historia y política; Ideas, procesos, y movimientos sociales* 11 (2004): 65–86; Daniel Cosío Villegas, *La constitución de 1857 y sus críticos* (México City: Fondo de Cultura Económica, 2013). For the antislavery provisions of the Constitution of 1857, see Karl Jacoby, *The Strange Career of William Ellis* (New York: Norton, 2016), 17–18; Rosalie Schwartz, *Across the Rio to Freedom*, 51.

30. Zarco, *Crónica*, 274–277; "Noticias: Congreso Constituyente, Julio 18 de 1856," *Diario Oficial* (July 19, 1856), 3; Mexican Constitution of 1857, Article 2, 10, 15, 30, 34; *Legislación del estado de Veracruz desde el año de 1824 hasta la presente época* (Jalapa, MX: Imprenta Veracruzana de Agustin Ruiz, 1881), 8.

31. *Dred Scott v. Sandford*, 60 US 393 (1857), 404–405. The best book on the case remains Don E. Fehrenbacher, *The Dred Scott Case: Its Significance in American Law and Politics* (Oxford: Oxford University Press, 1978). The claim to freedom that Dred Scott made was unexceptional, as shown by Kelly M. Kennington, *In the Shadow of Dred Scott: St. Louis Freedom Suits and the Legal Culture of Slavery in Antebellum America* (Athens: University of Georgia Press, 2017), and Ann Twitty, *Before Dred Scott: Slavery and Legal Culture in the American Confluence, 1787–1857* (Cambridge: Cambridge University Press, 2016). See also: Martha Jones, *Birthright Citizens: A History of Race and Rights in Antebellum America* (Cambridge: Cambridge University Press, 2019), 129–145. The case is known as *Dred Scott v. Sandford*, because a clerk misspelled the respondent's surname, "Sanford," and the court never corrected the error. John Vishneski, "What the Court Decided in Dred Scott v. Sandford," *The American Journal of Legal History* 32:4 (1988): 373–390.

32. Fehrenbacher, *Dred Scott*, 340, 351, 361–362; Leon Litwack, "The Federal Government and the Free Negro, 1790–1860," *The Journal of Negro History* 43:4 (October 1958), 273.

33. *Dred Scott v. Sandford*, 60 US 393 (1857), 452.

34. Pridgen, *Address to the People of Texas*, 10; "No Slave-Catching in Mexico," *Liberator* (May 15, 1857); "Petition of 500 'Texian Subscribers' to the House and Senate of the United States, March 24, 1858," printed in H. M'Bride Pridgen, *Address*, 15–16, BRBML.

35. Frederick Law Olmsted, *A Journey Through Texas; or a Saddle-Trip on the Southwestern Frontier: with a Statistical Appendix* (New York: Dix, Edwards, 1857), 110.

36. Ibid., 110, 114.

37. Bills and Resolutions, December 10, 1857, Records of the Seventh Legislature, TSA; Pridgen, *Address*, 14; "A bill for the reclamation of fugitive slaves," January 25, 1858, *Appendix to the Official Journal of the House of Representatives of the Seventh Legislature of the State of Texas* (Austin: John Marshall, 1858), 671.

38. "Runaway Negroes," *State Gazette* (February 19, 1859), 2; Testimony of Alexander Oswald and Isidro Martínez, September 19, 1860, folder 11, box 1153, Adjutant General Ranger Records, TSA; Testimony of Leanobra Zabar and José María López, December 1, 1860, folder 14, box 381, ibid.; Appraisal of Amos Morrille and John H. Pop, n.d., ibid.

39. *Reports of the committee of investigation sent in 1873 by the Mexican government to the frontier of Texas. Tr. from the official edition made in Mexico* (Mexico City: Comisión Pesquisadora de la Frontera del Norte, 1873), 243; Extracto de la causa seguida contra un americano y varios mejicanos que se llevaron por la fuerza al C, Anastacio Aguado, 3-5-13, SRE.

40. Diffenduffer to Cass, July n.d., 1859, vol. 1, reel 1, DUSC-Ciudad Juárez.

41. Testimonies of Antonio Saenz, Esteban Gómez, Francisco Longoria Guerra, and Antonio Uresti, C3-F8-E8-7F, FSXIX, AGEC.

42. Serapio Fragua to Sr Com Municipal de la Villa de Múzquiz, October 1, 1854, folder 102, box 9, Múzquiz Collection, BRBML; Aguilar to Governor of Coahuila, October 21, 1854, exp. 9, folder 7, box 8, FSXIX, AGEC; Ayuntamiento to Presidencia, November 8, 1851, f. 54, exp. 25, AMG, AGEC; *Reports of the committee of investigation*, 243; James David Nichols, *The Limits of Liberty: Mobility and the Making of the Eastern U.S.-Mexico Border* (Lincoln: University of Nebraska Press, 2018), 138; Manuel Rejón to Alcalde de Nava, October 28, 1860, exp. 5, folder 13, caja 32, FPMN, AGEC.

43. Paul Vanderwood, "Betterment for Whom? The Reform Period: 1855–1875," in *The Oxford History of Mexico*, eds. Michael C. Beezley and Lorenzo Meyer (Oxford: Oxford University Press, 2000), 235; Jan Bazant, *Alienation of Church Wealth in Mexico: Social and Economic Aspects of the Liberal Revolution, 1856–1875* (Cambridge: Cambridge University Press, 1971), 41–175; Robert J. Knowlton, *Church Property and the Mexican Reform, 1856–1910* (DeKalb: Northern Illinois University Press, 1976), 22–35; Margaret Chowning, *Wealth and Power in Provincial Mexico: Michoacán from the Late Colony to the Revolution* (Stanford, CA: Stanford University Press, 1999), 206–260; Jacqueline Covo, *Las ideas de la Reforma en México, 1855–1861* (Mexico City: Universidad Nacional Autónoma de México, 1983; Jaime Olveda, ed., *Los*

obispados de México frente a la Reforma liberal (Guadalajara, MX: El Colegio de Jalisco, 2007).

44. Ramón Múzquiz to Alcalde de Monclova, March 31, 1859, folder 7, box 6, series 4, FSXIX, AMM.

45. Kevin Mulroy, *Freedom on the Border: The Seminole Maroons in Florida, the Indian Territory, Coahuila, and Texas* (Lubbock: Texas Tech University Press, 1993), 84; "Mexico was a land of freedom," folder 3, box 23, Porter Papers, SCRBC.

46. Alcalde 1 de Villa de Rosas to Srio del Gobierno, September 5, 1857, f. 20, L-E-1596, SRE; Capitán Leon to Prefectura de Monclova, August 29, 1857, folder 132, box 11, Múzquiz Collection, BRBML; Ramón Múzquiz to Alcalde de Múzquiz, March 31, 1859, ibid.; Miguel Blanco to Srio de Guerra, March 13, 1859, ibid.; Ramón Múzquiz to Alcalde de Múzquiz, March 19, 1859, folder 127, box 11, ibid.

47. Ramón Múzquiz to Alcalde de Múzquiz, March 31, 1859, folder 132, box 11, Múzquiz Collection, BRBML.

48. Pablo Espinoza to Alcalde de Guerrero, April 6, 1859, exp. 8, folder 8, caja 2, FSXIX, AGEC. The Shields family, free blacks from the Carolinas, remained at Nacimiento, with the consent of the Seminoles. Manuel Rejón to Gob de Coahuila, November 24, 1860, folder 132, box 11, Múzquiz Collection, BRBML; Interviews with Dindie Factor, 1943; Julia Payne, 1942, Porter Papers, SCRBC; Múzquiz Mayor to Rosas Mayor, June 13, 1859, folder 117, box 10, Múzquiz Collection, BRBML; Múzquiz Mayor to San Buenaventura Mayor, June 18, 1859, ibid.

49. William Darlington, *Desultry Remarks on the Question Extending Slavery into Missouri* (West Chester, PA: Lewis Marshall, 1856), 24; James Henry Hammond, William Harper, Thomas Dew, and William Gilmore Simms, *The Pro-Slavery Argument: As Maintained by the Most Distinguished Writers of the Southern States* (Charleston, SC: Walker, Richards, 1852), 250.

50. Fehrenbacher, *Dred Scott*, 462, 469; James McPherson, *Battle Cry of Freedom: The Civil War Era* (Oxford: Oxford University Press, 1988), 168; Nicole Etcheson, *Bleeding Kansas: Contested Liberty in the Civil War Era* (Lawrence: University Press of Kansas, 2004), 141–181; David Potter, *The Impending Crisis, 1848–61* New York: Harper and Row, 1976), 316; Damon Wells, *Stephen Douglas: The Last Years, 1857–1861* (Austin: University of Texas Press, 1971), 50.

51. Fehrenbacher, *Dred Scott*, 479. For the compromise, see E. Duane Elbert, "The English Bill: An Attempt to Compromise the Lecompton Dilemma," *Kansas History* 1:4 (Winter 1978): 219–234.

52. Robert Russel, "The Issues in the Congressional Struggle over the Kansas-Nebraska Bill, 1854," *Journal of Southern History*, 189; John M. Berrien, "Slavery in the Territories," February 12, 1850, *CGA*, (31st Congress, 1st Session), 207; Wells, *Stephen Douglas*, 121.

53. Wells, *Stephen Douglas*, 218, 221; Lawrence T. McDonnell, *Performing Disunion: The Coming of the Civil War in Charleston, South Carolina* (Cambridge: Cambridge University Press, 2018), 198–199; Michael Holt, *The Election of 1860* (Lawrence: University Press of Kansas, 2017), 50–66.

CHAPTER 12: WAR

1. Douglas Egerton, *Year of Meteors: Stephen Douglas, Abraham Lincoln, and the Election that Brought on the Civil War* (New York: Bloomsbury Press, 2010), 129; Murat Halstead, *History of the National Political Conventions of 1860* (Columbus: Follett, Foster, 1860), 191.

2. Ibid.

3. Walter Stahr, *Seward: Lincoln's Indispensable Man* (New York: Simon & Schuster, 2012), 3–5.

4. James McPherson, *Battle Cry of Freedom: The Civil War Era* (Oxford: Oxford University Press, 1988), 216; Abraham Lincoln to Jesse W. Fell, December 20, 1859, *Collected Works of Abraham Lincoln*, Roy P. Basler, ed. (New Brunswick, NY: Rutgers University Press, 1953), 3:511.

5. Halstead, *National Political Conventions*, 149–151.

6. Michael Holt, *The Election of 1860* (Lawrence: University Press of Kansas, 2017), 115–133. Don E. Fehrenbacher, *The Dred Scott Case: Its Significance in American Law and Politics* (Oxford: Oxford University Press, 1978), 538.

7. Romero to Ministro de Relaciones Exteriores, September 5, 1860, *Correspondencia de la Legación Mexicana en Washington durante la intervención extranjera, 1860–1868* (Mexico City: Imprenta del Gobierno, 1870–1892), 1:177–178.

8. Egerton, *Year of Meteors*, 217; May S. Ringgold, "Robert Newman Gourdin and the '1860 Association,'" *Georgia Historical Quarterly* 55 (1971): 501–509; Charles Cauthen, *South Carolina Goes to War, 1860–1865* (Chapel Hill: University of North Carolina Press, 1950), 34–35; Jon L. Wakelyn, *Southern Pamphlets on Secession, November 1860–April 1861* (Chapel Hill: University of North Carolina Press, 2000), xvi–xvii.

9. *Charleston Mercury*, November 8, 1860; For the atmosphere in Charleston on the night of the election, see Paul Starobin, *Madness Rules the Hour: Charleston, 1860, and the Mania for War* (New York: Public Affairs, 2017), 119,

142; David Detzer, *Allegiance: Fort Sumter, Charleston, and the Beginning of the Civil War* (New York: Houghton Mifflin, 2002), 51; Russell McClintock, *Lincoln and the Decision for War: The Northern Response to Secession* (Chapel Hill: University of North Carolina Press, 2008), 15; Egerton, *Year of Meteors*, 214.

10. Egerton, *Year of Meteors*, 209–210; Holt, *The Election of 1860*, 174–176; Damon Wells, *Stephen Douglas: The Last Years, 1857–1861* (Austin: University of Texas Press, 1971), 257.

11. McClintock, *Lincoln and the Decision for War*, 16; Egerton, *Year of Meteors*, 219; Lawrence T. McDonnell, *Performing Secession: The Coming of the Civil War in Charleston, South Carolina* (Cambridge, Cambridge University Press, 2018), 140–141.

12. *Charleston Mercury*, October 11, 1860.

13. Egerton, *Year of Meteors*, 281–282. It's important to note that Lincoln made contradictory comments about racial equality over the course of his public career. See Eric Foner, *The Fiery Trial: Abraham Lincoln and American Slavery* (New York: Norton, 2010), 9, 77, 109, 122, 218; George Fredrickson, *Big Enough to Be Inconsistent: Abraham Lincoln Confronts Slavery and Race* (Cambridge, MA: Harvard University Press, 2008), 1–42; Republican Platform, 1860, in Henry Steele Commager, ed., *Documents of American History*, 8th ed. (New York: Appleton Century Crofts, 1968), 364.

14. Fehrenbacher, *Dred Scott*, 545–549; Mr. Crittenden, January 7, 1861, CG, 265.

15. Henry Wilson, *The Crittenden Compromise—a Surrender: Speech of Henry Wilson, of Mass., Delivered in the Senate, February 21st, 1861*, 11; Mr. Campbell, February 14, 1861, CG, 912; Horace Greeley, *The American Conflict* (Hartford, CT: O. D. Case, 1866), 1:378; *Macon Daily Telegraph*, January 31, 1861; Egerton, *Year of Meteors*, 312; Detzer, *Allegiance*, 75; David Potter, *The Impending Crisis, 1848–61* (New York: Harper and Row, 1976), 530–533, 553; Shearer Davis Bowman, *At the Precipice: Americans North and South during the Secession Crisis* (Chapel Hill: University of North Carolina Press, 2010), 261–288.

16. *New York Herald*, November 28, 1860, December 2, 1860; "Dangers of Good Nature," *New York Herald* (December 20, 1860).

17. Thomas Schoonover, ed., *The Mexican Lobby: Matías Romero in Washington, 1861–1867* (Lexington: University Press of Kentucky, 1986), 2; Henry Villard, *Memoirs of Henry Villard*, 2 vols. (New York: Houghton, Mifflin, 1904), 1:141. For a general description of the mud on the central Mexican plateau, see Otterbourg to Seward, September 28, 1864, vol. 11, reel 6, DUSC-Mexico City.

18. Harford Montgomery Hyde, *Mexican Empire: The History of Maximilian and Carlota of Mexico* (New York: Macmillan, 1946), 111; Matías Romero to Secretary of Foreign Relations, January 23, 1861, 29-15-29, SRE.

19. Ibid.; Melchor Ocampo to Matías Romero, December 22, 1860, *Correspondencia de la Legación Mexicana*, 1:274.

20. Potter, *The Impending Crisis*, 445; July 22, 1861, *CG* (37th Congress, 1st Session), 223; Matías Romero to Minister of Foreign Relations, June 6, 1861, *Correspondencia de la Legación Mexicana*, 1:411.

21. Egerton, *Year of Meteors*, 221, 223.

22. Samuel S. Cox, *Three Decades of Federal Legislation, 1855–1885* (Providence, RI: J. A. and R. A. Reid, 1885), 158.

23. Ibid.

24. Jasper Ridley, *Maximilian and Juárez* (New York: Ticknor & Fields, 1992), 64. For the French intervention, see Erika Pani, "Dreaming of a Mexican Empire: The Political Projects of the 'Imperialistas,'" *Hispanic American Historical Review* 82:1 (February 2002): 1–31; Erika Pani, *Para mexicanizar el Segundo Imperio. El imaginario político de los imperialistas* (Mexico City: El Colegio de México, 2001); Erika Pani, *El Segundo Imperio: Pasados de usos múltiples* (Mexico City: Centro de Investigación y Docencia Económicas, 2004); Erika Pani, *Una serie de admirables acontecimientos. México y el mundo en la época de la Reforma, 1848–1867* (Puebla, MX: Ediciones de Educación y Cultura, 2013); Arnold Blumberg, *The Diplomacy of the Second Empire, 1863–1867* (Philadelphia: Transactions of the American Philosophical Society, 1971); Robert Duncan, "Political Legitimation and Maximlian's Second Empire in Mexico, 1864–1867," *Mexican Studies/Estudios Mexicanos* XII:1 (Winter 1996): 27–66; Patricia Gaeleana, *Las relaciones iglesia-estado durante el Segundo Imperio* (Mexico City: Universidad Nacional Autónoma de México, 1991); Gerardo Gurza, *Una vecindad efímera: los Estados confederados de América y su política exterior hacia México, 1861–1865* (Mexico City: Instituto de Investigaciones, Dr. José María Luis Mora, 2001); Jean François Lecaillon, *Napoleon III et le Mexique: les illusions d'un grand dessein* (Paris: L'Harmattan, 1994).

25. John Elderfield, *Manet and the Execution of Maximilian* (New York: Museum of Modern Art, 2006), 32; Alexander Watkins Terrell, Reminiscences, f. 48, Box 1947/5, TSA; Quoted in Gene Smith, *Maximilian and Charlotte* (New York: Morrow, 1973), 139.

26. Hyde, *Mexican Empire*, 124; Percy Martin, *Maximilian in Mexico: The Story of the French Intervention, 1861–1867* (New York: Scribner's, 1914), 392.

27. McPherson, *Battle Cry of Freedom*, 410; Steven E. Woodworth, ed., *The Shiloh Campaign* (Carbondale: Southern Illinois University Press, 2009), 2–6.

28. Douglas Putnam Jr., "Reminiscences of the Battle of Shiloh," in *Sketches of War History, 1861–65*, ed. Robert Hunter (Cincinnati: R. Clarke, 1888), 3:205.

29. Winston Groom, *Shiloh, 1862* (Washington, DC: National Geographic Society, 2012), 358; U. S. Grant, *Personal Memoirs of U. S. Grant* (New York: Charles Webster, 1894), 1:211, 218.

30. Thomas Reynolds to Hon. E. J. Derrick, February 25, 1864, f. 112, reel 1, Thomas Reynolds Papers, LoC. McPherson, *Battle Cry of Freedom*, 471; Joseph Glathaar, *General Lee's Army: From Victory to Collapse* (New York: Free Press, 2009), 140; Glenn David Brasher, *The Peninsula Campaign and the Necessity of Emancipation: African Americans and the Fight for Freedom* (Chapel Hill: University of North Carolina Press, 2012).

31. Stève Sainlaude, *France and the American Civil War: A Diplomatic History*, trans. Jessica Edwards (Chapel Hill: University of North Carolina Press, 2019), 99–109; Howard Jones, *Union in Peril: The Crisis over British Intervention in the Civil War* (Lincoln: University of Nebraska Press, 1992), 138–161; Abraham Lincoln to Cuthbert Bullitt, July 28, 1862, *Colllected Works of Abraham Lincoln*, 5:346; "White kid-glove warfare," quoted in Allan G. Bogue, *Earnest Men: Republicans of the Civil War Senate* (Ithaca, NY: Cornell University Press, 1981), 162.

32. John Witt, *Lincoln's Code: The Laws of War in American History* (New York: Free Press, 2012), 220–249; Foner, *Fiery Trial*, 206–289; Burrus M. Carnahan, *Lincoln's Emancipation Proclamation and the Law of War* (Lexington: University Press of Kentucky, 2007), 93–132. For the Emancipation Proclamation, see Allen C. Guelzo, *Lincoln's Emancipation Proclamation: The End of Slavery in America* (New York: Simon & Schuster, 2004), and William Blair and Karen Fisher Younger, eds., *Lincoln's Proclamation: Emancipation Reconsidered* (Chapel Hill: University of North Carolina Press, 2009).

33. John David Smith, *Lincoln and the U.S. Colored Troops* (Carbondale: Southern Illinois University Press, 2013), 2–3. For Milliken's Bend, see Linda Barnickel, *Milliken's Bend: A Civil War Battle in History and Memory* (Baton Rouge: LSU Press, 2013). For Fort Wagner, see Russell Duncan, *Where Death and Glory Meet: Colonel Robert Gould Shaw and the 54th Massachusetts Infantry* (Athens: University of Georgia Press, 1999), 110–117. Douglas Egerton, *Thunder at the Gates: The Black Civil War Regiments that Redeemed America* (New York: Basic Books, 2016), 179–212; Lincoln to James Conkling, August 26, 1863, in *The War of the Rebellion* (Champaign: University of Illinois Press, 1899), 733.

34. Judith Giesberg, ed., *Emilie Davis's Civil War: The Diaries of a Free Black Woman in Philadelphia* (University Park, PA: Pennsylvania State University Press,

2014), 17; Adam Woog, *The Emancipation Proclamation: Ending Slavery in America* (New York: Infobase Publishing, 2009), 46; Thomas Wentworth Higginson, *Army Life in a Black Regiment* (Cambridge, MA: Riverside Press, 1900), 72.

35. Romero to Ministry of Foreign Relations, October 9, 1862, *Correspondencia de la Legación Mexicana*, 2:531–534; *El Siglo Diez y Nueve* (May 26, 1863), 2; William Shrie to Matías Romero, February 4, 1864, f. 7, exp. 2, leg. 65, AEMEUA, SRE.

36. For Fort Pillow, see John Cimprich, *Fort Pillow: A Civil War Massacre and Public Memory* (Baton Rouge: LSU Press, 2005); Andrew Ward, *River Run Red: The Fort Pillow Massacre in the American Civil War* (New York: Penguin, 2006); Brian Steel Wills, *The River Was Dyed With Blood: Nathan Bedford Forrest and Fort Pillow*. For the Overland Campaign, see Mark Grimsley, *And Keep Moving On: The Virginia Campaign, May–June 1864* (Lincoln: University of Nebraska Press, 2002), and Gary W. Gallagher and Caroline E. Janney, eds., *Cold Harbor to the Crater: The End of the Overland Campaign* (Chapel Hill: University of North Carolina Press, 2015).

37. Hyde, *Mexican Empire*, 143; Thomas Corwin to William Seward, May 28, 1864, vol. 30, reel 31, DUSM-Mexico; Corwin to Seward, May 28, 1864, ibid.

38. Hyde, *Mexican Empire*, 116, 124; Ridley, *Maximilian and Juárez*, 141; Erika Pani, "Juárez vs. Maximiliano: Mexico's Experiment with Monarchy," in Don Doyle, ed., *American Civil Wars: The United States, Latin America, Europe, and the Crisis of the 1860s* (Chapel Hill: University of North Carolina Press, 2017), 175–178.

39. Ripley, *Maximilian and Juárez*, 179; Hyde, *Mexican Empire*, 147.

40. "La France, le Mexique, et la Confederation," *L'estafette*, November 2, 1863; "Decreto para establecimiento de la Junta de Colonización" *L'estafette*, March 29, 1865; "Ministerio de Fomento," May 4, 1865, ibid.; Nicholas Guyatt, "The Future Empire of Our Freedmen: Republican Colonization Schemes in Texas and Mexico, 1861–65," *Civil War Wests: Testing the Limits of the United States*, ed. Adam Arenson and Andrew Graybill (Berkeley: University of California Press, 2015), 107.

41. "Junta de Colonización," *Diario del Imperio* (July 10, 1865), 2.

42. "Concluye la acta num. 15 del dia 14 de junio de 1865," *Diario del Imperio* (July 27, 1865), 2; "Junta de Colonización: Concluye la acta num; 16 del día 17 de junio de 1865" *Diario del Imperio* (July 29, 1865), 3.

43. Peones, trabajadores, jornaleros, Proyecto de leye para protegerlos, July 12, 1865, exp. 14bis, caja 10, Segundo Imperio, AGN. For this law, see Jaime del Arenal, "La protección del indígena en el Segundo Imperio mexicano: la

Junta Protectora de las Clases Menesterosas," *Ars Iuris* (1991): 1–33; Jack A. Dabbs, "The Indian Policy of the Second Empire," in *Essays in Mexican History*, Thomas E. Cotner and Carlos Castañeda, eds. (Austin: University of Texas Press, 1958); Aimer Granados, "Comunidad indígena, imaginario monárquico, agravio y economía moral durante el Segundo Imperio mexicano," *Secuencia. Revista de historia y ciencias sociales* 41 (May–August 1998): 45–73; Jean Meyer, "La Junta Protectora de las Clases Menesterosas; Indigenismo y agrarismo en el Segundo Imperio," in *Indio, anción y comunidad en el Mexico del siglo XIX*, Antonio Escobar, ed. (Mexico City: Centro de Estudios Mexicanos y Centroamericanos, 1993), 329–364.

44. Ley de Colonización, *Diario del Imperio* (November 3, 1865), 443.

45. "American Citizens Enslaved in Mexico," *Daily Alta California*, April 10, 1870.

46. Memorial of Burrill Daniel, May 17, 1870, "Correspondencia," AEMEUA, SRE; Testimony of Tomás, ibid.

47. Unsigned letter in Gwin's hand to the *New Orleans Times*, June 1, 1865; "Correspondencia," AEMEUA, SRE; William M. Gwin to mother, May 16, 1865, "Colonization Laws Passed by Maximilian Relating to the Confederacy," AEMEUA, SRE.

48. Estimates vary of the number of Confederate exiles in Mexico; Hanna and Hanna, "The Immigration Movement," *HAHR* XXVIII (May 1947), 234, estimate about one thousand Confederates fled to Mexico; Andrew Rolle, *The Lost Cause: The Confederate Exodus to Mexico* (Norman: University of Oklahoma Press, 1992), 80, puts the number around four thousand; Todd W. Wahlstrom, *The Southern Exodus to Mexico: Migration Across the Borderlands After the American Civil War* (Lincoln: University of Nebraska Press, 2015), 28, 37, estimates five thousand; Philip Henry Sheridan, *Personal Memoirs of Philip Henry Sheridan* (New York: D. Appleton, 1902), 2:206–208; Testimony of Reuben Creel, "Correspondencia," AEMEUA, SRE.

49. William W. Richmond to Matías Romero, May 26, 1865, f. 246, exp. 2, leg. 65, AEMEUA, SRE; J. B. Jones to Romero, May 15, 1865, f. 214, exp. 2, leg. 65, AEMEUA, SRE.

50. Anna Telez to Romero, May 14, 1865, f. 186, exp. 2, leg. 65, AEMEUA, SRE; William Richmond to Romero, May 26, 1865, f. 246, exp. 2, leg. 65, AEMEUA, SRE; H. William Russell to Romero, January 13, 1866, f. 43, exp. 2, leg. 66, AEMEUA, SRE; Horace G. Thomas to Simon [sic] Romero, May 9, 1865, f. 109, exp. 2, leg. 65, AEMEUA, SRE.

51. Corwin to Seward, September 10, 1865, vol. 30, reel 31, vol. 30, reel 31, DUSM-Mexico; Speed to Seward, October 21, 1865, 10-21-73, SRE.

52. Unsigned, El Emperador Maximiliano y la Esclavitud, n.d. (1865?) f. 10, folder 20, box 59, Segundo Imperio, AGN; "Actualidades," *La Sociedad* (November 12, 1865), 2; W. C. Hasbrook to Maury, August 27, 1865, vol. 23, Maury Papers, LoC; Anonymous (Gramercy Park House) to editors of the *Courrier des Etats Unis*, December 26, 1865, VII-1.3–4.178, CONDUMEX.

53. Edward Heaton to Romero, Novemeber 19, 1866, f. 375, exp. 2, leg. 66, AEMEUA, SRE; Ridley, *Maximilian and Juárez*, 120; Romero to Minister of Foreign Relations, December 10, 1865, *Correspondencia de la Legación Mexicana*, 5:883; *Shall our government act, or refrain from acting, in Mexican affairs?* (S. I., 1866), 6.

54. William H. Seward to John Bigelow, November 6, 1865, *Papers Relating to Foreign Affairs*, 3:422.

55. Romero to Mexican Minister of Foreign Affairs, October 5, 1865, *Correspondencia de la Legación Mexicana*, 5:667; R. Wentzel to Matías Romero, November 17, 1865, f. 286, exp. 2, leg. 65, AEMEUA, SRE; J. S. Compant to Matías Romero, November 3, 1865, f. 278, exp. 2, leg. 65, AEMEUA, SRE.

56. Sheridan to U. S. Grant, September 21, 1865, John Y. Simon, ed., *The Papers of Ulysses S. Grant* (Carbondale: Southern Illinois University Press, 1991), 17:366; Ridley, *Maximilian and Juárez*, 186, 213, 222–223, 250, 257, 262; George H. White to C. Wyke, October 25, 1863, PRO 30/22/74, NA-K.

57. Ridley, *Maximilian and Juárez*, 268–275.

58. "Mexique," *Le memorial diplomatique* (October 10, 1867), 1122; Ridley, *Maximilian and Juárez*, 277.

59. Memorial of Burrill Daniel, May 17, 1870, "Correspondencia," AEMEUA, SRE.

60. Testimony of Reuben Creel, "Correspondencia," AEMEUA, SRE.

61. Testimony of Mariana Daniel, "Correspondencia," AEMEUA, SRE; Testimony of Enrique Muller, ibid.; Testimony of Jacobo Hamburg, ibid.

62. Testimony of Reuben Creel, "Correspondencia," AEMEUA, SRE; Testimony of Mariana Daniel, ibid.

63. Testimony of Luis Daniel, "Correspondencia," AEMEUA, SRE; Testimony of Enrique Muller, ibid.; Testimony of Burrill Daniel, ibid.

64. Barbara Jeanne Fields, *Slavery and Freedom on the Middle Ground: Maryland During the Nineteenth Century* (New Haven, CT: Yale University Press, 1985), 174–176; Nell Irvin Painter, *Exodusters: Black Migration to Kansas After Reconstruction* (New York: Norton, 1992), 7; Eric Foner, *The Story of American Freedom* (New York: Norton, 1999), 113.

EPILOGUE

1. Kenneth Wiggins Porter to Beth Dillinghan, n.d., folder 3, box 241, Porter Papers, SCRBC.

2. August Meier and Elliott M. Rudwick, *Black History and the Historical Profession, 1815–1980* (Champaign-Urbana: University of Illinois Press, 1986), 106; Biographical information, Porter Papers, SCRBC.

3. Kenneth Wiggins Porter to Beth Dillinghan, n.d., folder 3, box 241, Porter Papers, SCRBC.

4. Undated notes, folder 3, box 23, Porter Papers, SCRBC.

5. Kenneth W. Porter, "Relations between Negroes and Indians within the Present Limits of the United States," *The Journal of Negro History* 17, no. 3 (July, 1932), 287; Undated notes, folder 3, box 23, Porter Papers, SCRBC.

6. Kenneth Wiggins Porter, *The Negro on the American Frontier* (New York: Arno, 1972). Porter was not the first to study African Americans in the West. For an example of earlier work on the subject, see R. R. Wright, "Negro Companions of the Spanish Explorers," *American Anthropologist* 4:2 (April–June 1902): 217–228. For later scholarship on African Americans in the West, see Nell Irvin Painter, *Exodusters: Black Migration to Kansas after Reconstruction* (New York: Knopf, 1977); Quintard Taylor, *In Search of the Racial Frontier: African Americans in the American West, 1528–1990* (New York: W. W. Norton, 1998); Arnoldo de León, *Racial Frontiers: Africans, Chinese, and Mexicans in Western America, 1848–1890* (Albuquerque: University of New Mexico Press, 2002); Quintard Taylor and Shirley Ann Wilson Moore, *African American Women Confront the West, 1600–2000* (Norman: University of Oklahoma Press, 2003); Douglas Flamming, *African Americans in the West* (New York: ABC-CLIO, 2009); William Loren Katz, *The Black West* (New York: Random House, 2005); Matthew C. Whitaker, *Race Work: The Rise of Civil Rights in the Urban West* (Lincoln: University of Nebraska Press, 2007); Albert S. Broussard, *Expectations of Equality: A History of Black Westerners* (Wheeling, IL: Harlan Davidson, 2012); Shirley Ann Wilson Moore, *Sweet Freedom's Plains: African Americans on the Overland Trails, 1841–1869* (Norman: University of Oklahoma Press, 2016); Herbert G. Ruffin and Dwayne A. Mack, eds., *Freedom's Racial Frontier: African Americans in the Twentieth-Century West* (Norman: University of Oklahoma Press, 2018).

7. "General Intelligence," *Vermont Chronicle* (December 4, 1829), 193; "Latest from Mexico," *Daily National Journal* 1905 (January 16, 1830); "Mexico; Government; Slavery; Abolition," *Connecticut Journal* (December 1, 1829),

3; "Speech of the Honorable Matias Romero," March 29, 1864, in Citizens of New York, *Proceedings of a Meeting of Citizens of New York to Express Sympathy and Respect for the Mexican Republic Exiles* (New York: J. A. Gray & Green, 1865). Discussion of the role of the US in Mexico's War with the French, February 8, 1866, AD 1874, Richard Clough Anderson Papers, HEH.

8. John Forsyth to Lerdo de Tejada, August 20, 1857, vol. 20, reel 21, DUSM-Mexico; "Mexico versus Texas," *Telegraph and Texas Register* (December 4, 1839), 4; Ashbel Smith to John C. Calhoun, June 19, 1843, *Papers of John C. Calhoun* (Columbia: University of South Carolina Press, 1959), 17:252–253; Morgan C. Hamilton to Earl of Aberdeen, n.d. (1841), f. 50, FO 75/2, NA-K; Charles Elliott to Earl of Aberdeen, July 28, 1845, f. 170, FO 75/13, NA-K; August 20, 1842, *CG* (27th Congress, 3rd Session), 2; *New Orleans Commercial Bulletin*, April 25, 1842. For the Monroe Doctrine, see Jay Sexton, *The Monroe Doctrine: Empire and Nation in Nineteenth-Century America* (New York: Hill & Wang, 2011), 85–122; William Ellery Channing, *A Letter to the Hon. Henry Clay on the Annexation of Texas to the United States* (Boston: J. Munroe, 1837), 40; Michel-Rolph Trouillot, *Silencing the Past: Power and the Production of History* (Boston: Beacon Press, 1995), 145.

9. "By the Express mail," *Charleston Courier,* June 3, 1837, 2; "We understand" *Telegraph and Texas Register* 1, no. 50 (January 3, 1837), 3.

10. For the argument that Mexico's emancipatory promise was empty, see Sarah Cornell, "Citizens of Nowhere," *Journal of American History* (September 2013), 351–374; James David Nichols, "The Line of Liberty: Runaway Slaves and Fugitive Peons in the Texas-Mexico Borderlands," *WHQ* 44 (Winter 2013), 413–433, and Mekala Shadd-Sartor Audain, "Mexican Canaan: Fugitive Slaves and Free Blacks on the American Frontier, 1804–1867" (unpublished PhD diss., Rutgers, The State University of New Jersey, 2014), 87–162. For the view that Mexico did maintain an antislavery stance to serve its political interests, see Gerardo Gurza Lavalle, "Against Slave Power? Slavery and Runaway Slaves in Mexico-United States Relations, 1821–1857," *Mexican Studies/Estudios Mexicanos* 35:2 (Summer 2019): 143–170. For scholarship on the British threat to slavery, see Matthew Karp, *This Vast Southern Empire: Slaveholders at the Helm of American Foreign Policy* (Cambridge, MA: Harvard University Press, 2016), 70–102; Steven Heath Mitton, "The Upshur Inquiry: Lost Lessons of the Great Experiment," *Slavery & Abolition* 27:1 (2006): 89–124.

11. Walt Whitman, *Poems of Walt Whitman (Leaves of Grass)* (New York: Thomas Y. Crowell, 1902), 245.

Index

ALICE L. BAUMGARTNER is assistant professor of history at the University of Southern California. She received an MPhil in history from Oxford, where she was a Rhodes Scholar, and a PhD in history from Yale University. She lives in Los Angeles, California.